Revised Regulations
for the
Army of the United States,
1861

ISSUED BY THE
WAR DEPARTMENT, UNITED STATES

DOVER PUBLICATIONS, INC.,
MINEOLA, NEW YORK

WAR DEPARTMENT,
WASHINGTON, AUGUST 10, 1861.

WHEREAS, it has been found expedient to revise the Regulations for the Army, and the same having been approved by the President of the United States, he commands that they be published for the information and government of the military service, and that, from and after the date hereof, they shall be strictly observed as the sole and standing authority upon the matter therein contained.

Nothing contrary to the tenor of these Regulations will be enjoined in any part of the forces of the United States by any commander whatsoever.

SIMON CAMERON,
Secretary of War.

Bibliographical Note

This Dover edition, first published in 2013, is an unabridged republication of *Revised Regulations for the United States Army, 1861,* first published in 1861 by J. G. L. Brown, Philadelphia. Pages 252 and 253 did not appear in the original publication.

Library of Congress Cataloging-in-Publication Data

United States. War Department.
    Revised regulations for the Army of the United States, 1861 : with a full index / by authority of the War Department. — Dover edition.
      p. cm.
    Includes index.
    ISBN-13: 978-0-486-49714-3
    ISBN-10: 0-486-49714-3
    1. United States. Army—Regulations. 2. Military law—United States. I. Title.

KF7305.A33 2013
343.73'0109034—dc23

2013009178

Manufactured in the United States by Courier Corporation
49714301   2013
www.doverpublications.com

PUBLISHER'S NOTE

When the Civil War started in April of 1861, the United States Army consisted of a total of about 15,000 officers and men spread out in many widely scattered and mostly very small posts. It's amazing to realize that just two years and four months later the Union was able to send over 80,000 men into battle at Gettysburg (against the Confederacy's 75,000). Casualties at Gettysburg alone numbered more than three times the size of the whole Union Army at the time of Fort Sumter. All of this is just to point out that the United States went almost overnight from having a very small army to needing a very big one. The book which the reader is holding in his hands is a historical document which brings back to life a major part of that military transformation.

Published in Philadelphia in 1861, the *Revised Regulations for the Army of the United States* assembles between its covers the basic organizational principles and rules on which the Union Army was set up, and above all, lays out the rules and regulations governing each area, also often including the actual forms for officers and men to use when needed, reporting on events that happened, arranging for transfers and discharges, ordering equipment when it was needed, and in many other ways. Covered in the *Revised Regulations* were matters concerning appointments for officers, rank and command, promotions, pay, military discipline, desertions, arrests and discharges, the resignation of officers, the care of fortifications and arms, the care of the sick and the processing and handling of deceased officers and soldiers, every possible subject concerning uniforms, insignia, horses and equipment, rations on the march and in camp of such staple items as candles, soap, bread, fresh meat and salt meat, depending on availability, beans and rice, one pound of potatoes three times a week per man when feasible, coffee and tea, when coffee not available.

The Union's Army was essentially built with volunteers who answered a series of calls for their services starting very soon after the Civil War began. At the start of the conflict, President Lincoln called for 75,000 members of various militia units to volunteer for a few months, which was all he could legally do at that time. Subsequent calls for volunteers were for a three-year enlistment, and many thousands signed up on those terms. The depths of the conflict in 1863 saw the first compulsory conscription in the nation's history, except that anyone drafted could send a substitute, if he could (for whatever inducement) find someone willing to take his place, and anyone drafted could, more simply, purchase an exemption to the draft from the government for $300. The new draft produced about 50,000 new recruits—more than twice that many sent substitutes and about 80,000 purchased exemptions.

All told, over two million men served in the Union Armies during the Civil War and over 350,000 of them died, about a third on the battlefields of the conflict and the greater number from diseases incurred. The Confederacy's numbers were smaller but still staggering—over a million soldiers of whom between a quarter and a third were killed in battle or died of disease. Any soldier contemplating serving in the Union Army, or facing the draft, could find out a lot about how his unit would be organized from reading this book after it was published in 1861, and copies occasionally turn up on the Civil War rare book market showing signs of having undergone some hard campaigning in their owners' saddlebags. It remains an indispensable source for the day to day, campaign to campaign, life of the Union soldier in the Civil War.

CONTENTS.

A FULL INDEX WILL BE FOUND AT THE END OF THIS WORK.

REVISED

REGULATIONS FOR THE ARMY.

ARTICLE I.
MILITARY DISCIPLINE.

1. ALL inferiors are required to obey strictly, and to execute with alacrity and good faith, the lawful orders of the superiors appointed over them.

2. Military authority is to be exercised with firmness, but with kindness and justice to inferiors. Punishments shall be strictly conformable to military law.

3. Superiors of every grade are forbidden to injure those under them by tyrannical or capricious conduct, or by abusive language.

ARTICLE II.
RANK AND COMMAND.

4. Rank of officers and non-commissioned officers:

1st. Lieutenant-General.	10th. Cadet.
2d. Major-General.	11th. Sergeant-Major.
3d. Brigadier-General.	12th. Quartermaster-Sergeant of a
4th. Colonel.	Regiment.
5th. Lieutenant-Colonel.	13th. Ordnance Sergeant and Hospital Steward.
6th. Major.	
7th. Captain.	14th. First Sergeant.
8th. First Lieutenant.	15th. Sergeant.
9th. Second Lieutenant.	16th. Corporal.

And in each grade by date of commission or appointment.

5. When commissions are of the same date, the rank is to be decided, between officers of the same regiment or corps by the order of appointment; between officers of different regiments or corps: 1st. by rank in actual service when appointed; 2d. by former rank and service in the

army or marine corps; 3d. by lottery among such as have not been in the military service of the United States. In case of equality of rank by virtue of a brevet commission, reference is had to commissions not brevet.

6. Officers having brevets, or commissions of a prior date to those of the regiment in which they serve, may take place in courts-martial and on detachments, when composed of diffi rent corps, according to the ranks given them in their brevets or dates of their former commissions; but in the regiment, troop, or company to which such officers belong, they shall do duty and take rank both in courts-martial and on detachments which shall be composed only of their own corps, according to the commissions by which they are mustered in the said corps.—(61st *Art. of War.*)

7. If, upon marches, guards, or in quarters, different corps of the army shall happen to join, or do duty together, the officer highest in rank of the *line* of the army, marine corps, or militia, by commission, there on duty or in quarters, shall command the whole, and give orders for what is needful to the service, unless otherwise specially directed by the President of the United States, according to the nature of the case.—(62d *Art of War.*)

8. An officer not having orders from competent authority cannot put himself *on duty* by virtue of his commission alone.

9. Officers serving *by commission* from any state of the Union take rank next after officers of the like grade *by commission* from the United States.

10. Brevet rank takes effect only in the following cases: 1st. by special assignment of the President in commands composed of *different corps;* 2d. on courts-martial or *detachments* composed of *different corps.* Troops are on *detachment,* only when sent out *temporarily* to perform a *special* service.

11. In regularly constituted commands, as garrisons, posts, departments; companies, battalions, regiments; corps, brigades, divisions, army corps, or the army itself, brevet rank cannot be exercised except by special assignment.

12. The officers of Engineers are not to assume nor to be ordered on any duty beyond the line of their immediate profession, except by the special order of the President.

13. An officer of the Pay or Medical Department cannot exercise command except in his own department; but, by virtue of their commissions, officers of these departments may command all *enlisted* men, like other commissioned officers.

14. Officers of the corps of Engineers or Ordnance, or of the Adjutant-General's, Inspector-General's, Quartermaster-General's, or Subsistence Department, though eligible to command according to the rank they

hold in the army of the United States, shall not assume the command of troops unless put on duty under orders which specially so direct by authority of the President.

ARTICLE III.
SUCCESSION IN COMMAND OR DUTY.

15. The functions assigned to any officer in these regulations by title of office, devolve on the officer acting in his place, except as specially excepted.

16. During the absence of the Adjutant-General, or of the chief of any military bureau of the War Department, his duties in the bureau, prescribed by law or regulations, devolve on the officer of his department empowered by the President to perform them in his absence.

17. An officer who succeeds to any command or duty, stands in regard to his duties in the same situation as his predecessor. The officer relieved shall turn over to his successor all orders in force at the time, and all the public property and funds pertaining to his command or duty, and shall receive therefor duplicate receipts, showing the condition of each article.

18. An officer in a temporary command shall not, except in urgent cases, alter or annul the standing orders of the regular or permanent commander without authority from the next higher commander.

ARTICLE IV.
APPOINTMENT AND PROMOTION OF COMMISSIONED OFFICERS.

19. All vacancies in established regiments and corps, to the rank of Colonel, shall be filled by promotion according to seniority, except in case of disability or other incompetency.

20. Promotions to the rank of Captain shall be made regimentally; to Major and Lieutenant-Colonel and Colonel, according to the arm, as infantry, artillery, &c., and in the Staff Departments and in the Engineers, Topographical Engineers, and Ordnance, according to corps.

21. Appointments to the rank of Brigadier-General and Major-General will be made by selection from the army.

22. The graduates of the Military Academy are appointed to vacancies of the lowest grade, or attached by brevet to regiments or corps, not to exceed one brevet to each company; and meritorious non-commissioned officers, examined by an Army Board, and found qualified for the duties

of commissioned officers, will, in like manner, be attached to regiments as Brevet Second Lieutenants.

23. Whenever the public service may require the appointment of any citizen to the army, a Board of Officers will be instituted, before which the applicant will appear for an examination into his physical ability, moral character, attainments, and general fitness for the service. If the Board report in favor of the applicant, he will be deemed eligible for a commission in the army.

ARTICLE V.

RESIGNATIONS OF OFFICERS.

24. No officer will be considered out of service on the tender of his resignation, until it shall have been duly accepted by the proper authority. Any officer who, having tendered his resignation, shall, prior to due notice of the acceptance of the same by the proper authority, and, without leave, quit his post or proper duties with the intent to remain permanently absent therefrom, shall be registered as a deserter, and punished as such.

25. Resignations will be forwarded by the commanding officer to the Adjutant-General of the army for decision of the War Department; and with them, where leave is given, the officer's address.

26. Resignations tendered under charges, when forwarded by any commander, will always be accompanied by a copy of the charges; or, in the absence of written charges, by a report of the case, for the information of the Secretary of War.

27. Before presenting the resignation of any officer, the Adjutant-General will ascertain and report to the War Department the state of such officer's accounts of money, as well as of public property, for which he may have been responsible.

28. In time of war, or with an army in the field, resignations shall take effect within thirty days from the date of the order of acceptance.

29. Leaves of absence will not be granted by commanding officers to officers on tendering their resignation, unless the resignation be unconditional and immediate.

ARTICLE VI.

EXCHANGE OR TRANSFER OF OFFICERS.

30. The transfer of officers from one regiment or corps to another will be made only by the War Department, on the mutual application of the parties desiring the exchange.

31. An officer shall not be transferred from one regiment or corps to another with prejudice to the rank of any officer of the regiment or corps to which he is transferred.

32. Transfers will be seldom granted—never except for cogent reasons.

ARTICLE VII.

APPOINTMENTS ON THE STAFF.

33. As far as practicable, all appointments and details on the staff will be equalized among the several regiments.

34. General Officers appoint their own Aides-de-camp.

35. Brevet Brigadier and Major Generals on duty as such, may, with the special sanction of the War Department, be allowed the aides-de-camp of their brevet grades.

36. An officer shall not fill any staff appointment, or other situation, the duties of which will detach him from his company, regiment, or corps, until he has served at least three years with his regiment or corps; nor shall any officer (aides-de-camp excepted) so remain detached longer than four years.

37. An officer of a mounted corps shall not be separated from his regiment, except for duty connected with his particular arm.

38. The senior Lieutenant present, holding the appointment of Assistant Commissary of Subsistence, is entitled to perform the duties.

ARTICLE VIII.

DISTRIBUTION OF THE TROOPS.

39. The military geographical departments will be established by the War Department. In time of peace, brigades or divisions will not be formed, nor the stations of the troops changed, without authority from the War Department.

ARTICLE IX.

CARE OF FORTIFICATIONS.

40. No person shall be permitted to walk upon any of the slopes of a fortification, excepting the ramps and glacis. If, in any case, it be necessary to provide for crossing them, it should be done by placing wooden steps or stairs against the slopes. The *occasional* walking of persons on a parapet will do no harm, provided it be not allowed to cut the surface into paths.

41. No cattle, horses, sheep, goat, or other animal, shall ever be permitted to go upon the slopes, the ramparts, or the parapets, nor upon the glacis, except within fenced limits, which should not approach the crest nearer than 30 feet.

42. All grassed surfaces, excepting the glacis, will be carefully and frequently mowed (except in dry weather), and the oftener the better, while growing rapidly—the grass never being allowed to be more than a few inches high. In order to cut the grass even and close, upon small slopes a light one-handed scythe should be used; and in mowing the steep slopes, the mower should stand on a light ladder resting against the slope, and not upon the grass. Crops of hay may be cut on the glacis; or, if fenced, it may be used as pasture; otherwise it should be treated as other slopes of the fortification. On all the slopes, spots of dead grass will be cut out and replaced by fresh sods. All weeds will be eradicated. A very little labor, applied steadily and judiciously, will maintain the grassed surfaces, even of the largest of our forts, in good condition.

43. The burning of grass upon any portion of a fortification is strictly forbidden.

44. Particular attention is required to prevent the formation of gullies in the parade, terreplein, and ramps, and especially in slopes where grass is not well established. If neglected, they soon involve heavy expense.

45. Earth, sand, or ashes must not be placed against wood-work; a free ventilation must be preserved around it; and all wooden floors, platforms, bridges, &c., will be kept clean swept.

46. The machinery of draw-bridges, gates, and posterns must be kept in good working order by proper cleaning and oiling of the parts; the bridges will be raised, and the gates and posterns opened as often as once a week.

47. The terrepleins of forts, the floors of casemates, caponniers, storerooms, barracks, galleries, posterns, magazines, &c., and the sidewalks in front of quarters and barracks, as well as other walks, are sometimes paved with bricks or stones, or formed of concrete. These surfaces must be preserved from injury with great care. In transporting guns and carriages, and in mounting them, strong way-planks will be used, and neither the wheels nor any other part of the carriages, nor any machinery, such as shears, gins, &c., nor any handspike or other implements, will be allowed to touch those surfaces. Unless protected in a similar manner, no wheelbarrow or other vehicle, no barrels, hogsheads, &c., will be rolled upon these surfaces. No violent work will be suffered to be done upon them, such as cutting wood, breaking coal, &c., and no heavy weight be thrown or permitted to fall thereon. In using machines, as gins, &c., in casemates, care must be taken not to injure the arch or ceiling, as well as the

floor. Neglect of these precautions may cause injuries slight in appearance but serious in effect from the leaking of water into masonry and casemates, and expensive to repair.

48. The doors and windows of all store-rooms and unoccupied casemates, quarters, barracks, &c., will be opened several times a week for thorough ventilation.

49. The masonry shot-furnaces will be heated only on the approach of an enemy. For ordinary practice with hot shot, iron furnaces are provided.

50. The foregoing matters involve but little expense; the labor is within the means of every garrison, and no technical knowledge is called for beyond what will be found among soldiers. Other repairs requiring small disbursements, such as repainting exposed wood or iron work, can be also executed by the garrison; but reports, estimates, and requisitions may be necessary to obtain the materials.

51. No alteration will be made in any fortification, or in its casemates, quarters, barracks, magazines, store-houses, or any other building belonging to it; nor will any building of any kind, or work of earth, masonry, or timber be erected within the fortification, or on its exterior within half a mile, except under the superintendence of the Engineer Department, and by the authority of the Secretary of War.

ARTICLE X.

CARE OF ARMAMENT OF FORTIFICATIONS.

52. At each permanent post with a fixed battery, and garrisoned by not more than one company, there will be kept mounted, for purposes of instruction and target practice, *three* heavy guns, and at posts garrisoned by more than one company, at the rate of *two* for each of the companies composing its garrison. The other guns dismounted will be properly placed (see page 21, Ordnance Manual for 1850) within their own traverse circles, and the carriages preserved from the weather.

53. All guns should be sponged clean and their vents examined to see that they are clear. The chassis should be traversed and left in a different position, the top carriage moved backward and forward and left alternately over the front and rear transoms of the chassis; the elevating screws or machines wiped clean, worked and oiled if required, and the nuts of all bolts screwed up tight. This should all be done regularly once in every week.

54. When tarpaulins, or pent houses, are placed over the guns, they should be removed once a week when the weather is fair, the carriages and guns brushed off, and, if damp, allowed to dry.

55. An old sponge-staff and head should be used for drill. The new

sponges should never be used unless the gun is fired. The implements should be kept in store, under cover, and be examined, wiped clean or brushed at least once a month. In the case of leather equipments, the directions for the preservation of harness in the Ordnance Manual should be followed.

56. The magazine should be frequently examined to see that the powder is well preserved. It should be opened every other day when the air is dry and clear. Barrels of powder should be turned and rolled occasionally. Under ordinary circumstances, only a few cartridges should be kept filled. If the paper body of the cartridge becomes soft or loses its sizing, it is certain that the magazine is very damp, and some means should be found to improve the ventilation. Cartridge bags may be kept in the magazine ready for filling; also port-fires, fuzes, tubes, and primers. Stands of grape, canisters, and wads for barbette guns, should be kept in store with the implements. For casemate guns, wads may be hung in bundles, and grape and canisters placed near the guns. Shot, well lacquered and clean, may be placed in piles near the guns.

ARTICLE XI.

ARTILLERY PRACTICE.

57. At all posts with fixed batteries, the position of every gun, mounted or to be mounted, will have its number, and this number be placed on the gun when in position.

58. For every such work a post-book of record will be kept, under the direction of the commander of the post, in which will be duly entered— the number of each mounted gun, its calibre, weight, names of founder and its inspector, and other marks; the description of its carriage and date of reception at the post; where from; and the greatest field of fire of the gun in its position.

59. Every commander of a fort or other fixed battery will, before entering on artillery practice, carefully reconnoitre and cause to be sketched for his record-book, the water-channels with their soundings, and other approaches to the work. Buoys or marks will be placed at the extreme and intermediate ranges of the guns, and these marks be numerically noted on the sketch. A buoy at every five hundred yards may suffice.

60. At the time of practice, a distinct and careful note will be made for the record-book of every shot or shell that may be thrown, designating the guns fired by their numbers, the charges of powder used, the times of flight of shots and shells, the ranges and ricochets, and the positions of guns in respect to the horizontal and vertical lines.

61. The time of flight of a shell may be noted with sufficient **accuracy**

by a stop-watch, or by counting the beats (previously ascertaining their value) of other watches, and the range may sometimes be computed by the time of flight. Other modes of ascertaining the range will readily occur to officers of science.

62. When charged shells with fuzes are thrown, the time of bursting will be noted. If they are intended to fall on land, only a blowing charge will be given to the shells, so that they may be picked up for further use.

63. On filling from the barrel, the proof range of powder will be marked on the cartridges.

64. The general objects of this practice are—to give to officers and men the ready and effective use of batteries; to preserve on record the more important results for the benefit of the same, or future commanders, and to ascertain the efficiency of guns and carriages.

65. Commanders of field artillery will also keep registers of their practice, so that not a shot or shell shall be thrown in the Army, for instruction, without distinct objects, such as range, accuracy of aim, number of ricochets, time of bursting, in the case of shells, &c.

66. Every company with a field battery will be allowed for annual practice as many blank cartridges for the instruction and drill as may be necessary for the purpose, on requisitions duly approved at the proper Departments. Companies with fixed batteries will be allowed 100 cartridges each, with seventy-five shots or shells. This ammunition will be expended in equal parts in the three months designated below, and if the company be mounted, eight blank cartridges will be allowed for each of the other months in the year. This allowance is intended only for companies *permanently* serving with batteries. The firing with field-guns by other Artillery companies must be confined to *blank* cartridges.

67. For all Artillery there will be annually three periods of practice in firing—*April, June,* and *October* for the latitude of Washington and south; and *May, July,* and *September* north of that latitude.

68. At the termination of each period of practice, the commanding officers of posts will transmit to the Adjutant-General full reports of the results, in order that proper tabular statements may be prepared for the War Department.

69. To determine accuracy of aim in firing shot and shell, butts or targets will be used. Where no natural butt presents itself, targets will be erected. A form for floating targets will be sent to the commanders of the several forts.

70. As practice in gunnery is a heavy expense to government, commanders of companies and their immediate superiors are charged with

the strict execution of the foregoing details; and all officers authorized to make tours of inspection will report, through the prescribed channels, on such execution.

ARTICLE XII.

REGIMENTS.

71. On the organization of a regiment, the companies receive a permanent designation by letters beginning with A, and the officers are assigned to companies; afterward, company officers succeed to companies, as promoted to fill vacancies. Companies take place in the battalion according to the rank of their captains.

72. Captains should be with their companies. Therefore, although subject to the temporary details of service, as for courts-martial, military boards, &c., they shall not, except for urgent reasons, be detailed upon any duty which may separate them for any considerable time from their companies.

73. The commander of a regiment will appoint the adjutant from the subalterns of the regiment. He will nominate the regimental quartermaster to the Secretary of War for appointment if approved. He will appoint the non-commissioned staff of the regiment; and, upon the recommendation of the company commanders, the sergeants and corporals of companies.

74. In cases of vacancy, and till a decision can be had from regimental head-quarters, the company commanders may make temporary appointments of non-commissioned officers.

75. Commanders of regiments are enjoined to avail themselves of every opportunity of instructing both officers and men in the exercise and management of field artillery; and all commanders ought to encourage useful occupations, and manly exercises and diversions among their men, and to repress dissipation and immorality.

76. Regiments serving on foot, being usually employed as light troops, will be habitually exercised in the system of U. S. Tactics for light infantry and riflemen adopted by the War Department, May 1, 1861.

NON-COMMISSIONED OFFICERS.

77. A board, to consist of the Professors of Mathematics and Ethics and the Commandant of Cadets, will convene at the Military Academy, on the first Monday of September in every year, for the examination of such non-commissioned officers, for promotion, as have already passed the regimental examination prescribed in General Orders No. 17, of October 4, 1854.

Non-Commissioned Officers.

78. It is enjoined upon all officers to be cautious in reproving non-commissioned officers in the presence or hearing of privates, lest their authority be weakened ; and non-commissioned officers are not to be sent to the guard-room and mixed with privates during confinement, but to be considered as placed in arrest, except in aggravated cases, where escape may be apprehended.

79. Non-commissioned officers may be reduced to the ranks by the sentence of a court-martial, or by order of the commander of the regiment on the application of the company commander. If reduced to the ranks by garrison courts, at posts not the head-quarters of the regiment, the company commander will immediately forward a transcript of the order to the regimental commander.

80. Every non-commissioned officer shall be furnished with a certificate or warrant of his rank, signed by the colonel and countersigned by the adjutant. Blank warrants, on parchment, are furnished from the Adjutant-General's office. The first, or orderly sergeant, will be selected by the captain from the sergeants.

81. When it is desired to have bands of music for regiments, there will be allowed for each, sixteen privates to act as musicians, in addition to the chief musicians authorized by law, provided the total number of privates in the regiment, including the band, does not exceed the legal standard. Regimental commanders will without delay designate the proportion to be subtracted from each company for a band, and the "number of recruits required" will be reported accordingly. The companies from which the non-commissioned officers of bands for artillery regiments shall be deducted, will in like manner be designated, and vacancies left accordingly. At the artillery school, Fort Monroe, the non-commissioned officers and privates of the band, will be apportioned among the companies serving at the post.

82. The musicians of the band will, for the time being, be dropped from company muster-rolls, but they will be instructed as soldiers, and liable to serve in the ranks on any occasion. They will be mustered in a separate squad under the chief musician, with the non-commissioned staff, and be included in the aggregate in all regimental returns.

83. When a regiment occupies several stations, the band will be kept at the head-quarters, *provided* troops (one or more companies) be serving there. The field music belonging to companies not stationed at regimental head-quarters will not be separated from their respective companies.

84. No man, unless he be a carpenter, joiner, carriage-maker, blacksmith, saddler, or harness-maker, will be mustered as an "artificer."

85. Every article, excepting arms and accoutrements, belonging to the regiment, is to be marked with the number and name of the regiment.

86. Such articles as belong to companies are to be marked with the letter of the company, and number and name of the regiment; and such as belong to men, with their individual numbers, and the letter of the company.

87. All orders and circulars from general, department, division, or brigade head-quarters, will be tied together in book form, and properly indexed as they are received; and afterwards bound in volumes of convenient size.

88. The books for each regiment shall be as follows:

1. *Regimental Order Book*, of three quires of paper, 16 inches by 10½ inches, to contain regimental orders, with an index.

2. *Letter Book*, of three quires of paper, 16 inches by 10½ inches, to contain the correspondence of the commanding officer on regimental subjects, with an index.

3. An index of letters required to be kept on file, in the following form:

No.	Name of writer.	Date.	Subject.
1	Captain A. B.....	July 15, 1860	Appointm't of non-com. officers.
2	Adjt. Gen. R. J..	Sept. 4, 1860	Recruiting service.
3	Captain F. G.....	Oct. 11, 1860	Error in company return.
4	Lieutenant C. D.	Nov. 2, 1860	Application for leave.

The date of receipt should be indorsed on all letters. They should be numbered to correspond with the index, and filed in regular order, for easy reference.

4. *Descriptive Book*, of five quires of paper, 16 inches by 10½ inches, to contain a list of the officers of the regiment, with their rank, and dates of appointment, and promotions; transfers, leaves of absence, and places and dates of birth. To contain, also, the names of all enlisted soldiers, entered according to priority of enlistments, giving their description, the dates and periods of their enlistment; and, under the head of remarks, the cause of discharge, *character*, death, desertion, transfer, *actions in which engaged*, &c.; in short, every thing relating to their *military history*. This book to be indexed, and when filled, and no longer needed with the company, to be forwarded to the Adjutant-General's office. One copy of the monthly returns will be filed.

POST BOOKS.

89. The following books will be kept at each post: a Morning Report Book, a Guard Report Book, an Order Book, a Letter Book, each two quires foolscap; also copies of the monthly post returns

ARTICLE XIII.

COMPANIES.

90. The captain will cause the men of the company to be numbered, in a regular series, including the non-commissioned officers, and divided into four squads, each to be put under the charge of a non-commissioned officer.

91. Each subaltern officer will be charged with a squad for the supervision of its order and cleanliness; and captains will require their lieutenants to assist them in the performance of *all* company duties.

92. As far as practicable, the men of each squad will be quartered together.

93. The utmost attention will be paid by commanders of companies to the cleanliness of their men, as to their persons, clothing, arms, accoutrements, and equipments, and also as to their quarters or tents.

94. The name of each soldier will be labeled on his bunk, and his company number will be placed against his arms and accoutrements.

95. The arms will be placed in the arm-racks, the stoppers in the muzzles, the cocks let down, and the bayonets in their scabbards; the accoutrements suspended over the arms, and the swords hung up by the belts on pegs.

96. The knapsack of each man will be placed on the lower shelf of his bunk, at its foot, packed with his effects, and ready to be slung; the great-coat on the same shelf, rolled and strapped; the coat, folded inside out, and placed under the knapsack; the cap on the second or upper shelf; and the boots well cleaned.

97. Dirty clothes will be kept in an appropriate part of the knapsack; no article of any kind to be put under the bedding.

98. Cooking utensils and table equipage will be cleaned and arranged in closets or recesses; blacking and brushes out of view; the fuel in boxes.

99. Ordinarily the cleaning will be on Saturdays. The chiefs of squads will cause bunks and bedding to be overhauled; floors dry rubbed; tables and benches scoured; arms cleaned; accoutrements whitened and polished, and every thing put in order.

100. Where conveniences for bathing are to be had, the men should bathe once or twice a week. The feet to be washed at least twice a week. The hair *kept short*, and beard neatly trimmed.

101. Non-commissioned officers, in command of squads, will be held more immediately responsible that their men observe what is prescribed above; that they wash their hands and faces daily; that they brush or

comb their heads; that those who are to go on duty put their arms, accoutrements, dress, &c., in the best order, and that such as have permission to pass the chain of sentinels are in the dress that may be ordered.

102. Commanders of companies and squads will see that the arms and accoutrements in possession of the men are always kept in good order, and that proper care be taken in cleaning them.

103. When belts are given to a soldier, the captain will see that they are properly fitted to the body; and it is forbidden to cut any belt without his sanction.

104. Cartridge-boxes and bayonet-scabbards will be polished with blacking; varnish is injurious to the leather, and will not be used.

105. All arms in the hands of the troops, whether browned or bright, will be kept in the state in which they are issued by the Ordnance Department. Arms will not be taken to pieces without permission of a commissioned officer. Bright barrels will be kept clean and free from rust without polishing them; care should be taken in rubbing not to bruise or bend the barrel. After firing, wash out the bore; wipe it dry, and then pass a bit of cloth, slightly greased, to the bottom. In these operations, a rod of wood with a loop in one end is to be used instead of the rammer. The barrel, when not in use, will be closed with a stopper. For exercise, each soldier should keep himself provided with a piece of sole leather to fit the cup or countersink of the hammer.

(For care of arms in service, see Ordnance Manual, page 185, &c.)

106. Arms shall not be left loaded in quarters or tents, or when the men are off duty, except by special orders.

107. Ammunition issued will be inspected frequently. Each man will be made to pay for the rounds expended without orders, or not in the way of duty, or which may be damaged or lost by his neglect.

108. Ammunition will be frequently exposed to the dry air, or sunned.

109. Special care shall be taken to ascertain that no ball-cartridges are mixed with the blank cartridges issued to the men.

110. All knapsacks are to be painted black. Those for the artillery will be marked in the centre of the cover with the number of the regiment only, in figures of one inch and a half in length, of the character called full face, with yellow paint. Those for the infantry will be marked in the same way, in white paint. Those for the ordnance will be marked with two cannon, crossing; the cannon to be seven and a half inches in length, in yellow paint, to resemble those on the cap. The knapsack straps will be black.

111. The knapsacks will also be marked upon the inner side with the letter of the company and the number of the soldier, on such part as may be readily observed at inspections

112. Haversacks will be marked upon the flap with the number and name of the regiment, the letter of the company, and number of the soldier, in black letters and figures. And each soldier must, at all times, be provided with a haversack and canteen, and will exhibit them at all inspections. It will be worn on the left side on marches, guard, and when paraded for detached service—the canteen outside the haversack.

113. The front of the drums will be painted with the arms of the United States, on a blue field for the infantry, and on a red field for the artillery. The letter of the company and number of the regiment, under the arms, in a scroll.

114. Officers at their stations, in camp or in garrison, will always wear their proper uniform.

115. Soldiers will wear the prescribed uniform in camp or garrison, and will not be permitted to keep in their possession any other clothing. When on fatigue parties, they will wear the proper fatigue dress.

116. In camp or barracks, the company officers must visit the kitchen daily and inspect the kettles, and at all times carefully attend to the messing and economy of their respective companies. The commanding officer of the post or regiment will make frequent inspections of the kitchens and messes. These duties are of the utmost importance—not to be neglected.

117. The bread must be thoroughly baked, and not eaten until it is cold. The soup must be boiled at least five hours, **and** the vegetables always cooked sufficiently to be perfectly soft and digestible.

118. Messes will be prepared by privates of squads, including private musicians, each taking his tour. The greatest care will be observed in washing and scouring the cooking utensils; those made of brass and copper should be lined with tin.

119. The messes of prisoners will be sent to them by the cooks.

120. No persons will be allowed to visit or remain in the kitchens, except such as may come on duty, or be occupied as cooks. The kitchen should always be under the particular charge of a non-commissioned officer.

121. Those detailed for duty in the kitchens will also be required to keep the furniture of the mess-room in order.

122. On marches and in the field, the only mess furniture of the soldier will be one tin plate, one tin cup, one knife, fork, and spoon, to each man, to be carried by himself on the march.

123. Tradesmen may be relieved from ordinary military duty to make, to alter, or to mend soldiers' clothing, &c. Company commanders will fix the rates at which work shall be done, and cause the men, for whose benefit it is done, to pay for it at the next pay day.

124. Each company officer, serving with his company, may take from it one soldier as waiter, with his consent and the consent of his captain. No other officer shall take a soldier as a waiter. Every soldier so employed shall be so reported and mustered.

125. Soldiers taken as officers' waiters shall be acquainted with their military duty, and at all times be completely armed and clothed, and in every respect equipped according to the rules of the service, and have all their necessaries complete and in good order. They are to fall in with their respective companies at all reviews and inspections, and are liable to such drills as the commanding officer shall judge necessary to fit them for service in the ranks.

126. Non-commissioned officers will, in no case, be permitted to act as waiters; nor are they, or private soldiers, not waiters, to be employed in any menial office, or made to perform any service not military, for the private benefit of any officer or mess of officers.

COMPANY BOOKS.

127. The following books are allowed to each company : one descriptive book, one clothing book, one order book, one morning report book, each one quire, sixteen inches by ten. One page of the descriptive book will be appropriated to the list of officers; two to the non-commissioned officers; two to the register of men transferred; four to register of men discharged; two to register of deaths; four to register of deserters—the rest to the company description list.

LAUNDRESS.

128. Four women will be allowed to each company as washerwomen, and will receive one ration per day each.

129. The price of washing soldiers' clothing, by the month, or by the piece, will be determined by the Council of Administration.

130. Debts due the laundress by soldiers, for washing, will be paid, or collected at the pay-table, under the direction of the captain.

ARTICLE XIV.
ORDNANCE SERGEANTS.

131. The Secretary of War selects from the sergeants of the *line* of the army, who may have faithfully served eight years (four years in the grade of non-commissioned officer), as many Ordnance Sergeants as the service may require, not exceeding one to each military post.

132. Captains will report to their colonels such sergeants as, by their conduct and service, merit such appointment, setting forth the descrip-

tion, length of service of the sergeant, the portion of his service he was a non-commissioned officer, his general character as to fidelity and sobriety, his qualifications as a clerk, and his fitness for the duties to be performed by an ordnance sergeant. These reports will be forwarded to the Adjutant-General, to be laid before the Secretary of War, with an application in the following form:

Head-Quarters, &c.

To the Adjutant-General:

Sir :—*I forward, for consideration of the proper authority, an application for the appointment of Ordnance Sergeant.*

Name and Regiment.	Letter of Company.	Length of Service.				Remarks.
		As non-commissioned Officer.		In the Army.		
		Years.	Months.	Years.	Months.	

Inclosed herewith you will receive the report of ————, the officer commanding the company in which the sergeant has been serving, to which I add the following remarks :

———— ————, *Commanding — Regiment.*

133. When a company is detached from the head-quarters of the regiment, the reports of the commanding officer in this matter will pass to the regimental head-quarters through the commanding officer of the post or detachment, and be accompanied by his opinion as to the fitness of the candidate.

134. Ordnance Sergeants will be assigned to posts when appointed, and are not to be transferred to other stations except by orders from the Adjutant-General's office.

135. At the expiration of their term of service, Ordnance Sergeants may be re-enlisted, provided they shall have conducted themselves in a becoming manner, and performed their duties to the satisfaction of the commanding officer. If the commanding officer, however, shall not think proper to re-enlist the Ordnance Sergeant of his post, he will communi-

cate to the Adjutant-General his reasons for declining to re-enlist him, in time to receive the decision of the War Department before the Sergeant may lawfully claim to re-enlist.

136. The officers interested must be aware, from the nature of the duties assigned to Ordnance Sergeants, that the judicious selection of them is of no small importance to the interests of the service; and that while the law contemplates, in the appointment of these non-commissioned officers, the better preservation of the ordnance and ordnance stores in deposit in the several forts, there is the further motive of offering a reward to those faithful and well-tried sergeants who have long served their country, and of thus giving encouragement to the soldier in the ranks to emulate them in conduct, and thereby secure substantial promotion. Colonels and Captains cannot, therefore, be too particular in investigating the characters of the candidates, and in giving their testimony as to their merits.

137. The appointment and removal of Ordnance Sergeants, stationed at military posts, in pursuance of the above provisions of law, shall be reported by the Adjutant-General to the chief of the Ordnance Department.

138. When a non-commissioned officer receives the appointment of Ordnance Sergeant, he shall be dropped from the rolls of the regiment or company in which he may be serving at the time.

139. The duty of Ordnance Sergeants relates to the care of the ordnance, arms, ammunition, and other military stores at the post to which they may be attached, under the direction of the commanding officer, and according to the regulations of the Ordnance Department.

140. If a post be evacuated, the Ordnance Sergeant shall remain on duty at the station, under the direction of the chief of the Ordnance Department, in charge of the ordnance and ordnance stores, and of such other public property as is not in charge of some officer or agent of other departments; for which ordnance stores and other property he will account to the chiefs of the proper departments until otherwise directed.

141. An Ordnance Sergeant in charge of ordnance stores at a post where there is no commissioned officer sha'l be held responsible for the safe-keeping of the property, and he shall be governed by the regulations of the Ordnance Department in making issues of the same, and in preparing and furnishing the requisite returns. If the means at his disposal are not sufficient for the preservation of the property, he shall report the circumstances to the chief of the Ordnance Department.

142. Ordnance Sergeants are to be considered as belonging to the non-commissioned staff of the post, under the orders of the commanding

officer. They are to wear the uniform of the Ordnance Department, with the distinctive badges prescribed for the non-commissioned staff of regiments of artillery; and they are to appear under arms with the troops at all reviews and inspections, monthly and weekly.

143. When serving at any post which may be the head-quarters of a regiment, Ordnance Sergeants shall be reported by name on the post returns, and mustered with the non-commissioned staff of the regiment; and at all other posts they shall be mustered and reported in some company stationed at the post at which they serve; be paid on the muster-roll, and be charged with the clothing and all other supplies previously received from any officer, or subsequently issued to them by the commanding officer of the company for the time being. Whenever the company may be ordered from the post, the Ordnance Sergeant will be transferred to the rolls of any remaining company, by the order of the commanding officer of the post.

144. In the event of the troops being all withdrawn from a post at which there is an Ordnance Sergeant, he shall be furnished with his descriptive roll and account of clothing and pay, signed by the proper officer last in command, accompanied by the remarks necessary for his military history; and on his exhibiting such papers to any Paymaster, with a letter from the Ordnance Office acknowledging the receipt of his returns, and that they are satisfactory, he will be paid on a separate account the amount which may be due him at the date of the receipt of the returns mentioned in such letter, together with commutation of rations, according to the regulations of the Subsistence Department. A certified statement of his pay account will be furnished the Ordnance Sergeant by the Paymaster by whom he may be last paid. When there are no troops at the post, the Ordnance Sergeant will report to the Adjutant-General's office, by letter, on the last day of every month.

ARTICLE XV.

TRANSFER OF SOLDIERS.

145. No non-commissioned officer or soldier will be transferred from one regiment to another without the authority of the commanding general.

146. The colonel may, upon the application of the captains, transfer a non-commissioned officer or soldier from one company to another of his regiment—with consent of the department commander in case of change of post.

147. When soldiers are authorized to be transferred, the transfer will take place on the first of a month, with a view to the more convenient settlement of their accounts.

Deceased Officers and Soldiers.

148. In all cases of transfer, a complete descriptive roll will accompany the soldier transferred, which roll will embrace an account of his pay, clothing, and other allowances; also, all stoppages to be made on account of the government, and debts due the laundress, as well as such other facts as may be necessary to show his character and military history.

ARTICLE XVI.
DECEASED OFFICERS.

149. Whenever an officer dies, or is killed at any military post or station, or in the vicinity of the same, it will be the duty of the commanding officer to report the fact direct to the Adjutant-General, with the date, and any other information proper to be communicated. If an officer die at a distance from a military post, any officer having intelligence of the same will in like manner communicate it, specifying the day of his decease; a duplicate of the report will be sent to Department Head-Quarters.

150. Inventories of the effects of deceased officers, required by the 94th Article of War, will be transmitted to the Adjutant-General.

151. If a legal administrator or family connection be present, and take charge of the effects, it will be so stated to the Adjutant-General.

ARTICLE XVII.
DECEASED SOLDIERS.

152. Inventories of the effects of deceased non-commissioned officers and soldiers, required by the 95th Article of War, will be forwarded to the Adjutant-General, by the commander of the company to which the deceased belonged, and a duplicate of the same to the colonel of the regiment. Final statements of pay, clothing, &c., will be sent with the inventories. When a soldier dies at a post or station absent from his company, it will be the duty of his immediate commander to furnish the required inventory, and, at the same time, to forward to the commanding officer of the company to which the soldier belonged, a report of his death, specifying the date, place, and cause; to what time he was last paid, and the money or other effects in his possession at the time of his decease; which report will be noted on the next muster-roll of the company to which the man belonged. Each inventory will be indorsed, "Inventory of the effects of ———— ————, late of company (—) ——- regiment of ——, who died at ————, the —— day of ————, 186-." If a legal representative receive the effects, it will be stated in the report. If the soldier leave no effects, the fact will be reported.

153. Should the effects of a deceased non-commissioned officer or

soldier not be administered upon within a short period after his decease, they shall be disposed of by a Council of Administration, under the authority of the commanding officer of the post, and the proceeds deposited with the Paymaster, to the credit of the United States, until they shall be claimed by the legal representatives of the deceased.

154. In all such cases of sales by the Council of Administration, a statement in detail, or account of the proceeds, duly certified by the Council and commanding officer, accompanied by the Paymaster's receipt for the proceeds, will be forwarded by the commanding officer to the Adjutant-General. The statement will be endorsed, "Report of the proceeds of the effects of ———— ————, late of company (—) —— regiment of ——, who died at ————, the —— day of ————, 186–."

ARTICLE XVIII.

DESERTERS.

155. If a soldier desert from, or a deserter be received at, any post other than the station of the company or detachment to which he belonged, he shall be promptly reported by the commanding officer of such post to the commander of his company or detachment. The time of desertion, apprehension, and delivery will be stated. If the man be a recruit, unattached, the required report will be made to the Adjutant-General. When a report is received of the apprehension or surrender of a deserter at any post other than the station of the company or detachment to which he belonged, the commander of such company or detachment shall immediately forward his description and account of clothing to the officer making the report.

156. A reward of five dollars will be paid for the apprehension and delivery of a deserter to an officer of the army at the most convenient post or recruiting station. Rewards thus paid will be promptly reported by the disbursing officer to the officer commanding the company in which the deserter is mustered, and to the authority competent to order his trial. The reward of five dollars will include the remuneration for all expenses incurred for apprehending, securing, and delivering a deserter.

157. When non-commissioned officers or soldiers are sent in pursuit of a deserter, the expenses necessarily incurred will be paid whether he be apprehended or not, and reported as in case of rewards paid.

158. Deserters shall make good the time lost by desertion, unless discharged by competent authority.

159. No deserter shall be restored to duty without trial, except by authority competent to order the trial.

160. Rewards and expenses paid for apprehending a deserter will be set against his pay, *when adjudged by a court-martial*, or when he is restored to duty without trial on such *condition*.

161. In reckoning the time of service, and the pay and allowances of a deserter, he is to be considered as again in service when delivered up as a deserter to the proper authority.

162. An apprehended deserter, or one who surrenders himself, shall receive no pay while waiting trial, and only such clothing as may be actually necessary for him.

ARTICLE XIX.

DISCHARGES.

163. No enlisted man shall be discharged before the expiration of his term of enlistment without authority of the War Department, except by sentence of a general court-martial, or by the commander of the Department or of an army in the field, on certificate of disability, or on application of the soldier after twenty years' service.

164. When an enlisted man is to be discharged, his company commander shall furnish him certificates of his account, usually called final statements, according to Form 4, Pay Department. And to *ensure* his being at the post to get these, no leave of absence, terminating with his service, will be given to him. He may, however, be discharged in advance of the latter, under the circumstances and conditions described in General Orders No. 24, from the War Department, of November 30, 1859.

165. Blank discharges on parchment will be furnished from the Adjutant-General's office. No discharge shall be made in duplicate, nor any certificate given in lieu of a discharge.

166. The cause of discharge will be stated in the body of the discharge, and the space at foot for character cut off, unless a recommendation is given.

167. Whenever a non-commissioned officer or soldier shall be unfit for the military service in consequence of wounds, disease, or infirmity, his captain shall forward to the commander of the Department or of the army in the field, through the commander of the regiment or post, a statement of his case, with a certificate of his disability signed by the senior surgeon of the hospital, regiment, or post, according to the form prescribed in the Medical Regulations.

168. If the recommendation for the discharge of the invalid be approved, the authority therefor will be indorsed on the " certificate of disability," which will be sent back to be completed and signed by the

commanding officer, who will then send the same to the Adjutant-General's office.

169. Insane soldiers will not be discharged, but sent, under proper protection, by the Department commander to Washington for the order of the War Department for their admission into the Government Asylum. The history of the cases, with the men's descriptive list, and accounts of pay and clothing, will be sent with them.

170. The date, place, and cause of discharge of *t.* soldier absent from his company will be reported by the commander of the post to his company commander.

171. Company commanders are required to keep the blank discharges and all certificates relating to discharge carefully in their *own custody.*

172. No volunteer will be discharged upon Surgeon's certificate of disability until the certificate shall have been submitted to the Medical Director, and shall have been approved and countersigned by him

ARTICLE XX.

TRAVELING ON DUTY.

173. Whenever an officer traveling under orders arrives at his post, he will submit to the commanding officer a report, in writing, of the time occupied in the travel, with a copy of the orders under which the journey was performed, and an explanation of any delay in the execution of the orders; which report the commanding officer shall transmit, with his opinion on it, to Department Head-Quarters. If the officer be superior in rank to the commander, the required report will be made by the senior himself.

174. Orders detaching an officer for a special duty, imply, unless otherwise stated, that he is thereafter to join his proper station.

ARTICLE XXI.

LEAVES OF ABSENCE TO OFFICERS.

175. In no case will leaves of absence be granted, so that a company be left without one of its *commissioned officers,* or that a garrisoned post be left without two commissioned officers and competent medical attendance; nor shall leave of absence be granted to an officer during the season of active operations, except on urgent necessity.

176. When not otherwise specified, leaves of absence will be considered as commencing on the day that the officer is relieved from duty at his post. He will report, monthly, his address for the next thirty days, to the commander of his post and of his regiment or corps, and to

Leaves of Absence to Officers.

the Adjutant-General, together with every change of address; and in his first report state the day when his leave of absence commenced. The expiration of his leave must find him at his station.

177. In time of peace, commanding officers may grant leaves of absence as follows : the commander of a post not to exceed seven days at one time, or in the same month; the commander of a geographical department not to exceed sixty days. Applications for leaves of absence for more than four months, or to officers of engineers, ordnance, or of the general staff, or serving on it (aides-de-camp excepted), for more than thirty days, must be referred to the Adjutant-General for the decision of the Secretary of War. In giving a permission to apply for the extension of a leave of absence, the term of the extension should be stated. The term of the extension approved by the Department commander will be regulated by the season and the usual opportunities for reaching the officer's station, so that he may not be absent during the time for active operations.

178. The War Department will not grant leaves to officers on applications made out of the proper military channel; or longer extensions of leave than are recommended by the competent authority.

179. The immediate commander of the officer applying for leave of absence, and all intermediate commanders, will indorse their opinion on the application before forwarding it.

180. The commander of a post may take leave of absence not to exceed seven days at one time, or in the same month, reporting the fact to his next superior.

181. Three months' leave of absence will be allowed to graduates, from the time of quitting (as cadet) the Military Academy.

182. No leave of absence exceeding seven days, except on extraordinary occasions, when the circumstances must be particularly stated (and except as provided in the preceding paragraph), shall be granted to any officer until he has joined his regiment or corps, and served therewith at least two years.

183. Officers will not leave the United States, to go beyond sea, without permission from the War Department.

184. All leaves of absence to Chaplains and Schoolmasters employed at military posts will be granted by the commanding officer, on the recommendation of the post Council of Administration, not to exceed four months.

185. An application for leave of absence on account of sickness must be accompanied by a certificate of the senior medical officer present, in the following form :

—— ——, *of the* —— *regiment of* ——, *having applied for a certificate on which to ground an application for leave of absence, I do hereby certify that I have carefully examined this officer, and find that* — [Here the nature of the disease, wound, or disability is to be fully stated, and the period during which the officer has suffered under its effects.] *And that, in consequence thereof, he is, in my opinion, unfit for duty. I further declare my belief that he will not be able to resume his duties in a less period than* —— [Here state candidly and explicitly the opinion as to the period which will probably elapse before the officer will be able to resume his duties. When there is no reason to expect a recovery, or when the prospect of recovery is distant and uncertain, or when a change of climate is recommended, it must be so stated.] *Dated at* ——, *this* —— *day of* ——.

Signature of the Medical Officer.

186. Leaves of absence on account of sickness will not be granted to officers to go beyond the limits of the Military Department within which they are stationed, unless the certificate of the medical officer shall explicitly state that a greater change is necessary to save life, or prevent *permanent* disability. Nor will sick leaves to go beyond the Department limits be given in any case, except of immediate urgency, without the previous sanction of the War Department.

187. On the expiration of a leave of absence given on account of sickness, if the officer *be able to travel*, he will forthwith proceed to his post, although his disability may not have been removed. Exceptions to this general rule must be made in each case by the War Department on full and explicit medical certificates setting forth the reasons for delay and the length of time delay is considered necessary.

188. When an officer is prevented by sickness from joining his station, he will transmit certificates in the above form monthly, to the commanding officer of his post and regiment or corps, and to the Adjutant-General; and when he cannot procure the certificates of a medical officer of the army, he will substitute his own certificate on honor to his condition, and a full statement of his case. If the officer's certificate is not satisfactory, and whenever an officer has been absent on account of sickness for one year, he shall be examined by a medical board, and the case specially reported to the President.

189. In all reports of absence, or applications for leave of absence on account of sickness, the officer shall state how long he has been absent already on that account, and by whose permission.

ARTICLE XXII.

FURLOUGHS TO ENLISTED MEN.

190. Furloughs will be granted only by the commanding officer of the post, or the commanding officer of the regiment actually quartered with it. Furloughs may be prohibited at the discretion of the officer in command, and are not to be granted to soldiers about to be discharged.

191. Soldiers on furlough shall not take with them their arms or accoutrements.

192. Form of furlough:

TO ALL WHOM IT MAY CONCERN.

The bearer hereof, —— ——, a Sergeant (corporal, or private, as the case may be) of Captain —— —— company, —— regiment of ——, aged — years, — feet — inches high, —— complexion, —— eyes, —— hair, and by profession a ——; born in the —— of ——, and enlisted at ——, in the —— of ——, on the — day of ——, eighteen hundred and ——, to serve for the period of ——, is hereby permitted to go to ——, in the county of ——, State of ——, he having received a Furlough from the — day of ——, to the — day of ——, at which period he will rejoin his company or regiment at ——, or wherever it then may be, or be considered a deserter.

Subsistence has been furnished to said —— —— to the — day of ——, and pay to the — day of ——, both inclusive.

Given under my hand, at ——, this — day of ——, 18—.

Signature of the officer ⎱
   giving the furlough. ⎰   —— ——.

ARTICLE XXIII.

COUNCILS OF ADMINISTRATION.

193. The commanding officer of every post shall, at least once in every two months, convene a *Post Council of Administration*, to consist of the *three* regimental or company officers next in rank to himself; or, if there be but two, then the *two* next; if but one, the *one* next; and if there be none other than himself, then he himself shall act.

194. The junior member will record the proceedings of the Council in a book, and submit the same to the commanding officer. If he disapprove the proceedings, and the Council, after a reconsideration, adhere to its decision, a copy of the whole shall be sent by the officer commanding to the next higher commander, whose decision shall be final, and entered

in the Council book, and the whole be published in orders for the information and government of all concerned.

195. The proceedings of Councils of Administration shall be signed by the president and recorder, and the recorder of each meeting, after entering the whole proceedings, together with the final order thereon, shal. deposit the book with the commanding officer. In like manner, the approval or objections of the officer ordering the Council will be signed with his own hand.

196. The Post Council shall prescribe the quantity and kind of clothing, small equipments, and soldiers' necessaries, groceries, and all articles which the sutlers may be required to keep on hand; examine the sutler's books and papers, and fix the tariff of prices of the said goods or commodities; inspect the sutler's weights and measures; fix the laundress' charges, and make regulations for the post school.

197. Pursuant to the 30th Article of War, commanding officers reviewing the proceedings of the Council of Administration will scrutinize the tariff of prices proposed by them, and take care that the stores actually furnished by the sutler correspond to the quality prescribed.

POST FUND.

198. A Post Fund shall be raised at each post by a tax on the sutler, not to exceed 10 cents a month for every officer and soldier of the command, according to the average in each month to be ascertained by the Council, and from the saving on the flour ration, ordinarily 33 per cent., by baking the soldiers' bread at a post bakery. Provided, that when want of vegetables or other reasons make it necessary, the commanding officer may order the flour saved, or any part of it, issued to the men, after paying expenses of baking.

199. The commanding officer shall designate an officer to be post treasurer, who shall keep the account of the fund, subject to the inspection of the Council and commanding officer, and disburse the fund on the warrants of the commanding officer, drawn in pursuance of specific resolves of the Council.

200. The following are the objects of expenditure of the post fund:—1st. Expenses of the bake-house; 2d. support of a band; 3d. the post school for soldiers' children; 4th. for formation of a library.

201. On the last day of April, August, and December, and when relieved from the duty, the treasurer shall make out his account with the fund since his last account, and submit it, with his vouchers, to the Council of Administration, to be examined by them, and recorded in the Council book, and then forwarded by the commanding officer to Department Head-Quarters.

202. At each settlement of the treasurer's account, the Council shall distribute the unexpended balance of the post fund to the several companies and other troops in the ratio of their average force during the period.

203. When a company leaves the post, it shall then receive its distributive share of the accrued fund.

204. The regulations in regard to a post fund will, as far as practicable, be applied in the field to a regimental fund, to be raised, administered, expended, and distributed in like manner, by the regimental commander and a regimental council.

COMPANY FUND.

205. The distributions from the post or regimental fund, and the savings from the company rations, constitute the Company Fund, to be disbursed by the captain for the benefit of the enlisted men of the company, pursuant to resolves of the Company Council, consisting of all the company officers present. In case of a tie vote in the Council, the commander of the post shall decide. The Council shall be convened once in two months by the captain, and whenever else he may think proper.

206. Their proceedings shall be recorded in a book, signed by all the Council, and open at all times to the inspection of the commander of the post. Every four months, and whenever another officer takes command of the company, and when the company leaves the post, the account of the company fund shall be made up, audited by the Council, recorded in the Council book, and submitted, with a duplicate, to the post commander, who shall examine it and forward the duplicate to Department Head-Quarters.

207. The supervision of the company fund by the post commander herein directed shall, in the field, devolve on the commander of the regiment.

ARTICLE XXIV.
CHAPLAINS.

208. One chaplain shall be allowed to each regiment of the army, to be appointed by the colonel, on the nomination of the company commanders. None but regularly ordained ministers of some Christian denomination, however, shall be eligible to appointment; and the wishes and wants of the soldiers of the regiment shall be allowed their *full* and *due* weight in making the selection. The proceedings in each case will be immediately forwarded to the Adjutant-General's office, the name and denomination of the chaplain being in every case reported. Chaplains will only be allowed to regiments which are embodied and serving together as one whole—not to regiments of which the companies are serving at different stations.

209. Chaplains, not to exceed thirty in number, are also allowed to

posts. The posts at which chaplains may be employed will be announced by the War Department, but the *appointment* will be made by the Council of Administration.

210. The Council of the post will, however, report to the Adjutant-General, for the approval of the Secretary of War, the rate of pay allowed to the person selected to officiate as Chaplain and perform the duties of Schoolmaster; the decision of the Secretary on this point will be notified to the commanding officer of the post by the Adjutant-General.

ARTICLE XXV.

SUTLERS.

211. Every military post may have one Sutler, to be appointed by the Secretary of War.

212. A Sutler shall hold his office for a term of three years, unless sooner removed; but the commanding officer may, for cause, suspend a Sutler's privilege until a decision of the War Department is received in the case.

213. In case of vacancy, a temporary appointment may be made by the commanding officer upon the nomination of the Council of Administration.

214. Troops in campaign, on detachment, or on distant service, will be allowed Sutlers, at the rate of one for every regiment, corps, or separate detachment; to be appointed by the commanding officer of such regiment, corps, or detachment, upon the recommendation of the Council of Administration, subject to the approval of the general or other officer in command.

215. No tax or burden in any shape, other than the authorized assessment for the post fund, will be imposed on the Sutler. If there be a spare building, the use of it may be allowed him, he being responsible that it is kept in repair. If there be no such building, he may be allowed to erect one; but this article gives the Sutler no claim to quarters, transportation for himself or goods, or to any military allowance whatever.

216. The tariff of prices fixed by the Council of Administration shall be exposed in a conspicuous place in the Sutler's store. No difference of prices will be allowed on cash or credit sales.

217. No Sutler shall sell to an enlisted man on credit to a sum exceeding *one-third* of his monthly pay, *within the same month*, without the written sanction of the company commander, or the commanding officer of the post or station, if the man does not belong to a company; and not exceeding *one-half* of the monthly pay with such permission.

218. Three days before the last of every month the Sutler shall render,

for verification, to the company commander, or to the commanding officer, as the case may be, according to the meaning of the preceding paragraph, a written and separate account in each case of any charges he may have against enlisted men for collection, and the officer shall submit the account to the soldier for acknowledgment and signature, and witness the same. In the case of death, desertion, or removal from the post (of the soldier), the account will be rendered immediately. If the soldier dispute the account and the Sutler insist, and in the case of death and desertion, the Sutler will be required to establish the account by affidavit indorsed on it before any officer authorized to administer an oath. Debts thus verified as due the Sutler are to be noted on the Muster Rolls, and will be paid by the Paymaster out of the arrearages due to the soldier at the time of death, desertion, discharge, or sentence of court-martial: the sums due the Government and laundress being first paid. Every facility will be afforded to the Sutler in the collection of the just debts contracted with him. He will, to this end, be allowed to take his place at the pay-table with his books and accounts.

219. Sutlers shall not farm out or underlet the business and privileges granted by their appointment.

ARTICLE XXVI.
MILITARY DISCUSSIONS AND PUBLICATIONS.

220. Deliberations or discussions among any class of military men, having the object of conveying praise, or censure, or any mark of approbation toward their superiors or others in the military service; and all publications relative to transactions between officers of a private or personal nature, whether newspaper, pamphlet, or hand-bill, are strictly prohibited.

ARTICLE XXVII.
ARRESTS AND CONFINEMENTS.

221. None but commanding officers have power to place officers under arrest except for offenses expressly designated in the 27th Article of War.

222. Officers are not to be put in arrest for light offenses. For these the censure of the commanding officer will, in most cases, answer the purposes of discipline.

223. An officer in arrest may, at the discretion of his commanding officer, have larger limits assigned him than his tent or quarters, on written application to that effect. Close confinement is not to be resorted to unless under circumstances of an aggravated character.

224. In ordinary cases, and where inconvenience to the service would

result from it, a medical officer will not be put in arrest until the court-martial for his trial convenes.

225. The arrest of an officer, or confinement of a soldier, will, as soon as practicable, be notified to his immediate commander.

226. All prisoners under guard, without written charges, will be released by the officer of the day at guard-mounting, unless orders to the contrary be given by the commanding officer.

227. On a march, company officers and non-commissioned officers in arrest will follow in the rear of their respective companies, unless otherwise particularly ordered.

228. Field officers, commissioned and non-commissioned staff officers, under the same circumstances, will follow in the rear of their respective regiments.

229. An officer under arrest will not wear a sword, or visit officially his commanding or other superior officer, unless sent for; and in case of business, he will make known his object in writing.

ARTICLE XXVIII.
HOURS OF SERVICE AND ROLL-CALLS.

230. In garrison, *reveille* will be sounded immediately after day-break; and *retreat* at sunset; the *troop, surgeon's call, signals* for breakfast and dinner at the hours prescribed by the commanding officer, according to climate and season. In the cavalry, *stable-calls* immediately after reveille, and an hour and a half before retreat; *water-calls* at the hours directed by the commanding officer.

231. In camp, the commanding officer prescribes the hours of reveille, reports, roll-calls, guard-mounting, meals, stable-calls, issues, fatigues, &c

232.   SIGNALS.

1. To go for fuel—*poing stroke and ten-stroke roll.*
2. To go for water—*two strokes and a flam.*
3. For fatigue party—*pioneer's march.*
4. Adjutant's call—*first part of the troop.*
5. First sergeant's call—*one roll and four taps.*
6. Sergeant's call—*one roll and three taps.*
7. Corporal's call—*one roll and two taps.*
8. For the drummers—*the drummer's call.*

233. The *drummer's call* shall be beat by the drums of the police guard five minutes before the time of beating the stated calls, when the drummers will assemble before the colors of their respective regiments,

and as soon as the beat begins on the right, it will be immediately taken up along the line.

ROLL-CALLS.

234. There shall be daily at least three roll-calls, viz., at *reveille, retreat,* and *tattoo.* They will be made on the company parades by the first sergeants, *superintended by a commissioned officer* of the company. The captains will report the absentees without leave to the colonel or commanding officer.

235. Immediately after *reveille* roll-call (after stable-duty in the cavalry), the tents or quarters, and the space around them, will be put in order by the men of the companies, superintended by the chiefs of squads, and the guard-house or guard-tent by the guard or prisoners.

236. The morning reports of companies, signed by the captains and First Sergeants, will be handed to the Adjutant before eight o'clock in the morning, and will be consolidated by the Adjutant within the next hour, for the information of the Colonel; and if the consolidation is to be sent to higher authority, it will be signed by the Colonel and the Adjutant.

ARTICLE XXIX.
HONORS TO BE PAID BY THE TROOPS.

237. The *President* or *Vice-President* is to be saluted with the highest honors—all standards and colors dropping, officers and troops saluting, drums beating and trumpets sounding.

238. A *General commanding-in-chief* is to be received—by cavalry, with sabres presented, trumpets sounding the march, and all the officers saluting, standards dropping; by infantry, with drums beating the march, colors dropping, officers saluting, and arms presented.

239. A *Major-General* is to be received—by cavalry, with sabres presented, trumpets sounding twice the trumpet-flourish, and officers saluting; by infantry, with three ruffles, colors dropping, officers saluting, and arms presented.

240. A *Brigadier-General* is to be received—by cavalry, with sabres presented, trumpets sounding once the trumpet-flourish, and officers saluting; by infantry, with two ruffles, colors dropping, officers saluting, and arms presented.

241. An *Adjutant-General* or *Inspector-General*, if under the rank of a General officer, is to be received at a review or inspection of the troops under arms—by cavalry, with sabres presented, officers saluting; by infantry, officers saluting and arms presented. The same honors to be paid

to any field-officer authorized to review and inspect the troops. When the inspecting officer is junior to the officer commanding the parade, no compliments will be paid: he will be received only with swords drawn and arms shouldered.

242. All guards are to turn out and present arms to *General officers* as often as they pass them, except the personal guards of General officers, which turn out only to the Generals whose guards they are, and to officers of superior rank.

243. To commanders of regiments, garrison, or camp, their own guard turn out, and present arms once a day; after which, they turn out with shouldered arms.

244. *To the members of the Cabinet; to the Chief Justice, the President of the Senate, and Speaker of the House of Representatives of the United States; and to Governors, within their respective States and Territories* —the same honors will be paid as to a General commanding-in-chief.

245. *Officers of a foreign service* may be complimented with the honors due to their rank.

246. *American and Foreign Envoys or Ministers* will be received with the compliments due to a Major-General.

247. The colors of a regiment passing a guard are to be saluted, the trumpets sounding, and the drums beating a march.

248. When General officers, or persons entitled to salute, pass in the rear of a guard, the officer is only to make his men stand shouldered, and not to face his guard about, or beat his drum.

249. When General officers, or persons entitled to a salute, pass guards while in the act of relieving, both guards are to salute, receiving the word of command from the senior officer of the whole.

250. All guards are to be under arms when armed parties approach their posts; and to parties commanded by commissioned officers, they are to present their arms, drums beating a march, and officers saluting.

251. No compliments by guards or sentinels will be paid between *retreat* and *reveille*, except as prescribed for *grand rounds*.

252. All guards and sentinels are to pay the same compliments to the officers of the navy, marines, and militia, in the service of the United States, as are directed to be paid to the officers of the army, according to their relative ranks.

253. It is equally the duty of non-commissioned officers and soldiers, *at all times* and *in all situations*, to pay the proper compliments to officers of the navy and marines, and to officers of other regiments, when in uniform, as to officers of their own particular regiments and corps.

254. Courtesy among military men is indispensable to discipline. Respect to superiors will not be confined to obedience on duty, but will be

extended to all occasions. It is always the duty of the inferior to accost or to offer first the customary salutation, and of the superior to return such complimentary notice.

255. Sergeants, with swords drawn, will salute by bringing them to a present--with muskets, by bringing the left hand across the body, so as to strike the musket near the right shoulder. Corporals out of the ranks, and privates not sentries, will carry their muskets at a shoulder as sergeants, and salute in like manner.

256. When a soldier without arms, or with side-arms only, meets an officer, he is to raise his hand to the right side of the visor of his cap, palm to the front, elbow raised as high as the shoulder, looking at the same time in a respectful and soldier-like manner at the officer, who will return the compliment thus offered.

257. A non-commissioned officer or soldier being seated, and without particular occupation, will rise on the approach of an officer, and make the customary salutation. If standing, he will turn toward the officer for the same purpose. If the parties remain in the same place or on the same ground, such compliments need not be repeated.

SALUTES.

258. The national salute is determined by the number of States composing the Union, at the rate of one gun for each State.

259. The *President of the United States* alone is to receive a salute of twenty-one guns.

260. The *Vice-President* is to receive a salute of seventeen guns.

261. The *Heads of the great Executive Departments of the National Government;* the *General commanding the army;* the *Governors of States and Territories,* within their respective jurisdictions, fifteen guns.

262. A *Major-General,* thirteen guns.

263. A *Brigadier-General,* eleven guns.

264. *Foreign ships of war* will be saluted in return for a similar compliment, gun for gun, on notice being officially received of such intention. If there be several posts in sight of, or within six miles of each other, the principal only shall reciprocate compliments with ships passing.

265. *Officers of the Navy* will be saluted according to relative rank.

266. *Foreign Officers* invited to visit a fort or post may be saluted according to their relative rank.

267. *Envoys and Ministers* of the United States and foreign powers are to be saluted with thirteen guns.

268. A General officer will be saluted but once in a year at each post and only when notice of his intention to visit the post has been given.

269. Salutes to individuals are to be fired on their arrival only.

270. A national salute will be fired at meridian on the anniversary of the Independence of the United States, at each military post and camp provided with artillery and ammunition.

ESCORTS OF HONOR.

271. Escorts of honor may be composed of cavalry or infantry, or both, according to circumstances. They are guards of honor for the purpose of receiving and escorting personages of high rank, civil or military. The troops for this purpose will be selected for their soldierly appearance and superior discipline.

272. The escort will be drawn up in line, the centre opposite to the place where the personage presents himself, with an interval between the wings to receive him and his retinue. On his appearance, he will be received with the honors due to his rank. When he has taken his place in the line, the whole will be wheeled into platoons or companies, as the case may be, and take up the march. The same ceremony will be observed, and the same honors paid, on his leaving the escort.

273. When the position of the escort is at a considerable distance from the point where he is expected to be received, as, for instance, where a court-yard or wharf intervenes, a double line of sentinels will be posted from that point to the escort, facing inward, and the sentinels will successively salute as he passes.

274. An officer will be appointed to attend him, to bear such communications as he may have to make to the commander of the escort.

FUNERAL HONORS.

275. On the receipt of official intelligence of the death of the *President of the United States*, at any post or camp, the commanding officer shall, on the following day, cause a gun to be fired at every half hour, beginning at sunrise, and ending at sunset. When posts are contiguous, the firing will take place at the post only commanded by the superior officer.

276. On the day of the interment of a *General commanding-in-chief*, a gun will be fired at every half hour, until the procession moves, beginning at sunrise.

277. The funeral escort of a *General commanding-in-chief* shall consist of a regiment of infantry, a squadron of cavalry, and six pieces of artillery.

278. That of a *Major-General*, a regiment of infantry, a squadron of cavalry, and four pieces of artillery.

279. That of a *Brigadier-General*, a regiment of infantry, one company of cavalry, and two pieces of artillery.

280 That of a *Colonel*, a regiment.

281. That of a *Lieutenant-Colonel*, six companies.

282 That of a *Major*, four companies.

283. That of a *Captain*, one company.

284. That of a *Subaltern*, half a company.

285. The funeral escort shall always be commanded by an officer of the same rank with the deceased; or, if none such be present, by one of the next inferior grade.

286. The funeral escort of a non-commissioned staff officer shall consist of sixteen rank and file, commanded by a Sergeant.

287. That of a Sergeant, of fourteen rank and file, commanded by a Sergeant.

288. That of a Corporal, of twelve rank and file, commanded by a Corporal; and,

289. That of a private, of eight rank and file, commanded by a Corporal.

290. The escort will be formed in two ranks, opposite to the quarters or tent of the deceased, with shouldered arms and bayonets unfixed; the artillery and cavalry on the right of the infantry.

291. On the appearance of the corpse, the officer commanding the escort will command,

Present—Arms!

when the honors due to the deceased will be paid by the drums and trumpets. The music will then play an appropriate air, and the coffin will then be taken to the right, where it will be halted. The commander will next order,

1. *Shoulder*—Arms! 2. *By company (or platoon), left wheel*. 3. March! 4. *Reverse*—Arms! 5. *Column, forward*. 6. *Guide right*. 7. March!

The arms will be reversed at the order by bringing the firelock under the left arm, butt to the front, barrel downward, left hand sustaining the lock, the right steadying the firelock behind the back; swords are reversed in a similar manner under the right arm.

292. The column will be marched in slow time to solemn music, and, on reaching the grave, will take a direction so as that the guides shall be next to the grave. When the centre of the column is opposite the grave, the commander will order,

1. *Column*. 2. Halt! 3. *Right into line, wheel*. 4. March!

The coffin is then brought along the front, to the opposite side of the grave, and the commander then orders,

1. *Shoulder*—ARMS! 2. *Present*—ARMS!

And when the coffin reaches the grave, he adds,

1. *Shoulder*—ARMS! 2. *Rest on*—ARMS!

The rest on arms is done by placing the muzzle on the left foot, both hands on the butt, the head on the hands or bowed, right knee bent.

293. After the funeral service is performed, and the coffin is lowered into the grave, the commander will order,

1. *Attention!* 2. *Shoulder*—ARMS! 3. *Load at will.* 4. LOAD!

When three rounds of small arms will be fired by the escort, taking care to elevate the pieces.

294. This being done, the commander will order,

1. *By company (or platoon), right wheel.* 2. MARCH! 3. *Column, forward.* 4. *Guide left.* 5. *Quick*—MARCH!

The music will not begin to play until the escort is clear of the inclosure.

295 When the distance to the place of interment is considerable, the escort may march in common time and in column of route, after leaving the camp or garrison, and till it approaches the burial-ground.

296. The pall-bearers, six in number, will be selected from the grade of the deceased, or from the grade or grades next above or below it.

297. At the funeral of an officer, as many in commission of the army, division, brigade, or regiment, according to the rank of the deceased, as can conveniently be spared from other duties, will join in the procession in uniform, and with side-arms. The funeral of a non-commissioned officer or private will be attended, in like manner, by the non-commissioned officers or privates of the regiment or company, according to the rank of the deceased, with side-arms only.

298. Persons joining in the procession follow the coffin in the inverse order of their rank.

299. The usual badge of military mourning is a piece of black crape around the left arm, above the elbow, and also upon the sword-hilt; and will be worn when in full or in undress.

300. As family mourning, crape will be worn by officers (when in uniform) only around the left arm.

301. The drums of a funeral escort will be covered with black crape, or thin black serge.

302. Funeral honors will be paid to deceased officers without military rank, according to their assimilated grades.

ARTICLE XXX.
INSPECTIONS OF THE TROOPS.

303. The inspection of troops, as a division, regiment, or other body composing a garrison or command, not less than a company, will generally be preceded by a review.

304. There will be certain periodical inspections, to wit:

1. The commanders of regiments and posts will make an inspection of their commands on the last day of every month.
2. Captains will inspect their companies every Sunday morning. No soldier will be excused from Sunday inspection except the guard, the sick, and the necessary attendants in the hospital.
3. Medical officers having charge of hospitals will also make a thorough inspection of them every Sunday morning.
4. Inspection when troops are mustered for payment.

305. Besides these inspections, frequent visits will be made by the commanding officer, company and medical officers, during the month, to the men's quarters, the hospital, guard-house, &c.

FORM OF INSPECTION.

306. The present example embraces a battalion of infantry. The inspecting officer and the field and staff officers will be on foot.

307. The battalion being in the order of battle, the Colonel will cause it to break into open column of companies, right in front. He will next order the ranks to be opened, when the color-rank and color-guard, under the direction of the Adjutant, will take post ten paces in front, and the band ten paces in rear of the column.

308. The Colonel, seeing the ranks aligned, will command,

1. *Officers and Sergeants, to the front of your companies.* 2. MARCH!

The officers will form themselves in one rank, eight paces, and the non-commissioned officers in one rank, six paces, in advance, along the whole fronts of their respective companies, from right to left, in the order of seniority; the pioneers and music of each company, in one rank, two paces behind the non-commissioned officers.

309. The Colonel will next command,

Field and staff, to the front--MARCH!

Form of Inspection.

The commissioned officers thus designated will form themselves in one rank, on a line equal to the front of the column, six paces in front of the colors, from right to left, in the order of seniority; and the non-commissioned staff, in a similar manner, two paces in rear of the preceding rank. The Colonel, seeing the movement executed, will take post on the right of the Lieutenant-Colonel, and wait the approach of the inspecting officer But such of the field officers as may be superior in rank to the Inspector will not take post in front of the battalion.

310. The Inspector will commence in front. After inspecting the dress and general appearance of the field and commissioned staff under arms, the Inspector, accompanied by these officers, will pass down the open column, looking at every rank in front and rear.

311. The Colonel will now command,

1. *Order Arms.* 2. REST!

when the Inspector will proceed to make a minute inspection of the several ranks or divisions, in succession, commencing in front.

312. As the Inspector approaches the non-commissioned staff, color-rank, the color-guard, and the band, the Adjutant will give the necessary orders for the inspection of arms, boxes, and knapsacks. The colors will be planted firm in the ground, to enable the color-bearers to display the contents of their knapsacks. The non-commissioned staff may be dismissed as soon as inspected; but the color-rank and color-guard will remain until the colors are to be escorted to the place from which they were taken.

313. As the Inspector successively approaches the companies, the Captains will command,

1. *Attention.* 2. *Company.* 3. *Inspection*—ARMS!

The inspecting officer will then go through the whole company, and minutely inspect the arms, accoutrements, and dress of each soldier. After this is done, the Captain will command,

Open—BOXES!

when the ammunition and the boxes will be examined.

314. The Captain will then command,

1. *Shoulder*—ARMS!   3. MARCH!
2. *Close order.*   4. *Order*—ARMS!

5. *Stack*—ARMS!
6. *To the rear, open order.*
7. MARCH!

8. *Frontrank*—ABOUT—FACE!
9. *Unsling—Knapsacks.*
10. *Open—Knapsacks.*

315. The Sergeants will face inward at the 2d command, and close upon the centre at the 3d, and stack their arms at the 5th command; at the 6th command they face outward, and resume their positions at the 7th. When the ranks are closed, preparatory to *take arms*, the Sergeants will also close upon the centre, and at the word, take their arms and resume their places.

316. The knapsacks will be placed at the feet of the men, the flaps from them, with the great-coats on the flaps, and the knapsacks leaning on the great-coats. In this position the Inspector will examine their contents, or so many of them as he may think necessary, commencing with the non-commissioned officers, the men standing at attention.

317. When the Inspector has passed through the company, the Captain will command,

Repack—Knapsacks;

when each soldier will repack and buckle up his knapsack, leaving it on the ground, the number upward, turned from him, and then stand at rest.

318. The Captain will then command,

1. *Attention.*   2. *Company.*   3. *Sling—Knapsacks.*

At the word *sling*, each soldier will take his knapsack, holding it by the inner straps, and stand erect; at the last word he will replace it on his back. The Captain will continue,

4. *Frontrank*—ABOUT—FACE!
5. *Close order.*
6. MARCH!
7. *Take*—ARMS!

8. *Shoulder*—ARMS!
9. *Officers and Sergeants, to your posts.*
10. MARCH!

and will cause the company to file off to their tents or quarters, except the company that is to re-escort the colors, which will await the further orders of the Colonel.

319. In an extensive column, some of the rearmost companies may, after the inspection of dress and general appearance, be permitted to *stack arms* until just before the Inspector approaches them, when they will be directed to *take arms* and resume their position.

320. The inspection of the troops being ended, the field and staff will

next accompany the Inspector to the hospital, magazine, arsenal, quarters, sutler's shop, guard-house, and such other places as he may think proper to inspect. The Captains and subalterns repair to their companies and sections to await the Inspector.

321. The hospital being at all times an object of particular interest, it will be critically and minutely inspected.

322. The men will be formed in the company quarters in front of their respective bunks, and on the entrance of the Inspector the word *Attention!* will be given by the senior non-commissioned officer present, when the whole will salute with the hand, without uncovering.

323. The Inspector, attended by the company officers, will examine the general arrangement of the interior of the quarters, the bunks, bedding, cooking and table utensils, and· such other objects as may present themselves; and afterward the exterior.

324. The Adjutant will exhibit to the Inspector the regimental books and papers, including those relating to the transactions of the Council of Administration. The company books and papers will also be exhibited, the whole together, generally at the Adjutant's office, and in the presence of the officers not otherwise particularly engaged.

325. The Inspector will examine critically the books and accounts of the administrative and disbursing officers of the command, and the money and property in their keeping.

326. The inspection of cavalry and artillery will conform to the principles laid down in the foregoing paragraphs, regard being had to the system of instruction for those arms of service respectively.

ARTICLE XXXI.

MUSTERS.

327. Troops will be mustered for pay on the last day of February, April, June, August, October, and December. The musters will be made by an Inspector-General, if present, otherwise by an officer specially designated by the Commander of the Army, Division, or Department; and in absence of either an Inspector-General or officer specially designated, the muster will be made by the commander of the post.

328. When one inspecting officer cannot muster all the troops himself on the day specified, the commanding officer will designate such other competent officers as may be necessary, to assist him.

329. All stated musters of the troops shall be preceded by a minute and careful *inspection* in the prescribed mode; and if the command be of more than a company, by a *review*, before inspection.

330. The mustering officer having inspected the companies in succession,

beginning on the right, returns to the first company to muster it. The company being at *ordered arms*, with open ranks, as when inspected, the Captain will, as the mustering officer approaches, command,

1. *Attention.*   2. *Company!*   3. *Shoulder—*ARMS!   4. *Support—*ARMS!

The mustering officer will then call over the names on the roll, and each man, as his name is called, will distinctly answer, *Here!* and bring his piece to a *carry* and to an *order.*

331. After each company is mustered, the Captain will order it to be marched to the company parade, and there dismissed to quarters to await the Inspector's visit.

332. After mustering the companies, 'the mustering officer, attended by the company commanders, will visit the guard and hospital, to verify the presence of the men reported there.

333. The muster and pay rolls will be made on the printed forms furnished from the Adjutant-General's office, and according to the directions given on them. On the muster-rolls companies are designated by the name of the Captain, whether present or absent. The pay-roll is left blank, to be filled by the Paymaster.

334. One copy of each muster-roll will be transmitted by the mustering officer to the Adjutant-General's office in the War Department within three days after the muster.

ARTICLE XXXII.
FORMS OF PARADE.

335. On all parades of ceremony, such as Reviews, Guard-mounting, at *Troop* or *Retreat* parades, instead of the word "*Rest,*" which allows the men to move or change the position of their bodies, the command will be "PARADE—REST!" At the last word of this command, the soldier will carry the right foot six inches in rear of the left heel, the left knee slightly bent, the body upright upon the right leg; the musket resting against the hollow of the right shoulder, the hands crossed in front, the backs of them outward, and the left hand uppermost. At the word "ATTENTION!" the soldier will resume the correct position at ordered arms. In the positions here indicated, the soldier will remain silent and motionless; and it is particularly enjoined upon all officers to cause the commands above given, on the part of the soldier, to be executed with great briskness and spirit.

336. Officers on all duties under arms are to have their swords drawn, without waiting for any words of command for that purpose

I. DRESS PARADE.

337. There shall be daily one dress parade, at *troop* or *retreat*, as the commanding officer may direct.

338. A signal will be beat or sounded half an hour before *troop* or *retreat*, for the music to assemble on the regimental parade, and each company to turn out under arms on its own parade, for roll-call and inspection by its own officers.

339. Ten minutes after that signal, the *Adjutant's call* will be given, when the Captains will march their companies (the band playing) to the regimental parade, where they take their positions in the order of battle. When the line is formed, the Captain of the first company, on notice from the Adjutant, steps one pace to the front, and gives to his company the command, *"Order—*ARMS! PARADE—REST!*"* which is repeated by each Captain in succession to the left. The Adjutant takes post two paces on the right of the line; the Sergeant-major two paces on the left. The music will be formed in two ranks on the right of the Adjutant. The senior officer present will take the command of the parade, and will take post at a suitable distance in front, opposite the centre, facing the line.

340. When the companies have ordered arms, the Adjutant will order the music to *beat off*, when it will commence on the right, beat in front of the line to the left, and back to its place on the right.

341. When the music has ceased, the Adjutant will step two paces to the front, face to the left, and command,

1. *Attention!*   2. *Battalion.*   3. *Shoulder—*ARMS!   4. *Prepare to open
ranks!*   5. *To the rear, open order!*   6. MARCH!

At the sixth command, the ranks will be opened according to the system laid down in the Infantry Tactics, the commissioned officers marching to the front, the company officers four paces, field officers six paces, opposite to their positions in the order of battle, where they will halt and dress. The Adjutant, seeing the ranks aligned, will command,

FRONT!

and march along the front to the centre, face to the right, and pass the line of company officers eight or ten paces, where he will come to the right-about, and command,

*Present—*ARMS!

when arms will be presented, officers saluting.

342. Seeing this executed, he will face about to the commanding officer, salute, and report, " *Sir, the parade is formed.*" The Adjutant will then, on intimation to that effect, take his station three paces on the left of the commanding officer, one pace retired, passing round his rear.

343. The commanding officer, having acknowledged the salute of the line by touching his hat, will, after the Adjutant has taken his post, draw his sword, and command,

1. *Battalion.*   2. *Shoulder*—ARMS!

and add such exercises as he may think proper, concluding with

Order—ARMS!

then return his sword, and direct the Adjutant to receive the reports.

344. The Adjutant will now pass round the right of the commanding officer, advance upon the line, halt midway between him and the line of company officers, and command,

1. *First Sergeants, to the front and centre.*   2. MARCH!

At the first command, they will *shoulder arms* as Sergeants, march two paces to the front, and face inward. At the second command, they will march to the centre, and halt. The Adjutant will then order,

1. *Front*—FACE.   2. *Report.*

At the last word, each in succession, beginning on the right, will salute by bringing the left hand smartly across the breast to the right shoulder, and report the result of the roll-call previously made on the company parade.

345. The Adjutant again commands,

1. *First Sergeants, outward*—FACE!   2. *To your posts*—MARCH!

when they will resume their places, and order arms. The Adjutant will now face to the commanding officer, salute, report absent officers, and give the result of the First Sergeants' reports. The commanding officer will next direct the orders to be read, when the Adjutant will face about and announce,

Attention to Orders.

He will then read the orders.

346. The orders having been read, the Adjutant will face to the commanding officer, salute, and report; when, on an intimation from the commander, he will face again to the line, and announce,

Parade is dismissed.

All the officers will now return their swords, face inward, and close on the Adjutant, he having taken position in their line, the field officers on the flanks. The Adjutant commands,

1. *Front*—FACE ! 2. *Forward*—MARCH !

when they will march forward, dressing on the centre, the music playing, and when within six paces of the commander, the Adjutant will give the word,

Halt !

The officers will then salute the commanding officer by raising the hand to the cap, and there remain until he shall have communicated to them such instructions as he may have to give, or intimates that the ceremony is finished. As the officers disperse, the First Sergeants will close the ranks of their respective companies, and march them to the company parades, where they will be dismissed, the band continuing to play until the companies clear the regimental parade.

347. All field and company officers and men will be present at *dress parades*, unless especially excused, or on some duty incompatible with such attendance.

348. A dress parade once a day will not be dispensed with, except on extraordinary and urgent occasions.

II. REVIEW OF A BATTALION OF INFANTRY.

349. Preparatory to a review, the Adjutant will cause a camp-color to be placed 80 or 100 paces, or more, according to the length of the line, in front of, and opposite to, where the centre of the battalion will rest, where the reviewing officer is supposed to take his station; and, although he may choose to quit that position, still the color is to be considered as the point to which all the movements and formations are relative.

350. The Adjutant will also cause points to be marked, at suitable distances, for the wheelings of the divisions; so that their right flanks, in marching past, shall only be about four paces from the camp-color, where it is supposed the reviewing officer places himself to receive the salute.

851. The battalion being formed in the order of battle, at *shouldered arms*, the Colonel will command,

1. *Battalion, prepare for review!* 2. *To the rear, open order.* 3. MARCH!

At the word MARCH, the field and staff officers dismount; the company officers and the color-rank advance four paces in front of the front rank, and place themselves opposite to their respective places, in the order of battle. The color-guard replace the color-rank. The staff officers place themselves, according to rank, three paces on the right of the rank of company officers, and one pace from each other; the music takes post as at parade. The non-commissioned staff take post one pace from each other, and three paces on the right of the front rank of the battalion.

352. When the ranks are aligned, the Colonel will command,

FRONT!

and place himself eight paces, and the Lieutenant-Colonel and Major will place themselves two paces, in front of the rank of company officers, and opposite to their respective places in the order of battle, all facing to the front.

353. When the reviewing officer presents himself before the centre, and is fifty or sixty paces distant, the Colonel will face about, and command,

Present—ARMS!

and resume his front. The men present arms, and the officers salute, so as to drop their swords with the last motion of the firelock. The non-commissioned staff salute by bringing the sword to a *poise*, the hilt resting on the breast, the blade in front of the face, inclining a little outward. The music will play, and all the drums beat, according to the rank of the reviewing officer. The colors only salute such persons as, from their rank and by regulation (see Article XXIX.), are entitled to that honor. If the reviewing officer be junior in rank to the commandant of the parade, no compliment will be paid to him, but he will be received with arms carried, and the officers will not salute as the column passes in review.

354. The reviewing officer having halted, and acknowledged the salute of the line by touching or raising his cap or hat, the Colonel will face about and command,

Shoulder—ARMS!

when the men shoulder their pieces; the officers and non-commissioned staff recover their swords with the last motion, and the Colonel faces to the front.

355. The reviewing officer will then go toward the right, the whole remaining perfectly steady, without paying any further compliment, while he passes along the front of the battalion, and proceeds round the left flank, and along the rear of the file-closers, to the right. While the reviewing officer is going round the battalion, the band will play, and will cease when he has returned to the right flank of the troops.

356. When the reviewing officer turns off, to place himself by the camp-color in front, the Colonel will face to the line and command,

1. Close Order. 2. MARCH!

At the first command, the field and company officers will face to the *right-about*, and at the second command, all persons, except the Colonel, will resume their places in the order of battle; the field and staff officers mount.

357. The reviewing officer having taken his position near the camp-color, the Colonel will command,

1. By company, right wheel. 2. Quick—MARCH! 3. Pass in review.
4. Column, forward. 5. Guide right. 6. MARCH!

The battalion, in column of companies, right in front, will then, in common time, and at *shouldered arms,* be put in motion; the Colonel four paces in front of the Captain of the leading company; the Lieutenant-Colonel on a line with the leading company; the Major on a line with the rear company; the Adjutant on a line with the second company; the Sergeant-Major on a line with the company next preceding the rear—each six paces from the flank (left) opposite to the reviewing officer; the staff officers in one rank, according to the order of precedency, from the right, four paces in rear of the column; the music, preceded by the principal musician, six paces before the Colonel; the pioneers, preceded by a Corporal, four paces before the principal musician; and the Quartermaster-Sergeant two paces from the side opposite to the guides, and in line with the pioneers.

358. All other officers and non-commissioned officers will march past in the places prescribed for them in the march of an open column. The guides and soldiers will keep their heads steady to the front in passing in review.

359. The color-bearer will remain in the ranks while passing and saluting.

360. The music will begin to play at the command to march, and after passing the reviewing officer, wheel to the left out of the column, and

take a position opposite and facing him, and will continue to play until the rear of the column shall have passed him, when it will cease, and follow in the rear of the battalion, unless the battalion is to pass in *quick time* also, in which case it will keep its position.

361. The officers will salute the reviewing officer when they arrive within six paces of him, and recover their swords when six paces past him. All officers, in saluting, will cast their eyes toward the reviewing officer.

362. The Colonel, when he has saluted at the head of the battalion, will place himself near the reviewing officer, and will remain there until the rear has passed, when he will rejoin the battalion.

363. The colors will salute the reviewing officer, if entitled to it, when within six paces of him, and be raised when they have passed by him an equal distance. The drums will beat a march, or ruffle, according to the rank of the reviewing officer, at the same time that the colors salute.

364. When the column has passed the reviewing officer, the Colonel will direct it to the ground it marched from, and command,

Guide left,

in time for the guides to cover. The column having arrived on its ground, the Colonel will command,

1. *Column.*   2. HALT !

form it in order of battle, and cause the ranks to be opened as in paragraph 351. The review will terminate by the whole saluting as at the beginning.

365. If, however, instructions have been previously given to march the troops past in *quick* time also, the Colonel will, instead of changing the guides, halting the column, and wheeling it into line, as above directed, give the command,

1. *Quick time.*   2. MARCH !

In passing the reviewing officer again, no salute will be offered by either officers or men. The music will have kept its position opposite the reviewing officer, and at the last command will commence playing, and as the column approaches, will place itself in front of, and march off with the column, and continue to play until the battalion is halted on its original ground of formation. The Review will terminate in the same manner as prescribed above.

366. The Colonel will afterward cause the troops to perform such exercises and manœuvres as the reviewing officer may direct.

367. When two or more battalions are to be reviewed, they will be formed in parade order, with the proper intervals, and will also perform the same movements that are laid down for a single battalion, observing the additional directions that are given for such movements when applied to the line. The Brigadier-General and his staff, on foot, will place themselves opposite the centre of the brigade; the Brigadier-General two paces in front of the rank of Colonels; his aid two paces on his right, and one retired; and the other brigade staff officers, those having the rank of field officers, in the rank of Lieutenant-Colonels and Majors; and those below that rank, in the rank of company officers.

368. In passing in review, a Major-General will be four paces in front of the Colonel of the leading battalion of his division; and the Brigadier-General will be on the right of the Colonels of the leading battalions of their brigades; staff officers on the left of their Generals.

369. When the line exceeds two battalions, the reviewing officer may cause them to march past in quick time only. In such cases the mounted officers only will salute.

370. A number of companies less than a battalion will be reviewed as a battalion, and a single company as if it were with the battalion. In the latter case, the company may pass in column of platoons.

371. If several brigades are to be reviewed together, or in one line, this further difference will be observed: the reviewing personage, joined by the General of the division, on the right of his division, will proceed down the line, parallel to its front, and when near the Brigadier-Generals respectively, will be saluted by their brigades in succession. The music of each, after the prescribed salute, will play while the reviewing person age is in front, or in rear of it, and only then.

372. In marching in review, with several battalions in common time, the music of each succeeding battalion will commence to play when the music of the preceding one has ceased, in order to follow its battalion. When marching in quick time, the music will begin to play when the rear company of the preceding battalion has passed the reviewing officer.

373. The reviewing officer or personage will acknowledge the salute by raising, or taking off, his cap or hat, when the commander of the troops salutes him; and also when the colors pass. The remainder of the time occupied by the passage of the troops he will be covered.

374. The review of Cavalry and Artillery will be conducted on similar principles, and according to the systems of instruction for those arms of service.

III. GUARD-MOUNTING.

375. Camp and garrison guards will be relieved every twenty-four hours. The guards at outposts will ordinarily be relieved in the same manner, but this must depend on their distances from camp, or other circumstances, which may sometimes require their continuing on duty several days. In such cases, they must be previously warned to provide themselves accordingly.

376. At the first call for guard-mounting, the men warned for duty turn out on their company parades for inspection by the First Sergeants; and at the second call, repair to the regimental or garrison parade, conducted by the First Sergeants. Each detachment, as it arrives, will, under the direction of the Adjutant, take post on the left of the one that preceded it, in open order, arms shouldered, and bayonets fixed; the supernumeraries five paces in the rear of the men of their respective companies; the First Sergeants in rear of them. The Sergeant-Major will dress the ranks, count the files, verify the details, and when the guard is formed, report to the Adjutant, and take post two paces on the left of the front rank.

377. The Adjutant then commands *Front*, when the officer of the guard takes post twelve paces in front of the centre, the Sergeants in one rank, four paces in the rear of the officers; and the Corporals in one rank, four paces in the rear of the Sergeants—all facing to the front. The Adjutant then assigns their places in the guard.

378. The Adjutant will then command,

> 1. *Officer and non-commissioned officers.* 2. ABOUT—FACE.
> 3. *Inspect your guards*—MARCH!

The non-commissioned officers then take their posts. The commander of the guard then commands,

> 1. *Order*—ARMS.   2. *Inspection*—ARMS.

and inspects his guard. When there is no commissioned officer on the guard, the Adjutant will inspect it. During inspection the band will play.

379. The inspection ended, the officer of the guard takes post as though the guard were a company of a battalion, in open order, under review; at the same time, also, the officers of the day will take post in front of the centre of the guard; the old officer of the day three paces on the right of the new officer of the day, one pace retired.

380. The Adjutant will now command,

1. *Parade*—REST! 2. *Troop*—*Beat off!*

when the music, beginning on the right, will beat down the line in front of the officer of the guard to the left, and back to its place on the right, where it will cease to play.

381. The Adjutant then commands,

1. *Attention!* 2. *Shoulder*—ARMS! 3. *Close order*—MARCH!

At the word "close order," the officer will face about; at "march," resume his post in line. The Adjutant then commands,

Present—ARMS!

At which he will face to the new officer of the day, salute, and report, "*Sir, the guard is formed.*" The new officer of the day, after acknowledging the salute, will direct the Adjutant to march the guard in review, or by flank to its post. But if the Adjutant be senior to the officer of the day, he will report without saluting with the sword then, or when marching the guard in review.

382. In review, the guard march past the officer of the day, according to the order of review, conducted by the Adjutant, marching on the left of the first division; the Sergeant-Major on the left of the last division.

383. When the column has passed the officer of the day, the officer of the guard marches it to its post, the Adjutant and Sergeant-Major retiring. The music, which has wheeled out of the column, and taken post opposite the officer of the day, will cease, and the old officer of the day salute, and give the old or standing orders to the new officer of the day. The supernumeraries, at the same time, will be marched by the First Sergeants to their respective company parades, and dismissed.

384. In bad weather, or at night, or after fatiguing marches, the ceremony of turning off may be dispensed with, but not the inspection.

385. Grand guards, and other brigade guards, are organized and mounted on the brigade parade by the staff officer of the parade, under the direction of the field officer of the day of the brigade, according to the principles here prescribed for the police guard of a regiment. The detail of each regiment is assembled on the regimental parade, verified by the Adjutant, and marched to the brigade parade by the senior officer of the detail. After inspection and review, the officer of the day directs the several guards to their respective posts.

386. The officer of the old guard, having his guard paraded, on the approach of the new guard commands,

Present—ARMS!

387. The new guard will marc'i, in quick time, past the old guard, at *shouldered arms*, officers saluting, and take post four paces on its right, where, being aligned with it, its commander will order,

Present—ARMS!

The two officers will then approach each other, and salute. They will then return to their respective guards, and command,

1. *Shoulder*—ARMS! 2. *Order*—ARMS!

388. The officer of the new guard will now direct the detail for the advanced guard to be formed and marched to its post, the list of the guard made and divided into three reliefs, experienced soldiers placed over the arms of the guard and at the remote and responsible posts, and the young soldiers in posts near the guard for instruction in their duties, and will himself proceed to take possession of the guard-house or guard-tent, and the articles and prisoners in charge of the guard.

389. During the time of relieving the sentinels and of calling in the small posts, the old commander will give to the new all the information and instructions relating to his post.

390. The first relief having been designated and ordered two paces to the front, the Corporal of the new guard will take charge of it, and go to relieve the sentinels, accompanied by the Corporal of the old guard, who will take command of the old sentinels, when the whole are relieved.

391. If the sentinels are numerous, the Sergeants are to be employed, as well as the Corporals, in relieving them.

392. The relief, with arms at a support, in two ranks, will march by a flank, conducted by the Corporal on the side of the leading front-rank man; and the men will be numbered alternately in the front and rear rank, the man on the right of the front rank being No. 1. Should an officer approach, the Corporal will command *carry arms*, and resume the *support arms* when the officer is passed.

393. The sentinels at the guard-house or guard-tent will be the first relieved and left behind: the others are relieved in succession.

394. When a sentinel sees the relief approaching, he will halt and face to it, with his arms at a shoulder. At six paces, the Corporal will command,

1. *Relief.* 2. HALT!

when the relief will halt and carry arms. The Corporal will then add, "No. 1," or "No 2," or "No. 3," according to the number of the post,

Arms—PORT!

The two sentinels will, with arms at *port*, then approach each other, when the old sentinel, under the correction of the Corporal, will whisper the instructions to the new sentinel. This done, the two sentinels will shoulder arms, and the old sentinel will pass, in quick time, to his place in rear of the relief. The Corporal will then command,

1. *Support*—ARMS! 2. *Forward.* 3. MARCH!

and the relief proceeds in the same manner until the whole are relieved.

395. The detachments and sentinels from the old guard having come in, it will be marched, at *shouldered arms*, along the front of the new guard, in quick time, the new guard standing at *presented arms;* officers saluting, and the music of both guards beating, except at the outposts.

396. On arriving at the regimental or garrison parade, the commander of the old guard will send the detachments composing it, under charge of the non-commissioned officers, to their respective regiments. Before the men are dismissed, their pieces will be drawn or discharged at a target. On rejoining their companions, the chiefs of squads will examine the arms, &c., of their men, and cause the whole to be put away in good order.

397. When the old guard has marched off fifty paces, the officer of the new guard will order his men to stack their arms, or place them in the arm-racks.

398. The commander of the guard will then make himself acquainted with all the instructions for his post, visit the sentinels, and question them and the non-commissioned officers relative to the instructions they may have received from other persons of the old guard.

ARTICLE XXXIII.

GUARDS.

399. Sentinels will be relieved every two hours, unless the state of the weather, or other causes, should make it necessary or proper that it be done at shorter or longer intervals.

400. Each relief, before mounting, is inspected by the commander of the guard or of its post. The Corporal reports to him, and presents the old relief on its return.

401. The *countersign*, or watchword, is given to such persons as are entitled to pass during the night, and to officers, non-commissioned

officers, and sentinels of the guard.   Interior guards receive the countersign only when ordered by the commander of the troops.

402. The *parole* is imparted to such officers only as have a right to visit the guards, and to make the grand rounds; and to officers commanding guards.

403. As soon as the new guard has been marched off, the officer of the day will repair to the office of the commanding officer and report for orders.

404. The officer of the day must see that the officer of the guard is furnished with the parole and countersign before *retreat.*

405. The officer of the day visits the guards during the day at such times as he may deem necessary, and makes his rounds at night at least once after 12 o'clock.

406. Upon being relieved, the officer of the day will make such remarks in the report of the officer of the guard as circumstances require, and present the same at head-quarters.

407. Commanders of guards leaving their posts to visit their sentinels, or on other duty, are to mention their intention, and the probable time of their absence, to the next in command.

408. The officers are to remain constantly at their guards, except while visiting their sentinels, or necessarily engaged elsewhere on their proper duty.

409. Neither officers nor soldiers are to take off their clothing or accoutrements while they are on guard.

410. The officer of the guard must see that the countersign is duly communicated to the sentinels a little before twilight.

411. When a fire breaks out, or any alarm is raised in a garrison, all guards are to be immediately under arms.

412. Inexperienced officers are put on guard as supernumeraries, for the purpose of instruction.

413. Sentinels will not take orders or allow themselves to be relieved, except by an officer or non-commissioned officer of their guard or party, the officer of the day, or the commanding officer; in which case the orders will be immediately notified to the commander of the guard by the officer giving them.

414. Sentinels will report every breach of orders or regulations they are instructed to enforce.

415. Sentinels must keep themselves on the alert, observing every thing that takes place within sight and hearing of their post.   They will carry their arms habitually at support, or on either shoulder, but will never quit them.   In wet weather, if there be no sentry-box, they will secure arms.

Form of Guard Report.

FORM OF GUARD REPORT.

Report of a Guard mounted at —, on the —, and relieved on the —.

Parole.	Lieutenants.	Sergeants.	Corporals.	Musicians.	Privates.	Total.	Aggregate.	Articles in Charge.			Received the fore-going articles. A. B—, Lieut. 1st Infantry.
Countersign.											
Detail.											

LIST OF THE GUARD.

Reliefs, and when posted.									Where posted.	Remarks
1st Relief. From — to — and — to —			2d Relief. From — to — and — to —			3d Relief. From — to — and — to —				
No.	Name.	Co.	Rt.	Name.	Co.	Rt.	Name.	Co.	Rt.		
1	C. D.	A	1st	I. J.	D	3d	O. P.	G	8th	Guard-House.	
2	E. F.	B	4th	K. L.	E	2d	Q. R.	H	9th	Magazine.	
3	G. H.	C	6th	M. N.	F	5th	S. T.	I	10th	Quarm'r Store.	
1	Sergeant W. V., Co. A, 1st Artillery.									Serg't Guard.	
2	Corporal W. X., Co. B, 1st Infantry.									Corp'l "	
3	Corporal Y. Z., Co. C, 3d Infantry.									" "	

LIST OF PRISONERS.

No.	Names.	Company.	Regiment.	Confined.		Charges.	Sentences.	Remarks
				When.	By whom.			
1								
2								
3								
4								
5								

A. B. C.,
Lieut. — Regt. ———,
Commanding the Guard.

416. No sentinel shall quit his post or hold conversation not necessary to the proper discharge of his duty.

417. All persons, of whatever rank in the service, are required to observe respect toward sentinels.

418. In case of disorder, a sentinel must call out *the guard;* and if a fire take place, he must cry—*"Fire!"* adding the number of his post. If in either case the danger be great, he must discharge his firelock before calling out.

419. It is the duty of a sentinel to repeat all calls made from posts more distant from the main body of the guard than his own, and no sentinel will be posted so distant as not to be heard by the guard, either directly or through other sentinels.

420. Sentinels will present arms to general and field officers, to the officer of the day, and to the commanding officer of the post. To all other officers they will carry arms.

421. When a sentinel in his sentry-box sees an officer approaching, he will stand at *attention,* and as the officer passes will salute him, by bringing the left hand briskly to the musket, as high as the right shoulder.

422. The sentinel at any post of the guard, when he sees any body of troops, or an officer entitled to compliment, approach, must call—*"Turn out the guard!"* and announce who approaches.

423. Guards do not turn out as a matter of compliment after sunset; but sentinels will, when officers in uniform approach, pay them proper attention, by facing to the proper front, and standing steady at *shouldered arms.* This will be observed until the evening is so far advanced that the sentinels begin challenging.

424. After retreat (or the hour appointed by the commanding officer), until broad daylight, a sentinel challenges every person who approaches him, taking, at the same time, the position of *arms port.* He will suffer no person to come nearer than within reach of his bayonet, until the person has given the countersign.

425. A sentinel, in challenging, will call out—*"Who comes there?"* If answered—*"Friend, with the countersign,"* and he be instructed to pass persons with the countersign, he will reply—*"Advance, friend, with the countersign!"* If answered—*"Friends!"* he will reply—*"Halt, friends! Advance one with the countersign!"* If answered—*"Relief,"* *"Patrol,"* or *"Grand rounds,"* he will reply—*"Halt! Advance, Sergeant (or Corporal), with the countersign!"* and satisfy himself that the party is what it represents itself to be. If he have no authority to pass ersons with the countersign, if the wrong countersign be given, or if

Duties of Sentinels.

the persons have not the countersign, he will cause them to stand, and call—" *Corporal of the guard!*"

426. In the daytime, when the sentinel before the guard sees the officer of the day approach, he will call—" *Turn out the guard! officer of the day.*" The guard will be paraded, and salute with presented arms.

427. When any person approaches a post of the guard at night, the sentinel before the post, after challenging, causes him to halt until examined by a non-commissioned officer of the guard. If it be the officer of the day, or any other officer entitled to inspect the guard and to make the rounds, the non-commissioned officer will call—" *Turn out the guard!*" when the guard will be paraded at shouldered arms, and the officer of the guard, if he thinks necessary, may demand the countersign and parole.

428. The officer of the day, wishing to make the rounds, will take an escort of a non-commissioned officer and two men. When the rounds are challenged by a sentinel, the Sergeant will answer—" *Grand rounds!*" and the sentinel will reply—" *Halt, grand rounds! Advance, Sergeant, with the countersign!*" Upon which the Sergeant advances and gives the countersign. The sentinel will then cry—" *Advance, rounds!*" and stand at a shoulder till they have passed.

429. When the sentinel before the guard challenges, and is answered —" *Grand rounds,*" he will reply—" *Halt, grand rounds! Turn out the guard; grand rounds!*" Upon which the guard will be drawn up at shouldered arms. The officer commanding the guard will then order a Sergeant and two men to advance; when within ten paces, the Sergeant challenges. The Sergeant of the grand rounds answers—" *Grand rounds!*" The Sergeant of the guard replies—" *Advance, Sergeant, with the countersign!*" The Sergeant of the rounds advances alone, gives the countersign, and returns to his round. The Sergeant of the guard calls to his officer—" *The countersign is right!*" on which the officer of the guard calls—" *Advance, rounds!*" The officer of the rounds then advances alone, the guard standing at shouldered arms. The officer of the rounds passes along the front of the guard to the officer, who keeps his post on the right, and gives him the parole. He then examines the guard, orders back his escort, and, taking a new one, proceeds in the same manner to other guards.

430. All material instructions given to a sentinel on post by persons entitled to make grand rounds, ought to be promptly notified to the commander of the guard.

431. Any General officer, or the commander of a post or garrison, may visit the guards of his command, and go the grand rounds, and be received in the same manner as prescribed for the officer of the day.

ARTICLE XXXIV.

ORDERS AND CORRESPONDENCE.

432. The orders of commanders of armies, divisions, brigades, regiments, are denominated orders of such army, division, &c., and are either general or special. Orders are numbered, general and special, in separate series, each beginning with the year.

433. General orders announce the time and place of issues and payments; hours for roll-calls and duties; the number and kind of orderlies, and the time when they shall be relieved; police regulations, and the prohibitions required by circumstances and localities; returns to be made, and their forms; laws and regulations for the army; promotions and appointments; eulogies or censures to corps or individuals, and generally, whatever it may be important to make known to the whole command.

434. Special orders are such as do not concern the troops generally, and need not be published to the whole command; such as relate to the march of some particular corps, the establishment of some post, the detaching of individuals, the granting requests, &c., &c.

435. A general order, and an important special order, must be read and approved by the officer whose order it is, before it is issued by the staff officer.

436. An order will state at the head the source, place, and date, and at the foot, the name of the commander who gives it; as for example:

Head-Quarters of the First Brigade, Second Division.
Camp at ———, 1st June, 1860.

GENERAL ORDERS, }
   No. ——. }

    By command of Brigadier-General A. B.
        C. D., Assistant Adjutant-General.

437. Orders may be put in the form of letters, but generally in the strict military form, through the office of the Adjutant or Adjutant-General of the command.

438. Orders are transmitted through all the intermediate commanders in the order of rank. When an intermediate commander is omitted, the officer who gives the order shall inform him, and he who receives it shall report it to his immediate superior.

439. Orders for any body of troops will be addressed to the commander, and will be opened and executed by the commander present, and published

or distributed by him when necessary; printed orders, however, are gene rally distributed direct to posts from the head-quarters where issued.

440. Orders assigning the stations of officers of engineers, ordnance, and of the staff departments, except as provided in the regulations for troops in the campaign, will be given by the Secretary of War, through the Adjutant-General's office, or by commanders of geographical departments, under the special authority of the War Department. The commander of a department, who, in consequence of the movement of troops or other necessity of the service, removes an officer from the station assigned to him by the Secretary of War, shall promptly report the case to the Adjutant-General.

441. A file of the printed orders will be kept with the head-quarters of each regiment, with each company, and at each military post, and will be regularly turned over by the commander, when relieved, to his successor.

442. If general orders are not received in regular succession, commanding officers will report the missing numbers to the proper head-quarters.

443. The orderly hours being fixed at each head-quarters, the staff officers and chiefs of the special services either attend in person, or send their assistants to obtain the orders of the day; and the first sergeants of companies repair for that purpose to the regimental or garrison head-quarters.

444. During marches and active operations, and when the regular orderly hours cannot be observed, all orders will be either sent direct to the troops, or the respective commanders of regiments or corps will be informed when to send to head-quarters for them. Under the same circumstances, orders will be read to the troops during a halt, without waiting for the regular parades.

445. Orders to any officer to make a tour of travel on duty, as for the inspection or payment of troops, &c., shall designate the troops and posts he shall visit, and the order in which he shall visit them, and the route of travel.

446. Every commander who gives an order involving an expenditure of public money, shall send a copy, without delay, to the bureau of the War Department to which the expenditure appertains, and if such commander be serving in a military department, he shall send a copy of the order to the head-quarters of the Department.

447. If a military commander shall give to a disbursing officer any order in conflict with orders received by him from the officer in charge of his department, at any superior head-quarters, such commander shall forthwith transmit the order to such head-quarters, with explanation of the necessity which justifies it.

448. Copies of all orders of the commanders of armies, departments, divisions, and detached brigades, and of the Superintendent of the recruiting service, will be forwarded at their dates, or as soon thereafter as practicable, in separate series, on full sheets of letter paper, or as printed, to the Adjutant-General's office.

449. Written communications from a commander to those under his command may be made by his staff officer. In all other cases by the officer himself.

450. In signing an official communication, the writer shall annex to his name his rank and corps. When he writes by order, he shall state by whose order.

451. All official correspondence between the heads of the different departments of the staff of any command, and its commander, must pass through the Adjutant-General, Assistant Adjutant-General, or Adjutant of the command, as the case may be. Communications to or from a commander, and those under his command, must pass through the Adjutant-General, Assistant Adjutant-General, or Adjutant on duty with it; excepting only such communications between a disbursing officer and the chief of his particular branch of the staff, as relate exclusively to the ordinary routine of business in their own department. All communications, whether from an inferior to a superior, or *vice versâ*, are, as a general rule, to be passed through the intermediate commanders. The same rule governs in verbal applications : for example, a Lieutenant seeking an indulgence must apply through his Captain, the Captain through the Adjutant, and so on.

452. Copies of all important communications from the bureaus of the War Department to disbursing officers, relating to the service in a military department, shall be sent from the bureau to the department commander.

453. Rolls and returns will be accompanied by a letter of transmittal, enumerating them, and referring to no other subject.

454. Generally, officers who forward communications indorse on them their remarks or opinion, without other letters of transmittal.

455. Official letters should generally refer to one matter only. In regard to an enlisted man, the company and regiment must be stated.

456. Letters on letter paper will be folded in three folds, parallel with the writing.

457. All communications on public service are to be marked on the cover, " *Official Business.*"

ARTICLE XXXV.

RETURNS AND REPORTS.

MONTHLY RETURNS.

458. Commanders of regiments, corps, and posts, will make to the Adjutant-General's office of the War Department monthly returns of their respective regiments, corps, and posts, on the forms furnished from that office, and according to the directions expressed on them. In like manner, Captains make monthly company returns to regimental head-quarters. All monthly returns will be forwarded on the 1st day of the next month, except regimental returns, which are forwarded as soon as all the company returns are received.

459. In campaign, monthly returns of divisions and detached brigades, and, generally, of all detached commands (see General Orders No. 1, of February 10, 1855), will be made to the Adjutant-General's office. They will exhibit separately the several regiments, and detachments, and staff corps, and the strength of each garrison within the command. These returns, and those of regiments, corps, and posts, in campaign, will, unless otherwise ordered, be transmitted through the intermediate commanders.

460. The established *printed* forms and blanks of all returns required from the commanders of divisions, brigades, regiments, corps, companies, and posts, will be furnished from the Adjutant-General's office, on their requisitions annually made, or oftener, if necessary. The receipt of these forms and blanks will be immediately acknowledged, and afterward ac-counted for on the next monthly returns.

461. Manuscript returns, rolls, certificates, and other documents, are prohibited, unless the proper *printed* forms have not been received in time. Regimental returns must be made out in the name of the Colonel, whether he be present or absent.

ANNUAL RETURNS—CASUALTIES.

462. This return will exhibit the various changes and alterations which may have taken place in the regiment during the preceding twelve months: that is to say—a statement of the number of resignations, transfers, deaths, &c., of commissioned officers; the number of men joined by enlistment, transferred, and discharged; the number tried by Courts-Martial or by the civil law, and the nature of their offenses; the number of discharges, deaths, dismissals, and desertions; number joined from desertion, pardoned, &c., &c.

RETURN OF DECEASED SOLDIERS.

463. To be forwarded to the Adjutant-General, by the Colonels of regiments, *quarterly*. Also a duplicate to the Second Auditor of the Treasury.

FIELD RETURNS.

464. Besides the stated returns of the troops, such other *field returns* and reports will be made as may be necessary to keep the government informed of the condition and strength of the forces.

465. After any action or affair, a return of the killed, wounded, and missing will be made, in which the name, rank, and regiment of each officer and soldier will be specified, with such remarks and explanations as may be requisite for the records of the Department of War, or be necessary to establish the just claims of any individual who may have been wounded, or of the heirs and representatives of any killed in action (taking care to specify the *nature of the wound*, the *time* and *place* of its occurrence, the company, regiment, or corps, and the name of the Captain, Colonel, or other commanding officer).

REPORTS.

466. The date of appointment, of detail, and of removal of all staff officers, or of officers selected for duty in staff departments, which may entitle them to receive additional pay, will be immediately reported by the officer making such appointment, detail, or removal, to the Adjutant-General, and to the Paymaster of the department or command to which such officers belong.

467. Whenever any change takes place in the position or location of troops, the fact will be immediately reported by the commanding officer to general, division, and department head-quarters, specifying the date of departure of the whole or any part of the troops, or of the arrival of any detachment; as well as all other circumstances connected with such changes in the command. These special reports will always be accompanied by an exact *return* of the troops according to the established printed forms. A similar report will be noted on the next monthly return of the post or station. If a new post or position be established, its situation, and the nearest post-office and proper route to it, should be reported.

468. Officers on detached duty will report, monthly, to the commanders of their posts, of their regiments or corps, and to the Adjutant-General, their stations, the nature of their duties, and the authority placing them thereon—likewise each *change* of *address*.

PRISONERS OF WAR—CAPTURED PROPERTY.

469. A return of prisoners, and a report of the number and description of the killed and wounded of the enemy, will be forwarded to the Adjutant-General's office, Washington.

470. A return of all property captured will be made by the commanding officer of the troops by whom such capture was made, to the Adjutant-General, at Washington, in order that it may be disposed of according to the orders of the War Department.

INSPECTION REPORTS.

471. Inspection reports will show the discipline of the troops; their instruction in all military exercises and duties: the state of their arms, clothing, equipments, and accoutrements of all kinds; of their kitchens and messes; of the barracks and quarters at the post; of the guard-house, prisons, hospital, bake-house, magazines, store-houses, and stores of every description; of the stables and horses; the condition of the post school; the management and application of the post and company funds; the state of the post, and regimental, and company books, papers, and files; the zeal and ability of the officers in command of troops; the capacity of the officers conducting the administrative and staff services, the fidelity and economy of their disbursements; the condition of all public property, and the amount of money in the hands of each disbursing officer; the regularity of issues and payments; the mode of enforcing discipline by courts-martial, and by the authority of the officers; the propriety and legality of all punishments inflicted; and any information whatsoever concerning the service, in any matter or particular that may merit notice, or aid to correct defects or introduce improvements.

472. Inspectors are required particularly to report if any officer is of intemperate habits, or unfit for active service by infirmity or any other cause.

ARTICLE XXXVI.

TROOPS IN CAMPAIGN.

ORGANIZATION OF AN ARMY IN THE FIELD.

473. The formation by divisions is the basis of the organization and administration of armies in the field.

474. A division consists usually of two or three brigades, either of infantry or cavalry, and troops of other corps in the necessary proportion.

475. A brigade is formed of two or more regiments. The first number takes the right.

476. Mixed brigades are sometimes formed of infantry and light cavalry, especially for the advanced guards.

477. As the troops arrive at the rendezvous, the general commanding-in-chief will organize them into brigades and divisions.

478. The light cavalry is employed as flankers and partisans, and generally for all service out of the line.

479. Heavy cavalry belongs to the reserve, and is covered, when necessary, in marches, camps, or bivouacs, by light troops, or infantry of the line.

480. The arrangement of the troops on parade and in order of battle is—1st, the light infantry; 2d, infantry of the line; 3d, light cavalry; 4th, cavalry of the line; 5th, heavy cavalry. The troops of the artillery and engineers are in the centre of the brigades, divisions, or corps to which they are attached; marines take the left of other infantry; volunteers and militia take the left of regular troops of the same arm, and among themselves, regiments of volunteers or militia of the same arm take place by lot. This arrangement is varied by the general commanding-in-chief, as the circumstances of war render expedient.

481. Brigades in divisions, and divisions in the army, are numbered from right to left; but in reports of military operations, brigades and divisions are designated by the name of the general commanding them.

482. The order of regiments in brigades and of brigades in divisions may be changed by the commander of the division for important reasons, such as the weakness of some corps, or to relieve one from marching too long at the rear of the column. Such changes must be reported to the general commanding-in-chief.

483. The general commanding-in-chief assigns the generals of divisions and of brigades to their respective commands, when the assignment is not made by the Department of War.

484. The general of brigade inspects his troops in detail, by companies, when he takes the command and at the opening of the campaign, and as often as may be necessary to ascertain exactly their condition. The general of division makes similar inspections when he thinks proper. At these inspections the generals examine the arms, clothing, equipments, harness, horses, &c., direct the necessary repairs, and designate the men and horses to remain in depôt, or march with the train.

485. Reports of inspections are made by the general of brigade to the general of division, and by the general of division to the general commanding-in-chief.

486. During marches and all active operations, generals of brigade keep themselves exactly informed, by reports of corps and by their inspections, of the actual strength of the regiments, so as always, and

especially after an engagement, to make accurate returns to the general of division.

487. Staff officers, and officers of engineers, ordnance, and artillery, according to the nature of the service, are assigned to the head-quarters of armies and divisions, and detached brigades, by order of the general commanding-in-chief, when the distribution of these officers has not been regulated by the War Department. The necessary staff will be assigned to commanders of brigades.

488. When an Engineer or other officer is charged with directing an expedition or making a reconnoissance, without having command of the escort, the commander of the escort shall consult him on all the arrangements necessary to secure the success of the operation.

489. Staff officers, and commanders of engineers, ordnance, and artillery, report to their immediate commanders the state of the supplies and whatever concerns the service under their direction, and receive their orders, and communicate to them those they receive from their superiors in their own corps.

490. The senior officer of engineers, of ordnance, and the departments of the general staff serving at the chief head-quarters in the field, will transmit to the bureau of his department at Washington, at the close of the campaign, and such other times as the commander in the field may approve, a full report of the operations of his department, and whatever information to improve its service he may be able to furnish.

The report of the officer of engineers will embrace plans of military works executed during the campaign, and, in case of siege, a journal of the attack or defense.

CONTRIBUTIONS.

491. When the wants of the army absolutely require it, and in other cases, under special instructions from the War Department, the general commanding the army may levy contributions in money or kind on the enemy's country occupied by the troops. No other commander can levy such contributions without written authority from the general commanding-in-chief.

ORDERLIES.

492. At the opening of a campaign, the commander of an army determines and announces in orders the number of orderlies, mounted or foot, for the Generals, and the corps or regiments by which they are to be supplied, and the periods at which they shall be relieved.

493. In marches, the mounted orderlies follow the Generals, and perform the duty of escorts, or march with orderlies on foot at the head of the division or brigade.

494. The staff officer who distributes the orderlies to their posts sends with them a note of the time and place of departure; those relieved receive a like note from the staff officer at the head-quarters.

495. Mounted soldiers are to be employed to carry dispatches only in special and urgent cases. (See par. 557.)

496. The precise time when the dispatch is sent off, and the rate at which it is to be conveyed, are to be written clearly on the covers of all letters transmitted by a mounted orderly, and the necessary instructions to him, and the rate of travel going and returning, are to be distinctly explained to him.

DEPÔTS.

497. The grand depôts of an army are established where the military operations would not expose them to be broken up. Smaller depôts are organized for the divisions and the several arms. They are commanded by officers temporarily disabled for field service, or by other officers when necessary, and comprise, as much as possible, the hospitals and depôts for convalescents. When conveniently placed, they serve as points for the halting and assembling of detachments. They receive the disabled from the corps on the march; and the officers in command of the depôts send with the detachments to the army those at the depôts who have become fit for service.

CAMPS.

498. A camp is the place where troops are established in tents, in huts, or in bivouac. Cantonments are the inhabited places which troops occupy for shelter when not put in barracks. The camping-party is a detachment detailed to prepare a camp.

499. Reconnoissances should precede the establishment of the camp. For a camp of troops on the march, it is only necessary to look to the health and comfort of the troops, the facility of the communications, the convenience of wood and water, and the resources in provisions and forage. The ground for an intrenched camp, or a camp to cover a country, or one designed to deceive the enemy as to the strength of the army, must be selected, and the camp arranged for the object in view.

500. The camping-party of a regiment consists of the regimental Quartermaster and Quartermaster-Sergeant, and a Corporal and two men per company. The General decides whether the regiments camp separately or together, and whether the police guard shall accompany the camping-party, or a larger escort shall be sent.

501. Neither baggage nor led horses are permitted to move with the camping-party.

502. When the General can send in advance to prepare the camp, he

Camps.

gives his instructions to the chief of the Quartermaster's Department, who calls on the regiments for their camping-parties, and is accompanied, if necessary, by an Engineer to propose the defenses and communications.

503. The watering-places are examined, and signals placed at those that are dangerous. Any work required to make them of easier access is done by the police guard or Quartermaster's men. Sentinels, to be relieved by the guards of the regiment when they come up, are placed by the camping-party over the water if it is scarce, and over the houses and stores of provisions and forage in the vicinity.

504. If the camping-party does not precede the regiment, the Quartermaster attends to these things as soon as the regiment reaches the camp.

505. On reaching the ground, the infantry form on the color front; the cavalry in rear of its camp.

506. The Generals establish the troops in camp as rapidly as possible, particularly after long, fatiguing marches.

507. The number of men to be furnished for guards, pickets, and orderlies; the fatigue parties to be sent for supplies; the work to be done, and the strength of the working parties; the time and place for issues; the hour of marching, &c., are then announced by the Brigadier-Generals to the Colonels, and by them to the field officers—the Adjutant and Captains formed in front of the regiment, the First Sergeants taking post behind their Captains. The Adjutant then makes the details, and the First Sergeants warn the men. The regimental officer of the day forms the picket, and sends the guards to their posts. The colors are then planted at the centre of the color line, and the arms are stacked on the line; the fatigue parties to procure supplies, and the working parties, form in rear of the arms; the men not on detail pitch the tents.

508. If the camp is near the enemy, the picket remains under arms until the return of the fatigue parties, and, if necessary, is re-enforced by details from each company.

509. In the cavalry, each troop moves a little in rear of the point at which its horses are to be secured, and forms in one rank; the men then dismount; a detail is made to hold the horses; the rest stack their arms and fix the picket rope; after the horses are attended to, the tents are pitched, and each horseman places his carbine at the side from the weather, and hangs his sabre and bridle on it.

510. The standard is then carried to the tent of the Colonel.

511. The terms front, flank, right, left, file, and rank, have the same meaning when applied to camps as to the order of battle.

512. The front of the camp is usually equal to the front of the troops.

Camp of Infantry.

The tents are arranged in ranks and files. The number of ranks varies with the strength of the companies and the size of the tents.

513. No officer will be allowed to occupy a house, although vacant and on the ground of his camp, except by permission of the commander of the brigade, who shall report it to the commander of the division.

514. The staff officer charged with establishing the camp will designate the place for the shambles. The offal will be buried.

CAMP OF INFANTRY.

515. Each company has its tents in two files, facing on a street perpendicular to the color line. The width of the street depends on the front of the camp, but should not be less than 5 paces. The interval between the ranks of tents is 2 paces; between the files of tents of adjacent companies, 2 paces; between regiments, 22 paces.

516. The color line is 10 paces in front of the front rank of tents. The kitchens are 20 paces behind the rear rank of company tents; the non-commissioned staff and sutler, 20 paces in rear of the kitchens; the company officers, 20 paces farther in rear; and the field and staff, 20 paces in rear of the company officers.

517. The company officers are in rear of their respective companies; the Captains on the right.

518. The Colonel and Lieutenant-Colonel are near the centre of the line of field and staff; the Adjutant, a Major and Surgeon, on the right; the Quartermaster, a Major and Assistant Surgeon, on the left.

519. The police guard is at the centre of the line of the non-commissioned staff, the tents facing to the front, the stacks of arms on the left.

520. The advanced post of the police guard is about 200 paces in front of the color line, and opposite the centre of the regiment, or on the best ground; the prisoners' tent about 4 paces in rear. In a regiment of the second line, the advanced post of the police guard is 200 paces in rear of the line of its field and staff.

521. The horses of the staff officers and of the baggage train are 25 paces in rear of the tents of the field and staff; the wagons are parked on the same line, and the men of the train camped near them.

522. The sinks of the men are 150 paces in front of the color line—those of the officers 100 paces in rear of the train. Both are concealed by bushes. When convenient, the sinks of the men may be placed in rear or on a flank. A portion of the earth dug out for sinks to be thrown back occasionally.

523. The front of the camp of a regiment of 1000 men in two ranks will be 400 paces, or one fifth less paces than the number of files, if the

Plate 1.

Camp of a Regiment of Infantry.

Cl.—Colonel.
Lt. Cl.—Lieut. Colonel.
M.—Major.
Surg.—Surgeon.

Ast. Surg.—Asst. Surgeon.
Adjt.—Adjutant.
Q. M.—Quarter Master.
n-c-s.—Non.-Com.-Staff.

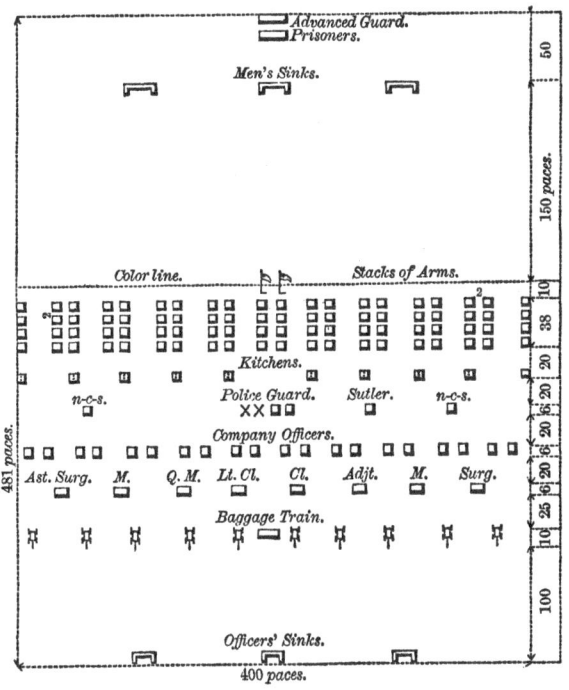

Plate 2.

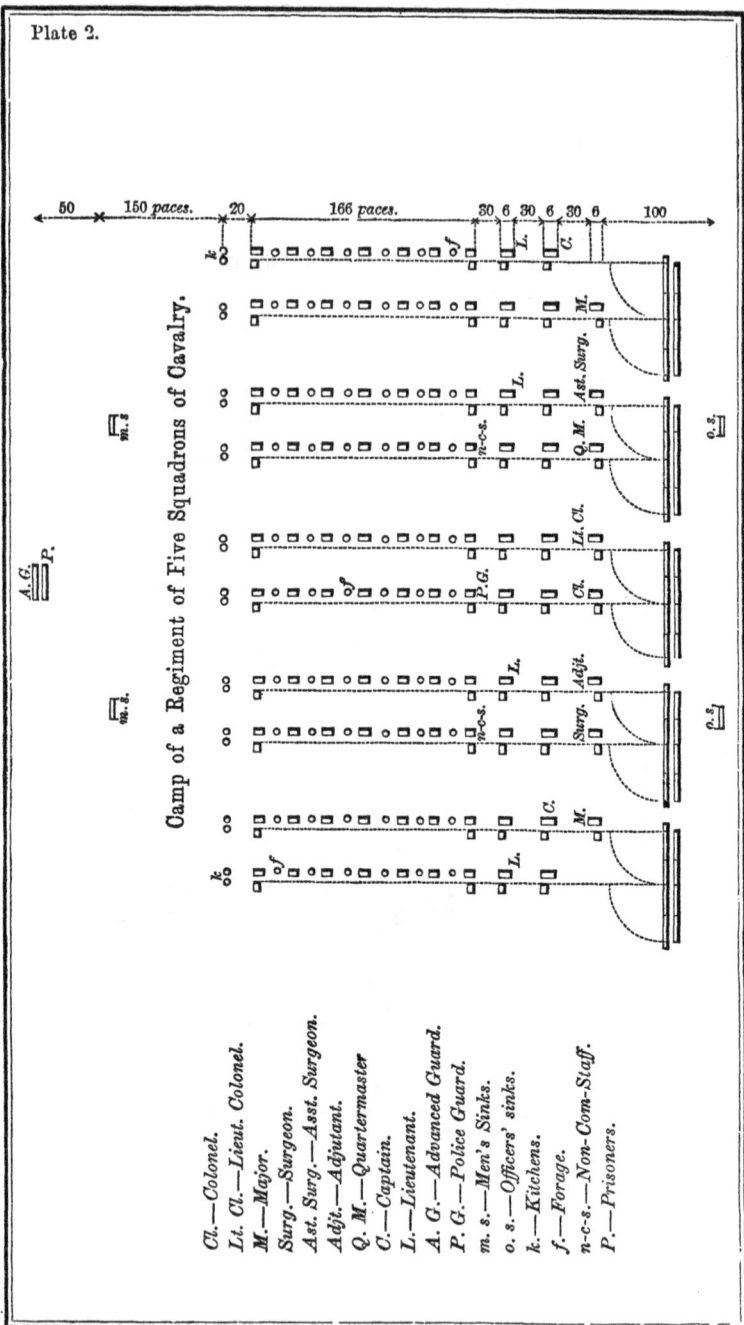

Camp of a Regiment of Five Squadrons of Cavalry.

Cl.—Colonel.
Lt. Cl.—Lieut. Colonel.
M.—Major.
Surg.—Surgeon.
Ast. Surg.—Asst. Surgeon.
Adjt.—Adjutant.
Q. M.—Quartermaster
C.—Captain.
L.—Lieutenant.
A. G.—Advanced Guard.
P. G.—Police Guard.
m. s.—Men's Sinks.
o. s.—Officers' sinks.
k.—Kitchens.
f.—Forage.
n-c-s.—Non-Com-Staff.
P.—Prisoners.

camp is to have the same front as the troops in order of battle. But the front may be reduced to 190 paces by narrowing the company streets to 5 paces; and if it be desirable to reduce the front still more, the tents of companies may be pitched in single file—those of a division facing on the same street.

CAMP OF CAVALRY.

524. In the cavalry, each company has one file of tents—the tents opening on the street facing the left of the camp.

525. The horses of each company are placed in a single file, facing the opening of the tents, and are fastened to pickets planted firmly in the ground, from 3 to 6 paces from the tents of the troops.

526. The interval between the file of tents should be such that, the regiment being broken into column of companies [as indicated in plate], each company should be on the extension of the line on which the horses are to be picketed.

527. The streets separating the squadrons are wider than those between the companies by the interval separating squadrons in line; these intervals are kept free from any obstruction throughout the camp.

528. The horses of the rear rank are placed on the left of those of their file-leaders.

529. The horses of the Lieutenants are placed on the right of their platoons; those of the Captains on the right of the company.

530. Each horse occupies a space of about 2 paces. The number of horses in the company fixes the depth of the camp, and the distance between the files of tents; the forage is placed between the tents.

531. The kitchens are 20 paces in front of each file of tents.

532. The non-commissioned officers are in the tents of the front rank. Camp-followers, teamsters, &c., are in the rear rank. The police guard in the rear rank, near the centre of the regiment.

533. The tents of the Lieutenants are 30 paces in rear of the file of their company; the tents of the Captains 30 paces in rear of the Lieutenants.

534. The Colonel's tent 30 paces in rear of the Captains', near the centre of the regiment; the Lieutenant-Colonel on his right; the Adjutant on his left; the Majors on the same line, opposite the 2d company on the right and left; the Surgeon on the left of the Adjutant.

535. The field and staff have their horses on the left of their tents, on the same line with the company horses; sick horses are placed in one line on the right or left of the camp. The men who attend them have a separate file of tents; the forges and wagons in rear of this file. The horses of the train and of camp-followers are in one or more files extending

to the rear, behind the right or left squadron. The advanced post of the police guard is 200 paces in front, opposite the centre of the regiment; the horses in one or two files.

536. The sinks for the men are 150 paces in front—those for officers 100 paces in rear of the camp.

CAMP OF ARTILLERY.

537. The artillery is encamped near the troops to which it is attached, so as to be protected from attack, and to contribute to the defense of the camp. Sentinels for the park are furnished by the artillery, and, when necessary, by the other troops.

538. For a battery of 6 pieces the tents are in three files—one for each section; distance between the ranks of tents 15 paces; tents opening to the front. The horses of each section are picketed in one file, 10 paces to the left of the file of tents. In the horse artillery, or if the number of horses makes it necessary, the horses are in two files on the right and left of the file of tents. The kitchens are 25 paces in front of the front rank of tents. The tents of the officers are in the outside files of company tents, 25 paces in rear of the rear rank—the Captain on the right, the Lieutenants on the left.

539. The park is opposite the centre of the camp, 40 paces in rear of the officers' tents. The carriages in files 4 paces apart; distance between ranks of carriages sufficient for the horses when harnessed to them; the park guard is 25 paces in rear of the park. The sinks for the men 150 paces in front; for the officers 100 paces in rear. The harness is in the tents of the men.

BIVOUACS.

540. A regiment of cavalry being in order of battle, in rear of the ground to be occupied, the Colonel breaks it by platoons to the right. The horses of each platoon are placed in a single row, and fastened as prescribed for camps; near the enemy, they remain saddled all night, with slackened girths. The arms are at first stacked in rear of each row of horses; the sabres, with the bridles hung on them, are placed against the stacks.

541. The forage is placed on the right of each row of horses. Two stable-guards for each platoon watch the horses.

542. A fire for each platoon is made near the color line, 20 paces to the left of the row of horses. A shelter is made for the men around the fire, if possible, and each man then stands his arms and bridle against the shelter.

543. The fires and shelter for the officers are placed in rear of the line of those for the men.

544. The interval between the squadrons must be without obstruction throughout the whole depth of the bivouac.

545. The interval between the shelters should be such that the platoons can take up a line of battle freely to the front or rear.

546. The distance from the enemy decides the manner in which the horses are to be fed and led to water. When it is permitted to unsaddle, the saddles are placed in the rear of the horses.

547. In infantry, the fires are made in rear of the *color line*, on the ground that would be occupied by the tents in camp. The companies are placed around them, and, if possible, construct shelters. When liable to surprise, the infantry should stand to arms at daybreak, and the cavalry mount until the return of the reconnoitring parties. If the arms are to be taken apart to clean, it must be done by detachments, successively.

CANTONMENTS.

548. The cavalry should be placed under shelter whenever the distance from the enemy, and from the ground where the troops are to form for battle, permit it. Taverns and farm-houses, with large stables and free access, are selected for quartering them.

549. The Colonel indicates the place of assembling in case of alarm. It should generally be outside the cantonment; the egress from it should be free; the retreat upon the other positions secure, and roads leading to it on the side of the enemy obstructed.

550. The necessary orders being given, as in establishing a camp, the picket and grand guards are posted. A sentinel may be placed on a steeple or high house, and then the troops are marched to the quarters. The men sleep in the stables, if it is thought necessary.

551. The above applies in the main to infantry. Near the enemy, companies or platoons should be collected, as much as possible, in the same houses. If companies must be separated, they should be divided by platoons or squads. All take arms at daybreak.

552. When cavalry and infantry canton together, the latter furnish the guards by night, and the former by day.

553. Troops cantoned in presence of the enemy should be covered by advanced guards and by natural or artificial obstacles. Cantonments taken during a cessation of hostilities should be established in rear of a line of defense, and in front of the point on which the troops would concentrate to receive an attack. The General commanding-in-chief assigns the limits of their cantonments to the divisions, the commanders of divisions to

brigades, and the commanders of brigades post their regiments. The position for each corps in case of attack is carefully pointed out by the Generals.

HEAD-QUARTERS.

554. Generals take post at the centre of their commands, on the main channels of communication. If troops bivouac in presence of the enemy, the Generals bivouac with them.

MILITARY EXERCISES.

555. When troops remain in camp or cantonment many days, the Colonels require them to be exercised in the school of the battalion and squadron. Regiments and brigades encamped by division are not united for drills without the permission of the General of division. The troops must not be exercised at the firings without the authority of the General commanding-in-chief. The practice of the drums must never begin with the "general," or the "march of the regiment;" nor the trumpets with the sound "to horse." The hour for practice is always announced.

ORDERS.

556. In the field, verbal orders and important sealed orders are carried by officers, and, if possible, by staff officers. When orders are carried by orderlies, the place and time of departure will be marked on them, and place and time of delivery on the receipt.

DISPATCHES.

557. Dispatches, particularly for distant corps, should be intrusted only to officers to whom their contents can be confided. In a country occupied by the enemy, the bearer of dispatches should be accompanied by at least two of the best mounted men; should avoid towns and villages, and the main roads; rest as little as possible, and only at out-of-the-way places. Where there is danger, he should send one of the men in advance, and be always ready to destroy his dispatches. He should be adroit in answering questions about the army, and not to be intimidated by threats.

WATCHWORDS.

558. The parole and countersign are issued daily from the principal head-quarters of the command. The countersign is given to the sentinels and non-commissioned officers of guards; the parole to the commissioned officers of guards. The parole is usually the name of a general, the countersign that of a battle.

559. When the parole and countersign cannot be communicated daily to a post or detachment which ought to use the same as the main body, a series of words may be sent for some days in advance.

560. If the countersign is lost, or one of the guard deserts with it, the commander on the spot will substitute another, and report the case at once to the proper superior, that immediate notice may be given to head-quarters.

ISSUES.

561. At what time and for what period issues are made, must depend on circumstances, and be regulated in orders. When an army is not moving, rations are generally issued for four days at a time. Issues to the companies of a regiment, and the fatigues to receive them, are superintended by an officer detailed from the regiment. Issues are made from one end of the line to the other, beginning on the right and left, alternately. An issue commenced to one regiment will not be interrupted for another entitled to precedence if it had been in place.

THE ROSTER, OR DETAILS FOR SERVICE.

562. The duties performed by detail are of three classes. The *first class* comprises, 1st. grand guards and outposts; 2d. interior guards, as of magazine, hospital, &c.; 3d. orderlies; 4th. police guards.

The *second class* comprises, 1st. detachments to protect laborers on military works, as field works, communications, &c.; 2d. working parties on such works; 3d. detachments to protect fatigues.

The *third class* are all fatigues, without arms, in or out of camp.

In the cavalry, stable-guards form a separate roster, and count before fatigue.

563. The rosters are distinct for each class. Officers are named on them in the order of rank. The details are taken in succession in the order of the roster, beginning at the head.

564. Lieutenants form one roster, and first and second Lieutenants are entered on it alternately. The senior first Lieutenant is the first on the roster; the senior second Lieutenant is the second, &c. The Captains form one roster, and are exempt from fatigues, except to superintend issues. A Captain commanding a battalion temporarily is exempt from detail, and duty falling to him passes. Lieutenant-Colonels and Majors are on one roster. They may be detailed for duties of the first and second classes, when the importance of the guards and detachments requires it Their roster is kept at division and brigade head-quarters. In the company, sergeants, corporals, and privates form distinct rosters.

565. Officers, non-commissioned officers, and soldiers take duties of the first class in the order stated, viz., the first, for the detail, takes the grand

guards; the next, the interior guards; the last, the police guard; and the same rule in regard to the details and duties of the second class. In the details for the third class, the senior officer takes the largest party. The party first for detail takes the service out of camp.

566. When the officer whose tour it is, is not able to take it, or is not present at the hour of marching, the next after him takes it. When a guard has passed the chain of sentinels, or an interior guard has reached its post, the officer whose tour it was cannot then take it. He takes the tour of the officer who has taken his. When an officer is prevented by sickness from taking his tour, it passes. These rules apply equally to non-commissioned officers and soldiers.

567. Duties of the first and second classes are credited on the roster when the guards or detachments have passed the chain of sentinels, or an interior guard has reached its post; fatigue duties when the parties have passed the chain or begun the duties in camp.

568. Every officer, non-commissioned officer, or soldier, on duty of the first class, or who is of the next detail for such duty, takes, when relieved, the duty of the second or third class that has fallen to him during that time, unless he has marched for detachment of more than twenty-four hours.

569. Soldiers march with knapsacks on all duties of the first class; and with arms and equipments complete on all working parties out of the camp, unless otherwise ordered. In the cavalry, horses are packed for all mounted service.

570. In the cavalry, dismounted men, and those whose horses are not in order, are preferred for the detail for dismounted service. Those who are mounted are never employed on those services, if the number of the other class are sufficient.

571. Every non-commissioned officer and soldier in the cavalry detailed for dismounted service must, before he marches, take to the First Sergeant of the troop, or Sergeant of his squad, his horse equipments and his valise ready packed. In case of alarm, the First Sergeant sees that the horses of these men are equipped and led to the rendezvous.

572. These rules in regard to the roster apply also to service in garrison.

POLICE GUARD.

573. In each regiment a police guard is detailed every day, consisting of two sergeants, three corporals, two drummers, and men enough to furnish the required sentinels and patrols. The men are taken from all the companies, from each in proportion to its strength. The guard is commanded by a Lieutenant, under the supervision of a Captain, as regimental officer of the day. It furnishes ten sentinels at the camp:

one over the arms of the guard; one at the Colonel's tent; three on the color front, one of them over the colors; three, fifty paces in rear of the field officers' tents; and one on each flank, between it and the next regiment. If it is a flank regiment, one more sentinel is posted on the outer flank.

574. An advanced post is detached from the police guard, composed of a sergeant, a corporal, a drummer, and nine men to furnish sentinels and the guard over the prisoners. The men are the first of the guard roster from each company. The men of the advanced post must not leave it under any pretext. Their meals are sent to the post. The advanced post furnishes three sentinels; two a few paces in front of the post, opposite the right and left wing of the regiment, posted so as to see as far as possible to the front, and one over the arms.

575. In the cavalry, dismounted men are employed in preference on the police guard. The mounted men on guard are sent in succession, a part at a time, to groom their horses. The advanced post is always formed of mounted men.

576. In each company, a corporal has charge of the stable-guard. His tour begins at retreat, and ends at morning stable-call. The stable-guard is large enough to relieve the men on post every two hours. They sleep in their tents, and are called by the corporal when wanted. At retreat he closes the streets of the camp with cords, or uses other precautions to prevent the escape of loose horses.

577. The officer of the day is charged with the order and cleanliness of the camp: a fatigue is furnished to him when the number of prisoners is insufficient to clean the camp. He has the calls beaten by the drummer of the guard.

578. The police guard and the advanced post pay the same honors as other guards. They take arms when an armed body approaches.

579. The sentinel over the colors has orders not to permit them to be moved except in presence of an escort; to let no one touch them but the color-bearer, or the sergeant of the police guard when he is accompanied by two armed men.

580. The sentinels on the color front permit no soldier to take arms from the stacks, except by order of some officer, or a non-commissioned officer of the guard. The sentinel at the Colonel's tent has orders to warn him, day or night, of any unusual movement in or about the camp.

581. The sentinels on the front, flanks, and rear, see that no soldier leaves camp with horse or arms unless conducted by a non-commissioned officer. They prevent non-commissioned officers and soldiers from passing out at night, except to go to the sinks, and mark if they return. They arrest, at any time, suspicious persons prowling about the camp, and at

night, every one who attempts to enter, even the sold'ers of other corps. Arrested persons are sent to the officer of the guard, who sends them, if necessary, to the officer of the day.

582. The sentinels on the front of the advanced post have orders to permit neither non-commissioned officers nor soldiers to pass the line, without reporting at the advanced post; to warn the advanced post of the approach of any armed body, and to arrest all suspicious persons. The sergeant sends persons so arrested to the officer of the guard, and warns him of the approach of any armed body.

583. The sentinel over the arms at the advanced post guards the prisoners and keeps sight of them, and suffers no one to converse with them without permission. They are only permitted to go to the sinks one at a time, and under a sentinel.

584. If any one is to be passed out of camp at night, the officer of the guard sends him under escort to the advanced post, and the sergeant of the post has him passed over the chain.

585. At retreat, the officer of the guard has the roll of his guard called, and inspects arms, to see that they are loaded and in order; and visits the advanced post for the same purpose. The sergeant of the police guard, accompanied by two armed soldiers, folds the colors and lays them on the trestle in rear of the arms. He sees that the sutler's stores are then closed, and the men leave them, and that the kitchen fires are put out at the appointed hour.

586. The officer of the day satisfies himself frequently during the night, of the vigilance of the police guard and advanced post. He prescribes patrols and rounds to be made by the officer and non-commissioned officers of the guard. The officer of the guard orders them when he thinks necessary. He visits the sentinels frequently.

587. At reveille, the police guard takes arms; the officer of the guard inspects it and the advanced post. The Sergeant replants the colors in place. At retreat and reveille the advanced post takes arms; the Sergeant makes his report to the officer of the guard when he visits the post.

588. When necessary, the camp is covered at night with small outposts, forming a double chain of sentinels. These posts are under the orders of the commander of the police guard, and are visited by his patrols and rounds.

589. The officer of the guard makes his report of his tour of service, including the advanced post, and sends it, after the guard is marched off, to the officer of the day.

590. When the regiment marches, the men of the police guard return to their companies, except those of the advanced post. In the cavalry, at the sound "boot and saddle," the officer of the guard sends one-half the

men to saddle and pack; when the regiment assembles, all the men join it.

591. When the camping-party precedes the regiment, and the new police guard marches with the camping-party, the guard, on reaching the camp, forms in line thirty paces in front of the centre of the ground marked for the regiment. The officer of the guard furnishes the sentinels required by the commander of the camping-party. The advanced post takes its station.

592. The advanced post of the old police guard takes charge of the prisoners on the march, and marches, bayonets fixed, at the centre of the regiment. On reaching camp, it turns over the prisoners to the new advanced post.

THE PICKET.

593. The detail for the picket is made daily, after the details for duty of the first class, and from the next for detail on the roster of that class. It is designed to furnish detachments and guards unexpectedly called for in the twenty-four hours; it counts as a tour of the first class to those who have marched on detachment or guard, or who have passed the night in bivouac.

594. The officers, non-commissioned officers, and soldiers of the picket are at all times dressed and equipped; the horses are saddled, and knapsacks and valises ready to be put on.

595. Detachments and guards from the picket are taken from the head of the picket-roll in each company, and, if possible, equally from each company. The picket of a regiment is composed of a Lieutenant, two Sergeants, four Corporals, a drummer, and about forty privates. For a smaller force, the picket is in proportion to the strength of the detachment.

596. Officers and men of the picket who march on detachment or guard before retreat will be replaced.

597. The picket is assembled by the Adjutant at guard-mounting; it is posted twelve paces in rear of the guard, and is inspected by its own commander. When the guard has marched in review, the commandant of the picket marches it to the left of the police guard, where it stacks its arms, and is dismissed; the arms are under charge of the sentinel of the police guard.

598. The picket is only assembled by the orders of the Colonel or officer of the day. It forms on the left of the police guard.

599. The officer of the day requires the roll of the picket to be called frequently during the day; the call is sounded from the police guard. At roll-calls and inspections, infantry pickets assemble with knapsacks on, cavalry on foot. The picket is assembled at retreat; the officer has the

roll called, and inspects the arms. The picket sleep in their tents, but without undressing.

600. The picket does not assemble at night except in cases of alarm, or when the whole or a part is to march; then the officer of the day calls the officers, the latter the non-commissioned officers, and these the men, for which purpose each ascertains the tents of those he is to call; they are assembled without beat of drum or other noise. At night, cavalry pickets assemble mounted.

601. Pickets rejoin their companies whenever the regiment is under arms for review, drill, march, or battle.

GRAND GUARDS AND OTHER OUTPOSTS.

602. Grand guards are the advanced posts of a camp or cantonment, and should cover the approaches to it. Their number, strength, and position are regulated by the commanders of brigades; in detached corps, by the commanding officer. When it can be, the grand guards of cavalry and infantry are combined, the cavalry furnishing the advanced sentinels. When the cavalry is weak, the grand guards are infantry, but furnished with a few cavalry soldiers, to get and carry intelligence of the enemy.

603. The strength of the grand guard of a brigade will depend on its object and the strength of the regiments, the nature of the country, the position of the enemy, and the disposition of the inhabitants. It is usually commanded by a Captain.

604. Under the supervision of the Generals of Division and Brigade, the grand guards are specially under the direction of a field officer of the day in each brigade. In case of necessity, Captains may be added to the roster of Lieutenant-Colonels and Majors for this detail.

605. Staff officers, sent from division head-quarters to inspect the posts of grand guards, give them orders only in urgent cases, and in the absence of the field officer of the day of the brigade.

606. Grand guards usually mount at the same time as the other guards, but may mount before daybreak if the General of Brigade thinks it necessary to double the outposts at that time. In this case they assemble and march without noise, and during their march throw out scouts; this precaution should always be taken in the first posting of a grand guard. The doubling of guards weakens the corps and fatigues the men, and should seldom be resorted to, and never when preparing to march or fight.

607. A grand guard is conducted to its post, in the first instance, by the field officer of the day, guided by a staff officer who accompanied the General in his reconnoissance. After the post has been established, the commander sends to the field officer of the day, when necessary, a soldier of the guard to guide the relieving guard to the post. He also sends to

him in the evening a corporal or trusty man of the guard for the note containing the parole and countersign, and sends them before dark to the detached posts. He will not suffer his guard to be relieved except by a guard of the brigade, or by special orders.

608. If there is no pass to be observed or defended, the grand guards are placed near the centre of the ground they are to observe, on sheltered, and, if possible, high ground, the better to conceal their strength and observe the enemy; they ought not to be placed near the edge of a wood. When, during the day, they are placed very near or in sight of the enemy, they fall back at night on posts selected farther to the rear.

609. In broken or mountainous countries, and particularly if the inhabitants are ill disposed, intermediate posts must be established when it is necessary to post the grand guard distant from the camp.

610. Grand guards are chiefly to watch the enemy in front; their flanks are protected by each other, and the camp must furnish posts to protect their rear and secure their retreat.

611. Grand guards are seldom intrenched, and never without the orders of the General, except by a barricade or ditch when exposed in a plain to attacks of cavalry.

612. The General of Division, if he thinks proper, changes the stations and orders of these guards, and establishes posts to connect the brigades or protect the exterior flanks.

613. After a grand guard is posted, the first care of the commander and of the field officer of the day is to get news of the enemy; then to reconnoitre his position, and the roads, bridges, fords, and defiles. This reconnoissance determines the force and position of the small posts and their sentinels day and night. These posts, according to their importance, are commanded by officers or non-commissioned officers; the cavalry posts may be relieved every four or eight hours.

614. The commander of a grand guard receives detailed instructions from the General and field officer of the day of the brigade, and instructs the commanders of the small posts as to their duties and the arrangements for defense or retreat. The commanders of grand guards may, in urgent cases, change the positions of the small posts. If the small posts are to change their positions at night, they wait until the grand guard have got into position and darkness hides their movements from the enemy; then march silently and rapidly under the charge of an officer.

615. In detached corps, small posts of picked men are at night sent forward on the roads by which the enemy may attack or turn the position. They watch the forks of the roads, keep silence, conceal themselves, light no fires, and often change place. They announce the approach of the

enemy by signals agreed upon, and retreat, by routes examined during the day, to places selected, and rejoin the guard at daybreak.

616. Grand guards have special orders in each case, and the following in all cases: to inform the nearest posts and the field officer of the day, or the General of Brigade, of the march and movements of the enemy, and of the attacks they receive or fear; to examine every person passing near the post, particularly those coming from without; to arrest suspicious persons, and all soldiers and camp-followers who try to pass out without permission, and to send to the General, unless otherwise directed, all country people who come in.

617. All out-guards stand to arms at night on the approach of patrols, rounds, or other parties; the sentinel over the arms has orders to call them out.

618. Advanced posts will not take arms for inspection or ceremony when it would expose them to the view of the enemy.

619. Grand guards are often charged with the care and working of telegraphic signals.

620. The sentinels and vedettes are placed on points from which they can see farthest, taking care not to break their connection with each other or with their posts. They are concealed from the enemy as much as possible by walls, or trees, or elevated ground. It is generally even of more advantage not to be seen than to see far. They should not be placed near covers, where the enemy may capture them.

621. A sentinel should always be ready to fire; vedettes carry their pistols or carbines in their hands. A sentinel must be sure of the presence of an enemy before he fires; once satisfied of that, he must fire, though all defense on his part be useless, as the safety of the post may depend on it. Sentinels fire on all persons deserting to the enemy.

622. If the post must be where a sentinel on it cannot communicate with the guard, a Corporal and three men are detached for it, or the sentinels are doubled, that one may communicate with the guard. During the day the communication may be made by signals, such as raising a cap or handkerchief. At night sentinels are placed on low ground, the better to see objects against the sky.

623. To lessen the duty of rounds, and keep more men on the alert at night, sentinels are relieved every hour. To prevent sentinels from being surprised, it is sometimes well to precede the countersign by signals, such as striking the musket with the hand, striking the hands together, &c.

624. On the approach of any one at night, the sentinel orders— "*Halt!*" If the order is not obeyed after once repeated, he fires. If obeyed, he calls— "*Who goes there?*" If answered—"*Rounds*" or

"*Patrol*," he says—"*Stand: Advance one with the countersign.*" If more than one advance at the same time, or the person who advances fails to give the countersign or signal agreed on, the sentinel fires, and falls back on his guard. The sentinel over the arms, as soon as his hail is answered, turns out the guard, and the Corporal goes to reconnoitre. When it is desirable to hide the position of the sentinel from the enemy, the hail is replaced by signals; the sentinel gives the signal, and those approaching the counter signal.

625. With raw troops, or when the light troops of the enemy are numerous or active, and when the country is broken or wooded, the night stormy or dark, sentinels should be doubled. In this case, while one watches, the other, called a flying sentinel, moves about, examining the paths and hollows. .

626. The commandants of grand guards visit the sentinels often change their positions when necessary; make them repeat their orders teach them under what circumstances and at what signals to retire, and particularly not to fall back directly on their guard if pursued, but to lead the enemy in a circuit.

627. At night, half the men of the grand guard off post watch under arms, while the rest lie down, arms by their side. The horses are always bridled; the horsemen hold the reins, and must not sleep.

628. When a grand guard of cavalry is so placed as not to be liable to a sudden attack from the enemy, the General may permit the horses to be fed during the night, unbridling for this purpose a few at a time— the horsemen being vigilant to prevent them from escaping.

629. An hour before break of day, infantry grand guards stand to arms, and cavalry mount. At the advanced posts, some of the infantry are all night under arms, some of the cavalry on horseback.

630. The commander of a grand guard regulates the numbers, the hours, and the march of patrols and rounds, according to the strength of his troop and the necessity for precaution; and, accompanied by those who are to command the patrols and rounds during the night, he will reconnoitre all the routes they are to follow.

631. Patrols and rounds march slowly, in silence, and with great precaution; halt frequently to listen and examine the ground. The rounds consist of an officer or non-commissioned officer, and two or three men.

632. Toward break of day the patrols ought to be more frequent, and sent to greater distances. They examine the hollow-ways and ground likely to conceal an enemy, but with great caution, to avoid being cut off, or engaged in an unequal combat; if they meet the enemy, they fire and attempt to stop his march. While the patrols are out, the posts are under arms.

633. Cavalry patrols should examine the country to a greater distance than infantry, and report to the infantry guard every thing they observe. The morning patrols and scouts do not return until broad daylight; and when they return, the night sentinels are withdrawn, and the posts for the day resumed.

634. When patrols are sent beyond the advanced posts, the posts and sentinels should be warned.

635. On their return, commanders of patrols report in regard to the ground and every thing they have observed of the movements of the enemy, or of his posts, and the commandant of the grand guard reports to the field officer of the day.

636. The fires of grand guards should be hidden by a wall, or ditch, or other screen. To deceive the enemy, fires are sometimes made on ground not occupied. Fires are not permitted at small posts liable to surprise.

637. The horses of cavalry guards are watered or fed by detachments; during which the rest are ready to mount.

638. If a body of troops attempt to enter the camp at night, unless their arrival has been announced, or the commander is known to, or is the bearer of a written order to the commander of the grand guard, he stops them, and sends the commander under escort to the field officer of the day, and warns the posts near him.

639. Bearers of flags are not permitted to pass the outer chain of sentinels; their faces are turned from the post or army; if necessary, their eyes are bandaged; a non-commissioned officer stays with them to prevent indiscretion of the sentinels.

640. The commandant of the grand guard receipts for dispatches, and sends them to the field officer of the day or General of Brigade, and dismisses the bearer; but if he has discovered what ought to be concealed from the enemy, he is detained as long as necessary.

641. Deserters are disarmed at the advanced posts, and sent to the commander of the grand guard, who gets from them all the information he can concerning his post. If many come at night, they are received *cautiously, a few at a time.* They are sent in the morning to the field officer of the day, or to the nearest post or camp, to be conducted to the General of the brigade. All suspected persons are searched by the commanders of the posts.

642. When an enemy advances to attack, unless he is in too great force, or the grand guard is to defend an intrenched post or a defile, it will take the positions and execute the movements to check the enemy, acting as skirmishers, or fighting in close or open order, as may be best

The guard joins its corps when in line, or when a sufficient number of troops have reached the ground it defends.

INTRENCHED POSTS.

643. Unless the army be acting on the defensive, no post should be intrenched, except to cover the weak parts of the line, or at points which the enemy cannot avoid, or in mountain warfare, or to close a defile, or cover winter quarters.

644. Posts connected with the operations of an army are intrenched only by order of the General commanding-in-chief or a General of Division.

645. Any intrenchment that requires artillery is considered as a post, and a guard or garrison and commander are assigned to it.

646. The General who establishes an intrenched post gives to its commander detailed instructions in regard to its defense, and the circumstances under which the defense should cease.

647. The commander reconnoitres his post; distributes the troops; posts the officers and non-commissioned officers; forms a reserve; gives orders for all contingencies he can foresee; supposes an attack, and arranges his troops for defense, so as to prepare them for attack, day or night.

648. In dark weather he redoubles his vigilance, and changes the hours and direction of the rounds and patrols. He permits no flags of truce, deserters, or strangers to enter. If a flag ought to pass his post, he bandages his eyes. He refuses admittance to a relief or any other party until he has carefully examined them. In case of an attack, he does not wait for orders or hold a council. Having defended his post to the last extremity, or till the purpose of the defense, according to his instructions, is answered, he may then spike his guns and rejoin the army under cover of night, or by cutting his way through the enemy.

DETACHMENTS.

649. When a detachment is to be formed from the different regiments of a brigade, the Assistant Adjutant-General of the brigade assembles it, and turns it over to the commander.

650. When a detachment is to be formed from different brigades, the Assistant Adjutant-General in each forms the contingent of the brigade, and sends it to the place of assembling.

651. Detachments are generally formed by taking battalions, squadrons, companies, platoons in turn, according to the roster for such detail.

652. When the detachment is to consist of men from every company or troop, the first on the roster for guard are taken.

653. Officers, non-commissioned officers, and soldiers, whose tour it is to go on detachment, if employed otherwise at the time, are relieved from the duty they are on, if they can reach camp in time to march with the detachment.

654. When detachments meet, the command is regulated while they serve together as if they formed one detachment. But the senior officer cannot prevent the commander of any detachment from moving, when he thinks proper, to execute the orders he has received.

655. On the return of a detachment, the commander reports to the head-quarters from which he received his orders.

RECONNOISSANCES.

656. Near an enemy, daily reconnoissances are made to observe the ground in front, and to discover whether the advanced guards of the enemy have been increased or put in motion, or any other sign of his preparation for march or action.

657. They are made by small parties of cavalry and infantry, from the brigade, under direction of the General of Division or the General of a separate brigade, and to less distance by the patrols of the grand guard, and are not repeated at the same hour or by the same route. On the plain, reconnoissances are made by cavalry; among mountains, by infantry, with a few horsemen to carry intelligence.

658. Reconnoitring parties observe the following precautions: to leave small posts, or sentinels at intervals, to transmit intelligence to the advanced posts of the army, unless the return is to be by a different route; to march with caution, to avoid fighting; and see, if possible, without being seen; to keep an advanced guard; to send well-mounted men ahead of the advanced guard, and on the flank of the party; to instruct the scouts that no two should enter a defile or mount a hill together, but to go one at a time, while one watches to carry the news if the other is taken.

659. Before daybreak the advanced guard and scouts are drawn closer; the party then march slowly and silently, stop frequently to listen, and keep the horses that neigh in the rear. The party should enter no wood, defile, village, or inclosure, until it has been fully examined by the scouts.

660. Special reconnoissances are made under the instruction of the General in command, by such officers and with such force as he may direct.

661. Offensive or forced reconnoissances are to ascertain with certainty points in the enemy's position, or his strength. They are sometimes preludes to real actions, and sometimes only demonstrations. They drive in his outposts, and sometimes engage special corps of his line. They are

only made by the order of the General commanding-in-chief, or the commander of an isolated corps.

662. In all reports of reconnoissances, the officer making them shall distinguish expressly what he has seen from the accounts he has not been able to verify personally.

663. In special and offensive reconnoissances, the report must be accompanied by a field-sketch of the localities, the dispositions and defenses of the enemy.

PARTISANS AND FLANKERS.

664. The operations of partisan corps depend on the nature and theatre of the war; they enter into the general plan of operations, and are conducted under the orders of the General commanding-in-chief.

665. The composition and strength of partisan corps and detachments of flankers depend on the object, the difficulties, the distance, and the probable time of the expedition.

666. The purpose of these isolated corps is to reconnoitre at a distance on the flanks of the army, to protect its operations, to deceive the enemy, to interrupt his communications, to intercept his couriers and his correspondence, to threaten or destroy his magazines, to carry off his posts and his convoys, or, at all events, to retard his march by making him detach largely for their protection.

667. While these corps fatigue the enemy and embarrass his operations, they endeavor to inspire confidence and secure the good will of the inhabitants in a friendly country, and to hold them in check in an enemy's country.

668. They move actively, appear unexpectedly on different points in such a manner as to make it impossible to estimate their force, or to tell whether they are irregular forces or an advanced guard.

669. These operations require vigilance, secrecy, energy, and promptness. The partisan commander must frequently supply by stratagem and audacity what he wants in numbers.

670. These detachments are sometimes composed of different arms, but the service belongs more particularly to the light cavalry, which can move to a distance by rapid marches, surprise the enemy, attack unexpectedly, and retire as promptly.

671. Stormy weather, fogs, extreme heat, and the night above all, are favorable to the success of ambuscades; when the enemy are careless, the break of day is the best time. A partisan commander should communicate to his second in command his secret orders, the direction and object of the expedition, and the different points of junction with the army.

672. Guides of the country and spies are often necessary to the parti-

san. They are examined separately, and confronted if their accounts differ. When there is but one guide, he marches with the advanced guard, guarded by two men, and bound if necessary. Peddlers and smugglers are specially suitable for spies.

673. A fit time to attack a convoy is at a halt, or when they begin to park, cr when they are watering, or passing a wood or a defile; at a bend of the road, a bridge, or steep ascent.

674. The attacking party may be principally cavalry, with some infantry. The first object is to disperse the escort. A part of the detachment attacks the main body of the escort, another the wagons, and a third is in reserve; skirmishers line the road, and try to cut the traces, and to seize the front and rear wagons, and turn them across the road, to prevent the train from advancing or retreating.

675. If the convoy is parked, the cavalry surrounds it, assails the escort, and tries to draw it away from the train. The infantry then engage the troops remaining at the park, slip under the wagons, and get into the park. When the cavalry is alone and the enemy are shaken, they dismount a portion of the men to supply the want of infantry.

676. If it is a large convoy, the principal attack is made on the centre; the most valuable wagons are also selected, and additional horses are put to them if the attack is successful. Those that cannot be carried off are burned.

MARCHES.

677. The object of the movement and the nature of the ground determine the order of march, the kind of troops in each column, and the number of columns.

678. The force is divided into as many columns as circumstances permit, without weakening any one too much. They ought to preserve their communications, and be within supporting distance of each other. The commander of each column ought to know the strength and direction of the others.

679. The advance and rear guards are usually light troops; their strength and composition depend on the nature of the ground and the position of the enemy. They serve to cover the movements of the army, and to hold the enemy in check until the General has time to make his arrangements.

680. The advance guard is not always at the head of the column; in a march to a flank, it takes such positions as cover the movement. Sappers are attached to the advanced guard if required.

681. The "*general,*" sounded one hour before the time of marching, is the signal to strike tents, to load the wagons, and pack horses, and send them to the place of assembling. The fires are then put out, and care taken

to avoid burning straw, &c., or giving to the enemy any other indication of the movement.

682. The "march" will be beat in the infantry, and the "advance" sounded in the cavalry, in succession, as each is to take its place in the column.

683. When the army should form suddenly to meet the enemy, the "*long roll*" is beat, and "*to horse*" sounded. The troops form rapidly in front of their camp.

684. Batteries of artillery and their caissons move with the corps to which they are attached; the field train and ambulances march at the rear of the column; and the baggage with the rear guard.

685. Cavalry and infantry do not march together, unless the proximity of the enemy makes it necessary.

686. In cavalry marches, when distant from the enemy, each regiment, and, if possible, each squadron, forms a separate column, in order to keep up the same gait from front to rear, and to trot, when desirable, on good ground. In such cases, the cavalry may leave camp later, and can give more rest to the horses, and more attention to the shoeing and harness. Horses are not bridled until the time to start.

687. When necessary, the orders specify the rations the men are to carry in their haversacks. The field officers and Captains make inspections frequently during the march; at halts they examine the knapsacks, valises, and haversacks, and throw away all articles not authorized. The officers and non-commissioned officers of cavalry companies attend personally to the packs and girths.

688. When it can be avoided, troops should not be assembled on high-roads or other places where they interrupt the communication.

689. Generals of Division and commanders of detached corps send a staff officer to the rendezvous, in advance, to receive the troops, who, on arriving, take their place in the order of battle, and form in close column, unless otherwise ordered. Artillery, or trains halted on the roads, form in file on one side.

690. The execution of marching orders must not be delayed. If the commander is not at the head of his troops when they are to march, the next in rank puts the column in motion.

691. If possible, each column is preceded by a detachment of sappers, to remove obstacles to the march, aided, when necessary, by infantry, or the people of the country. The detachment is divided into two sections: one stops to remove the first obstacle, the other moves on to the next.

692. In night marches, and at bad places, and at cross-roads, when necessary, intelligent non-commissioned officers are posted to show the way, and are relieved by the regiments as they come up.

Marches.

693. On the march no one shall fire a gun, or cry "*halt*" or "*march*" without orders.

694. Soldiers are not to stop for water; the canteens should be filled before starting.

695. It is better to avoid villages; but, if the route lies through them, officers and non-commissioned officers are to be vigilant to prevent straggling. Halts should not take place at villages.

696. Besides the rear guard, the General sometimes takes a detachment from the last regiment, and adds to it non-commissioned officers from each regiment, to examine villages and all hiding-places on the route, to bring up stragglers and seize marauders.

697. In night marches, the Sergeant-Major of each regiment remains at the rear with a drummer, to give notice when darkness or difficulty stops the march. In cavalry, a trumpet is placed in rear of each squadron, and the signal repeated to the head of the regiment.

698. The General and field officers frequently stop, or send officers to the rear, to see that the troops march in the prescribed order, and keep their distances. To quicken the march, the General warns the Colonels, and may order a signal to be beat. It is repeated in all the regiments.

699. In approaching a defile, the Colonels are warned; they close their regiments as they come up; each regiment passes separately, at an accelerated pace, and in as close order as possible. The leading regiment having passed, and left room enough for the whole column in close order, then halts, and moves again as soon as the last regiment is through. In the cavalry, each squadron, before quickening the pace to rejoin the column, takes its original order of march.

700. When the distance from the enemy permits, each regiment, after closing up in front and rear of the defile, stacks arms.

701. Halts to rest and re-form the troops are frequent during the day, depending on the object and length of the march. They are made in preference after the passage of defiles.

702. No honors are paid by troops on the march or at halts.

703. The sick march with the wagons.

704. Led horses of officers, and the horses of dismounted men, follow their regiment. The baggage wagons never march in the column. When the General orders the field train and ambulances to take place in the column, he designates the position they shall take.

705. If two corps meet on the same road, they pass to the right, and both continue their march, if the road is wide enough; if it is not, the first in the order of battle takes the road, the other halts.

706. A corps in march must not be cut by another. If two corps meet at cross-roads, that which arrives last halts if the other is in motion.

A corps in march passes a corps at a halt, if it has precedence in the order of battle, or if the halted corps is not ready to move at once.

707. A column that halts to let another column pass resumes the march in advance of the train of this column. If a column has to pass a train, the train must halt, if necessary, till the column passes. . The column which has precedence must yield it if the commander, on seeing the orders of the other, finds it for the interest of the service.

JOURNAL.

708. Commanding officers of troops marching through a country little known, will keep journals of their marches according to the form and directions hereto annexed. At the end of the march a copy of the journal will be retained at the station where the troops arrive, and the original will be forwarded to the head-quarters of the Department, or *corps d'armée*. Thence, after a copy has been taken, it will be transmitted, through the head-quarters of the army, to the Adjutant-General, for the information of the War Department.

709. The object of the journal is to furnish data for maps, and information which may serve for future operations. Every point of practical importance should therefore be noted, even though not indicated in these directions.

DIRECTIONS FOR KEEPING THE JOURNAL.

710. The journal should be kept in a pocket note book; or, if one cannot be obtained, in a book made of sheets of paper folded to half the letter size.

711. The record is to run from the bottom to the top of each page.

712. The horizontal divisions in the column headed *"Route"* represent portions of a day's march. The distance, in miles, between each of the horizontal divisions, will be noted in the column headed *"Distance,"* which will be summed up at the top of each column, and the sum carried to the bottom of the next column.

713. The notes within each horizontal division are to show the general direction of the march, and every object of interest observed in its course. All remarkable features of the country, therefore, such as hills, streams, fords, springs, houses, villages, forests, marshes, &c., and the places of encampment, will be sketched in their relative positions, as well as noted by name.

714. The *"Remarks"* corresponding to each division will be upon the soil, productions, quantity and quality of timber, grass, water, fords, nature of the roads, &c., and important incidents. They should show where provisions, forage, fuel, and water can be obtained; whether the

Journal.

FORM OF

JOURNAL of the march of [*here insert the names of the regiments* from [*here insert the point of departure*] to [*the stopping-place*],

Date.	Hour.	Weather	Distance.	Route.
1860.			Total, 19	
			3	
July 8.	5. a. m.			
	1 p. m.		8	
	10.		8	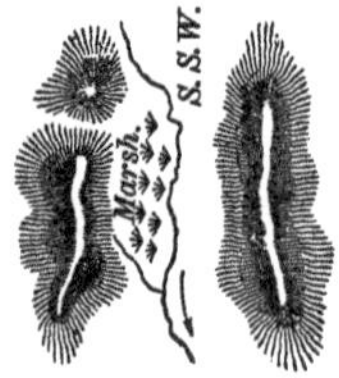
	6.80.		1	
	6.		4	
July 7.	4.80.			

(Weather column, vertical text: Cloudy, with wind.—Cold early in morning.—Cloudy.)

JOURNAL.

or companies composing the column], commanded by —— ——,
pursuant to [*here give the No. and date of order for the march*].

Remarks.

Road rocky; but little grass; good water. Plenty of timber on summit of hills, extending three miles; road to right of hills.

Good shelter for camp at foot of peak; fuel plenty. Springs of sweet water, with good grass near. Road to this point rather more sandy.

Road runs through a cañon ½ mile long, to right of a small stream; marsh on left of stream; water sweet; grass excellent. Halted to graze two hours. No Indian signs.

Companies F, G, and I, 3d ——, detached at Mount P——, under command of —— —— (see par. 3, General Orders No. ——), to take road to ——.
A small creek, easily forded.

Road turns short to right at top of hill after crossing river; crossing good, but a little boggy on the right bank. This bottom shows signs of recent overflow, when it must have been impassable; banks low; water sweet; no wood near crossing; road hard and good up to river.

Journal.

JOURNAL—

Date.	Hour.	Weather.	Distance.	Route.
1860.			Total, 47	
			5	
July 9.	4.30 a. m.	Rain.		Fork in Road.
	4.30 p. m.		3	Camp No. 2. Springs. Ravine. S. S. E
	3 p. m.	Very pleasant; cloudy in the p. m.	15	+Grave. Mt. T. S. S. E.
	9		5	Springs. S. S. W.
July 8.	6.30 a. m.			
			19	

Journal.

Continued.

Remarks.

At the point where the road forks, turn to the right. The left-hand road leads to a deep ravine, which cannot be crossed.

After the road strikes the ravine, it runs one mile along its bank before coming to the crossing-place. The camping-ground is at springs, half a mile beyond the ravine. Old Indian signs at the springs.

Road less rocky; last three miles rather sandy; no water. Passed at the point marked † an Indian grave.

Road still rocky; good springs, where casks should be filled. No more water for twenty miles after leaving spr'ngs. Occasional hills to left of road; no wood or grass streams to be crossed are fordable, miry, have quicksands or steep banks, and whether they overflow their banks in wet seasons; also the quality of the water; and, in brief, every thing of practical importance.

715. When a detachment leaves the main column, the point on the *"Route"* will be noted, and the reason given in the *Remarks.* The commander of the detachment will be furnished with a copy of the journal up to that point, and will continue it over his new line of march.

POSTS.

716. Whenever a new post is established, or a camp, meant to be occupied for some time, the commanding officer will forward to the Adjutant-General's office, as well as to the head-quarters of the Department, or *corps d'armée* if in the field, an accurate description of its locality, of its distance and bearings from the nearest known point, and the manner of reaching it by mail, together with a sketch of the country in its immediate vicinity.

717. Military posts will be named by the Secretary of War.

BATTLES.

718. Dispositions for battle depend on the number, kind, and quality of the troops opposed, on the ground, and on the objects of the war; but the following rules are to be observed generally:

719. In attacking, the advanced guard endeavors to capture the enemy's outposts, or cut them off from the main body. Having done so, or driven them in, it occupies, in advancing, all the points that can cover or facilitate the march of the army, or secure its retreat, such as bridges, defiles, woods, and heights; it then makes attacks, to occupy the enemy, without risking too much, and to deceive them as to the march and projects of the army.

720. When the enemy is hidden by a curtain of advanced troops, the commandant of the advanced guard sends scouts, under intelligent officers, to the right and left, to ascertain his position and movements. If he does not succeed in this way, he tries to unmask the enemy by demonstrations; threatens to cut the advance from the main body; makes false attacks; partial and impetuous charges in echelon; and if all fail, he makes a real attack to accomplish the object.

721. Detachments left by the advanced guard to hold points in the rear rejoin it when other troops come up. If the army takes a position, and the advanced guard is separated from it by defiles or heights, the communication is secured by troops drawn from the main body.

722. At proper distance from the enemy, the troops are formed for the attack in several lines; if only two can be formed, some battalions in

column are placed behind the wings of the second line. The lines may be formed of troops in column or in order of battle, according to the ground and plan of attack.

723. The advanced guard may be put in the line or on the wings, or other position, to aid the pursuit or cover the retreat.

724. The reserve is formed of the best troops of foot and horse, to complete a victory or make good a retreat. It is placed in the rear of the centre, or chief point of attack or defense.

725. The cavalry should be distributed in echelon on the wings and at the centre, on favorable ground.

726. It should be instructed not to take the gallop until within charging distance; never to receive a charge at a halt, but to meet it, or, if not strong enough, to retire manoeuvring; and in order to be ready for the pursuit, and prepared against a reverse, or the attacks of the reserve, not to engage all its squadrons at once, but to reserve one-third, in column or in echelon, abreast of or in the rear of one of the wings; this arrangement is better than a second line with intervals.

727. In the attack, the artillery is employed to silence the batteries that protect the position. In the defense, it is better to direct its fire on the advancing troops. In either case, as many pieces are united as possible, the fire of artillery being formidable in proportion to its concentration.

728. In battles and military operations it is better to assume the offensive, and put the enemy on the defensive; but to be safe in doing so requires a larger force than the enemy, or better troops, and favorable ground. When obliged to act on the defensive, the advantage of position and of making the attack may sometimes be secured by forming in rear of the ground on which we are to fight, and advancing at the moment of action. In mountain warfare, the assailant has always the disadvantage; and even in offensive warfare in the open field, it may frequently be very important, when the artillery is well posted, and any advantage of ground may be secured, to await the enemy and compel him to attack.

729. The attack should be made with a superior force on the decisive point of the enemy's position, by masking this by false attacks and demonstrations on other points, and by concealing the troops intended for it by the ground, or by other troops in their front.

730. Besides the arrangements which depend on the supposed plan of the enemy, the wings must be protected by the ground, or supported by troops in echelon; if the attack of the enemy is repulsed, the offensive must at once be taken, to inspire the troops, to disconcert the enemy, and often to decide the action In thus taking the offensive, a close column should

be pushed rapidly on the wing or flank of the enemy. The divisions of this column form in line of battle successively, and each division moves to the front as soon as formed, in order, by a rapid attack in echelon, to prevent the enemy from changing front or bringing up his reserves. In all arrangements, especially in those for attack, it is most important to conceal the design until the moment of execution, and then to execute it with the greatest rapidity. The night, therefore, is preferred for the movement of troops on the flank or rear of the enemy, otherwise it is necessary to mask their march by a grand movement in front, or by taking a wide circuit.

731. In making an attack, the communications to the rear and for retreat must be secured, and the General must give beforehand all necessary orders to provide for that event.

732. When a success is gained, the light troops should pursue the enemy promptly and rapidly. The other troops will restore order in their columns, then advance from position to position, always prepared for an attack or to support the troops engaged.

733. Before the action, the Generals indicate the places where they will be; if they change position, they give notice of it, or leave a staff officer to show where they have gone.

734. During the fight the officers and non-commissioned officers keep the men in the ranks, and enforce obedience if necessary. Soldiers must not be permitted to leave the ranks to strip or rob the dead,—nor even to assist the wounded unless by express permission, which is only to be given after the action is decided. The highest interest and most pressing duty is to win the victory, by winning which only can a proper care of the wounded be ensured.

735. Before the action, the Quartermaster of the division makes all the necessary arrangements for the transportation of the wounded. He establishes the ambulance depôts in the rear, and gives his assistants the necessary instructions for the service of the ambulance wagons and other means of removing the wounded.

736. The ambulance depôt, to which the wounded are carried or directed for immediate treatment, is generally established at the most convenient building nearest the field of battle. A *red flag* marks its place, or the way to it, to the conductors of the ambulances and to the wounded who can walk.

737. The active ambulances follow the troops engaged to succor the wounded and remove them to the depôts; for this purpose the conductors should always have the necessary assistants, that the soldiers may have no excuse to leave the ranks for that object.

738. The medical director of the division, after consultation with the

Quartermaster-General, distributes the medical officers and hospital attendants at his disposal, to the depôts and active ambulances. He will send officers and attendants, when practicable, to the active ambulances, to relieve the wounded who require treatment before being removed from the ground. He will see that the depôts and ambulances are provided with the necessary apparatus, medicines, and stores. He will take post and render his professional services at the principal depôt.

739. If the enemy endanger the depôt, the Quartermaster takes the orders of the General to remove it or to strengthen its guard.

740. The wounded in the depôts and the sick are removed, as soon as possible, to the hospitals that have been established by the Quartermaster-General of the army on the flanks or rear of the army.

741. After an action, the officers of ordnance collect the munitions of war left on the field, and make a return of them to the General. The Quartermaster's Department collects the rest of the public property captured, and makes the returns to head-quarters.

742. Written reports for the General commanding-in-chief are made by commandants of regiments, batteries, and separate squadrons, and by all commanders of a higher grade, each in what concerns his own command, and to his immediate commander.

743. When an officer or soldier deserves mention for conduct in action, a special report shall be made in his case, and the General commanding-in-chief decides whether to mention him in his report to the government and in his orders. But he shall not be mentioned in the report until he has been mentioned in the orders to the army. These special reports are examined with care by the intermediate commanders, to verify the facts, and secure commendation and rewards to the meritorious only.

744. The report of battles, which must frequently be made before these special reports of persons are scrutinized, is confined to general praise or blame, and an account of the operations.

PRISONERS OF WAR.

745. Prisoners of war will be disarmed and sent to the rear, and reported as soon as practicable to the head-quarters. The return of prisoners from the Head-Quarters of the Army to the War Department will specify the number, rank, and corps.

746. The private property of prisoners will be duly respected, and each shall be treated with the regard due to his rank. They are to obey the necessary orders given them. They receive for subsistence one ration each, without regard to rank; and the wounded are to be treated with

the same care as the wounded of the army.　Other allowances to them will depend on conventions with the enemy.　Prisoners' horses will be taken for the army.

747. Exchanges of prisoners and release of officers on parole depend on the orders of the General commanding-in-chief, under the instructions of government.

CONVOYS AND THEIR ESCORTS.

748. The strength and composition of the escort of a convoy depend on the country, the nature and value of the convoy, and the dangers it may incur.　A larger escort is required for a convoy of powder, that the defense may not be near the train.

749. Cavalry is employed in escorts chiefly to reconnoitre; the proportion is larger as the country is more open.

750. Pioneers or working-parties are attached to convoys to mend roads, remove obstacles, and erect defenses.　The convoys should always be provided with spare wheels, poles, axles, &c.

751. The commandant of the escort should receive detailed instructions in writing.

752. As far as the defense permits, the commander of the escort shall refer to the officer in charge of the convoy for the hours of departure, the halts, the parking and order of the train, and the precautions against accidents.

753. Officers who accompany the convoy, but do not belong to the escort, shall exercise no authority in it except by consent of the commander.　If these officers are junior to the commander, he may assign them to duty if the defense requires it.

754. Large convoys are formed into divisions, each with a conductor. The distance between the wagons is four paces.　A small party of infantry is attached to each division.

755. Generally, munitions of war are at the head of the convoy, subsistence next, and then other military stores; the sutler last.　But always that part of the convoy which is most important to the army shall be where it is most secure from danger.

756. The commandant should send out reconnoitring parties, and never put the convoy in motion until their reports have been received. He always forms an advance and rear guard, and keeps the main body under his immediate order at the most important point, with small guards or posts at other points.

757. In an open country the main body marches by the side of the road, opposite the centre of the convoy; in other cases at the head or rear of the column, as the one or the other is more exposed.

758. The advance guard precedes the convoy far enough to remove all obstacles to its advance. It examines the woods, defiles, and villages, and by mounted men gives information to the commander, and receives his orders. It reconnoitres places for halts and parks.

759. If the head of the column is threatened, the advanced guard seizes the defiles and places which the enemy might occupy, and holds them until the main body advances to the front and relieves it; the main body holds the positions until the head of the convoy arrives, and then leaves detachments which are relieved by the parties marching with the divisions; the posts are not abandoned until the whole convoy has passed and the position is no longer important.

760. When the rear is threatened, like measures are taken; the rear guard defends the ground and retards the enemy by breaking the bridges and blocking the road.

761. If the flanks are threatened, and the ground is broken, and many defiles are to be passed, the defense of the convoy becomes more difficult; the advance and rear guards must be reduced, the flanks strengthened, and positions which will cover the march of the convoy must be occupied by the main body of the troops before the head of the convoy reaches them, and until it has passed.

762. If the convoy is large, and has to pass places that the force and position of the enemy make dangerous, the loss of the whole convoy must not be risked; it must pass by divisions, which reunite after the passage. In this case the greater part of the troops guard the first division; they seize the important points, and cover them with light troops, or, if necessary, with small posts, and hold them until all the divisions have passed.

763. If there is artillery in the convoy, the commander of the escort uses it for the defense.

764. To move faster and make the defense easier, the wagons move in double file whenever the road allows it. If a wagon breaks, it is at once removed from the road; when repaired, it takes the rear; when it cannot be repaired, its load and horses are distributed to some of the other wagons kept in the rear for that purpose.

765. Convoys by water are escorted on the same principles. Each boat has a small infantry guard; one portion of the escort precedes or follows the convoy in boats. The cavalry march opposite the convoy; the advance and rear guard move by land, and all are connected by flankers with the convoy. Where a river runs through a narrow valley, the body of the infantry moves by land to prevent the enemy from occupying the heights and disturbing the convoy.

766. Convoys halt every hour to let the horses take breath and the wagons close up. Long halts are made but seldom, and only in places

that have been reconnoitred and found favorable for defense. At night the park is arranged for defense, and in preference at a distance from inhabited places, if in an enemy's country.

767. The wagons are usually parked in ranks, axle against axle, the poles in the same direction, and with sufficient space between the ranks for the horses. If an attack is feared, they are parked in square, the hind-wheels outside, and the horses inside.

768. On the appearance of the enemy during the march, the commander closes up the wagons and continues his march in order; he avoids fighting; but if the enemy seizes a position that commands his road, he attacks vigorously with the mass of his force, but is not to continue the pursuit far from the convoy. The convoy halts, and resumes the march when the position is carried.

769. When the enemy is too strong to be attacked, the convoy is parked in square if there is room; if not, closed up in double file; at the front and rear the road is blocked by wagons across it. The drivers are dismounted at the heads of the horses. They are not permitted to make their escape. The light troops keep the enemy at a distance as long as possible, and are supported when necessary, but prudently, as the troops must be kept in hand to resist the main attack.

770. If a wagon takes fire in the park, remove it if possible; if not, remove first the ammunition wagons, then those to leeward of the fire.

771. When a whole convoy cannot be saved, the most valuable part may sometimes be by abandoning the rest. If all efforts fail, and there is no hope of succor, the convoy must be set on fire and the horses killed that cannot be saved; the escort may then cut its way through.

772. If the convoy is of prisoners of war, every effort should be made to reach a village or strong building where they may be confined; if forced to fight in the field, the prisoners must be secured and made to lie down until the action is over.

BAGGAGE TRAINS.

773. The baggage train of general head-quarters and the trains of the several divisions are each under the charge of an officer of the Quartermaster's Department. These officers command and conduct the trains under the orders they receive from their respective head-quarters. When the trains of different divisions march together, or the train of a division marches with the train of general head-quarters, the senior Quartermaster directs the whole.

774. The Regimental Quartermaster has charge of the wagons, horses equipments, and all means of transport employed in the service of the regiment. Under the orders of the Colonel, he assembles them for the

march, and maintains the order and police of the train in park and on the march. On marches, the regimental trains are under the orders of the Quartermaster of the division. When the march is by brigade, the senior Regimental Quartermaster in the brigade, or the Quartermaster of the brigade, has the direction of the whole. The necessary wagon-masters, or non-commissioned officers to act as such, are employed with the several trains.

775. None but the authorized wagons are allowed to march with the train. The wagons of the several head-quarters, the regimental wagons, and the wagons of sutlers authorized by orders from head-quarters to march with the train, are all to be conspicuously marked.

776. When the train of head-quarters is to have a guard, the strength of the guard is regulated by the General. Generals of Brigade guard their trains by the men attached to the train of the first regiment of their brigades. The regimental trains are loaded, unloaded, and guarded, as far as practicable, by convalescents and men not effective in the ranks; in the cavalry, by dismounted men. When the guard of a train is the escort for its defense, the regulations in regard to convoys and escorts take effect.

777. Habitually each division is followed by its train, the regimenta trains uniting at the brigade rendezvous. When otherwise, the order for the movement of the divisions, brigades, and regiments contains the necessary directions in regard to the assembling and marching of the respective trains. The several trains march in an order analogous to the rank of the generals, and the order of battle of the troops to which they belong. Trains are not allowed in any case to be in the midst of the troops, or to impede the march of the troops.

778. The wagon-masters, under the orders of the officers of the Quartermaster's Department, exercise the necessary restraints over the teamsters and servants who leave their teams, or do not properly conduct them; or who ill treat their horses, or who attempt to pillage, or run away in case of attack.

779. The General commanding the army and the Generals of Division will not permit any general or staff officer, or regiment under their orders, or any person whatsoever, attached to their command, to have more than the authorized amount or means of transportation. For this purpose they will themselves make, and cause to be made, frequent reviews and inspections of the trains. They will see that no trooper is employed to lead a private horse, no soldier to drive a private vehicle, and that no trooper is put on foot to lend his horse to an officer. They will not permit the wagons of the artillery or of the train to be loaded with any thing foreign to their proper service, nor any public horse, for any occasion, to be harnessed to a private carriage.

780. The officers of the Quartermaster's Department, the wagon-masters, and all conductors of trains, are charged with watching that the regulations respecting transportation allowances are strictly observed.

GENERAL POLICE.

781. When necessary, the General-in-chief or General of Division may appoint a provost marshal to take charge of prisoners, with a suitable guard, or other police force.

782. Private servants, not soldiers, will not be allowed to wear the uniform of any corps of the army, but each will be required to carry with him a certificate from the officer who employs him, verified, for regimental officers, by the signature of the Colonel; for other officers under the rank of Colonel, by the chief of their corps or department.

783. Laundresses permitted to follow the army will be furnished with certificates, signed as in the preceding paragraph, and no woman of bad character will be allowed to follow the army. Other persons with the army, not officers or soldiers, such as guides of the country, interpreters, &c., will carry about them similar certificates from the head-quarters that employs them.

784. Deserters from the enemy, after being examined, will be secured for some days, as they may be spies in disguise; as opportunities offer, they will be sent to the rear; after which, if they are found lurking about the army, or attempting to return to the enemy, they will be treated with severity.

785. The arms and accoutrements of deserters will be turned over to the Ordnance Department, and their horses to the corps in want of them, after being branded with the letters "U. S." The compensation to be accorded to deserters, for such objects, will be according to appraisement, made under the direction of the Quartermaster's Department. The enlistment of deserters, without express permission from general headquarters, is prohibited.

786. It is forbidden to purchase horses without ascertaining the right of the party to sell. Stolen horses shall be restored. Estrays, in the enemy's country, when the owner is not discovered, are taken for the army.

787. Plundering and marauding, at all times disgraceful to soldiers, when committed on the persons or property of those whom it is the duty of the army to protect, become crimes of such enormity as to admit of no remission of the awful punishment which the military law awards against offenses of this nature.

SAFEGUARDS.

788. Safeguards are protections granted to persons or property in

foreign parts by the commanding general, or by other commanders within the limits of their command.

789. Safeguards are usually given to protect hospitals, public establishments, establishments of religion, charity, or instruction, museums, depositories of the arts, mills, post-offices, and other institutions of public benefit; also to individuals whom it may be the interest of the army to respect.

790. A safeguard may consist of one or more men of fidelity and firmness, generally non-effective non-commissioned officers, furnished with a paper setting out clearly the protection and exemptions it is intended to secure, signed by the commander giving it, and his staff officer; or it may consist of such paper, delivered to the party whose person, family, house, and property it is designed to protect. These safeguards must be numbered and registered.

791. The men left as safeguards by one corps may be replaced by another. They are withdrawn when the country is evacuated; but if not, they have orders to await the arrival of the enemy's troops, and apply to the commander for a safe-conduct to the outposts.

792. Form of a safeguard:

By authority of ——— ———,

A safeguard is hereby granted to [A. B———, or the house and family of A. B———, or to the college, mills, or property; stating precisely the place, nature, and description of the person, property, or buildings]. All officers and soldiers belonging to the army of the United States are therefore commanded to respect this safeguard, and to afford, if necessary, protection to [the person, family, or property of ———, as the case may be].

Given at Head-Quarters, the — day of ———.

A. B———, Major-General commanding-in-chief.

By command of the General.

C. D———, Adjutant-General.

55th Article of the Rules and Articles of War.

"Whosoever belonging to the armies of the United States, employed in foreign parts, shall force a safeguard, shall suffer death."

SIEGES.

793. In the following regulations the besieging force is supposed to be two divisions of infantry and a brigade of cavalry. The same principles govern in other cases.

794. The Brigadier-Generals of infantry serve, in turn, as Generals of the trenches; one or more of them are detailed daily, according to the

front and number of attacks; they superintend the operations, and dispose the guards of the trenches to repulse sorties and protect the works. Officers of the general staff are assigned to them to transmit their orders and attend to the details of service.

795. The Colonels and Lieutenant-Colonels of infantry alternate for duty in the trenches; one or more are detailed daily; they superintend the service of the guards and workmen in the part of the work to which the General of the trenches assigns them, being posted with troops of their own regiments in preference. The commandant of the siege may place the Colonels on the roster with the Brigadier-Generals.

796. The commandants of engineers and artillery accompany the first troops before the place to examine the works and the approaches. When the engineers have completed the reconnoissance of the works, and of each front as far as practicable, the commandant of engineers makes a plan of the works as exact and detailed as possible, and, under the instructions of the General commanding the siege, draws up the general plan of the siege, and discusses it with the commandant of artillery in regard to the best employment of that arm. These officers then submit their joint or separate opinions to the General, who decides on the plan of the siege, and gives the orders for the execution. The commandant of engineers directs the construction of all the works of siege, under the authority of the General, and lays before him every day a report of his operations, and a plan showing the progress of the attack. The commandant of artillery also makes daily reports to the General of all that relates to his branch of the service.

797. The Quartermaster-General establishes the hospitals, and organizes the means for transporting the wounded to them.

798. The commanding General appoints a field officer of the trenches, who is aided by one or two Captains or Lieutenants.

799. The field officer of the trenches is charged with all the details relative to the assembling of the guards and the workmen. He distributes the guards on the different points of the attack agreeably to the orders of the General of the trenches, and forms the detachments of workmen for the engineers and artillery; that he may be prepared for this distribution, he receives every day from the Adjutant-General a statement of the details for the next day.

800 On the arrival of the General of the trenches, the field officer of the trenches gives him all the information necessary to enable him to station the troops, attends him in his visit to the trenches, and takes his orders on the changes to be made in the position of the troops. The execution is intrusted to the commandants of the troops.

801. The field officer of the trenches sees that men and litters are

always ready to bring off the wounded. One or more companies of the guards of the trenches are put under his immediate orders for the preservation of order and police in the trenches.

802. The divisions, brigades, regiments, and battalions are encamped during the siege in the order of battle. The service of camp is conducted as heretofore prescribed.

803. The infantry has two kinds of siege service,—the guard of the trenches and the work of the trenches.

804. The guards of the trenches mount every day by battalions, in such order of detail that all the troops may take an equal share, and no part of the line be left too weak. If only one battalion is required, each division furnishes it alternately; if two are required, each division gives one; if three, one division furnishes two, the other one, alternately. The two battalions of the same division are not taken from the same brigade.

805. The detail for work of the trenches is by company, from all the regiments at one time, or in turn, and continues generally twelve hours. The detail from any regiment should never be less than a company. If only half a company would be needed from all the regiments at a time, every other regiment furnishes a full company alternately.

806. The battalions for guard are detailed at least twelve hours in advance; they furnish no other details during this tour. If the whole regiment is called out, it leaves a sufficient police guard in camp.

807. Twenty-four hours, or twelve at least, before mounting guard in the trenches, the battalions detailed for guard do not furnish workmen; and the companies of those battalions whose tour it would have been to work in the trenches, do not go there for twenty-four hours after guard, if possible, or at the least twelve.

808. The workmen who are required for other work than that of the trenches are taken from the roster for fatigue from the battalions and companies not employed in the trenches.

809. The battalions first for detail for guard of the trenches, and the companies first for detail for work in the trenches, furnish no other details, and are held on picket, ready to march at the call of the field officer of the trenches.

810. Materials for the siege, such as fascines, gabions, hurdles, pickets, &c., are furnished by the different corps, in the proportion ordered by the General.

811. Guards and workmen going to the trenches march without beat of drum or music.

812. At all times, and especially on the day the trenches are opened,

every thing is avoided likely to attract the attention of the enemy. With this view, the General may vary the hour of relieving guards.

813. The chiefs of engineers and artillery make requisitions for work-men in advance, that the details may be made in time to prevent any delay in the work. They should exceed the number strictly required, that there may be a reserve for unforeseen wants. If this reserve is found insufficient, the General directs the field officer of the trenches to call on the picket.

814. Before the guards and workmen march, the field officer of the trenches arranges them so that each detachment can reach its ground without confusion. The troops are posted in the trenches according to the position of their regiments in the order of battle, and, as far as pos-sible, the companies of workmen in like order. The reserves of workmen are placed at the depôt of the trenches, or the nearest suitable place to the works.

815. The workmen leave their knapsacks and swords in camp, and march with their firearms and cartridge-boxes, which they place near them while at work. They always carry their overcoats, to cover them in resting or when wounded.

816. The guards always enter the trenches with arms *trailed*, and the workmen also, unless they carry materials or tools, when the arms are in the sling.

817. The guards and detachments of workmen send a Corporal to the openings of the trenches to guide the relief. They march out of the trenches by the flank, with trailed arms.

818. Sand-bags, forming loop-holes, are placed at intervals on the parapet to cover the sentinels; they are more numerous than the senti-nels, so that the enemy may not know where the sentinels are placed.

819. When detachments are placed at night in advance of the trenches, to cover the workmen, the men sit or lie down, with their firearms in their hands, to hide themselves better from the enemy; the sentinels put their ears to the ground frequently, that they may hear troops coming out of the place. To prevent mistakes, the workmen are told what troops cover them.

820. No honors are paid in the trenches. When the General com-manding the siege visits them, the guards place themselves in rear of the banquette, and rest on their arms. The colors are never carried to the trenches unless the whole regiment marches to repulse a sortie or make an assault. Even in this case they are not displayed until the General commanding the siege gives a formal order.

821. The materials of the siege of all kinds, together with the tools, are collected in part at the depôts of the trenches, and in part at the

openings of the trenches, or in such other place as has been appointed for the convenience of the service by the field officer of the trenches, on the advice of the chiefs of artillery and engineers. They are in charge of officers of engineers and of artillery, with guards or non-commissioned officers of both corps. But if these corps cannot furnish them, the chiefs apply for assistance from the infantry.

822. The workmen, in going to the trenches, carry such tools and materials as are required by the artillery and engineers. In this case, the field officer of the trenches has notice and superintends it.

823. The soldiers sent to the trenches go with their cartridge-boxes filled. Cartridges, when needed, are sent to the trenches on the requisition of commanders of battalions, approved by the General of the trenches.

824. In the case of a sortie, the guards move rapidly to the places that have been designated by the General of the trenches, and which afford the best defense for the head of the works, the batteries, the communications, or the flanks, or best enable them to take the sortie itself in flank or reverse. Having lined the banquette to fire on the enemy, the troops form on the reverse of the trench to receive him. The workmen take arms, retain their positions, or retire with their tools, as ordered. The officers commanding the detachments of workmen see that their movements are made promptly and in good order, so as to avoid all confusion in the communications.

825. The troops that advance beyond the trenches to repulse the sortie must not follow in pursuit. The General takes care that they return to the trenches before the retreat of the sortie allows the artillery of the place to open on them. When the workmen return, the officers and non-commissioned officers of the detachments call the roll without interrupting the work, which is immediately resumed.

826. When it is necessary to dismount cavalry and send them to the trenches, they should be employed as near their camp as possible, and posted between the detachments of infantry.

827. Men belonging to the cavalry may, in assaults, be employed in carrying fascines and other materials to fill ditches and make passages.

828. The general officers of cavalry are more particularly employed in the service of posts and detachments placed in observation to protect the siege. They and the field officers of this arm are employed in the command of escorts to convoys, of whatever arms the escorts may be composed. When these duties are not sufficient to employ them, they take their share of the duty of the trenches.

829. The officers of engineers and artillery of the trenches make to the General of the trenches a return of all losses in their troops, and such

other reports on the work as he requires, in addition to the reports direct to their respective chiefs on the details of the service.

830. At the end of each tour, the field officer of the trenches draws up a report for the twenty-four hours to the General of the trenches. The General of the trenches reports to the General commanding the siege.

831. The commanders of the several corps in the trenches report, when relieved, to their respective head-quarters the losses during the tour, and the conduct of the officers and men.

832. However practicable the breach may appear, or however ruined the works in rear of it, the heads of columns must always be supplied with ladders to get over unexpected obstacles.

833. The General commanding the siege designates picked companies to protect property and persons, and prevent pillage and violence, from the moment the place is carried. The officers exert themselves to restrain the men.

834. The General designates the places requiring particular protection, such as churches, asylums, hospitals, colleges, schools, and magazines. The order for their protection should remind the soldiers, at the time, of the penalty of disobeying it.

835. Whether the place be taken by assault or by capitulation, the provisions and military stores, and the public funds, are reserved for the use of the army.

836. The commander of engineers will keep a journal of the siege, showing the operations of each day in detail, the force employed on the work, the kind and quantity of materials used in them, &c. He will also mark on a plan of the ground the daily progress of the works, and make the necessary drawings explanatory of their construction.

837. The commander of the artillery will keep a daily journal of the operations under his direction, showing—the number and kind of pieces in battery, the force employed in serving them, the kind and quantity of ammunition expended, the number of rounds fired from each piece of ordnance, the effect of the fire, and all other particulars relative to his branch of the service.

838. These journals and drawings will be sent, after the siege, with the report of the General, to the War Department.

DEFENSE OF FORTIFIED PLACES.

839. In war, every commander of a fortified place shall always hold himself prepared with his plan of defense, as if at any time liable to attack. He arranges this plan according to the probable mode of attack; determines the posts of the troops in the several parts of the works, the

reliefs, the reserves, and the details of service in all the corps. He draws up instructions for a case of attack, and exercises the garrison according to his plan of defense. In sea-coast works, he provides the instructions for the different batteries on the approach of ships.

840. In framing his plan, he studies the works and the exterior within the radius of attack and investment, the strength of the garrison, the artillery, the munitions of war, subsistence and supplies of all kinds, and takes immediate measures to procure whatever is deficient of troops or supplies, either by requisition on the government or from the means put at his disposal.

841. On the approach of an enemy, he removes all houses and other objects, within or without the place, that cover the approaches, or interrupt the fire of the guns or the movements of the troops. He assures himself personally that all posterns, outlets, embrasures, &c., are in proper state of security.

842. He shall be furnished by the Department of War with a plan of the works, showing all the details of the fortifications and of the exterior within the radius of attack; with a map of the environs within the radius of investment; with a map of the vicinity, including the neighboring works, roads, water-channels, coasts, &c.; with a memoir explaining the situation and defense of the place, and the relations and bearings of the several works on each other, and on the approaches by land and water—all which he carefully preserves, and communicates only to the council of defense.

843. He consults his next in rank, and the senior officer of the engineers and of the artillery, either separately or as a council of defense. In the latter case he designates an officer to act as secretary to the council, and to record their proceedings and their joint or separate opinions, which are to be kept secret during the siege. The members may record their opinions under their own signature. In all cases, the commander decides on his own responsibility.

844. The commander of the place, and the chiefs of engineers and of artillery, shall keep journals of the defense, in which shall be entered, in order of date, without blank or interlineation, the orders given or received, the manner in which they are executed, their results, and every event and circumstance of importance in the progress of the defense. These journals and the proceedings of the council of defense shall be sent after the siege to the Department of War.

845. There shall be kept in the office of the commandant of the place, to be sent after the siege to the Department of War, a map of the environs, a plan of the fortifications, and a special plan of the front of attack, on which the chief engineer will trace, in succession, the positions

occupied, and the works executed by the enemy from the investment; and also the works of counter approach or defense, and the successive positions of the artillery and other troops of the garrison during the progress of the siege.

846. The commander shall defend in succession the advanced works, the covered way and outworks, the body of the work, and the interior intrenchments. He will not be content with clearing away the foot of the breaches, and defending them by abattis, mines, and all the means used in sieges; but he shall begin in good time, behind the bastions or front of attack, the necessary intrenchments to resist assaults on the main work.

847. He shall use his means of defense in such manner as always to have a reserve of fresh troops, chosen from his best soldiers, to resist assaults, retake the outworks, and especially to resist the assaults on the body of the place; and a reserve of provisions for the last period of the siege, and of ammunition for the last attacks.

848. He must, in every case, compel the besieging force to approach by the slow and successive works of siege, and must sustain at least one assault on a practicable breach in the body of the place.

849. When the commander thinks that the end of the defense has come, he shall still consult the council of defense on the means that may remain to prolong the siege. But in all cases he alone will decide on the time, manner, and terms of the surrender. In the capitulation, he shall not seek or accept better terms for himself than for the garrison, but shall share their fate, and exert his best endeavors for the care of the troops, and especially of the sick and wounded.

850. No commander in the field shall withdraw troops or supplies from any fortified place, or exercise any authority over its commandant, unless it has been put subject to his orders by competent authority.

ARTICLE XXXVII.

TROOPS ON BOARD OF TRANSPORTS.

851. Military commanders charged with the embarkation of troops, and officers of the Quartermaster's Department intrusted with the selection of the transports, will take care that the vessels are entirely seaworthy and proper for such service, and that suitable arrangements are made in them for the health and comfort of the troops.

852. If, in the opinion of the officer commanding the troops to be embarked, the vessel is not proper or suitably arranged, the officer charged with the embarkation shall cause her to be inspected by competent and experienced persons.

Troops on board of Transports.

853. Immediately after embarking, the men will be assigned to quarters, equal parties on each side of the ship, and no man will be allowed to loiter or sleep on the opposite side. As far as practicable, the men of each company will be assigned to the same part of the vessel, and the squads, in the same manner, to contiguous berths.

854. Arms will be so placed, if there be no racks, as to be secure from injury, and enable the men to handle them promptly—bayonets unfixed and in scabbard.

855. Ammunition in cartridge-boxes to be so placed as to be entirely secure from fire; reserve ammunition to be reported to the master of the transport, with request that he designate a safe place of deposit. Frequent inspections will be made of the service ammunition, to insure its safety and good condition.

856. No officer is to sleep out of his ship, or to quit his ship, without the sanction of the officer commanding on board.

857. The guard will be proportioned to the number of sentinels required. At sea the guard will mount with side-arms only. The officer of the guard will be officer of the day.

858. Sentinels will be kept over the fires, with buckets of water at hand, promptly to extinguish fires. Smoking is prohibited *between decks or in the cabins*, at all times; nor shall any lights be allowed between decks, except such ship lanterns as the master of the transport may direct, or those carried by the officer of the day in the execution of his duty.

859. Regulations will be adopted to enable companies or messes to cook in turn; no others than those whose turn it is, will be allowed to loiter around or approach the galleys or other cooking places.

860. The commanding officer will make arrangements, in concert with the master of the vessel, for calling the troops to quarters, so that in case of alarm, by storm, or fire, or the approach of the enemy, every man may repair promptly to his station. But he will take care not to crowd the deck. The troops not wanted at the guns or to assist the sailors, and those who cannot be advantageously employed with small arms, will be formed as a reserve between decks.

861. All the troops will turn out at ———, A.M., without arms or uniform, and (in warm weather) without shoes or stockings; when every individual will be clean, his hands, face, and feet washed, and his hair combed. The same personal inspection will be repeated thirty minutes before sunset. The cooks alone may be exempted from *one* of these inspections per day, if necessary.

862. Recruits or awkward men will be exercised in the morning and evening in the use of arms, an hour each time, when the weather will permit.

863. Officers will enforce cleanliness as indispensable to health. When the weather will permit, bedding will be brought on deck every morning for airing. Tubs may be fixed on the forecastle for bathing, or the men may be placed in the *chains* and have buckets of water thrown over them.

864. *Between decks* will not be washed oftener than once a week, and only when the weather is fine. The boards of the lower berths will be removed once or twice a week to change the straw. Under the direction of the Surgeon and the officer of the day, frequent fumigations will be performed between decks. The materials required are—common salt, four ounces; powdered oxide of manganese, one ounce; sulphuric acid, one ounce, diluted with two ounces of water. The diluted acid is poured over the other ingredients in a basin placed in a hot sand-bath. Solutions of chloride of lime and chloride of zinc are excellent disinfecting agents.

865. During voyages in hot weather, the master of the vessel will be desired to provide wind-sails, which will be kept constantly hung up, and frequently examined, to see that they draw well and are not obstructed.

866. During cooking hours, the officers of companies visit the camboose, and see that the messes are well prepared. The coppers and other cooking utensils are to be regularly and well washed, both *before* and *after* use.

867. The bedding will be replaced in the berths at sunset, or at an earlier hour when there is a prospect of bad weather; and at *tattoo* every man not on duty will be in his berth. To insure the execution of this regulation, the officer of the day, with a lantern, will make a tour between decks.

868. Lights will be extinguished at *tattoo*, except such as are placed under sentinels. The officer of the day will see to it, and report to the commanding officer. The officers' lights will be extinguished at 10 o'clock, unless special permission be given to continue them for a longer time, as in case of sickness or other emergency.

869. For the sake of exercise, the troops will be occasionally called to quarters by the beat *to arms*. Those appointed to the guns will be frequently exercised in the use of them. The arms and accoutrements will be frequently inspected. The metallic parts of the former will be often wiped and greased again.

870. The men will not be allowed to sleep on deck in hot weather or in the sun; they will be encouraged and required to take exercise on deck, in squads by succession, when necessary.

871. At morning and evening parades, the Surgeon will examine the men, to observe whether there be any appearance of disease.

872. The sick will, as far as practicable, be separated from the healthy men. On the first appearance of mal'gnant contagion, a signal will be made for the hospital vessel (if there be one in company), and the diseased men removed to her.

873. A good supply of hospital stores and medicines will be taken on each vessel, and used only for the sick and convalescent.

874. The Surgeon will guard the men against costiveness on approaching a hot climate. In passing through the West Indies, to the southern coast for instance, and for some weeks after landing in those latitudes, great care is required in the use of fruit, as strangers would not be competent to judge of it, and most kinds, after long voyages, are prejudicial.

875. In harbor, where there is no danger from sharks, the men may bathe; but not more than ten at a time, and attended by a boat.

876. In fitting up a vessel for the transportation of horses, care is to be taken that the requisite arrangements are made for conveniently feeding and cleaning them, and to secure them from injury in rough weather by ropes attached to breast-straps and breeching, or by other suitable means; and especially that proper ventilation is provided by openings in the upper deck, wind-sails, &c. The ventilation of steamers may be assisted by using the engine for that purpose.

877. Horses should not be put on board after severe exercise or when heated. In hoisting them on board, the slings should be made fast to a hook at the end of the fall, or the knot tied by an expert seaman, so that it may be well secured and easily loosened. The horse should be run up quickly, to prevent him from plunging, and should be steadied by guide ropes. A halter is placed on him before he is lifted from the ground.

878. On board, care is to be taken that the horses are not over-fed; bran should form part of their ration. The face, eyes, and nostrils of each horse are to be washed at the usual stable hours, and, occasionally, the mangers should be washed and the nostrils of the horses sponged with vinegar and water.

879. In loading vessels with stores for a military expedition, the cargo of each should be composed of an assortment of such stores as may be available for service in case of the non-arrival of others, and they should be placed on board in such a manner that they may be easily reached, in the order in which they are required for service. Each store-ship should be marked, at the bow and stern, on both sides, in large characters, with a distinctive letter and number. A list is to be made of the stores on board of each vessel, and of the place where they are to be found in it; a copy of this list to be sent to the chief officer of the proper department in the expedition, or at the place of destination.

ARTICLE XXXVIII.

COURTS-MARTIAL.

880. In appointing a general court-martial, as many members will be detailed, from five to thirteen inclusively, as can be assembled without manifest injury to the service.

881. The decision of the officer appointing the court, as to the number that can be assembled without manifest injury to the service, is conclusive.

882. A President of the court will not be appointed. The officer highest in rank present will be President.

883. Form of Order appointing a general court-martial; the last paragraph omitted when the court can be kept up with thirteen members.

Head-Quarters, ———, &c.

A General Court-martial is hereby appointed to meet at ———, on the — day of ———, or as soon thereafter as practicable, for the trial of ——— and such other prisoners as may be brought before it.

Detail for the Court:

1. ———	8. ———
2. ———	9. ———
3. ———	10. ———
4. ———	11. ———
5. ———	12. ———
6. ———	13. ———
7. ———	——— ———, Judge Advocate.

No other officers than those named can be assembled without manifest injury to the service.

By order of ——— ———, commanding ———.

——— ———, Assistant Adjutant-General.

884. In the detail the members will be named, and they will take place in the court, in the order of their rank. A decision of the proper authority in regard to the rank of the members cannot be reversed by the court.

885. The place of holding a court is appointed by the authority convening it.

886. Application for delay or postponement of trial must, when practicable, be made to the authority convening the court. When made to the court, it must be before plea, and will then, if in the opinion of the court well founded, be referred to the authority convening the court, to

decide whether the court should be adjourned or dissolved, and the charges reserved for another court.

887. Upon application by the accused for postponement on the ground of the absence of a witness, it ought distinctly to appear on his oath, 1st. that the witness is material, and how; 2d. that the accused has used due diligence to procure his attendance; and, 3d. that he has reasonable ground to believe, and does believe, that he will be able to procure such attendance within a reasonable time stated.

888. The President of a court-martial, besides his duties and privileges as member, is the organ of the court, to keep order and conduct its business. He speaks and acts for the court in each case where the rule has been prescribed by law, regulation, or its own resolution. In all their deliberations the law secures the equality of the members.

889. The 76th Article of War does not confer on a court-martial the power to punish its own members. For disorderly conduct, a member is liable as in other offenses against military discipline; improper words are to be taken down, and any disorderly conduct of a member reported to the authority convening the court.

890. The Judge Advocate shall summon the necessary witnesses for the trial; but he shall not summon any witness at the expense of the United States, nor any officer of the army, without the order of the court, unless satisfied that his testimony is material and necessary to the ends of justice.

891. Every court-martial shall keep a complete and accurate record of its proceedings, to be authenticated by the signatures of the President and Judge Advocate; who shall also certify, in like manner, the sentence pronounced by the court in each case. The record must show that the court was organized as the law requires; that the court and Judge Advocate were duly sworn in the presence of the prisoner; that he was previously asked whether he had any objection to any member, and his answer thereto. A copy of the order appointing the court will be entered on the record in each case.

892. Whenever the same court-martial tries more prisoners than one, and they are arraigned on separate and distinct charges, the court is to be sworn at the commencement of each trial, and the proceedings in each case will be made up separately.

893. The record shall be clearly and legibly written; as far as practicable, without erasures or interlineations. The pages to be numbered, with a margin of one inch on the left side of each page, and at the top of the odd and bottom of the even pages; through this last margin the sheets to be stitched together; the documents accompanying the pro-

ceedings to be noted and marked in such manner as to afford an easy reference.

894. No recommendation will be embraced in the body of the sentence. Those members only who concur in the recommendation will sign it.

895. The legal punishments for soldiers by sentence of a court-martial according to the offense, and the jurisdiction of the court, are—death; confinement; confinement on bread and water diet; solitary confinement; hard labor; ball and chain; forfeiture of pay and allowances; discharges from service; and reprimands, and, when non-commissioned officers, reduction to the ranks. Ordnance Sergeants and Hospital Stewards, however, though liable to discharge, may not be reduced. Nor are they to be tried by regimental or garrison courts-martial, unless by special permission of the department commander. Solitary confinement, or confinement on bread and water, shall not exceed fourteen days at a time, with intervals between the periods of such confinement not less than such periods; and not exceeding eighty-four days in any one year.

896. The Judge Advocate shall transmit the proceedings, without delay, to the officer having authority to confirm the sentence, who shall state, at the end of the proceedings in each case, his decision and orders thereon.

897. The original proceedings of all general courts-martial, after the decision on them of the reviewing authority, and all proceedings that require the decision of the President under the 65th and 89th Articles of War, and copies of all orders confirming or disapproving, or remitting, the sentences of courts-martial, and all official communications for the Judge Advocate of the army, will be addressed to "*The Adjutant-General of the Army, War Department,*" marked on the cover, "*Judge Advocate.*"

898. The proceedings of garrison and regimental courts-martial will be transmitted without delay by the garrison or regimental commander to the department head-quarters for the supervision of the department commander.

899. The power to pardon or mitigate the punishment ordered by a court-martial is vested in the authority confirming the proceedings, and in the President of the United States. A superior military commander to the officer confirming the proceedings may suspend the execution of the sentence when, in his judgment, it is void upon the face of the proceedings, or when he sees a fit case for executive clemency. In such cases, the record, with his order prohibiting the execution, shall be transmitted for the final orders of the President.

900. When a court-martial or court of inquiry adjourns without day,

the members will return to their respective posts and duties unless otherwise ordered.

901. When a court adjourns for three days, the Judge Advocate shall report the fact to the commander of the post or troops, and the members belonging to the command will be liable to duty during the time.

ARTICLE XXXIX.

WORKING-PARTIES.

902. When it is necessary to employ the army at work on fortifications, in surveys, in cutting roads, and other constant labor of not less than ten days, the non-commissioned officers and soldiers so employed are enrolled as extra-duty men, and are allowed twenty-five cents a day when employed as laborers and teamsters, and forty cents a day when employed as mechanics, clerks, storekeepers, &c., at all stations east of the Rocky Mountains, and thirty-five and fifty cents per day, respectively, at all stations west of those mountains. But no man shall be rated and paid as a clerk or mechanic, who is not *skilled* in his particular employment; nor any man as a storekeeper, &c., whose trust is not of sufficient importance. Mere strikers, inferior workmen, &c. shall be rated as *laborers.* Commanding officers will particularly see to this; nor shall any soldier be rated at the higher pay, except by their order.

903. Enlisted men of the Ordnance and Engineer Departments, and artificers of artillery, are not entitled to this allowance when employed in their appropriate work.

904. Soldiers will not be employed as extra-duty men for any labor in camp or garrison which can properly be performed by fatigue parties.

905. No extra-duty men, except those required for the ordinary service of the Quartermaster, Commissary, and Medical Departments, and saddlers in mounted companies, will be employed without previous authority from department head-quarters, except in case of necessity, which shall be promptly reported to the department commander.

906. Extra-duty men should attend the weekly and monthly inspections of their companies, and, if possible, one drill in every week.

907. Extra-duty pay of the saddler in a mounted company will be charged on the company muster-roll, to be paid by the Paymaster and refunded by the Ordnance Department. Extra-duty pay of cooks and nurses in the hospital service will be paid by the quartermaster, in the absence of a medical disbursing officer, and refunded by the Medical Department.

908. The officer commanding a working-party will conform to the

directions and plans of the engineer or other officer directing the work, without regard to rank.

909. A day's work shall not exceed ten hours in summer, nor eight in winter. Soldiers are paid in proportion for any greater number of hours they are employed each day. Summer is considered to commence on the 1st of April, and winter on the 1st of October.

910. Although the necessities of the service may require soldiers to be ordered on working-parties as a duty, commanding officers are to bear in mind that fitness for military service by instruction and discipline is the object for which the army is kept on foot, and that they are not to employ the troops when not in the field, and especially the mounted troops, in labors that interfere with their military duties and exercises, except in case of immediate necessity, which shall be forthwith reported for the orders of the War Department.

ARTICLE XL.

RECRUITING SERVICE.

911. The recruiting service will be conducted by the Adjutant-General, under the direction of the Secretary of War.

912. Field officers will be detailed to superintend the recruiting districts, and lieutenants to take charge of the recruiting parties. The Adjutant-General will select the field officers, and announce in orders the number of Captains and Lieutenants to be selected for this duty from each regiment by the Colonel.

913. A recruiting party will consist generally of one lieutenant, one non-commissioned officer, two privates, and a drummer and fifer. The parties will be sent from the principal depôts, and none but suitable men selected.

914. Officers on the general recruiting service are not to be ordered on any other duty, except from the Adjutant-General's office.

DUTIES OF SUPERINTENDENTS.

915. As soon as a recruiting station is designated, the superintendent sends estimates for funds to the Adjutant-General, and requisitions on the proper departments (through the Adjutant-General) for clothing, camp equipage, arms, and accoutrements.

916. Subsequent supplies for the station in his district are procured by the superintendent on consolidated estimates; these are made quarterly for funds, and every six or twelve months for clothing, equipage, arms, and accoutrements   Estimates for funds will be in the following form :

Recruiting Service.——Superintendents.

Estimate of Recruiting Funds required for the
during the quarter ending   , 18   .

Names.	Rank.	Regiment.	Station.	Amount expended last quarter.		Amount on hand.		Amount required.		Remarks.
				$	Cts.	$	Cts.	$	Cts.	
Total amount required...										

———— ————, *Superintendent.*

917. Funds and supplies of clothing, camp and garrison equipage, arms and accoutrements, when ordered, will be sent direct to each station.

918. For subsistence to recruiting stations, see regulations of the Subsistence Department. When army rations are issued for recruits, savings on the rations shall be applied for their benefit, as in companies.

919. The superintendents will transmit to the Adjutant-General consolidated monthly returns of the recruiting parties under their superintendence, according to directions on the printed blanks, accompanied by one copy of the enlistment of each recruit enlisted within the month.

920. When recruits should be sent to regiments, a superintendent will report to the Adjutant-General for instructions in reference thereto.

921. When recruits are sent from a depôt or rendezvous to a regiment or post, *a muster and descriptive roll*, and an *account of clothing* of the detachment, will be given to the officer assigned to the command of it. And a duplicate of the muster and descriptive roll will be forwarded to the Adjutant-General by the superintendent, who will note on it the names of all the officers on duty with the detachment, and the day of its departure from the depôt or rendezvous.

922. The superintendent will report all commissioned or non-commissioned officers who may be incapable or negligent in the discharge of their functions. Where a recruiting party fails to get recruits from any cause other than the *fault* of the officer, the superintendent will recommend another station for the party.

923. When a rendezvous is closed, the superintendent will give the necessary instructions for the safe-keeping or disposal of the public property, so as not to involve any expense for storage.

924. Tours of inspection by superintendents will be made only on instructions from the Adjutant-General's Off `e. Officers on the recruit-

ing service will not be sent from place to place without orders from the same source.

DUTIES OF RECRUITING OFFICERS.

925. Success in obtaining recruits depends much on the activity and *personal attention* of recruiting officers, and they will not entrust to enlisted men the duties for which themselves only are responsible. They will in no case absent themnselves from their stations without authority from the superintendent.

926. They will not allow any man to be deceived or inveigled into the service by false representations, but will in person explain the nature of the service, the length of the term, the pay, clothing, rations, and other allowances to which a soldier is entitled by law, to every man before he signs the enlistment.

927. If minors present themselves, they are to be treated with great candor; the names and residences of their parents or guardians, if they have any, must be ascertained, and these will be informed of the minor's wish to enlist, that they may make their objections or give their consent.

928. With the sanction of superintendents, recruiting officers may insert, in not exceeding two newspapers, brief notices directing attention to the rendezvous for further information.

929. Any free white male person above the age of eighteen and under thirty-five years, being at least five feet three inches high, effective, ablebodied, sober, free from disease, of good character and habits, and with a competent knowledge of the English language, may be enlisted. This regulation, so far as respects the *height* and *age* of the recruit, shall not extend to musicians or to soldiers who may *"re-enlist,"* or have served honestly and faithfully a previous enlistment in the army.

930. No man having a wife or child shall be enlisted *in time of peace* without special authority obtained from the Adjutant-General's Office, through the superintendent. This rule is not to apply to soldiers who *"re-enlist."*

931. No person under the age of twenty-one years is to be enlisted or re-enlisted without the written consent of his parent, guardian, or master. The recruiting officers must be very particular in ascertaining the true age of the recruit.

932. After the nature of the service and terms of enlistment have been fairly explained to the recruit, the officer, before the enlistments are filled up, will read to him, and offer for his signature, the annexed declaration, to be appended to each copy of his enlistment:

I, ——, desiring to enlist in the Army of the United States for the period of five years, do declare that I am —— years and —— months of age; that I have neither wife nor child; that I have never

Duties of Recruiting Officers.

been discharged from the United States service on account of disability, or by sentence of a court-martial, or by order before the expiration of a term of enlistment; and I know of no impediment to my serving honestly and faithfully as a soldier for five years. —— ——

Witness:

—— ——

933. If the recruit be a minor, his parent, guardian, or master must sign a consent to his enlisting, which will be added to the preceding declaration, in the following form:

I, ——, do certify that I am the (*father, only surviving parent, legal master, or guardian, as the case may be*) of ——; that the said —— is —— years of age; and I do hereby freely give my consent to his enlisting as a soldier in the Army of the United States for the period of five years. —— ——

Witness:

—— ——

934. The forms of declaration, and of consent in case of a minor, having been signed and witnessed, the recruit will then be duly examined by the recruiting officer, and surgeon if one be present, and, if accepted, the 20th and 87th Articles of War will be read to him; after which he will be allowed time to consider the subject until his mind appears to be fully made up before the oath is administered to him.

935. As soon as practicable, and at least within six days after his enlistment, the following oath will be administered to the recruit:

"I, A— B—, do solemnly swear or affirm (as the case may be) that I will bear true allegiance to the United States of America, and that I will serve them honestly and faithfully against all their enemies or opposers whatsoever, and observe and obey the orders of the President of the United States, and the orders of the officers appointed over me, according to the rules and articles for the government of the armies of the United States." (See 10th Art. of War.)

936. Under the 11th section of the act of 3d August, 1861, chap. 42, the oath of enlistment and re-enlistment may be administered by any commissioned officer of the army.

937. It is the duty of the recruiting officer to be present at the examination of the recruit by the medical officer. (See par. 1261.)

938. Recruiting officers will not employ private physicians without authority from the Adjutant-General's Office, for the special purpose of examining the recruits prior to their enlisting.

939. If it be necessary, as in case of sickness, to employ a physician, the recruiting officer may engage his services by contract on reasonable terms, "by the visit," or by the month. If by the month, the examina-

tion of the recruits must be stated in the contract as part of his duty. In vouchers for medical attendance and medicines, the name of each patient, date of, and charge for, each visit, and for medicine furnished, must be given, and the certificate of the physician added, that the rates charged are the usual rates of the place. The physician will be paid from the recruiting funds.

940. Enlistments must, in all cases, be taken in triplicate. The recruiting officer will send one copy to the Adjutant-General with his quarterly accounts, a second to the superintendent with his monthly return, and a third to the depôt at the time the recruits are sent there. In cases of soldiers re-enlisted in a regiment, or of regimental recruits, the third copy of the enlistment will be sent at its date to regimental head-quarters for file.

941. When ordnance sergeants re-enlist, the recruiting officer will immediately send the second copy of the enlistment direct to the Adjutant-General, and the third copy to the station of the ordnance sergeant for file.

942. Enlistments must, in no case, be ante-dated so as to entitle a soldier who applies after the period for "re-enlisting" has expired, to any additional pay therefor.

943. The recruiting officer will see that the men under his command are neat in their personal appearance, and will require the permanent party to wear their military dress in a becoming manner, especially when permitted to go abroad.

944. Only such articles of clothing as are indispensable for immediate use will be issued to recruits at the rendezvous. Their equipment will not be made complete till after they have passed the inspection subsequent to their arrival at the depôt.

945. The instruction of the recruits will commence at the rendezvous from the moment of enlistment. The general superintendent will see that all recruiting officers give particular attention to this subject.

946. Recruits will be sent from rendezvous to depôts every ten days, or oftener if practicable, provided the number disposable exceeds three The detachments of recruits will be sent from rendezvous to depôts under charge of a non-commissioned officer.

947. Before recruits are sent from recruiting depôts to regiments or companies, the amounts due by them to the laundress and sutler, having been verified and audited, will be entered on a roll made for the purpose, and will be paid by the paymaster on his next visit at the post, the receipts of the laundress and sutler to the amounts paid being the voucher: Provided the recruits have a clear amount of pay due them, over and above their dues to the government, equal to the claims of the laundress

and sutler. The same amounts will be entered on the muster and descriptive roll of the recruits as "amount paid laundress, or sutler," (*naming them*,) to be deducted from the pay of the soldiers at their first subsequent payment.

948. Every officer commanding a recruiting party will procure the necessary transportation, forage, fuel, straw, and stationery, taking the requisite vouchers.

949. The transportation of recruits to depôts, and from one recruiting station to another, will be paid from the recruiting funds; transportation of officers and enlisted men on the recruiting service will be paid in the same manner, except when first proceeding to join that service, or returning to their regiments after having been relieved.

950. No expenses of transportation of officers will be admitted that do not arise from orders emanating from the Adjutant-General's office, except they be required to visit branch or auxiliary rendezvous under their charge, when they will be allowed the stage, steamboat, or railroad fare, porterage included.

951. Whenever an officer is relieved or withdrawn from the recruiting service, he will pay over the balance of any unexpended recruiting funds in his possession to the officer appointed to succeed him, or to the paymaster, if no officer be so designated; and if there be no paymaster or other proper officer convenient to receive such balance, the amount will be deposited to the credit of the Treasurer of the United States, with the most convenient Assistant Treasurer, or other depositary of public moneys. In either case the officer will forward to the Adjutant-General the evidence of the disposition he may make of the funds, and report the fact to the superintendent, or to his Colonel, if on regimental recruiting service.

RENDEZVOUS, QUARTERING AND SUBSISTING RECRUITS.

952. Written contracts will be made by recruiting officers for the rent of a rendezvous upon the most reasonable terms possible. The rent will be paid from the recruiting funds. The terms of the contract will be immediately reported to the Adjutant-General.

953. For the manner of subsisting recruits, see regulations of the Subsistence Department.

BLANKS.

954. Officers on recruiting service will make timely requisitions for printed blanks, direct, as follows:

To the Adjutant-General.—For enlistments; re-enlistments; forms for medical inspection of recruits; muster-rolls; muster and descriptive rolls;

monthly returns; tri-monthly reports; recruiting accounts current; accounts of clothing issued; posters or handbills.

To the Quartermaster-General.—For estimates of clothing, camp and garrison equipage; clothing receipt rolls; quarterly returns of clothing, camp and garrison equipage.

955. Of the blanks above named, none but the printed forms furnished will be used. Other blanks, when required, must be ruled.

956. Blanks for the regimental recruiting service are furnished to the company commanders.

FURNITURE AND STATIONERY.

957. The articles of furniture and police utensils which may be absolutely necessary at a recruiting station may be procured by the officer in charge of the rendezvous, on the special authority of the superintendent.

958. Necessary stationery will be purchased monthly or quarterly, not to exceed, per quarter at each station, six quires of paper, twenty-four quills, or twenty-four steel pens and two holders, half an ounce of wafers, one paper of ink-powder, one bottle of red ink, four ounces of sealing-wax, one quire of cartridge paper, or one hundred envelopes, one-fourth quire of blotting-paper, and one piece of tape. If necessary, an additional supply of one-fourth of these rates will be allowed to the recruiting officer having charge of one or more auxiliary rendezvous distant from his permanent station. At the principal depôts the allowance must be fixed by the wants of the public service.

959. To each office table is allowed one inkstand, one wafer stamp, one wafer box, one paper-folder, one ruler, and as many lead-pencils as may be required, not exceeding four per annum.

960. Such blank books as may be necessary are allowed to the general superintendent and at permanent recruiting depôts; also, one descriptive book for the register of recruits at each permanent station. Blank books will be purchased by recruiting officers, under instructions from the superintendent.

961. When a recruiting officer is relieved, the blanks, books, and unexpended stationery, with all the other public property at the station, will be transferred to his successor, who will receipt for the same.

ACCOUNTS, RETURNS, ETC.

962. The following are the accounts, returns, &c. to be rendered by officers on recruiting service:

To the Adjutant-General.

1. *Recruiting accounts current*, quarterly, with abstract, (Form C,) vouchers, (Form D,) and one set of enlistments. An account will

be rendered by every officer who may receive funds, whether he makes expenditures or not during the quarter.

2. *A quarterly return* of stationery, books, fuel, straw, and such other property as may have been purchased with the recruiting funds.

3. *A monthly summary statement* of money received, expended, and remaining on hand, (Form E,) to be transmitted on the last day of each month.

4. *A muster-roll* of all enlisted men at the rendezvous, including the names of all who may have joined, died, deserted, been transferred or discharged, during the period embraced in the muster-roll.

5. *Tri-monthly reports* of the state of the recruiting service, according to the prescribed form.

To the Superintendent.

6. *A monthly return* of recruits and of the recruiting party, accompanied with one copy of the enlistment of every recruit enlisted within the month.

7. Duplicate *muster-rolls for pay* of the permanent recruiting party, which may be sent direct to the nearest paymaster, when authorized by the superintendent. A triplicate of this roll will be retained at the station.

8. *Muster and descriptive rolls* and an *account of clothing* of every detachment of recruits ordered to the principal depôt. If the recruits be ordered to proceed from the rendezvous *direct*, to join any regiment or post, these rolls and accounts of clothing will be delivered to the officer in command of the detachment, a duplicate of each muster and descriptive roll only being then made and sent to the superintendent.

9. Copy of the quarterly abstract of contingent expenses; to be forwarded within three days after the expiration of each quarter.

10. *Quarterly estimates* for funds.

11. *Estimates* for clothing, and camp and garrison equipage, and for arms and accoutrements, for six or twelve months, or for such times as may be directed by the superintendent.

12. Copy of the return No. 13.

To the Quartermaster-General.

13. *A quarterly return* of clothing and camp and garrison equipage, and of all quartermaster's property in his possession, not including such as is purchased with the recruiting funds.

To the Ordnance Department.

14. *A quarterly return* of arms, accoutrements, ammunition, and of all ordnance stores.

RULES FOR MAKING ACCOUNTS AND PAPERS.

963. The following rules must be observed in making out and forwarding accounts and papers:

1. Letters addressed to the Adjutant-General "*on recruiting service,*" will be so endorsed on the envelopes, under the words "official business."

2. Each voucher must be separately entered on the abstract of contingent expenses, (Form C,) and only the gross amount of the abstract must be entered on the account current.

3. No expenditure must be charged without a proper voucher to support it. (See Form D.)

4. The receipt to the voucher must be signed, when practicable, by a principal. When this is not practicable, the recruiting officer will add to his own certificate a statement that the agent is duly authorized to sign the receipt.

5. When an individual makes "his mark" instead of signing his name to the receipt, it must be witnessed by a third person.

6. Expenditures must be confined to items stated in the Regulations. In an unforeseen emergency, requiring a deviation from this rule, a full explanation must be appended to the voucher for the expenditure; and, if this be not satisfactory, the account will be charged in the Treasury against the recruiting officer.

7. In all vouchers, the different items, with dates, and cost of each, must be given. To vouchers for transportation of officers, a copy of the order under which the journey was performed, must be appended.

8. In vouchers for medical attendance and medicines, the name of each patient, date of, and charge for, each visit, and for medicine furnished, must be given, and the certificate of the physician added, that the rates charged are the usual rates of the place.

9. To each voucher for notices inserted in newspapers a copy of the notice will be appended.

10. Quarterly accounts current must exhibit the numbers of Treasury drafts and dates of their receipt; and when funds are transferred, the names of officers from whom they are received, or to whom they are turned over, with the dates of transfer.

11. Fractions of cents are not to be taken up on accounts current.

12. Enlistments must be filled up in a fair and legible hand The

real name of the recruit must be ascertained, correctly spelled, and written in the same way wherever it occurs; the *Christian* name must not be abbreviated. Numbers must be written, and not expressed by figures. Each enlistment must be endorsed as follows:—

No. —.

A——— B———

enlisted at

_____

January —, 186-,

By Lt. C——— D———,

— Regiment of — -.

The number *in each month* to correspond with the names alphabetically arranged.

13. Whenever a soldier re-enters the service, the officer who enlisted him will endorse on the enlistment, next below his own name and regiment, "second (or third) enlistment," as the case may be, together with the name of the regiment and the letter of the company in which the soldier last served, and date of discharge from former enlistment. This information the recruiting officer must obtain, if possible, from the soldier's discharge, which he should in all cases be required to exhibit. (See 22d Art. of War.)

14. Re-enlistments must be forwarded with recruiting accounts, although the bounty due on them may not be paid. When the bounty is subsequently paid, the soldier's receipt is to be taken on a voucher showing date and place of re-enlistment, company and regiment, and by whom re-enlisted.

15. The filling up of, and endorsement on, the enlistment, will be in the handwriting of the recruiting officer, or done under his immediate inspection.

16. To facilitate the final settlement of accounts of discharged soldiers, the name of the *State*, as well as the town, where each recruit is enlisted, will be recorded on all muster, pay, and descriptive rolls.

DEPÔTS FOR COLLECTING AND INSTRUCTING RECRUITS.

964. The depôts for recruits are established by orders from the Adjutant-General's Office.

965. To each *depôt* there will be assigned a suitable number of officers to command and instruct the recruits; and, when necessary, such number of enlisted men as may be designated at the Adjutant-General's Office, will be selected for the permanent party, to do garrison duty and for drill-masters.

966. The number of recruits at depôts to be assigned to each arm and regiment is directed from the Adjutant-General's Office.

967. The recruits are to be *dressed in uniform* according to their respe:tive arms, and will be regularly mustered and inspected. They are to be well drilled in the Infantry Tactics, through the school of the soldier to that of the battalion, and in the exercise of field and garrison pieces. Duty is to be done according to the strict rules of service.

968. The general superintendent will cause such of the recruits as are found to possess a natural talent for music, to be instructed (besides the drill of the soldier) on the fife, bugle, and drum, and other military instruments; and boys of twelve years of age, and upward, may, under his direction, be enlisted for this purpose. But as recruits under eighteen years of age and under size must be discharged, if they are not capable of learning music, care should be taken to enlist those only who have a natural talent for music, and, if practicable, they should be taken on trial for some time before being enlisted.

969. Regiments will be furnished with field music on the requisitions of their commanders, made, from time to time, direct on the general superintendent; and, when requested by regimental commanders, the superintendents will endeavor to have suitable men selected from the recruits, or enlisted, for the regimental bands.

970. At every depôt pains will be taken to form from the permanent party a body of competent cooks; some of whom will be sent with every large draft of recruits ordered to regiments.

971. To give encouragement to the recruits, and hold out inducements to good conduct, the commanding officer of the depôt may promote such of them as exhibit the requisite qualifications to be *lance corporals* and *lance sergeants*, not exceeding the proper proportion to the number of recruits at the depôt. These appointments will be announced in orders in the usual way, and will be continued in force until they join their regiments, unless sooner revoked. No allowance of pay or emoluments is to be assigned to these appointments : they are only to be considered as recommendations to the captains of companies and colonels of regiments for the places in which the recruits may have acted; but such non-commissioned officers are to be treated with all the respect and to have all the authority which may belong to the stations of sergeant and corporal.

972. *Permanent* parties at depôts, and *recruiting parties* and recruits, will be mustered, inspected, and paid in the same manner as other soldiers. Recruits will be mustered for pay only at depôts, and, when paid there, one-half of their monthly pay will be retained until they join their regiments.

973. When recruits are received at a garrisoned post, the commanding officer will place them under the charge of a commissioned officer.

974. Recruits are not to be put to any labor or work which would interfere with their instruction, nor are they to be employed otherwise than as soldiers, in the regular duties of garrison and camp.

975. The Rules and Articles of War are to be read to the recruits every month, after the inspection; and so much thereof as relates to the duties of non-commissioned officers and soldiers will be read to them every week.

INSPECTION OF RECRUITS AT DEPÔTS AND POSTS.

976. The superintendent or commanding officer will cause a minute and critical inspection to be made of every recruit received at a depôt, two days after his arrival; and should any recruit be found unfit for service, or to have been enlisted contrary to law or regulations, he shall assemble a *Board of Inspectors*, to examine into the case. A board may also be assembled in a special case, when a concealed defect may become manifest in a recruit, at any time during his detention at the depôt.

977. Every draft of recruits ordered from a depôt to any regiment or post, shall, immediately preceding its departure, be critically inspected by the superintendent or commanding officer, and surgeon; and, when necessary, a Board of Inspectors will be convened.

978. Recruits received at a military post or station shall be carefully inspected by the commanding officer and surgeon, on the third day after their arrival; and if, on such inspection, any recruit, in their opinion, be unsound or otherwise defective, in such degree as to disqualify him for the duties of a soldier, then a Board of Inspectors will be assembled to examine into and report on the case. (See paragraphs 979, 980, 981.)

979. *Boards* for the inspection of recruits will be composed of the commanding officer, the senior medical officer of the army present, and, if possible, the three senior regimental officers present on duty with the troops.

REJECTED RECRUITS.

980. In all cases of *rejection*, the reasons therefor will be stated at large in a special *report*, to be made by the board; which, together with the surgeon's certificate of disability for service, will be forwarded by the superintendent or commandant of the post direct to the Adjutant-General. In all such cases the commanding officer will cause the articles of clothing, which may have been issued to the recruit, with the price of each article, to be endorsed on the certificates of disability. If the recommendation of the board for the discharge of the recruit be approved, the authority therefor will be endorsed on the certificate, which will be sent back to be filled up and signed by the commanding officer, who will return the same to the Adjutant-General's Office.

981. The board will state in the report whether the disability, or other cause of rejection, existed before his enlistment; and whether with *proper care and examination* it might not have been discovered.

RECRUITS SENT TO REGIMENTS.

982. An officer intrusted with the command of recruits ordered to regiments, will, on arriving at the place of destination, forward the following papers:

1. To the *Adjutant-General* and the *Superintendent,* each, a descriptive roll and an account of clothing of such men as may have deserted, died, or been left on the route from any cause whatever, with date and place; also, a special report of the date of his arrival at the post, the strength and condition of the party when turned over to the commanding officer, and all circumstances worthy of remark which may have occurred on the march.

2. To the *Commanding Officer* of the regiment, or post, the muster and descriptive roll furnished him at the time of setting out, properly signed and completed by recording the names of the recruits *present,* and by noting in the column for remarks, opposite the appropriate spaces, the time and place of death, desertion, apprehension, or other casualty that may have occurred on the route.

983. Should an officer be relieved in charge of a party of recruits *en route,* before it reaches its destination, the date and place, and name of the officer by whom he is relieved, must be recorded on the roll of the party. Without the evidence of such record, no charge for extra pay on account of clothing accountability of the party, where equal to a company, will be allowed.

984. The "original muster and descriptive roll" of every draft, with remarks showing the final disposition of each recruit, and the regiment and letter of the company to which he may be assigned, will be signed and forwarded to the Adjutant-General by the commanding officer who makes the assignment. If the recruits embraced in one roll happen to be assigned to different posts, the original roll is to continue with the last party to its destination, each commander completing it so far as concerns the recruits left at his post. When this is not practicable, extracts from the original roll are to be made by the authority which distributes the recruits, to accompany the several parties, and to be forwarded to the Adjutant-General as in case of the original roll.

REGIMENTAL RECRUITING SERVICE.

985. The regimental recruiting will be conducted in the manner prescribed for the general service.

Regimental Recruiting Service.

986. Every commander of a regiment is the superintendent of the recruiting service for his regiment, and will endeavor to keep it up to its establishment; for which purpose he will obtain the necessary funds, clothing, &c., by requisition on the Adjutant-General.

987. At every station occupied by his regiment, or any part of it, the colonel will designate a suitable officer to attend to the recruiting duties; which selection will not relieve such officer from his company or other ordinary duties. The officer thus designated will be kept constantly furnished with funds, and, when necessary, with clothing and camp equipage.

988. The regimental recruiting officer will, with the approbation of the commanding officer of the station, enlist all suitable men. He will be governed, in rendering his accounts and returns, by the rules prescribed for the general service; and, when leaving a post, will turn over the funds in his hands to the senior company officer of his regiment present, unless some other be appointed to receive them.

FORM A.

Dr. THE UNITED STATES,

To ————, Special Contractor.

For rations issued to recruits under the command of ————, at ————, from ———— to ————, as per accompanying abstract:

———— complete rations, at ——— cents - $ ⋅ ⋅ ⋅ ⋅ ⋅ ⋅ ⋅ ⋅

———— lbs. extra soap, at ——— cents - ⋅ ⋅ ⋅ ⋅ ⋅ ⋅ ⋅ ⋅ ⋅

———— lbs. extra candles, at ——— cents ⋅ ⋅ ⋅ ⋅ ⋅ ⋅ ⋅ ⋅

Due contractor $ ⋅ ⋅ ⋅ ⋅ ⋅ ⋅

Received from the United States ———— dollars and ——— cents, in full of the above account.

————, Special Contractor.

Recruiting Service.——Forms.

FORM B.

Abstract of rations issued to recruits stationed at ———, under command of ———, from ——— to ———, by ———, Special Contractor.

Date.	No. of return.	No. of men.	No. of women.	Commencing.	Ending.	No. of days drawn for.	No. of complete rations.	REMARKS.

Total number of complete rations..............

I certify that I have carefully compared the above abstract with the original returns now in my possession, and they amount to ——— complete rations.

FORM C.

Abstract of disbursements on account of contingencies of the recruiting service, by —— ——, in the quarter ending ——, 18—, at ——.

No. of voucher.	Date of payment.	To whom paid.	On what account.	Amount.	
				Dolls.	Cts
			$		

Recruiting Officer.

FORM D.

THE UNITED STATES,

To   DR.

Date.		Dolls.	Cts.
	For		

I certify that the above account is correct.

Recruiting Officer.

Received ——— this —— day of ———, 18—, of ——— ———, recruiting officer, ——— dollars and ——— cents, in full of the above account.

$ ———   (DUPLICATE.)

Recruiting Service.——Forms.

FORM E.

MONTHLY SUMMARY STATEMENT.

THE UNITED STATES *in account with* ———, *at* ———, *in the month of* ———, 18—.

DR.

To amount of expenditures within the month............	
To amount of advance made to............	
Balance due the United States, carried to next statement............	$

CR.

By balance per last statement...............	
By cash received from ———	
By cash received from Treasurer of the United States, being amount of warrant No. ———............	
	$

I certify that the above is a true statement of all the moneys which have come into my hands, on account of the recruiting service, during the month of ———, 18—, and that the disbursements have been faithfully made. The balance due the United States is deposited in ———.

———————, *Recruiting Officer.*

NOTE.—No vouchers accompany this statement.

ARTICLE XLI

PUBLIC PROPERTY, MONEY, AND ACCOUNTS.

989. All officers of the Pay, Commissary, and Quartermaster's Departments, and military store-keepers, shall, previous to their entering on the duties of their respective offices, give good and sufficient bonds to the United States fully to account for all moneys and public property which they may receive, in such sums as the Secretary of War shall direct; and the officers aforesaid shall renew their bonds every four years, and oftener if the Secretary of War shall so require, and whenever they receive a new commission or appointment.

990. The sureties to the bond shall be bound jointly and severally for the whole amount of the bond, and shall satisfy the Secretary of War that they are worth jointly double the amount of the bond, by the affidavit of each surety, stating that he is worth, over and above his debts and liabilities, the amount of the bond or such other sum as he may specify; and each surety shall state his place of residence.

991. The chiefs of disbursing departments who submit requisitions for money to be remitted to disbursing officers, shall take care that no more money than actually needed is in the hands of any officer.

992. The Treasury Department having provided, by arrangement with the assistant treasurers at various points, secure depositories for funds in the hands of disbursing officers, all disbursing officers are required to avail themselves, as far as possible, of this arrangement, by depositing with the assistant treasurers such funds as are not wanted for immediate use, and drawing the same in convenient sums as wanted.

993. No public funds shall be exchanged except for gold and silver. When the funds furnished are gold and silver, all payments shall be in gold and silver. When the funds furnished are drafts, they shall be presented at the place of payment, and paid according to law; and payments shall be made in the funds so received for the drafts, unless said funds or said drafts can be exchanged for gold and silver at par. If any disbursing officer shall violate any of these provisions, he shall be suspended by the Secretary of War, and reported to the President, and promptly removed from office or restored to his trust and duties as to the President may seem just and proper. (Act August 6, 1846.)

994. No disbursing officer shall accept, or receive, or transmit to the Treasury to be allowed in his favor, any receipt or voucher from a creditor of the United States without having paid to such creditor, in such funds as he received for disbursement, or such other funds as he is

authorized by the preceding article to take in exchange, the full amount specified in such receipt or voucher; and every such act shall be deemed to be a conversion to his own use of the amount specified in such receipt or voucher. And no officer in the military service charged with the safe-keeping, transfer, or disbursement of public money, shall convert to his own use, or invest in any kind of merchandise or property, or loan with or without interest, or deposit in any bank, or exchange for other funds, except as allowed in the preceding article, any public money intrusted to him; and every such act shall be deemed to be a felony and an embezzlement of so much money as may be so taken, converted, invested, used, loaned, deposited, or exchanged. (Act August 6, 1846.)

995. Any officer who shall directly or indirectly sell or dispose of, for a premium, any Treasury note, draft, warrant, or other public security in his hands for disbursement, or sell or dispose of the proceeds or avails thereof without making returns of such premium and accounting therefor by charging it in his accounts to the credit of the United States, will forthwith be dismissed by the President. (Act August 6, 1846.)

996. If any disbursing officer shall bet at cards or any game of hazard, his commanding officer shall suspend his functions, and require him to turn over all the public funds in his keeping, and shall immediately report the case to the proper bureau of the War Department.

997. All officers are forbid to give or take any receipt in blank for public money or property; but in all cases the voucher shall be made out in full, and the true date, place, and exact amount of money, in words, shall be written out in the receipt before it is signed.

998. When a signature is not written by the hand of the party, it must be witnessed.

999. No advance of public money shall be made, except advances to disbursing officers, and advances by order of the War Department to officers on distant stations, where they cannot receive their pay and emoluments regularly; but in all cases of contracts for the performance of any service, or the delivery of articles of any description, payment shall not exceed the value of the service rendered, or of the articles delivered, previously to such payment.

1000. No officer disbursing or directing the disbursement of money for the military service shall be concerned, directly or indirectly, in the purchase or sale, for commercial purposes, of any article intended for, making a part of, or appertaining to the department of the public service in which he is engaged, nor shall take, receive, or apply to his own use any gain or emolument, under the guise of presents or otherwise, for negotiating or transacting any public business, other than what is or may be allowed by law.

1001. No wagon-master or forage-master shall be interested or concerned, directly or indirectly, in any wagon or other means of transport employed by the United States, nor in the purchase or sale of any property procured for or belonging to the United States, except as the agent of the United States.

1002. No officer or agent in the military service shall purchase from any other person in the military service, or make any contract with any such person to furnish supplies or services, or make any purchase or contract in which such person shall be admitted to any share or part, or to any benefit to arise therefrom.

1003. No person in the military service whose salary, pay, or emoluments is or are fixed by law or regulations, shall receive any additional pay, extra allowance, or compensation in any form whatever, for the disbursement of public money, or any other service or duty whatsoever, unless the same shall be authorized by law, and explicitly set out in the appropriation.

1004. All accounts of expenditures shall set out a sufficient explanation of the object, necessity, and propriety of the expenditure.

1005. The facts on which an account depends must be stated and vouched by the certificate of an officer, or other sufficient evidence.

1006. If any account paid on the certificate of an officer to the facts is afterward disallowed for error of fact in the certificate, it shall pass to the credit of the disbursing officer, and be charged to the officer who gave the certificate.

1007. An officer shall have credit for an expenditure of money or property made in obedience to the order of his commanding officer. If the expenditure is disallowed, it shall be charged to the officer who ordered it.

1008. Disbursing officers, when they have the money, shall pay cash, and not open an account. Heads of bureaus shall take care, by timely remittances, to obviate the necessity of any purchases on credit.

1009. When a disbursing officer is relieved, he shall certify the outstanding debts to his successor, and transmit an account of the same to the head of the bureau, and turn over his public money and property appertaining to the service from which he is relieved to his successor, unless otherwise ordered.

1010. The chief of each military bureau of the War Department shall, under the direction of the Secretary of War, regulate, as far as practicable, the employment of hired persons required for the administrative service of his department.

1011. When practicable, persons hired in the military service shall be paid at the end of the calendar month, and when discharged. Separate pay-rolls shall be made for each month.

1012. When a hired person is discharged and not paid, a certified statement of his account shall be given him.

1013. Property, paid for or not, must be taken up on the return, and accounted for when received.

1014. No officer has authority to insure public property or money.

1015. Disbursing officers are not authorized to settle with heirs, executors, or administrators, except by instructions from the proper bureau of the War Department upon accounts duly audited and certified by the proper accounting officers of the Treasury.

1016. Public horses, mules, oxen, tools, and implements shall be branded conspicuously U. S. before being used in service, and all other public property that it may be useful to mark; and all public property having the brand of the U. S. when sold or condemned, shall be branded with the letter C.

1017. No public property shall be used, nor labor hired for the public be employed, for any private use whatsoever not authorized by the regulations of the service.

1018. When public property becomes damaged, except by fair wear and tear, or otherwise unsuitable for use, or a deficiency is found in it, the officer accountable for the same shall report the case to the commanding officer, who shall, if necessary, appoint a Board of Survey.

1019. Boards of Survey shall have no power to *condemn* public property. They are called only for the purpose of establishing data by which questions of administrative responsibility may be determined, and the adjustment of accounts facilitated; as, for example, to assess the amount and kind of damage or deficiency which public property may have sustained from any extraordinary cause, not ordinary wear, either in transit or in store, or in actual use, whether from accident, unusual wastage, or otherwise, and to set forth the circumstances and fix the responsibility of such damage, whether on the carrier, or the person accountable for the property or having it immediately in charge; to make inventories of property ordered to be abandoned, when the articles have not been enumerated in the orders; to assess the prices at which damaged clothing may be issued to troops, and the proportion in which supplies shall be issued in consequence of damage that renders them at the usual rate unequal to the allowance which the Regulations contemplate; to verify the discrepancy between the invoices and the actual quantity or description of property transferred from one officer to another, and ascertain, as far as possible, where and how the discrepancy has occurred, whether in the hands of the carrier or the officer making the transfer; and to make inventories and report on the condition of public property in the possession of officers at the time of their death. The action of the board for these authorized objects will be complete with the approval of the commanding officer, provided that neither he nor any of the board are interested parties; but will be subject to revision by higher authority. In no case, however, will the report of the board supersede the depositions which the law requires with reference to deficiencies and damage.

1020. Boards of Survey will not be convened by any other than the commanding officer present, and will be composed of as many officers, not exceeding three, as may be present for duty, exclusive always of the commanding officer and the officer responsible in the matter to be reported on; but in case the two latter only are present, then the one not responsible will perform the duties, and the responsible officer will perform them only if there be no other recourse. The proceedings of the board will be signed by each member, and a copy forwarded by the approving officer to the head-quarters of the department or army in the field, as the case may be, duplicates being furnished to the officer accountable for the property.

1021. All surveys and reports having in view the *condemnation* of public property, for whatever cause, will be made by the commanding officers of posts or other separate commands, or by Inspectors-General, or inspectors specially designated by the commander of a department or an army in the field, or by higher authority. Such surveys and reports having a different object from those of Boards of Survey, will be required independently of any preliminary action of a board on the same matter.

1022. When public property is received by any officer, he will make a careful examination to ascertain its quality and condition, but without breaking packages until issues are to be made, unless there should be cause to suppose the contents defective; and in any of the cases supposed in the preceding paragraph, he will apply for a Board of Survey for the purposes therein set forth. If he deem the property unfit for use and that the public interest requires it to be *condemned*, he will, in addition, report that fact to the commanding officer, who will make, or cause to be made, a critical inspection of it—according as he may be commander of a post only, or have a higher command. If the inspector deem the property fit, it shall be received and used. If not, he will forward a formal inspection report to the commander empowered to give orders in the case. The same rule will be observed, according to the nature of the case, with reference to property already on hand. The person accountable for the property, or having it in charge, will submit an inventory, which will accompany or be embodied in the inspection report, stating how long the property has been in his possession, how long in use, and from whom it was received. The inspector's report will state the exact condition of each article, and what disposition it is expedient to make of it: as, to be destroyed, to be dropped as being of no value, to be broken up, to be repacked or repaired, or to be sold. The inspector will certify on his report that he has examined each article, and that its condition is as stated. If the commanding officer, who ordinarily would be the inspector, is himself accountable for the property, the next officer in rank present for duty will act as the inspector. The authority to inspect and condemn will not, without special instructions, be exercised by commanding officers of arsenals with reference to ordnance and ordnance stores, but only in regard to other unserviceable supplies.

1023. An officer commanding a department, or an army in the field, may give orders, on the report of the authorized inspectors, to sell, destroy, or make such other disposition of any condemned property as the case may require—ordnance and ordnance stores alone excepted, for which the orders of the War Department must always be taken. But if the property be of very considerable value, and there should be reason to suppose that it could be advantageously applied or disposed of elsewhere than within his command, he will refer the matter to the Chief of the Staff Department to which it belongs, for the orders of the War Department. No other persons than those above designated, or the General-in-chief, will order the final disposition of condemned property; saving only in the case of horses which should be killed at once to prevent contagion, and of provisions or other stores which are rapidly deteriorating, when the immediate commander may have to act perforce. Inventories of condemned property will be made in triplicate, one to be retained by the person accountable, one to accompany his accounts, and one to be forwarded through the department or other superior head-quarters to the Chief of the Staff Department to which the property belongs. Separate inventories must be made of the articles to be repaired, of those to be broken up, those to be sold, to be dropped, &c.

1024. Every inspector, member of a Board of Survey, and commander acting on their proceedings, shall be answerable that his action has been proper and judicious, according to the Regulations and the circumstances of the case.

1025. As far as practicable, every officer in charge of public property, whether it be in use or in store, will endeavor by timely repairs to keep it in serviceable condition, for which purpose the necessary means will be allowed on satisfactory requisitions; and property in store so repaired will be issued for further use. Unserviceable arms will be sent to an arsenal for repair. Provisions and other perishable stores will be repacked whenever it may be necessary for their preservation and their value will justify the expense, which will be a legitimate charge against the department to which they belong. Public animals will not be condemned for temporary disease or want of condition, but may, by order of the commanding officer after inspection, be turned in for rest and treatment, if unfit for the service for which they are immediately required.

1026. Public property shall not be transferred gratuitously from one staff department to another; nor shall the funds of one be used to liquidate the debts of another.

1027. If any article of public property be lost or damaged by neglect or fault of any officer or soldier, he shall pay the value of such article, or amount of damage, or cost of repairs, at such rates as a Board of Survey, with the approval of the commanding officer, may assess, according to the place and circumstances of the loss or damage. And he shall, moreover, be proceeded against as the Articles of War provide, if he demand a trial by court-martial, or the circumstances should require it.

1028. Charges against a soldier shall be set against his pay on the muster-roll—but only on clear proof, and never without an inquiry, if he demand it. Charges against an officer to be set against his pay shall be promptly reported to the Secretary of War.*

1029. If any article of public property be embezzled, or by neglect lost or damaged, by any person hired in the public service, the value or damage, as ascertained, if necessary, by a Board of Survey, shall be charged to him, and set against any pay or money due him.

1030. Public property lost or destroyed in the military service must be accounted for by affidavit, or the certificate of a commissioned officer, or other satisfactory evidence.

1031. Affidavits or depositions may be taken before any officer in the list, as follows, when recourse cannot be had to any before named on said list, which fact shall be certified by the officer offering the evidence: 1st. a civil magistrate competent to administer oaths; 2d. a judge advocate; 3d. the recorder of a garrison or regimental court-martial; 4th. the adjutant of a regiment; 5th. a commissioned officer.

1032. Military stores and other army supplies regularly condemned, and ordered for sale, shall be sold for cash at auction, on due public notice, and in such market as the public interest may require. The officer making the sale will bid in and suspend the sale when, in his opinion, better prices may be got. Expenses of the sale will be paid from its proceeds. The auctioneer's certified account of the sales in detail, and the vouchers for the expenses of the sale, will be reported to the

---

* If the pay of any officer or soldier is wrongfully withheld for arrears or liabilities to the United States, a civil remedy is provided by the act of January 25, 1828.

chief of the department to which the property belonged. The net proceeds will be applied as the Secretary of War may direct.

1033. No officer making returns of property shall drop from his return any public property as worn out or unserviceable until it has been condemned, after proper inspection, and ordered to be so dropped.

1034. An officer issuing stores shall deliver or transmit to the receiving officer an exact list of them in duplicate invoices, and the receiving officer shall return him duplicate receipts.

1035. When an officer to whom stores are forwarded has reason to suppose them miscarried, he shall promptly inform the issuing and forwarding officer, and the bureau of the department to which the property appertains.

1036. When stores received do not correspond in amount or quality with the invoice, they will be examined by a Board of Survey, and a copy of the report of the board be communicated to the proper bureau, to the issuing and forwarding officer, and to the officer authorized to pay the transportation account. Damages recovered from the carrier or other party liable, will be refunded to the proper department.

1037. On the death of any officer in charge of public property or money, the commanding officer shall appoint a Board of Survey to take an inventory of the same, which he shall forward to the proper bureau of the War Department, and he shall designate an officer to take charge of the said property or money till orders in the case are received from the proper authority.

1038. When an officer in charge of public property is removed from the care of it, the commanding officer shall designate an officer to receive it, or take charge of it himself, till a successor be regularly appointed. Where no officer can remain to receive it, the commanding officer will take suitable means to secure it, and report the facts to the proper authority.

1039. Every officer having public money to account for, and failing to render his account thereof quarter-yearly, with the vouchers necessary to its correct and prompt settlement, within three months after the expiration of the quarter if resident in the United States, and within six months if resident in a foreign country, will be promptly dismissed by the President, unless he shall explain the default to the satisfaction of the President. (Act January 31, 1823.)

1040. Every officer intrusted with public money or property shall render all prescribed returns and accounts to the bureau of the department in which he is serving, where all such returns and accounts shall pass through a rigid administrative scrutiny before the money accounts

Contracts and Purchases.

are transmitted to the proper offices of the Treasury Department for settlement.

1041. The head of the bureau shall cause his decision on each account to be endorsed on it. He shall bring to the notice of the Secretary of War all accounts and matters of account that require or merit it. When an account is suspended or disallowed, the bureau shall notify it to the officer, that he may have early opportunity to submit explanations or take an appeal to the Secretary of War.

1042. When an account is suspended or disallowed in the proper office of the Treasury Department, or explanation or evidence required from the officer, it shall be promptly notified to him by the head of the military bureau. And all vouchers, evidence, or explanation returned by him to the Treasury Department shall pass through the bureau.

1043. Chiefs of the disbursing departments shall, under the direction of the Secretary of War, designate, as far as practicable, the places where the principal contracts and purchases shall be made and supplies procured for distribution.

1044. All purchases and contracts for supplies or services for the army, except personal services, when the public exigencies do not require the immediate delivery of the article or performance of the service, shall be made by advertising a sufficient time previously for proposals respecting the same.

1045. The officer advertising for proposals shall, when the intended contract or purchase is considerable, transmit forthwith a copy of the advertisement and report of the case to the proper bureau of the War Department.

1046. Contracts will be made with the lowest responsible bidder, and purchases from the lowest bidder who produces the proper article. But when such lowest bids are unreasonable, they will be rejected, and bids again invited by public notice; and all bids and advertisements shall be sent to the bureau.

1047. When sealed bids are required, the time of opening them shall be specified, and bidders have privilege to be present at the opening.

1048. When immediate delivery or performance is required by the public exigency, the article or service required may be procured by open purchase or contract at the places and in the mode in which such articles are usually bought and sold, or such services engaged, between individuals.

1049. Contracts shall be made in quadruplicate; one to be kept by the officer, one by the contractor, and two to be sent to the military bureau, one of which for the office of the Second Comptroller of the Treasury.

1050. The contractor shall give bond, with good and sufficient security, for the true and faithful performance of his contract; and each surety shall state his place of residence.

1051. An express condition shall be inserted in contracts that no member of Congress shall be admitted to any share or part therein, or any benefit to arise therefrom.

1052. No contract shall be made except under a law authorizing it, or an appropriation adequate to its fulfilment, except contracts by the Secretary of War for the subsistence or clothing of the army, or the Quartermaster's Department, which shall not exceed the necessities of the current year.

1053. It is the duty of every commanding officer to enforce a rigid economy in the public expenses.

1054. The commander of a geographical district or department shall require abstracts to be rendered to him, at least once in each quarter, by every officer under his orders who is charged with the care of public property or the disbursement of public money, showing all property received, issued, and expended by the officer rendering the account, and the property remaining on hand, and all moneys received, paid, or contracted to be paid by him, and the balances remaining in his hands; and where such officer is serving under any intermediate commander, as of the post, regiment, &c., the abstracts shall be revised by such commander; and both the accounting officer and the commanding officer shall accompany the abstracts with full explanations of every circumstance that may be necessary to a complete understanding, by the commander of the department, of all the items on the abstracts. These abstracts, where the accounting officer is serving in more than one staff department, will be made separately for each.

1055. The commander of the department shall promptly correct all irregularities and extravagances which he may discover. He shall also forward, as soon as practicable, the money abstracts to the bureau of the War Department to which the accounts appertain, with such remarks as may be necessary to explain his opinions and action thereon.

1056. All estimates for supplies of property or money for the public service within a department shall be forwarded through the commander of the department, and carefully revised by him. And all such estimates shall go through the immediate commander, if such there be, of the officer rendering the estimate, as of the post or regiment, who shall be required by the department commander to revise the estimates for the service of his own command.

1057. The administrative control exercised by department commanders shall, when troops are in the field, devolve on the commanders of divisions; or, when the command is less than a division, on the commander of the whole.

1058. No land shall be purchased for the United States except under a law authorizing such purchase.

1059. No public money shall be expended for the purchase of any land, nor for erecting armories, arsenals, forts, fortifications, or other permanent public buildings, until the written opinion of the Attorney-General shall be had in favor of the validity of the title to the land or site, nor, if the land be within any State of the United States, until a cession of the jurisdiction by the Legislature of the State.

1060. No permanent buildings for the army, as barracks, quarters, hospitals, store-houses, offices, or stables, or piers, or wharves, shall be erected but by order of the Secretary of War, and according to the plan directed by him, and in consequence of appropriations made by law. And no alteration shall be made in any such public building without authority from the War Department.

1061. Complete title papers, with full and exact maps, plans, and drawings of the public lands purchased, appropriated, or designed for permanent military fortifications, will be collected, recorded, and filed in the Bureau of the Corps of Engineers; of the public lands appropriated or designated for armories, arsenals, and ordnance depôts, will be collected, recorded, and filed in the Ordnance Bureau; of all other land belonging to the United States, and under the charge of the War Department for barracks, posts, cantonments, or other military uses, will be collected, recorded, and filed in the office of the Quartermaster-General of the army.

1062. A copy of the survey of the land at each post, fort, arsenal, and depôt, furnished from the proper bureau, will be carefully preserved in the office of the commanding officer.

SIGNAL OFFICER.

1063. The signal officer shall have charge, under the direction of the Secretary of War, of all signal duty, and of all books, papers, and apparatus connected therewith.

ARTICLE XLII.
QUARTERMASTER'S DEPARTMENT.

1064. This department provides the quarters and transportation of the army; storage and transportation for all army supplies; army clothing; camp and garrison equipage; cavalry and artillery horses; fuel; forage; straw; material for bedding, and stationery.

1065. The incidental expenses of the army paid through the Quartermaster's Department include per diem to extra-duty men; postage on public service; the expenses of courts-martial, of the pursuit and apprehension of deserters, of the burials of officers and soldiers, of hired escorts, of expresses, interpreters, spies, and guides, of veterinary surgeons and medicines for horses, and of supplying posts with water; and generally the proper and authorized expenses for the movements and operations of an army not expressly assigned to any other department.

BARRACKS AND QUARTERS.

1066. Under this head are included the permanent buildings for the use of the army, as barracks, quarters, hospitals, store-houses, offices, stables.

1067. When barracks and quarters are to be occupied, they will be allotted by the quartermaster at the station, under the control of the commanding officer.

1068. The number of rooms and amount of fuel for officers and men are as follows:

	Rooms.			Cords of wood per month.*	
	As quarters.	As kitchen.	As office.	From May 1 to Sept. 30.	From Oct. 1 to April 30.
A Major-General	5	1	...	1†	5
A Brigadier-General or Colonel	4	1	...	1	4
A Lieutenant-Colonel or Major	3	1	...	1	3½
A Captain or Chaplain	2	1	...	¾	3
Lieutenant	1	1	...	½	2
Military store-keeper	1	1	...	.	...
The General commanding the army	...	...	3	...	3
The commanding officer of a division or department, an assistant or deputy Quartermaster-General	...	...	2	...	2

* Or coal, at the rate of 1500 lbs. anthracite, or 30 bushels bituminous, to the cord.

† Two cords of pine wood for fuel may, at the discretion of a department commander be issued in lieu of one cord of oak, provided the cost be not greater.

Quartermaster's Department.——Barracks and Quarters.

	As quarters.	As kitchen.	As office.	From May 1 to Sept. 30.	From Oct. 1 to April 30.
	Rooms.			Cords of wood per month.	
The commanding officer of a regiment or post, Quartermaster, Assistant-Quartermaster, or Commissary of Subsistence	...	...	1	...	1
The senior Ordnance Officer stationed at the Head-Quarters of a Military Department...	...	...	1	...	1
The Assistant Adjutant-General at the Head-Quarters of the Army, the Assistant Adjutant-General, the Medical Director and Medical Purveyor of a Military Department, each..	...	...	1	...	‘
Officers of the Pay Department...	...	...	1	...	1
An acting Assistant-Quartermaster, when approved by the Quartermaster-General...	...	...	1	...	1
Wagon and forage master, Sergeant-Major, Ordnance Sergeant, Quartermaster-Sergeant, Medical Cadet, or Principal Musician...	1	...	...	$\frac{1}{2}$	1
Each non-commissioned officer, musician, private, officer's servant, and washerwoman..	...	...	...	$\frac{1}{12}$	$\frac{1}{6}$
Each necessary fire for the sick in hospital, to be regulated by the surgeon and commanding officer, *not exceeding*......	...	...	...	$\frac{1}{2}$	2
Each guard-fire, to be regulated by the commanding officer, not exceeding..	...	...	...	...	3
A commissary or quartermaster's store-house, when necessary, *not exceeding*..	...	...	...	...	1
A regiment or post mess..	1	...	...	...	1
To every six non-commissioned officers, musicians and privates, servants and washerwomen, 225 square feet of room north of 38° N., and 256 square feet south of that latitude.					

1069. Merchantable hard wood is the standard; the cord is 128 cubic feet.

1070. A particular set of quarters will be set apart at every chaplain-post for the chaplain. He will not be disturbed in these further than by a reduction of his allowance when that of the other officers is reduced Nor will he be allowed to choose other quarters.

1071. No officer shall occupy more than his proper quarters, except by order of the commanding officer when there is an excess of quarters at the station; which order the quartermaster shall forward to the Quartermaster-General, to be laid before the Secretary of War. But the amount of quarters shall be reduced *pro rata* by the commanding officer when the number of officers and troops make it necessary; and when the public buildings are not sufficient to quarter the troops, the commanding officer shall report to the commander of the department for authority to hire quarters, or other necessary orders in the case. The department commander shall report the case, and his orders therein, to the Quartermaster-General.

1072. A mess-room, and fuel for it, are allowed only when a majority of the officers of a post or regiment unite in a mess; never to less than three officers, nor to any who live in hotels or boarding-houses. Fuel for a mess-room shall not be used elsewhere, or for any other purpose.

1073. Fuel issued to officers or troops is public property for their use; what they do not actually consume shall be returned to the quartermaster and taken up on his quarterly return. With this exception, however: that the fuel issued to troops, and not actually used in quarters, may be used in baking their bread.

1074 In November, December, January, and February, the fuel is increased one-fourth at stations from the 39th degree to the 43d degree north latitude, and one-third at stations north of the 43d degree.

1075. Fuel shall be issued only in the month when due.

1076. In allotting quarters, officers shall have choice according to rank, but the commanding officer may direct the officers to be stationed convenient to their troops.

1077. An officer may select quarters occupied by a junior; but, having made his choice, he must abide by it, and shall not again at the post displace a junior, unless himself displaced by a senior.

1078. The set of rooms to each quarters will be assigned by the quartermaster, under the control of the commanding officer; attics not counted as rooms.

1079. Officers cannot choose rooms in different sets of quarters.

1080. When public quarters cannot be furnished to officers at stations without troops, or to enlisted men at general or department head-quarters, quarters will be commuted at a rate fixed by the Secretary of War, and fuel at the market price delivered. When fuel and quarters are commuted to an officer by reason of his employment on a civil work, the commutation shall be charged to the appropriation for the work. No commutation of rooms or fuel is allowed for offices or messes.

1081. The following rates of monthly commutation for quarters, when officers are serving without troops and at posts where there are no public quarters which they can occupy, have been established:

1. At Boston, New York, Philadelphia, Baltimore, Washington City, Charleston, Key West, Mobile, and New Orleans, and at all posts and stations in Texas, and in the Territories of New Mexico, Oregon, and Washington, $9 per room.

2. At Detroit, Chicago, and St. Louis, and at all places east of the Rocky Mountains, not heretofore enumerated, $8 per room.

8. At San Francisco, $20 per room, and at all other places in California, $12 per room.

1082. An officer is not deprived of his quarters and fuel, or commutation, at his station, by temporary absence on duty.

1083. Officers absent from their appropriate duties for a period exceeding six months, either with or without leave, shall not receive the allowances authorized by the existing laws for servants, forage, transportation of baggage, fuel, and quarters, either in kind or in commutation. (Act 5 Aug. 1861, chap. 38, sect. 20.)

1084. Officers and troops in the field are not entitled to commutation for quarters or fuel.

1086. An officer arriving at a station shall make requisition on the quartermaster for his quarters and fuel, accompanied by a copy of the order putting him on duty at the station. If in command of troops, his requisition shall be for the whole, and designate the number of officers of each grade, of non-commissioned officers, soldiers, servants, and washerwomen.

1087. Bunks, benches, and tables provided for soldiers' barracks and hospitals, are not to be removed from them, except by the quartermaster of the station, or order of the commanding officer, and shall not be removed from the station except by order of the Quartermaster-General.

1088. The furniture for each office will be two common desks or tables, six common chairs, one pair common andirons, and shovel and tongs.

1089. Furniture will be provided for officers' quarters when special appropriations for that purpose are made. Sales to officers of materials for furniture may be made at cost, at posts where they cannot be otherwise obtained.

1090. When buildings are to be occupied or allotted, an inspection of them shall be made by the commanding officer and quartermaster. Statements, in triplicate, of their condition, and of the fixtures and furniture in each room, shall be made by the quartermaster, and revised by the commanding officer. One of these shall be retained by the commanding officer, one by the quartermaster, and the third forwarded to the Quartermaster-General.

1091. Like inspection of all buildings in the use of troops will be made at the monthly inspections of the troops, and of all buildings which have been in the use of officers or troops, whenever vacated by them. Damages will be promptly repaired if the quartermaster has the means Commanding officers will take notice, as a military offense, of any neglect by any officer or soldier to take proper care of the rooms or furniture in his use or occupancy; but such officer or soldier may be allowed to pay the cost of the repairs when the commanding officer deems that sufficient in the case. Commanding officers are required to report to the Quartermaster-General their proceedings in all cases of neglect under this regulation.

1092. An annual inspection of the public buildings at the several stations shall be made at the end of June by the commanding officer and quartermaster, and then the quartermaster shall make the following reports: 1st. of the condition and capacity of the buildings, and of the additions, alterations, and repairs that have been made during the past year; 2d. of the additions, alterations, and repairs that are needed, with plans and estimates in detail.

These reports the commanding officer shall examine and forward, with his views, to the Quartermaster-General.

1093. Necessary repairs of public buildings, not provided for in the appropriations, can only be made by the labor of the troops.

1094. When private buildings occupied as barracks or quarters, or lands occupied for encampments, are vacated, the commanding officer and quartermaster shall make an inspection of them, and a report to the Quartermaster-General of their condition, and of any injury to them by the use of the United States.

1095. Military posts evacuated by the troops, and lands reserved for military use, will be put in charge of the Quartermaster's Department, unless otherwise specially ordered.

ARMY TRANSPORTATION.

1096. When troops are moved, or officers travel with escorts or stores, the means of transport provided shall be for the whole command. Proper orders in the case, and an exact return of the command, including officers' servants and company women, will be furnished to the quartermaster who is to provide the transportation.

1097. The baggage to be transported is limited to camp and garrison equipage, and officers' baggage. Officers' baggage shall not exceed (mess-chest and all personal effects included) as follows :

	In the field.	Changing stations.
General officers...............................	125 pounds.	1000 pounds.
Field officers...................................	100 "	800 "
Captains	80 "	700 "
Subalterns......................................	80 "	600 "

These amounts shall be reduced *pro rata* by the commanding officer when necessary, and may be increased by the Quartermaster-General on transports by water, when proper in special cases.

1098. The regimental and company desk prescribed in army regula-tions will be transported; also for staff officers, the books, papers, and instruments necessary to their duties; and for medical officers, their medical chest. In doubtful cases under this regulation, and whenever baggage exceeds the regulated allowance, the conductor of the train, or officer in charge of the transportation, will report to the commanding officer, who will order an inspection, and all excess to be rejected.

1099. Estimates of the medical director, approved by the commanding officer, for the necessary transportation to be provided for the hospital service, will be furnished to the quartermaster.

1100. The sick will be transported on the application of the medical officers.

1101. Certified invoices of all public stores to be transported will be furnished to the quartermaster by the officer having charge of them. In doubtful cases, the orders of the commanding officer will be required.

1102. Where officers' horses are to be transported, it must be authorized in the orders for the movement.

1103. The baggage trains, ambulances, and all the means of transport continue in charge of the proper officers of the Quartermaster's Depart-ment, under the control of the commanding officers.

1104. In all cases of transportation, whether of troops or stores, an exact return of the amount and kind of transportation employed will be made by the quartermaster to the Quartermaster-General, accompanied by the orders for the movement, a return of the troops, and an invoice of the stores.

1105. Wagons and their equipments for the transport service of the army will be procured, when practicable, from the Ordnance Department, and fabricated in the government establishments.

1106. Spring wagons or carriages will not be used except on extra-ordinary occasions, and then only on the written order of a department commander or the commander of an army in the field, a copy of which order will be transmitted to the Quartermaster-General. The purchase of this description of conveyance is prohibited, unless specially authorized by the War Department.

1107. When army supplies are turned over to a quartermaster for transportation, each package shall be directed and its contents marked on it; and duplicate invoices and receipts in bulk will be exchanged between the issuing and forwarding officer.

1108. On transports, cabin passage will be provided for officers, and reasonable and proper accommodation for the troops, and, when possible, separate apartment for the sick.

1109. An officer who travels not less than ten miles without troops, escort, or military stores, and under special orders in the case from a superior, or a summons to attend a military court, shall receive ten cents mileage, or, if he prefer it, the actual cost of his transportation and of the transportation of his allowance of baggage for the whole journey, provided he has traveled in the customary reasonable manner. Mileage will not be allowed where the travel is by government conveyances, which will be furnished in case of necessity.

1110. If the journey be to cash treasury drafts, the necessary and actual cost of transportation only will be allowed; and the account must describe the draft and state its amount, and set out the items of expense, and be supported by a certificate that the journey was necessary to procure specie for the draft at par.

1111. If an officer shall travel on urgent public duty without orders, he shall report the case to the superior who had authority to order the journey; and his approval, if then given, shall allow the actual cost of transportation. Mileage is computed by the shortest mail route, and the distance by the General Post-Office book. When the distance cannot be so ascertained, it shall be reckoned subject to the decision of the Quartermaster-General.

1112. Orders to an officer on leave of absence to rejoin the station or troops he left, will not carry transportation.

1113. In changes of station, an officer entitled to mileage, or actual cost of transportation, shall be entitled to actual cost of transportation of his authorized servants; and in other cases than change of station, an officer entitled to transportation, who, from wounds or disability, requires and takes one servant, shall be entitled to the actual cost of his transportation.

1114. The Inspectors-General, when on tours of inspection where they are obliged to take a servant, shall be entitled to the actual cost of his transportation.

1115. Citizens receiving military appointments join their stations without expense to the public.

1116. But assistant surgeons approved by an examining board and commissioned, receive transportation in the execution of their first order to duty, and graduates of the Military Academy receive transportation from the academy to their stations.

1117. When officers are permitted to exchange stations, or are transferred at their own request from one regiment or company to another, the public will not be put to the expense of their transportation. They must bear it themselves.

1118. A paymaster's clerk will receive the actual expenses of his transportation while traveling under orders in the discharge of his duty, upon his affidavit to the account of expenses, and the certificate of the paymaster that the journey was on duty.

1119. Travel of officers on business of civil works will be charged to the appropriation for the work.

1120. No officer shall have orders to attend personally at Washington to the settlement of his accounts, except by order of the Secretary of War on the report of the bureau, or of the Treasury, showing a necessity therefor.

FORAGE.

1121. The forage ration is fourteen pounds of hay and twelve pounds of oats, corn, or barley. For mules, fourteen pounds of hay and nine pounds of oats, corn, or barley.

1122. The allowance of forage to mounted officers will apply for mules equally as for horses, when the exigencies of the service make it necessary to use the former instead of the latter. This will not authorize officers to make the substitution on drills and parades, or, under ordinary circumstances, on any duty under arms.

1123. Forage shall be issued to officers only in the month when due, and at their proper stations, and for the horses actually kept by them in service, not exceeding in number as follows: In time of war, Major-General, seven horses; Brigadier-General, five; Colonels who have the cavalry allowance, five; other Colonels, four; Lieutenant-Colonels and Majors who have the cavalry allowance, four; other Lieutenant-Colonels and Majors, three; Captains who have the cavalry allowance, three; all other officers entitled to forage, two; and in time of peace, general and field officers, three horses; officers below the rank of field officers in the regiments of dragoons, cavalry, and mounted riflemen, two horses; all other officers entitled to forage, one horse.

1124. No officer shall sell forage issued to him. Forage issued to public horses or cattle is public property; what they do not actually consume is to be properly accounted for.

1125. Whenever the state of the supplies or circumstances of the service make it necessary to issue a part, only, of the ration, in kind, commanding officers will prescribe what part shall be so issued.

STRAW.

1126. In barracks, twelve pounds of straw per month for bedding will be allowed to each man, servant, and company woman.

1127. The allowance and change of straw for the sick is regulated by the surgeon.

1128. One hundred pounds per month is allowed for bedding to each horse in public service.

1129. At posts near prairie land owned by the United States, hay will be used instead of straw, and provided by the troops.

Straw not actually used as bedding shall be accounted for as other public property.

STATIONERY.

1130. Issues of stationery are made quarterly, in amount as follows:

	Quires of writing-paper.	Quires of envelope paper.	Number of quills.	Ounces of wafers.	Ounces of sealing-wax.	Papers of ink-powder.	Pieces of office tape.
Commander of an army, department, or division (what may be necessary for himself and staff for their public duty.)							
Commander of a brigade, for himself and staff......	12	1	50	1	8	2	2
Officer commanding a regiment or post of not less than five companies, for himself and staff.........	10	1	40	1	6	2	2
Officer commanding a post of more than two and less than five companies.............................	8	½	30	½	5	1	1
Commanding officer of a post of two companies....	6	½	25	½	4	1	1
Commanding officer of a post of one company or less, and commanding officer of a company.......	5	½	20	½	3	1	1
A Lieutenant-Colonel or Major not in command of a regiment or post......	3	¼	12	¼	2	1	1
Officers of the Inspector-General's, Pay, and Quartermaster's Department (the prescribed blank books and printed forms, and the stationery required for their public duty).							
All officers, including Chaplains, not enumerated above, when on duty and not supplied by their respective departments..............................	1½	⅛	6	⅛	1	½	½

Steel pens, with one holder to 12 pens, may be issued in place of quills, and envelopes in place of envelope paper, at the rate of 100 to the quire.

1131. When an officer is relieved in command, he shall transfer the office stationery to his successor.

1132. To each office table is allowed one inkstand, one stamp, one paper-folder, one sand-box, one wafer-box, and as many lead-pencils as may be required, not exceeding four per annum.

1133. Necessary stationery for military courts and boards will be furnished on the requisition of the recorder, approved by the presiding officer.

1134. The commander of an army, department, or division, may direct orders to be printed, when the requisite dispatch and the number to be distributed make it necessary. The necessity will be set out in the order for the printing, or certified on the account.

1135. Regimental, company, and post books, and printed blanks for the officers of Quartermaster and Pay Departments, will be procured by timely requisition on the Quartermaster-General.

1136. Printed matter procured by the Quartermaster-General for use out of Washington may be procured elsewhere, at a cost not to exceed the rates prescribed by Congress for the public printing increased by the cost of transportation.

EXPENSES OF COURTS-MARTIAL.

1137. An officer who attends a general court-martial or court of inquiry, convened by authority competent to order a general court-martial, will be paid, if the court is not held at the station where he is at the time serving, one dollar a day while attending the court and traveling to and from it if entitled to forage, and one dollar and twenty-five cents a day if not entitled to forage.

1138. The Judge Advocate or Recorder will be paid, besides, a per diem of one dollar and twenty-five cents for every day he is necessarily employed in the duty of the court. When it is necessary to employ a clerk to aid the Judge Advocate, the court may order it; a soldier to be procured when practicable.

1139. A citizen witness shall be paid his actual transportation or stage fare, and three dollars a day while attending the court and traveling to and from it, counting the travel at fifty miles a day.

1140. The certificate of the Judge Advocate shall be evidence of the time of attendance on the court, and of the time he was necessarily employed in the duty of the court. Of the time occupied in traveling, each officer will make his own certificate.

EXTRA-DUTY MEN.

1141. Duplicate rolls of the extra-duty men, to be paid by the Quartermaster's Department, will be made monthly, and certified by the quartermaster, or other officer having charge of the work, and countersigned by the commanding officer. One of these will be transmitted direct to the Quartermaster-General, and the other filed in support of the pay-roll.

PUBLIC POSTAGE.

1142. Postage and dispatches by telegraph, on public business, paid by an officer, will be refunded to him on his certificate to the account, and to the necessity of the communication by telegraph. The amount for postage, and for telegraph dispatches, will be stated separately. The telegraph should be used only in cases of urgent and imperative necessity, where the delay of the mail would be prejudicial to the public interest. Copies of the telegrams must accompany vouchers for their payment.

HORSES FOR MOUNTED OFFICERS.

1143. In the field, on the frontier, or in active service, the commanding officer may authorize a mounted officer to take from the public stables one or two horses at a price one-third greater than the average cost of the lot from which he selects, or at the actual cost of the horse when that can be ascertained; providing he shall not take the horse of any trooper. A horse so taken shall not be exchanged or returned. Horses of mounted officers shall be shod by the public farrier or blacksmith.

1144. The horses of a field battery will be shod by the artificers of the company, one of whom shall be a farrier. No other compensation than the pay and allowances of that grade will be made for these services.

CLOTHING, CAMP AND GARRISON EQUIPAGE.

1145. Supplies of clothing and camp and garrison equipage will sent by the Quartermaster-General from the general depôt to the officers of his department stationed with the troops.

1146. The contents of each package, and the sizes of clothing in it, will be marked on it.

1147. The receiving quartermaster will give duplicate receipts for the clothing as invoiced to him, if the packages as received and marked agree with the invoice, and appear rightly marked, and in good order; if otherwise, an inspection will be made by a board of survey, whose report in case of damage or deficiency will be transmitted, one copy to the Quartermaster-General and one to the officer forwarding the supplies. In case of damage, the board will assess the damage to each article.

1148. ALLOWANCE OF CAMP AND GARRISON EQUIPAGE.

	Tents, in the field.	Spades.	Axes.	Pickaxes.	Hatchets.	Camp-kettles.	Mess-pans.
A General..	3	...	1	...	1	...	...
Field or staff officer above the rank of Captain......	2	...	1	...	1	...	...
Other staff officers or Captains........................	1	...	1	...	1	...	...
Subalterns of a company, to every two..............	1	...	1	...	1	...	...
To every 15 foot and 13 mounted men...............	1	2	2	2	2	2	5

1149. Bed-sacks are provided for troops in garrison, and iron pots may be furnished to them instead of camp-kettles. Requisitions will be sent to the Quartermaster-General for the authorized flags, colors, standards, guidons, drums, fifes, bugles, and trumpets.

ALLOWANCE OF CLOTHING.

1150. A soldier is allowed the uniform clothing stated in the following table, or articles thereof of equal value. When a balance is due him at the end of a year, it is added to his allowance for the next:

Quartermaster's Department.——Allowance of Clothing.

CLOTHING.	FOR FIVE YEARS.					Total in the five years.
	1st.	2d.	3d.	4th.	5th.	
Cap, complete..	2	1	2	1	1	7
Hat with trimmings complete.	1	1	1	1	1	5
Fatigue forage caps, of pattern in the Quartermaster-General's Office, will be issued, in addition to hats	1	1	1	1	1	5
Pompon..	1	...	1	...	...	2
Eagle and ring..	1	...	1	...	...	2
Cover...	1	1	1	1	1	5
Coat..	2	1	2	1	2	8
Trowsers..	3	2	3	2	3	13
Flannel shirt..	3	3	3	3	3	15
" drawers..	3	2	2	2	2	11
Bootees,* pair..	4	4	4	4	4	20
Stockings, pair..	4	4	4	4	4	20
Leather stock..	1	...	1	...	...	2
Great-coat..	1	...	...	...	...	1
Stable-frock (for mounted men)..............................	1	...	1	...	...	2
Fatigue overalls (for engineers and ordnance).........	1	1	1	1	1	5
Blanket..	1	...	1	...	...	2

* Mounted men may receive *one* pair of "boots" and *two* pairs of "bootees" instead of *four* pairs of bootees.

1151. One sash is allowed to each company for the first sergeant, and one knapsack with straps, haversack, and canteen with straps, to each enlisted man.   These and the metallic scales, letters, numbers, castles, shells, and flames, and the camp and garrison equipage, will not be returned as issued, but borne on the return while fit for service.   They will be charged to the person in whose use they are, when lost or destroyed by his fault.

1152. Commanders of companies draw the clothing of their men, and the camp and garrison equipage for the officers and men of their company.   The camp and garrison equipage of other officers is drawn on their own receipts.

1153. When clothing is needed for issue to the men, the company commander will procure it from the quartermaster on requisition, approved by the commanding officer.

1154. Ordinarily the company commander will procure and issue clothing to his men twice a year; at other times, when necessary in special cases.

1155. Such articles of clothing as the soldier may need will be issued to him.   When the issues equal in value his allowance for the year, further issues are extra issues, to be charged to him on the next muster-roll.

1156. The talmas furnished the mounted troops will be accounted for as company property, and the men to whom they are issued will be held responsible for their preservation.

1157. The money value of the clothing, and of each article of it, will be ascertained annually, and announced in orders from the War Department.

1158. Officers receiving clothing, or camp and garrison equipage, will render quarterly returns of it to the Quartermaster-General.

1159. Commanders of companies will take the receipts of their men for the clothing issued to them, on a receipt-roll, witnessed by an officer, or, in the absence of an officer, by a non-commissioned officer; the witness to be witness to the fact of the issue and the acknowledgment and signature of the soldier. The several issues to a soldier to be entered separately on the roll, and all vacant spaces on the roll to be filled with a cipher. This roll is the voucher for the issue to the quarterly return of the company commander. Extra issues will be so noted on the roll.

1160. Each soldier's clothing account is kept by the company commander in a company book. This account sets out only the money value of the clothing which he received at each issue, for which his receipt is entered in the book, and witnessed as in the preceding paragraph.

1161. When a soldier is transferred or detached, the amount due to or by him on account of clothing will be stated on his descriptive list.

1162. When a soldier is discharged, the amount due to or by him for clothing will be stated on the duplicate certificates given for the settlement of his accounts.

1163. Deserters' clothing will be turned into store. The invoice of it, and the quartermaster's receipt for it, will state its condition, and the name of the deserter.

1164. The inspection report on damaged clothing shall set out, with the amount of damage to each article, a list of such articles as are fit for issue, at a reduced price stated.

1165. Commanding officers may order necessary issues of clothing to prisoners and convicts, taking deserters' or other damaged clothing when there is such in store.

1166. Officers of the army may purchase, at the regulation price, from the quartermaster of their post, such articles of uniform clothing as they actually need—certifying that the articles so drawn are intended solely for their own personal use.

1167. But—with the exception of under-clothing and shoes, of which, when there are no other means of procuring them, a reasonable quantity may, on the officers' certificate to that effect, be purchased for them from the quartermaster—no officer's private servant, not a soldier, shall be permitted to draw or to wear the uniform clothing issued to the troops.

1168. In all cases of deficiency, or damage of any article of clothing, or camp or garrison equipage, the officer accountable for the property is required by law "to show by one or more depositions setting forth the

circumstances of the case that the deficiency was by unavoidable accident or loss in actual service, without any fault on his part, and, in case
of damage, that due care and attention were exerted on his part, and
that the damage did not result from neglect."

RETURNS IN THE QUARTERMASTER'S DEPARTMENT.

1169. All officers and agents having money and property of the Department to account for, are required to make the monthly and quarterly
returns to the Quartermaster-General prescribed in the following articles:

1170. Monthly returns, to be transmitted within five days after the
month to which they relate, viz.: A summary statement (Form 1); report of persons and things (Form 2); roll of extra-duty men (Form 3);
report of stores for transportation, &c. (Form 4); return of animals,
wagons, harness, &c. (Form 5); report of forage (Form 6); report of
fuel and quarters commuted (Form 7); report of pay due (Form 8); an
estimate of funds for one month (Form 9) will be sent with the monthly
returns. It will be for the current month, or such subsequent month as
may give time to receive the remittance. Other special estimates will be
transmitted when necessary.

1171. Quarterly returns, to be transmitted within twenty days after
the quarter to which they relate, viz.: An account current of money
(Form 10), with abstracts and vouchers, as shown in Forms Nos. 11 to
22; a return of property (Form 23), with abstracts and vouchers, as shown
in Forms Nos. 24 to 45; a duplicate of the property return without
abstracts or vouchers; and a quarterly statement of the allowances paid
to officers (Form 46).

1172. A distinct account current will be returned of money received
and disbursed under the appropriation for "contingencies of the army."
(See Forms Nos. 47, 48, and 22, for the forms of the account current,
abstracts, and vouchers.) Necessary expenditures by the quartermaster
for the Medical Department are entered on Abstract C. (See Forms 49
and 50.) The account will, ordinarily, be transferred from "army contingencies" to the appropriation for the Medical and Hospital Department, in the Treasury.

1173. Forms 51 and 52 are the forms of the quarterly returns of clothing, camp and garrison equipage, and the receipt-roll of issues to soldiers.

1174. When persons and articles hired in the Quartermaster's Department are transferred, a descriptive list (Form 53) will be forwarded with
them to the quartermaster to whom they are sent.

1175. Officers serving in the Quartermaster's Department will report
to the Quartermaster-General useful information in regard to the routes
and means of transportation and of supplies.

Quartermaster's Department.——Forms.

No. 1.

MONTHLY SUMMARY STATEMENT.

The United States in account with ———, at ———, in the month of ———, 186 .

DR.		CR.

DR.

To amount of purchases within the month..........
To amount of expenditures within the month..........................
To amount of advances made to officers, per abstract..........................

Balance due the United States, carried to next statement.....................

$

CR.

By balance per last statement...............
By cash received from..............
By cash received from Treasurer of the United States, being amount of warrant No. ——.......................

$

I certify that the above is a true statement of all the moneys which have come into my hands on account of the Quartermaster's Department, during the month of ———, 186 , and that the disbursements have been faithfully made. The balance due the United States is deposited in ———.

A. B., *Quartermaster.*

NOTE.—No vouchers accompany this statement; abstracts of advances or transfers only, when the number of them makes the abstract necessary.

Quartermaster's Department.——Forms.

No. 2.

Report of Persons and Articles employed and hired at ———,

Running numbers.	No. of each class.	Names of persons and articles.	Designation and occupation.	Service during the month.			Rate of hire or compensation.		Date of contract, agreement, or entry into service.
				From.	To.	Day.	Amount.	Day, month, or voyage.	
1	1	House, 3 rooms	Quarters...	1	31	31	$40 00	Month.	July 1,1860.
2	2	House, 4 rooms	Storehouse	3	31	29	31 00	Month.	Dec. 3,1859.
3	3	House, 2 rooms	Guard "	1	31	31	10 00	Month.	Dec. 3,1859.
1	1	Ship Fanny....	Transport.	1	31	31	22,000 00	Voyage	May 3,1860.
2	2	Schr. Heroine.	Transport.	1	31	31	700 00	Month.	June 4,1860.
1	1	Wagon & team	....	1	31	31	100 00	Month.	Jan. 1,1860.
1	1	Chas. James...	Clerk.......	1	31	31	75 00	Month.	Dec. 3,1860.
2	1	Isaac Lowd....	Interpreter	7	10	4	2 00	Day.	Jan. 7,1861.
3	1	Peter Keene ...	Express....	7	12	6	40 00	Month.	Jan. 7,1861.
4	1	John Peters ...	Blacksmith	22	31	7	2 00	Day.	Jan. 1,1861.
5	1	Thos. Cross....	Laborer....	1	31	31	20 00	Month.	May 3,1860.
		United States Steamer Fashion							
1	1	Jas. Corwin ...	Captain....	1	31	31	150 00	Month.	Dec. 1,1860.
2	1	Geo. Pratt......	Engineer..	1	31	31	100 00	Month.	Dec. 1,1860.
3	1	John Paul......	Mate	1	31	31	50 00	Month.	Dec. 1,1860.

Amount of rent and hire during the month ....

I certify that the above is a true report of all the persons and articles employed the head of Remarks, and the statement of amounts due and remaining unpaid, Examined.

C. D ,

Commanding.

No. 2.

during the month of ——, 186 , *by* ——.

By whom owned.	Amount of rent or pay in the month.	Remarks showing by whom the buildings were occupied, and for what purpose, and how the vessels and men were employed during the month. (Transfers and discharges will be noted under this head.)	Time and amount due and remaining unpaid.		
			From.	To.	Am't.
A. Byrne...	$40 00	Major 3d Infantry..............	1860. Dec. 1.	1861. Jan. 31.	$80 00
Jas. Black.	29 00	Subsistence Store and Office...	Dec. 3.	Jan. 31.	60 00
Jas. Black.	10 00	Companies I & K, 3d Infantry	....	....	....
G. Wilkins.	....	Transporting stores to Benicia	Voyage	not	completed.
T. Browne.	700 00	Transporting stores to Brazos.	1861. Jan. 1.	1861. Jan. 31.	700 00
Jas. Barry.	100 00	Hauling stores to San Antonio	Jan. 1.	Jan. 31.	100 00
	75 00	Quartermaster's Office	....	....	....
	8 00	Employed by Com'ing General	....	....	....
	7 74	Express to Indianola	....	....	....
	14 00	Shoeing public horses..........	....	....	....
	20 00	Helping blacksmith	....	....	....
	150 00	} Steamship sent to Brazos... {	July 1.	July 31.	150 00
	100 00		July 1.	July 31.	100 00
	50 00		July 1.	July 31.	50 00
....	1308 74	Total amount due and remaining unpaid.........			1240 00

and hired by me during the month of ——, 186 , and that the observations under are correct.

E. F.,
Asst. Qr. Master.

Quartermaster's Department.——Forms.

No. 3.

Roll of Non-commissioned Officers and Privates employed on extra duty, as mechanics and laborers, at ——, during the month of ——, 186 , by ——.

No.	Names.	Rank or designation.	Company.	Regiment.	By whose order employed.	Nature of service.	Term of service.			Rate of pay or compensation.			How employed.
							From.	To.	No. days.	Per diem. Cts.	Dolls. Cts		REMARKS.
												$	

I certify that the above is a correct roll of non-commissioned officers, musicians, and privates, employed on extra duty, under my direction, during the month of ——, 186 , and that the remarks opposite their names are accurate and just.

A. B.,

Quartermaster (or officer commanding detachment).

Examined.   C. D., Commanding.

Quartermaster's Department.—Forms.

No. 4.

Report of Stores received for Transportation and Distribution at ——, by ——, in the month of ——, 186 .

Time received.	Marks.	No.	Contents.	From whom received.	By whom received.	Time sent.	To whom sent, and where.	With whom sent.	Intermediate destination.	Ultimate destination.	Remarks.
186 . June 1.	W. S. &c.	1 to 3.	Clothing.	Capt. A. B., Asst. Quartermaster, Boston.	Sloop Sally, Capt. A. W.	186 . June 3.	Capt. C., Asst. Qunr'master, St. Louis.	Ship George, Capt. I. B.	......	......	Received in good order.

I certify that the above report is correct.

E. A. O., *Quartermaster.*

Quartermaster's Department.—Forms.

No. 5.

Monthly Return of Public Animals, Wagons, Harness, and other means of transportation in the possession of ———, at ———, during the month of ————, 186 .

Date.		Horses.	Mules.	Oxen.	Wagons.	Ambulances.	Carts.	Wheel harness, single sets of.	Lead harness, single sets of.	Wagon saddles.	Ships.	Schooners.	Sloops.	Steamers.	Boats and barges.	Skiffs and bateaux.	Remarks.
	On hand..........																18 horses purchased; average cost $——. Wagons purchased at ——. 6 horses received from ——.
	Purchased during the month......																
	Received from officers................																
	Total to be accounted for...........																
	Transferred...........................																Horses transferred to ——. Wagons transferred to ——. 1 horse sold; — horses died on the road to ——.
	Sold and worn out..................																
	Died and lost........................																
	Total issued and expended.........																
	Remaining on hand.................																

I certify that the above return is correct.

NOTE.—No other articles than those above enumerated will be placed on this return.

A. B., Quartermaster.

No. 6.

Monthly Report of Forage which has been issued to Horses, Mules, and Oxen in the public service at ——, by ——, during the month of ——, 186 .

Date.	To whom issued.	Public Horses.	Public Mules.	Public Oxen.	Private Horses.	Private Mules.	Total Animals.	Corn Pounds.	Oats Pounds.	Hay Pounds.	Fodder Pounds.	Corn, per bush. (56 lbs.) $	c.	Oats, per bush. (32 lbs.) $	c.	Hay, per 100 pounds. $	c.	Fodder, per 100 pounds. $	c.	Remarks.
	Field and staff officers......	6	...	...	12	...	18	6,480	...	......	......		1 00		50		50		1 00	Hay purchased at ——, at —— per 100 pounds.
	Company A, 1st Dragoons..	61	...	...	4	...	65	23,400	...	1,350 2,240										Corn purchased at ——, and hauled at —— per bush.
	" B, 2d "	47	...	...	4	...	51	18,360	...	2,100										Fodder delivered at the post, at —— per 100 lbs.
	" K, 1st Artillery..	45	...	...	6	...	51	18,360	...											
	Qr. Master's Department...	60	300	80	...	...	440	158,400	...	33,000	1,640									
	Total......	219	300	80	26	...	625	225,000	...	38,690	1,640									

I certify that the above report is correct

A. B., *Quartermaster.*

No. 7.

Report of Officers of the Army stationed at ———, whose Quarters and Fuel are commuted, for the month of ———, 186 , by ———.

Names.	Rank.	Corps.	Period.		Quarters.					Fuel.								Under what order.	Remarks.
			From.	To.	Room No.	Rate per month. Dolls.	Cts.	Amount. Dolls.	Cts.	Wood. Cords.	Feet.	Ins.	Price per cord. Dolls.	Cts.	Amount. Dolls.	Cts.			
																			Paid—
								Amount of Quarters, $							Amount of Fuel, $				

I certify, that the above report is correct.

A. B., *Quartermaster.*

Quartermaster's Department.——Forms.

No. 8.

Report of Persons Hired and Employed in the Quartermaster's Department at ————, who have deceased, deserted, or
have been discharged the service with pay due, during the month of ————, 186 , by ————.

No.	Names.	Occupation.	RATE OF PAY OR HIRE.			TIME FOR, AND AMOUNT REMAINING UNPAID.				REMARKS.
			Dolls.	Cts.	Per day or month.	From.	To.	Dolls.	Cts.	
11	George Peters	Blacksmith	2	00	Day..........	1 Aug., 1860.	30 Sept., 1860.	52	00	Discharged 30th Sept., 1860; certificates given.
27	John Smith...	Teamster...	25	00	Month	1 Sept.,1860.	15 Sept., 1860.	12	50	Deserted 16th September, 1860.
39	Peter Davis...	Laborer	20	00	Month	1 Sept., 1860.	15 Sept., 1860.	10	00	Died 24th September, 1860.
								$ 74	50	

I certify that the above is a true report of all persons hired and employed by me in the Quartermaster's Department, who have deceased, deserted, or been discharged the service with pay due, and that the statement of time for, and amount remaining unpaid, and the remarks, are correct and just.

A. B., *Quartermaster.*

NOTE.—This report must contain all the information required, to enable the Department to pay the legal representatives of the deceased persons, to examine into the cases of deserters, and to examine and verify the correctness of payments made on certificates of discharge.

Quartermaster's Department.——Forms.

No. 9.

Estimate of Funds required for the service of the Quartermaster's Department at ——— , by ——— , in the month of ——— , 186 .

		Dolls.	Cts.
1	For Fuel...		
2	Forage...		
3	Straw..		
4	Stationery...		
5	Materials for building. (State what, and for what purpose.)..		
6	Hire of mechanics. (State for what work.).............		
7	Hire of laborers. (State for what service.).............		
8	Hire of teamsters. (State on what service.)............		
9	Pay of extra-duty men. (State for what work.)........		
10	Pay of wagon and forage masters.........................		
11	Hire of clerks, guides, escorts, expenses of courts-martial, of burials, of apprehending deserters, and other incidental expenses............................		
12	Hire or commutation of officers' quarters.................		
13	Hire of quarters for troops, or ground for encampment or use of military stations..........................		
14	Hire of store-houses, offices, &c. (For what use.).....		
15	Mileage to officers...		
16	Army transportation,—viz.:		
	Of troops and their baggage........................		
	Of Quartermasters', subsistence, ordnance, and hospital stores..................................		
17	Purchase of horses and mules (Q. M. Dept.).............		
18	Purchase of wagons and harness do.		
19	Purchase of horses for mounted troops,—viz.:		
	Horses for Company —— Dragoons.......................		
	Horses for Company —— Artillery, &c., &c...........		
20	Outstanding debts..		
	Deduct actual or probable balance on hand......................		

Quartermaster's Department.——Forms.

No. 10.

The United States in account current with ———, Quartermaster United States, on account of the Quartermaster's Department at ———, in the quarter ending on the ——— day of ———, 186 .

Dr.			Cr.
186 .		186 .	
March 31.	To amount of purchases, per Abstract A...	Jan. 1.	By balance on hand, per last account.
" 31.	To amount of expenditures, per Abstract B.	" 15.	By cash received from Treasurer of the United States, being amount of warrant No. ——
" 31.	To amount of transfers to officers, per abstract B b.............	March 31.	By cash received of sundry officers, per abstract B b b..............
" 31.	To balance due the United States carried to new account.............	" 31.	By cash received from sales of public property, as per account herewith.
	$		$

I certify that the above is a true account of all the moneys that have come into my hands, on account of the Quartermaster's Department, during the quarter ending on the ——— day of ———, 186 , and that the disbursements have been faithfully made.

A. B., Quartermaster.

NOTE.—Moneys for clothing, camp and garrison equipage, and contingencies of the army, are not accounted for in this account current. Abstracts B b and B b b are used only where the number of transfers make them necessary.

Quartermaster's Department.——Forms.

No. 11.—(ABSTRACT A.)

Abstract of Purchases paid for at ——— in the quarter ending on the ———, 186—, by ———.

Date.	No. of voucher.	Classes. From whom purchased.	Amount. Dolls.	Cts.	Fuel. Wood. Cords.	Feet.	Ins.	Coal. Lbs.	Forage. Corn. Bu.	Oats. Bu.	Hay. Lbs.	Straw. Pounds.	Stationery.
		Purchased prior to the quarter....											
		Purchased within the quarter.....											
		Total paid within the quarter.....											

NOTE.—This abstract will be supported by vouchers (Form 12), and must exhibit all the articles paid for in the quarter, whether purchased within or prior to the quarter, except purchases of clothing, camp and garrison equipage, and purchases for "army contingencies."

Quartermaster's Department.——Forms.

No. 12.—(Voucher for Purchases to Abstract A.)

The United States, To ————.   Dr.

Date of purchase.		Dollars.	Cents.
	For—		
June 3, 1860......	20 cords of wood, at —— per cord............		
" 10, "	20,352 pounds of straw, at —— per 100 lbs............		
" 29, "	100 bushels of coal, at —— per bushel............		
		$	

I certify that the above account is correct and just; the articles are to be (or have been) accounted for on my property return for the —— quarter ending on the —— day of ————, 186 .

A. B., Quartermaster.

Received at ——, the —— of ————, 186 , of C. D., Quartermaster U. S. Army, —— dollars and —— cents, in full of the above account.

E. F.

(Signed duplicates.)

Note.—The certificate made by the officer who purchased the property. The receipt taken by the officer who paid it.

Q 2

Quartermaster's Department.——Forms.

No. 13.—(ABSTRACT B.)

Abstract of Expenditures on account of the Quartermaster's Department, by ———, at ———, in the quarter ending on the ——— of ———, 186 .

Date of payment.	No. of voucher.	To whom paid.	On what account.	AMOUNT.	
				Dolls.	Cts.
				$	

I certify that the above abstract is correct.

A. B., *Quartermaster.*

NOTE.—This abstract contains all payments in the account current, except purchases (Abstract A) and transfers of funds.

No. 14.—(ABSTRACT B b.)

Abstract of Advances made to officers for disbursement, on account of the Quartermaster's Department, by ———, in the quarter ending the ———, 186 .

Date of the advance.	No. of the receipt or voucher.	To what officer.	By whose order, or for what purpose.	AMOUNT.	
				Dolls.	Cts.
				$	

Quartermaster's Department.——Forms.

No. 15.—(Voucher to Abstract B.)

We, the subscribers, do hereby acknowledge to have received of ———, Assistant Quartermaster U. S. Army at ———, the sums opposite to our names respectively, being in full of our pay for the period herein expressed, having signed duplicates hereof.

Date.	No.	Name.	Occupation.	Period of service.				Rate of pay.			Amount of pay.		Am't of stop'ges.		Amount received.		Signers' names.	Witnesses.	Remarks.
				From.	To.	Months.	Days.	Dollars.	Cents.	Per month or day.	Dollars.	Cents.	Dollars.	Cents.	Dollars.	Cents.			

I certify, that the above receipt-roll is correct and just.

A. B., *Quartermaster.*

No. 18.—(Voucher to Abstract B.)

The United States,

To ————.

Dr.

	Dollars.	Cents.
Date.		
From —— of —— to —— of ——		
For mileage from —— to ————, being ———— miles, at ———— cents per mile........		

I certify that the above account is correct and just; that I performed the journey, and under the order hereto annexed, and not returning from leave of absence to the station or troops I had left; that I have not been furnished with public transportation, nor received money in lieu thereof, for any part of the route.

Received, ————, 186 , of ————. ———— dollars and ———— cents in full of the above account.

(Signed duplicates.)

Quartermaster's Department.——Forms.

No. 17.—(VOUCHER TO ABSTRACT B.)

The United States,

To ———————.

Dr.

Date.		Dollars.	Cents.
	For expenses incurred for transportation of self and allowance of baggage, and porterage in traveling from ———— to ————, per annexed statement..................		
	$		

I certify that the above account is correct and just; that I have performed the journey, and on urgent public duty, without orders, for the purpose of ————, and necessarily incurred the expenses as stated; that I have traveled in the customary reasonable manner, and not returning from leave of absence to the station or troops I left; that I have not been furnished with public transportation, nor money in lieu thereof, for any part of the route. The approval of the journey by the proper authority is hereto annexed.

Received at ————, the ———— of ————, 186 , of ————, Assistant Quartermaster U. S. Army, ———— dollars and ———— cents, in full of the above account.

(Signed in duplicate.)

Dolls. $\frac{1}{100}$

Certificate in case of journey under orders.

I certify that this account is correct and just; that I performed the journey, and under the order hereto annexed, and necessarily incurred the expenses as stated: that I traveled in the customary reasonable manner; that I was not returning from leave of absence to the station or troops I had left; that I have not been furnished with public transportation, nor money in lieu thereof, for any part of the route.

No. 18.—(Voucher to Abstract B.)

The United States,   To ————,

Dr.

Date.		Dollars.	Cents.
	For mileage from ——— to ———, pursuant to annexed copy of Orders No. ———, convening (or annexed summons to attend) a court-martial at ———, distance being ——— miles, at ——— cents per mile.............. ——— days' attendance on said court-martial, being from the ——— of ——— to the ——— of ———, 186 , inclusive (per annexed certificate), at $———.............. ——— days' traveling on the ——— of ———, going to, and on the ——— of ———, return-ing from, the court, at $———..............		
		$	

I certify that the above account is correct and just; that I have actually performed the journeys therein charged for on the days stated, in obedience to the authority hereunto annexed; that I have not been furnished with public transportation, nor received money in lieu thereof, for any part of the route charged for.

Received at ———, the ——— of ———, 186 , of ———, Assistant Quartermaster U. S. Army, ——— dollars and ——— cents, in full of the above account.

(Signed in duplicate.)

Quartermaster's Department.——Forms.

No. 19.—(Voucher to Abstract B.)

Dr.

The United States, *To* —————,

Date.		Dollars.	Cents.
	For the actual expense of his transportation, while traveling under orders in the discharge of his duty as clerk to Major ————, Paymaster United States Army, from ———— to ————, per annexed statement...		

$

————, *Paymaster U. S. Army.*

I certify that ———— was, during the time above specified, employed as a clerk in the Pay Department, United States Army, and that the journeys charged for in the above account were performed by him in the discharge of his official duties, under my orders.

————————, *Paymaster U. S. Army.*

———— COUNTY, *ss.*

On this ———— day of ————, one thousand eight hundred and sixty ————, personally appeared before me, the subscriber, a justice of the peace in and for the county aforesaid, ————, and made oath in due form of law, that the above account is correct and just, and exhibits the actual expense of his transportation for and during the journey above specified.

(Subscribed in duplicate.)

————————, *Justice of the Peace.*

Received at ————, the ———— of ————, 186 , of ————, Assistant Quartermaster United States Army, ———— dollars and ———— cents, in full of the above account.

(Signed in duplicate.)

Dollars ——

Quartermaster's Department.——Forms.

No. 20.—(Voucher to Abstract B.)

The United States

To ——————.

Dr.

Date.		Dollars.	Cents.
	For cash paid for postage on letters and packages on public service, received and sent by him from the —— of ——, 186 , to the —— of ——, 186 , inclusive........		
		$	

I certify that the foregoing account is correct and just; that the letters and packages on which postage has been paid, as therein stated, were all on public service; that I have actually paid the amount charged.

E. F
——————, Assistant Quartermaster U. S. Army,

Received at ——, the —— of ——, 186 , of ——, Assistant Quartermaster U. S. Army, —— dollars and —— cents, in full of the above account.

E. F.

(Signed in duplicate.)

No. 21.—(VOUCHER TO ABSTRACT B.)

The United States,

    To ——— .

DR.

Date.		Dollars.	Cents.
	For commutation of quarters at ———, from the ——— of ———, 186 , to the ——— of ———, 186 , inclusive..............		
	For rooms, at ——— dollars each, per month.......		
	For commutation of fuel for the same period:		
	For myself, ——— cords ——— feet ——— inches, at ——— dollars per cord......		
	For my servant, ——— cords ——— feet ——— inches, at ——— dollars per cord......		
	$		

I certify that there were no quarters owned or hired by the public at the above station which could be assigned to ——— during the above period, and that the fuel is charged at the average market price for the month.

A. B., *Quartermaster.*

I certify that the above account is correct and just; that I have been regularly stationed on duty at ———, by ———, during the period charged for; that I have not been furnished with quarters, rent, or fuel by the public, nor received commutation of money in lieu thereof.

C. D

Received at ———, the ——— of ———, 186 , of ———, Quartermaster of the U. S. Army, ——— dollars and ——— cents, in full of the above account.

C. D.

(Signed in duplicate.)

NOTE.—The certificate must show by whose order the officer was stationed, and the first account to be accompanied by a copy of the order.

Quartermaster's Department.——Forms.

No. 22.—(Voucher.)

The United States,

To ————.

Dr.

Date.		Dollars.	Cents.

$

I certify that the above account is correct and just; that the services were rendered as stated, and that they were necessary for the public service.

A. B., Quartermaster.

Received ————, 186 , of ————, ———— dollars and ———— cents, in full of the above account.

E. F.

(Signed duplicates.)

NOTE.—This form will be used for miscellaneous disbursements, and will be entered in Abstract B or C, according to the nature of the expenditure.

No. 23.

QUARTERLY RETURN OF QUARTERMASTER'S STORES

received, issued, and remaining on hand at ————, *in the quarter ending on the* ———— *of* ————, 186 .

A. B., *Quartermaster.*

NOTE.

The property on this return (which does not include clothing, camp and garrison equipage) will be classed as follows :

1. Fuel.
2. Forage.
3. Straw.
4. Stationery.
5. Barrack, Hospital, and Office Furniture.
6. Means of Transportation, including Harness, &c.
7. Building Materials.
8. Veterinary Tools and Horse Medicines.
9. Blacksmiths' Tools.
10. Carpenters' Tools.
11. Wheelwrights' Tools.
12. Masons' and Bricklayers' Tools.
13. Miscellaneous Tools for Fatigue and Garrison Purposes.
14. Stores for Expenditure, such as Iron, Steel, Horse-Shoes, Rope, &c., &c., to be classed alphabetically.

Quartermaster's Department.——Forms.

No. 23.

Quarterly Return of Quartermaster's Stores, received and issued at by ——.

Classes			1. Fuel.				
			Wood.			Coal.	
Date.	Abstracts, &c.		Cords.	Feet.	Inches.	Anthracite.	Bituminous.
			No.	No.	No.	Lbs.	Bu.
Per last return.	On hand...........................						
Abstract D......	Received by purchase......						
" E......	" from officers....						
" N......	Fabricated, taken up, &c.						
	Total to be accounted for.................						
Per Abstract F..	Fuel...........................						
" G..	Forage...........................						
" H..	Straw...........................						
" I...	Stationery						
" K..	Special issues..............						
" L..	Expended, sold, &c..........						
" M.	Transferred.................						
	Total issued and·expended................						
	Total remaining on hand................						
Condition 1..............	In good order................						
" 2..............	Unfit for service, but repairable.....................						
" 3..............	Totally unfit for service...						

Quartermaster's Department.——Forms.

No. 23.

————, *in the quarter ending on the* ———— *of* ————, 186 , Continued.

2. Forage.				3. Straw.	4. Stationery.						
Corn.	Oats.	Hay.	Fodder.	For Bedding.	Foolscap Paper.	Letter Paper.	Folio Post Paper.	Envelope Paper.	Envelopes.	Two-quire blank-books.	Three-quire blk. books.
Lbs.	Lbs.	Lbs.	Lbs.	Pounds.	Qrs.	Qrs.	Qrs.	Qrs.	No.	No.	No.

No. 23.

Quarterly Return of Quartirmaster's Stores, received and issued ut

4. Stationery.

Abstracts, &c.	Four-quire blank-books.	Ink.	Ink-powder.	Wafers.	Sealing-wax.	Steel pens.	Quills.	Lead-pencils.	Office tape.	Inkstands.	Wafer-stamps.
	No.	Bottles.	Papers.	Ozs.	Ozs.	No.	Gross.	No.	Pieces.	No.	No.
O. H............											
D..............											
E..............											
N...............											
F.............											
G.............											
H											
I..............											
K.............											
L.............											
M											

Quartermaster's Department.——Forms.

No. 23.

———, *in the quarter ending on the* ——— *of* ———, 186 , *by* Continued.

4. Stationery.

Erasers.	Paper-folders.	Sand-boxes.	Wafer-boxes.											
No.	No.	No.	No.											

I certify that the foregoing return exhibits a true and correct statement of all the property which has come into my hands on account of the Quartermaster's Department dur'ng the quarter ending on the ——— of ———, 186 .

A. B., *Quartermaster.*

Quartermaster's Department.——Forms.

No. 24.—(Abstract D.)

Abstract of Articles purchased at ——, in the quarter ending on the —— of ——, 186 , by ——.

Date.	No. of voucher.	From whom purchased.	Amount.		Fuel.				Forage.	Straw.	Stationery.			
						Wood.		Coal.						
			Dolls.	Cts.	Cords.	Feet.	Ins.	Bu'ls.						
		Classes.................												
		Articles purchased and paid for......												
		Articles purchased and not paid for												
		Total purchased within the quarter												

I certify that the above abstract is correct.

A. B., *Quartermaster.*

Note.—This abstract appertains exclusively to the *Property Return,* and is designed to show all the supplies purchased by the Quartermaster, *whether paid for or not.* No vouchers of the purchases paid for accompany this abstract. They are in the second division of Abstract A. Purchases not paid for are vouched as in Form No. 25.

Quartermaster's Department.——Forms.

No. 25.—(Voucher to Abstract D.)

The United States,

To ——————,

Dr.

Date of purchase.		Dolls.	Cts.
	For —— cords of wood, at —— per cord........		
	For —— pounds of hay, at —— per 100 lbs........		

I certify that the above account is correct and just; that I purchased the articles above enumerated of the said ——, at the prices therein charged, amounting to —— dollars and —— cents, and that I have not paid the account. (Here state the cause of non-payment.)

A. B., Quartermaster.

Quartermaster's Department.——Forms.

No. 26.—(Abstract E.)

Abstract of Articles received from officers at ——, in the quarter ending on the —— of ——, 186 , by ——

Date.	No. of voucher.	Classes...............	From whom received.	Fuel. Wood. Cords.	Feet.	Inches.	Coal. Bushels.	Forage.	Straw.	Stationery.
		Total received...............								

I certify that the above abstract is correct.

A. B., Quartermaster.

Note.—All property received from other officers will be entered on this abstract, whether receipted for or not. For vouchers, see Form No. 27.

No. 27.—(VOUCHER TO ABSTRACT E.)

List of Quartermaster's Stores, &c., delivered by ——— to ——— , at ——— , on the ——— day of ——— , 186 .

Number or quantity.	Articles.	Cost when new.	Condition when delivered.	Remarks.
40	Forty......	Felling axes......	$1 00 each......	New...............
300	Three hundred pounds......	Bar iron, assorted.	6 per pound......	New...............
1,000	One thousand pounds......	Cut nails......	5 per pound......	New...............
656	Six hundred and fifty-six bushels......	Corn......	1 00 per bushel......	Good...............
30,500	Thirty thousand five hundred pounds......	Hay......	1 00 per hundred...	Good...............
10	Ten......	Wheelbarrows......	4 00 each...........	Half-worn......
5	Five......	Wagons (4-horse)...	150 00 each...........	Half-worn......
5	Five......	Wagons do........	150 00 each...........	New...............

I certify that I have this day delivered to A. B., Quartermaster United States Army, the articles specified in the foregoing list.

C. D., *Quartermaster.*

NOTE.—When no invoice is received, the receiving officer will substitute for this form of voucher a list of the stores received, certified by himself. When the person responsible for the property entered without invoice is known, it will be entered in his name.

Quartermaster's Department.——Forms.

No. 28.—(ABSTRACT F.)

Abstract of Fuel issued at ——, in the quarter ending on the —— of ——, 186 , by ——.

Date.	No. of voucher.	To whom issued.	For what period.	Wood.			Coal.		Remarks.
				Cords.	Feet.	Inches.	Pounds.	Bushels.	
		Total issued..........................							

I certify that the above abstract is correct.

A. B., *Quartermaster.*

NOTE.—For vouchers, see Forms No. 29 and No. 30. All fuel issued is entered on this abstract. Fuel transferred to other officers, to be accounted for by them, is entered on Abstract M.

Quartermaster's Department.——Forms.

No. 29.—(VOUCHER TO ABSTRACT F.)

Requisition for Fuel for —— Company, —— Regiment of ——, commanded by ——, for the month of ——, 186 .

Station.	Captains.	Subalterns.	Non-commissioned officers, musicians, and privates.	Laundresses and servants.	Total.	Monthly allowance to each, in cords.	TOTAL ALLOWANCE.						Remarks.
							Wood.			Coal.			
							Cords.	Feet.	Inches.	Bushels.	Pounds.		
Total													

I certify that the above requisition is correct and just, and that fuel has not been drawn for any part of the time above charged.

R. S., Commanding Company.

Received, ——, 186 , of ——, Assistant Quartermaster U. S. Army, —— cords —— feet —— inches of wood and —— of coal, in full of the above requisition.

(Signed duplicates.)

R. S., Commanding Company.

No. 30.—(Voucher to Abstract F.)

Requisition for Fuel for ——, stationed at ——, for the month of ——, 186 .

	Wood			Coal		Remarks.
	Cords.	Feet.	Inches.	Bushels.	Pounds.	
For myself............						
For private servant......						
Total........						

I certify that the above requisition is correct and just, and that I have not drawn fuel for any part of the time above charged.

Received, ——, 186 , of ——, Assistant Quartermaster United States Army, —— cords —— feet —— inches of wood and —— of coal, in full of the above requisition.

NOTE.—This form will be used for individual officers, hospitals, guards. &c.

Quartermaster's Department.——Forms.

No. 31.—(ABSTRACT G.)

Abstract of Forage issued at ———, in the quarter ending on the ——— of ———, 186 , by ———.

Date.	Number of voucher.	To whom issued.	For what period.		Number of horses.	Number of mules.	Number of oxen.	Total.	Total allowance.						Remarks.
			From —	To —					Corn.		Oats.		Hay.	Fodder.	Public. Private.
									Bushels, (56 lbs.)	Pounds.	Bushels, (32 lbs.)	Pounds.	Pounds.	Pounds.	
		Total............													

I certify that the above abstract is correct.

A. B., *Quartermaster.*

NOTE.—For vouchers, see Forms Nos. 32, 33, 34. All forage issued will be entered on this abstract. Forage transferred to other officers, to be accounted for by them, will be entered on Abstract M.

Quartermaster's Department.——Forms.

No. 32.—(Voucher to Abstract G.)

Requisition for Forage for Public Horses, Mules, and Oxen, in the service of —— for —— days, commencing the —— of ——, 186 , and ending on the —— of ——, 186 , at ——.

Date of requisition.	Number of horses.	Number of mules.	Number of oxen.	Total number of animals.	Number of days.	Number of rations.	Daily allowance to each animal.					Total allowance.					Remarks.
							Pounds of corn.	Pounds of barley.	Pounds of oats.	Pounds of hay.	Pounds of fodder.	Corn. Pounds of.	Barley. Pounds of.	Oats. Pounds of.	Hay. Pounds of.	Fodder. Pounds of.	

Required...............

On hand, to be deducted...............

To be supplied...............

I certify that the above requisition is correct and just; that I have now in service the number of animals for which forage is required; and that forage has not been received for any part of the time specified.

Received at ——, on the —— day of ——, 186 , of ——, Quartermaster United States Army, —— pounds of corn, —— pounds of barley, —— pounds of oats, —— pounds of hay, —— pounds of fodder, in full of the above requisition.

(Signed duplicates.)

Quartermaster's Department.——Forms.

No. 33.—(VOUCHER TO ABSTRACT G.)

Requisition for Forage for —— Private Horses in the service of ——, U. S. Army, at ——, for —— days, commencing the —— of ——, and ending the —— of ——, 186 .

Date.	Period.		Number of horses.	Daily allowance for each.			Total allowance.						Remarks.
	From.	To.		Corn. Pounds.	Oats. Pounds.	Hay. Pounds.	Corn. Bushels, (56 lbs.)	Corn. Pounds.	Oats. Bushels, (32 lbs.)	Oats. Pounds.	Hay. Pounds.	Fodder. Pounds.	
Total..........													

I certify that the above requisition is correct and just, and that I have not drawn forage for any part of the time above charged.

Received at ——, the —— of ——, 186 , of ——, Assistant Quartermaster U. S. Army, —— $\frac{5}{6}$ bushels corn, —— $\frac{3}{2}$ bushels oats, —— pounds hay, —— pounds fodder, in full of the above requisition.

(Signed duplicates.)

Quartermaster's Department --——Forms.

No. 34.—(Voucher to Abstract G.)

Statement of Forage issued to and consumed by the Public Animals under my direction at ——, during the month of ——, 186 .

| Period. | | | Number of animals. | | | | Quantity of, consumed. | | | | | Remarks. |
From.	To.	No. of days.	Horses.	Mules.	Oxen.	Total.	Corn. Pounds.	Oats. Pounds.	Barley. Pounds.	Hay. Pounds.	Fodder. Pounds.	

Total.... ....

I certify that the above statement is correct ; that the forage was issued to the Public Animals as stated, and that the issues were necessary.

Approved :

         R. S., *Commanding.*

         A. B., *Quartermaster.*

Quartermaster's Department.——Forms.

No. 35.—(Abstract H.)

Abstract of Straw issued at ———, in the quarter ending on the ——— of ———, 18 , by ———.

Date.	No. of voucher	To whom issued.	For what period.		Non-commissioned officers, musicians, and privates.	Laundresses.	Servants.	Hospital.	Total allowance.	Remarks.
			From—	To —					Pounds.	
		Total..								

I certify that the above abstract is correct.

A. B., *Quartermaster.*

Note.—For voucher, see Form No. 36.   Issues on this abstract.   Transfers on Abstract M.

No. 36.—(VOUCHER TO ABSTRACT H.)

Requisition for Straw for — Company, — Regiment of —, commanded by —, for the month of ——, 18 .

Station.	Non-commissioned officers, musicians, and privates.	Laundresses.	Servants.	Total drawn for.	Monthly allowance to each.		Total allowance.		Remarks.
					Pounds.		Pounds.		
Total......									

I certify that the above return is correct and just, and that straw has not been drawn for any part of the time charged.

G. H., *Commanding Company.*

Received at ——, the —— of ——, 18 , of ——, U. S. Army, —— pounds of straw, in full of the above requisition.

G. H., *Commanding Company.*

(Signed duplicates.)

Quartermaster's Department.——Forms.

No. 37.—(Abstract I.)

Abstract of Stationery issued at ——, in the quarter ending on the —— of ——, 186 , by ——.

Date.	No. of voucher.	To whom issued.	For what period.		Writing-paper, quires.	Cartridge paper, sheets.	Quills, number.	Wafers, ounces.	Sealing-wax, ounces.	Ink-powder, papers.	Blank-books, number.			Remarks.
			From.	To.										
Total.............														

I certify that the above abstract is correct.

A. B., *Quartermaster.*

NOTE.—For voucher, see Form No. 38. The stationery used by the Quartermaster in the public service is entered on this abstract, and all issues by him. Transfers on Abstract M

No. 38.—(Voucher to Abstract I.)

Requisition for Stationery for ——, stationed at ——, for the ——, commencing on the —— of ——, and ending on the —— of ——, 186 .

Quires of letter-paper.	Quires of foolscap paper.	Sheets of cartridge paper.	Number of quills.	Ounces of wafers.	Ounces of sealing-wax.	Pieces of tape.	Papers of ink-powder.						

I certify that the above requisition is correct, and that I have not drawn stationery for any part of the time specified.

Received at ——, on the —— of ——, 186 , of ——, Assistant Quartermaster U. S. Army, —— quires of letter-paper, —— quires of foolscap paper, —— quills, —— ounces of wafers, —— ounces of sealing-wax, —— pieces of tape, —— sheets of cartridge paper, —— papers of ink-powder.

(Signed duplicates.)

Quartermaster's Department.——Forms.

No. 39.—(Abstract K.—For all issues except Fuel, Forage, Straw, and Stationery.)

Abstract of Articles issued on Special Requisitions at ——, in the quarter ending on the —— of ——, 18 , ōy ——.

Date.	To whom issued.	Classes				

Total.........................

I certify that the above abstract is correct.

A. B., Quartermaster.

Note.—For voucher, see Form No. 40.   Transfers on Abstract M.

No 40.—(Voucher to Abstract K.)

SPECIAL REQUISITION.

For

I certify that the above requisition is correct, and that the articles specified are absolutely requisite for the public service, rendered so by the following circumstances: [here the officer will insert such reasons as he may think fit to give, tending to show the necessity for the supplies.]

Captain J. B, Assistant Quartermaster United States Army, will issue the articles specified in the above requisition.

C. D., *Commanding.*

Received at ———, the ——— of ———, 18—, of ———, Assistant Quartermaster United States Army ⌜here insert the articles⌝ in full of the above requisition.

(Signed duplicates.)

NOTE.—The cost of articles issued on special requisitions, and orders of commanding officers, will be entered on the requisition and on the list or invoice furnished the receiving officer.

Quartermaster's Department.——Forms.

No. 41.—(ABSTRACT L.)

Abstract of Articles Expended, Lost, Destroyed, in the public service, sold, &c., at ——, under the direction of ——, in the quarter ending on the —— of ——, 186 .

Classes............

By whom made.

No. of Certificate.

Date.

Total............

I certify that the above abstract is correct.

A. B., Quartermaster.

Quartermaster's Department.——Forms.

No. 42.—(VOUCHER TO ABSTRACT L.)

List of Quartermaster's Stores expended in public service at ——— under the direction of ——— , in the month of ——— , 186 .

No. or quantity.	Articles.	Application.

I certify that the several articles of Quartermaster's stores, above enumerated, have been necessarily expended in the public service, at this station, as indicated by the marginal remarks annexed to them respectively.

(Signed duplicates.)

A. B., *Quartermaster.*

Approved: R. S., *Commanding.*

NOTE.—This list should be made out monthly, to enable the Quartermaster to know the exact state of his supplies.

Quartermaster's Department.——Forms.

No. 43.—(Voucher to Abstract L.)

List of Articles Lost or Destroyed in the public service at ———, while in the possession and charge of ———, in the month of ———, 186 .

No. or quantity.	Articles.	Circumstances and cause.

I certify that the several articles of Quartermaster's stores, above enumerated, have been unavoidably lost or destroyed while in the public service, as indicated by the remarks annexed to them respectively.

A. B., *Quartermaster.*

Approved : C. D., *Commanding*

No. 44.—(Voucher to Abstract L.)

Account Sales of articles of public property sold at public auction at ——, *under the direction of* ——, *on the* —— *of* ——, 186 .

Number or quantity.	Articles.	Purchaser.	Amount.
			$

I certify that the above account sales is accurate and just.

A. B., *Auctioneer.*

I certify that the above enumerated articles were sold at public auction as above stated, pursuant to—[state the orders or authority.]

C. D., *Quartermaster*

Quartermaster's Department.——Forms.

No. 45.—(ABSTRACT M.)

Abstract of Articles transferred to ———, at ———, in the quarter ending on the ——— of ———, 18 , by ———.

Classes............	No. of voucher.	Date.	To whom transferred.					
Total.........								

I certify that the above abstract is correct.

A. B., *Quartermaster.*

NOTE.—This abstract contains all transfers of stores to other officers, to be accounted for by them; the vouchers will be their receipts. When these are not received in time, the Quartermaster will substitute his own certified list of the stores sent, and the bill of lading. The receipts he will afterward transmit when he receives them.

No. 45.—(Abstract N.)

Abstract of Articles received from various sources at ——, during the quarter ending the —— day of ——, 18 .

Date.	No. of invoice, &c.	From whence received.	Classes	Fuel — Wood. Cords.	Fuel — Wood. Feet.	Fuel — Wood. Inches.	Fuel — Coal.	Forage — Corn. Bushels. (56 lbs.)	Forage — Oats. Bushels. (32 lbs.)	Forage — Hay. Pounds.	Straw. Pounds.	Stationery.
		Found at the post										
		Manufactured										
		Parts of articles broken up										
		Heretofore issued, but not consumed										
		Captured from the enemy										
		Total										

I certify that the above abstract is correct.

A. B., *Quartermaster.*

NOTE.—This abstract contains all Quartermaster's property found at the post, not borne on the previous return ; all that may come to the Quartermaster's possession without his knowing who may be accountable for it ; articles manufactured in the quarter ; material or parts of articles that have been condemned or broken up ; fuel and forage issued but not consumed, &c., &c., &c. Separate lists of each class, with the necessary explanation, will be filed with the abstract.

No. 46.

Quarterly Statement of Allowances paid to Officers of the Army in Money,
the quarter end-

Officers' names.	Rank and Corps. (Rank being that for which they were paid, or allowances furnished.)	For Fuel.		Quarters.				
		Period.	Am't. $ c.	In money.		In kind.		
				Period.	$ c.	Period.	No. Rooms.
		1861.		1861.		1861.	
W. S....	Maj. Genl.....	July, Aug., Sep..	96 00	July, Aug., Sep..	120 00	....	...
J. T.....	Brig. Genl....	July.................	30 00	July, Aug., Sep..	80 00	....	...
K. J....	Col. Ajt. Gl..	August...............	30 00	July, Aug., Sep..	90 00	....	...
T. M...	Col. Q.M. D..	August..............	30 00	July, Aug., Sep..	80 00	....	...
T. L....	Maj. Pay Dt.	July, Aug., Sep..	30 00	Aug., Sep..........	80 00	July.........	3
L. B....	Col. Engrs...	July, Aug., Sep..	30 00	....	80 00	....	...
B. L....	Mj. T. Engs..	....	......	....	....	....	...
B.B. M.	Col. Drags....	....	......	....	....	July, Aug..	4
J. C.....	Col. Art.......	July, Aug..........	20 00	....	....	July, Aug..	4
F. E....	Maj. Infty....	July, Aug..........	12 00	....	....	July, Aug..	4

Quartermaster's Department.——Forms.

No. 46.

or furnished in kind, with the money value thereof, by ———, at———, in ing ———, 186 .

Rent.	For transportation of baggage.	Per diem on court-martial.	For forage issued in kind.	Straw for servants.	Stationery.	Total amount.	Abstract and voucher.	Remarks.
$ c	$ c.	$ c.	$ c.	$ c.	$ c.	$ c.		
....	120 00	40 00	....	....	20 00	396 00	B 1, 7, 9—I 9..	
....	90 00	....	....	....	15 00	215 00	B 2, 11, 14—I 4.	
....	....	....	....	....	....	120 00	B 17.............	
....	....	....	....	....	....	110 00	B 21.............	
30 00	60 00	....	30 00	....	....	230 00	B 4, 20—G 13.	
....	....	....	....	....	....	130 00	B 19.............	
....	100 00	....	....	....	....	110 00	B 26, 27.........	
30 00	30 00	40 00	37 50	2 00	....	139 50	B 27, 30—G 14.	
35 00	70 00	....	....	1 50	....	126 50	B 28, 32—H 2.	
....	....	....	....	50	....	12 50	F 4—H 6........	Public quarters.

I certify that the above is correct.

A. B., *Quartermaster.*

NOTE.—When officers occupy quarters owned by the public, the number of rooms only will be reported.

No. 47.

The United States in account current with ——; for expenditures on account of Contingencies of the Army, and of other Departments, in the quarter ending on the —— of —— 186 .

DR.

Date.		Dolls.	Cts.
Sept. 30.	To amount of expenditures, per Abstract C.		
Sept. 30.	To balance due the United States, carried to new account..................		
		$	

CR.

Date.		Dolls.	Cts.
July 1.	By balance on hand, as per last account..		
July 8.	By cash received of ——............		
Aug. 4.	By cash received from the Treasurer of the United States, being amount of Warrant No. ——.............		
		$	

I certify that the above exhibits a true account of all moneys which have come into my hands on account of contingencies of the army, during the quarter ending on the —— of ——, 18—, and that the disbursements have been faithfully made.

A. B., *Quartermaster.*

Quartermaster's Department.——Forms.

No. 48.—(Abstract C.)

" Abstract of Disbursements on account of Contingencies of the Army, and of other departments, by ——, in the quarter ending on the —— of ——, 186 , at ——.

Date of payment.	No. of voucher.	To whom paid.	On what account.	Amount.	
				Dollars.	Cents.
				$	

A. B., Quartermaster.

Note.—For vouchers, see Forms 49, 50 All payments for apprehending deserters must also be entered in this Abstract.

No. 49.—(Voucher to Abstract C.)

Requisition on the Quartermaster's Department for extra Supplies of Medicines and Hospital Stores.

I certify that the medicines and hospital stores above required are necessary for the use of the sick at this post, in consequence [here insert whether from loss, damage, &c.], and that the requisition is agreeable to the supply table.

A. B., *Assistant Surgeon.*

Approved.

C. D., *Commanding Officer.*

Received of ———, on the ——— of ———, 186—, the articles above enumerated.

(Signed duplicates.)

A. B., *Assistant Surgeon.*

Quartermaster's Department.——Forms.

No. 50.—(Voucher to Abstract C.)

Bill of Medicine, &c., when purchased by an officer of the Quartermaster's Department

The United States,   *To* ——————.

Dr.

Date of purchase.	For	Dollars.	Cents.

$

I certify that the prices of the articles above charged, for the use of the sick at ——, agreeable to the foregoing requisition, are reasonable and just.

A. B., *Surgeon.*

Received, ——, 186 , of ——, —— dollars and —— cents, in full of the above account.

E. F.

(Signed duplicates.)

Note.—The above certificate may be signed by the surgeon making the requisition, or by any surgeon or assistant surgeon belonging to the army. The requisition on which the purchase may be made must be attached to the bill of purchase, which will be entered in Abstract C, and the articles not noticed in the property returns.

Quartermaster's Department.——Forms.

No. 51.

Quarterly Return of Clothing, Camp, and Garrison Equipage of ——, 186 ,

WHEN RECEIVED.	No. of invoice.	OF WHOM RECEIVED.	Cavalry hats.	Caps and bands.	Cap-letters, castle, shell and flame.	Cap-covers.	POMPONS Color.	
		On hand per last return						
Total to be accounted for........................								

WHEN ISSUED.	No. of roll.	TO WHOM ISSUED.						
Total issued..								
On hand to be accounted for........								

Quartermaster's Department.——Forms.

No. 51.

received and issued at —— , *in the quarter ending on the* —— *day*
by —— .

CLOTHING.

Eagle and rings.	Plumes for cavalry.	COATS.									METALLIC SEALS.			Sashes.	UNIFORM JACKETS.		
		Sergeant-majors'.	Quartermaster-sergeants'.	Ordnance sergeants'.	Chief musicians'.	First sergeants'.	Sergeants'.	Corporals'.	Musicians'.	Privates'.	Non-commissioned staff.	Sergeants'.	Corporals' and privates'.		Sergeant-majors'.	Quartermaster-sergeants'.	First sergeants'.

Quartermaster'ℓ Department.——Forms.

No. 51.

Quarterly Return of Clothing, Camp and Garrison

CLOTHING.

UNIFORM JACKETS.			Trowsers.	Yards of binding.		Flannel shirts.	Drawers, pairs of.	Boots, cavalry, pairs of.	Boots, infantry, pairs of.	Stockings, pairs of.	Leather stocks.	Great-coats.	Great-coat straps, number of.	Talmas.	Blankets.	Knapsacks and straps.	Haversacks.
Sergeants'.	Corporals'.	Privates'.															

No. 51.

Equipage, received and issued, &c.—Continued.

EQUIPAGE.

Canteens and straps.		BED-SACKS.		Axes.	Axe-helves.	Spades.	Camp kettles.	Mess pans.	Camp hatchets.	Hatchet handles.	Garrison flag.	Garrison flag halliards,	Storm flag.	Recruiting flags.	Recruiting flag halliards.	Camp colors.	Guidons.
		Single.	Double.														

Quartermaster's Department.——Forms.

No. 51.

Quarterly Return of Clothing, Camp and Gar

EQUIPAGE.

Trumpets.	Bugles, with extra mouth-pieces.	Fifes.	DRUMS.								Wall-tents.	Wall-tent flies.	Wall-tent poles and pins, sets.	Common tents.	Common-tent poles and pins, sets.	Iron pots.	Pickaxes.
			Complete.	Heads, batter.	Heads, snare.	Slings.	Sticks, pairs.	Drum-stick carriages.	Cords.	Snares, sets.							

Quartermaster's Department.——Forms.

No. 51.

rison Equipage, received and issued, &c.—Continued.

	BOOKS AND BLANKS.						
Pickaxe-handles.	Clothing account-book.	Descriptive book.	Order-book.	Clothing returns.	Receipt-rolls.	Final statements.	

Quartermaster's Department.——Forms.

No. 52.

We, the undersigned Non-commissioned Officers, Artificers, Musicians, and
several articles of Clothing set

Date of the issue.	Name and designation of the soldier.	Caps.	Cap-covers.	Pompons.	Eagles and rings.	N. C. S.	UNIFORM COATS.				UNIFORM JACKETS.			
							Sergeants'	Corporals'	Musicians'	Privates'	Sergeants'	Corporals'	Musicians'	Privates'

NOTES.——Erasures and alterations of entries are prohibited.

Regular and extra issues will be distinguished on the receipt-roll.

Each signature, whether written by the soldier or acknowledged *by mark*, must be witnessed.

Vacant space will be filled by a cipher.

Mounted men may receive *one* pair of "boots" and *two* pairs of "bootees," instead of *four* pairs of bootees.

Quartermaster's Department.——Forms.

No. 52.—Continued.

Privates of ———, do hereby acknowledge to have received of ——— the opposite our respective names.

Trowsers, pairs.	Flannel shirts.	Drawers, pairs.	Boots, cavalry, pair.	Bootees, infantry, pairs.	Stockings, pairs.	Leather stocks.	Great-coats.	Fatigue overalls.	Stable-frocks.	Blankets.							Signatures.	Witness.

As the metallic shoulder-scales, letters, numbers, castles, and shells and flames will last for many years, they will be borne on the returns as company property, in the same manner as are sashes, knapsacks and straps, haversacks, canteens and straps, and other articles of camp and garrison equipage, and will be charged to the soldier only when lost or destroyed through neglect.

Quartermaster's Department.——Forms.

No. 53.

Descriptive List of Persons and Articles employed and hired in the Quartermaster's Department, and transferred by ———, at ———, to ———, Quartermaster at ———, on the ——— day of ———, 186–.

Number of each class.	Articles and names of persons.	Designation and occupation.	Period for which pay is due.				Rate of hire or compensation.			Amount due.		Date of contract, agreement, or entry into service.	By whom owned, and where.	Remarks.
			From—	To—	Month.	Days.	Dollars.	Cents.	Month, day, or voyage.	Dollars.	Cents.			

Total amount due ....

I certify that the above is a true list of persons and articles transferred by me to ——— at ———, on the ——— day of ———, 186–; and that the periods of service, rates of hire or compensation, and amounts due, are correctly stated.

ARTICLE XLIII.

SUBSISTENCE DEPARTMENT.

SUPPLIES.

1176. Subsistence stores for the army, unless in particular and urgent cases the Secretary of War shall otherwise direct, shall be procured by contract, to be made by the Commissary-General on public notice, to be delivered on inspection in the bulk, and at such places as shall be stipulated; the inspector to give duplicate inspection certificates (see Form 15), and to be a legal inspector where there is such officer.

1177. Purchases, to supply such corps and posts as by reason of their position, the climate, or for other sufficient cause the Secretary of War may specially direct to be supplied in that way, will be made in open market, on public notice, from the lowest bidder who produces the proper article.

1178. And whenever a deficiency of subsistence stores makes it necessary to buy them, the commissary, where they are needed, will make a requisition for that purpose on the proper purchasing commissary, or buy them himself of good quality corresponding with the contract.

1179. When subsistence is received under contract, the commissary will receipt for it on the inspection certificates (see Form 15). He will deliver one of these to the contractor, and forward the other to the Commissary-General, with a report on the quality of the provisions and the condition of the packages.

1180. Whenever subsistence stores are purchased, the advertisements and bids, and a copy of the bill of purchase, with a statement of the cause of purchase, will be forwarded by the purchasing officer to the Commissary-General. This rule does not apply to the ordinary purchase of hospital supplies. Pork, salt beef, and flour must be inspected before purchase by a legal inspector where there is such officer. Duplicate certificates of inspection (see Form 15) will be taken as sub-vouchers to the vouchers for the payment.

1181. Fresh beef, when it can be procured, shall be furnished as often as the commanding officer may order, at least twice a week: to be procured by the commissary, when practicable, by contract. (For form of contract and bond, see Forms 20 and 21.) When it can be provided at not more than six and a quarter cents per pound, net weight, or at not more than an equivalent proportion of salt pork, it will be issued to the troops five times per week. When beef is taken on the hoof, it will be accounted for on the provision return by the number of cattle and their estimated weight. When the pasture is insufficient, hay, corn, and other forage will be procured for public cattle.

1182. When circumstances are favorable, and it can be done with advantage to the government, the Subsistence Department will keep beef cattle to supply the issues.

1183. Good and sufficient store-room for the subsistence stores will be procured by the commissary from the quartermaster. Care shall be taken to keep the store-rooms dry and ventilated. Packages shall be so stored as to allow circulation of air among and beneath them. The flour should occasionally be rolled out into the air.

1184. Before submitting damaged commissary stores to boards of survey, the commissary shall separate and repack sound parts.

1185. Wastage on issues, or from evaporation or leakage, will be ascertained quarterly, or when it can be, most conveniently; and the actual wastage thus found will be charged on the monthly return. Loss, from whatever cause, exceeding ordinary waste, must be accounted for by the certificate of an officer, or other satisfactory evidence. Ordinary waste on issues should not exceed, say 3 per cent. on pork, bacon, sugar, vinegar, and soap; and 1 per cent. on hard bread, beans, rice, coffee, and salt.

1186. No wastage is admitted on issues of fresh beef furnished the company, detachment, or regiment directly from the butcher. But in beef on the hoof, errors in estimated weight, and losses on cattle strayed, stolen, or which have died, will be accounted for by the certificate of an officer, or other satisfactory evidence. When cattle are transferred, they should be appraised, and loss in weight reported as wastage by the officer delivering them. Fair wastage in transportation of stores is accounted for by the receiving officer.

1187. When practicable, cattle presented for acceptance must be weighed upon the scales. From the live weight of a steer, thus ascertained, his net weight shall be determined by deducting forty-five per centum when his gross weight exceeds thirteen hundred (1300) pounds, and fifty per centum when it is less than that and not under eight hundred (800) pounds.

1188. When it is impracticable to weigh upon the scales, one or more *average* steers must be selected, killed, and dressed in the usual manner. The average net weight of these (necks and shanks excluded) will be accepted as the average net weight of the herd.

1189. In all written instruments for the delivery of cattle on the hoof, the manner prescribed above for ascertaining net weight must, in express terms, be inserted; in verbal agreements, it must be understood and accepted by the party delivering the cattle.

1190. Vouchers for the payment of cattle will state the method observed in determining their net weight, except where payment is made on the certificate of an officer, when it must be stated in the certificate.

THE RATION.

1191. The ration is three-fourths of a pound of pork or bacon, or one and a fourth pound of fresh or salt beef; eighteen ounces of bread or flour, or twelve ounces of hard bread, or one and a fourth pound corn meal; and at the rate, to one hundred rations, of eight quarts of beans, or, in lieu thereof, ten pounds of rice, or, in lieu thereof, twice per week, one hundred and fifty ounces of desiccated potatoes, and one hundred ounces of mixed vegetables; ten pounds of coffee, or, in lieu thereof, one and one-half pound of tea; fifteen pounds of sugar; four quarts of vinegar; one pound of sperm candles, or one and one-fourth pound of adamantine candles, or one and one-half pound of tallow candles; four pounds of soap, and two quarts of salt.

1192. The table on page 280 shows the quantity of each part of the ration in any number of rations from one to one hundred thousand.

1193. On a campaign, or on marches, or on board of transports, the ration of hard bread is one pound.*

ISSUES.

1194. Returns for issues to companies will, when practicable, be consolidated for the post or regiment (see Form 14). At the end of the month the issuing commissary will make duplicate abstracts of the issues, which the commanding officer will compare with the original returns, and certify (see Form 2). This abstract is a voucher of the issue for the monthly return.

1195. Issues to the hospital will be on returns by the medical officer, for such provisions only as are actually required for the sick and the attendants. The cost of such parts of the ration as are issued will be charged to the hospital at contract or cost prices, and the hospital will be credited by the whole number of complete rations due through the month at contract or cost prices (see note 7, page 248); the balance, constituting the *Hospital Fund,* or any portion of it, may be expended by the commissary, on the requisition of the medical officer, in the purchase of any article for the subsistence or comfort of the sick, not authorized to be otherwise

---

* During the rebellion in the Southern States the ration is to be increased as follows : Twenty-two ounces of bread or flour, or one pound of hard bread, instead of the present issue; fresh beef shall be issued as often as the commanding officer of any detachment or regiment shall require it, when practicable, in place of salt meat; beans and rice shall be issued in the same ration in the proportions now provided by the regulation, and one pound of potatoes per man shall be issued at least three times a week, if practicable; and when these articles cannot be issued in these proportions, an equivalent in value shall be issued in some other proper food, and a ration of tea may be substituted for a ration of coffee upon the requisition of the proper officer.

Subsistence Department.——Issues.

furnished (see Form 3). At large depôts or general hospitals, this fund may be partly expended for the benefit of dependent posts or detachments, on requisitions approved by the medical director or senior surgeon of the district. On the 1st of January, each year, one-fourth of every hospital fund, if less than $150, and one-half, if more, will be dropped by the commissary from the fund (Form 3), and will be paid over to the treasurer of the Soldiers' Home by the Commissary-General.

1196. The articles purchased for the hospital, as well as those issued from the subsistence store-house, will be included in the surgeon's certificate of issues to the hospital, and borne on the monthly return of provisions received and issued. Vouchers for purchases for the hospital must either be certified by the surgeon or accompanied by his requisition.

1197. There may be allowed in hospitals, to be provided under such rules as the Surgeon-General of the army, with the approval of the Secretary of War, may prescribe, such quantities of fresh or preserved fruits, milk or butter, and of eggs, as may be necessary for the proper diet of the sick.

1198. Abstracts of the issues to the hospital will be made by the commissary, certified by the surgeon, and countersigned by the commanding officer (see Form 3).

1199. In order that the authorized women of companies may draw their rations while temporarily separated from their companies, the officer commanding the company must make a report to the commanding officer of the post where the women may be left, designating such as are to draw rations as attached to his company. Their rations are not commuted, and they can only draw them at a military post or station where there are supplies.

1200. When provisions can be spared from the military supplies, commanding officers have discretion to order issues to Indians visiting military posts on the frontiers, or in their respective nations, and to order sales of subsistence to Indian agents for issues to Indians. The returns for issues, where there is no Indian agent, will be signed by the commanding officer. The sales will be for cash, at cost, including all expenses; to be entered on the monthly return, and credited on the quarterly account current.

1201. Issues to *volunteers* and *militia*, to *sailors*, to *marines*, to *citizens* employed by any of the departments, or to *Indians*, will be entered on separate abstracts to the monthly return.

1202. An issue (extra) of ten pounds of sperm candles, or twelve pounds of adamantine candles, or fifteen pounds of tallow candles per month, may be made to the principal guard of each camp or garrison, on the order of the commanding officer, and salt, in small quantities, may be issued to public cattle. Occasional issues (extra) of molasses are made of two quarts to one hundred rations. (One gill of whisky is allowed daily, in case of excessive fatigue and exposure.) Troops at sea are recommended to draw rice in lieu of beans. Fresh vegetables (potatoes, onions, &c.), pickles, krout, and dried fruits, can only be purchased and paid for out of the hospital fund and issued to the sick.

1203. When men leave their company, the rations they have drawn, and left with it, will be deducted from the next return for the company; a like rule, when men are discharged from the hospital, will govern the hospital return.

RECRUITING SERVICE.

1204. When subsistence cannot be issued by the Commissariat to recruiting parties, it will be procured by the officer in charge, on written contracts for complete rations, or wholesome board and lodging. (See Form 19.)

1205. The contractor will send monthly or quarterly, as he may choose, his account for rations issued, to the Commissary-General for payment, vouched by the abstract of issues (Form 17) certified by the officer.

1206. When convenience and economy require that the contract shall be for board and lodging, the officer in charge shall estimate the cost of the ration, for which the contractor shall be paid as before directed, and shall pay the amount due to lodging from the recruiting fund.

1207. At temporary rendezvous, advertising may be dispensed with, and a contract made, conditioned to be terminated at the pleasure of the officer or the Commissary-General.

1208. The recruiting officer will be required, when convenient, to receive and disburse the funds for the subsistence of his party, and to render his accounts quarterly to the Commissary-General.

1209. When a contract cannot be made, the recruiting officer may pay the necessary expenses of subsisting and boarding his party.

1210. The expenses of subsistence at branch rendezvous, and all expenses of advertising for proposals, will be paid by the contractor at the principal station, and included in his accounts.

1211. Issues of provisions will be made on the usual provision returns, and board will be furnished on a return showing the number of the party, the days, and dates.

1212. A ration in kind may be allowed to one laundress at each principal rendezvous.

SUBSISTENCE TO OFFICERS.

1213. An officer may draw subsistence stores, paying cash for them at contract or cost prices, without including cost of transportation, on his certificate that they are for his own use and the use of his family. Commanding officers of companies may, in the same way, when authorized by the post commander, purchase subsistence stores for their company mess. These certified lists the commanding officer shall compare with the monthly abstracts of sales, which he shall countersign (see Form 5).

The commissary will enter the sales on his monthly return, and credit the money in his quarterly account current.

1214. When savings on company rations cannot otherwise be disposed of, the commissary is authorized to deduct their amount from the next ssue and pay their value into the company fund.

BACK RATIONS.

1215. When the supplies warrant it, back rations may be drawn, if the full rations could not have been issued at the time. The return for back rations shall set out the facts, and the precise time when rations were not issued.

COMMUTATION OF RATIONS.

1216. When a soldier is detached on duty, and it is impracticable to carry his subsistence with him, it will be commuted at seventy-five cents a day, to be paid by the commissary when due, or in advance, on the order of the commanding officer. The officer detaching the soldier will certify, on the voucher, that it is impracticable for him to carry his rations; and the voucher will show on its face the nature and extent of the duty the soldier was ordered to perform.   (See Form 18.)

1217. The expenses of a soldier placed temporarily in a private hospital, on the advice of the senior surgeon of the post or detachment, sanctioned by the commanding officer, will be paid by the Subsistence Department, not to exceed seventy-five cents a day.

1218. The ration of a soldier stationed in a city, with no opportunity of messing, will be commuted at seventy-five cents.   The rations of the non-commissioned regimental staff, when they have no opportunity of messing, and of soldiers on furlough, or stationed where rations cannot be issued in kind, may be commuted at the cost or value of the ration at the post.

1219. The ration of an Ordnance Sergeant may be commuted at thirty cents, except when serving with troops, or on furlough, when it may be commuted at cost at his post (exclusive of transportation).

1220. When a soldier on duty has necessarily paid for his own subsistence, he may be refunded the cost of the ration.   When more than the cost of the ration is claimed, the account must be submitted to the Commissary-General.

EXTRA-DUTY MEN.

1221. The commanding officer will detail a suitable non-commissioned officer or soldier for extra duty, under the orders of the commissary, and to be exempt from ordinary company and garrison duty.   All extra-duty men employed in the Commissariat will be paid the regulated allowance (see General Regulations) by the commissary.

1222. Barrels, boxes, hides, &c., will be sold, and the proceeds credited in the quarterly account current.

ACCOUNTS.

1223. The following are the accounts and returns required in the Subsistence Department:

Monthly.

Return of provisions and forage received and issued in the month	Form	1
Abstracts of issues to troops, &c. (see par. 1201)	"	2
Abstract of issues to hospital	"	3
Abstract of extra issues	"	4
Abstract of sales to officers	"	5
Distinct abstracts of other sales.		
Summary statement of money received and expended during the month	"	6

Quarterly.

Account current	"	7
Abstract of all purchases of provisions and forage during the quarter	"	8
Abstract of all expenditures in the quarter, except for purchase of provisions and forage	"	9
Consolidated abstract of sales to officers during the quarter	"	10
Distinct abstracts of other sales.		
Estimate of funds required for next quarter	"	11
Quarterly return of all property in the department, except provisions and forage for cattle	"	12

1224. The abstracts of issues will show the corps or detachment. When abstracts require more than one sheet, the sheets will be numbered in series, and not pasted together; the total at the foot of each carried to the head of the next, &c. All quarterly account currents, monthly summary statements, abstracts, property returns, &c., with the vouchers relating thereto, must be folded (in three parts for letter-paper) and fully endorsed.

1225. All lists of subsistence shall run in this order: meat, breadstuff, rice and beans, coffee, tea, sugar, vinegar, candles, soap, salt, desiccated potatoes, mixed vegetables, whisky, molasses, forage, purchases for hospital.

1226. No charge for printing blanks, as forms, will be allowed.

1227. A book will be kept by the commissary at each post, in which will be entered the monthly returns of provisions received and issued (Form 1). It will show from whom the purchases have been made, and whether paid for. It is called the Commissary's book, and will not be removed from the post.

1228. When any officer in the Subsistence Department is relieved, he shall certify the outstanding debts to his successor, and transmit an account of the same to the head of his bureau, and turn over his public property and funds, unless otherwise ordered; his property accounts he will close; his money accounts will be kept open till the end of the quarter, unless he cease to do duty in the department.

1229. Commissaries of subsistence in charge of principal depôts will render quarterly statements of the cost and quality of the ration, in all its parts, at their stations.

NOTES.

1. Stores longest on hand will be issued first.

2. Armorers, carriage-makers, and blacksmiths, of the Ordnance Department, are entitled to one and a half ration per day; all other enlisted men, one ration. Laundresses, one ration. No hired person shall draw more than one ration.

3. One ration a day may be issued to any person employed with the army, when the terms of his engagement allow it, or on paying the full cost of the ration, when he cannot otherwise procure food. Commutation can only be paid to those persons entitled to rations by law.

4. Lamps and oil to light a fort or garrison are not allowed from the Subsistence Department.

5. In purchasing pork for the Southern posts, a preference will be given to that which is put up in small pieces, say from four to six pounds each, and not very fat.

6. As soldiers are expected to preserve, distribute, and cook their own subsistence, the hire of citizens for any of these duties is not allowed, except in extreme cases. The expenses of bakeries are paid from the post fund, to which the profits accrue by regulations (see par. 198 page 35), such as purchase of hops, yeast, furniture; as sieves, cloths, &c., and the hire of bakers. *Ovens* may be built or paid for by the Subsistence Department, but not bake-houses.

7. Mode of ascertaining the hospital ration: 100 complete rations consist of, say—

			Cost.
68 rations of	pork is 51 lbs. at 6 cents		$3 06
32 "	fresh beef is 40 lbs. at 4 cents		1 60
100 "	flour is 112 lbs. at 2 cents		2 25
100 or 100 "	beans is 8 quarts at 4 cents... 32 rice is 10 lbs. at 6 cents........ 60		0 46
100 or 100 "	coffee is 10 lbs. at 15 cents......... tea is 1½ lb. at $1.....................		1 50
100 "	sugar is 15 lbs. at 10 cents		1 50
100 "	vinegar is 4 quarts at 5 cents		0 20
100 "	tallow candles is 1½ lb. at 12 cents		0 18
100 "	soap is 4 lbs. at 6 cents		0 24
100 "	salt is 2 quarts at 3 cents		0 06
	Cost of 100 rations		$11 05

or, one ration costs eleven cents and a half mill

Subsistence Department.——Forms.

FORM 1.

Return of Provisions received, issued, and remaining on hand at Assistant Commissary of Subsistence,

DATE. (1861.)	No. of voucher.	FROM WHOM RECEIVED.	PORK.			FRESH BEEF.	SALT BEEF.		BEEF CATTLE.	BACON.	HAMS.	FLOUR.	HARD BREAD.	CORN MEAL.	BEANS.		RICE.	COFFEE.
			Barrels. Pounds. Ounces.	Pounds. Ounces.	Barrels. Pounds. Ounces.	No. of	Pounds. Ounces.	Pounds. Ounces.	Barrels. Pounds. Ounces.	Pounds. Ounces.	Pounds. Bushels. Quarts. Gills.	Pounds. Ounces.	Pounds. Ounces.					
		Balance on hand, as per last return															
Oct.16	1	2d Lieut: J B, 4th Infantry, A. A. C. S....															
" 20	2	H C, Agent Subsistence Department															
" 31	3	Major T W L., C. S., U. S. A................															
" "		W J R, contractor for fresh beef..............															
" "		Purchased this month, as per abstract															
" "		Gained in issuing........															
		Total to be accounted for......															
Oct.31	1	To troops (regulars), as per abstract..........															
" "	2	To volunteers, as per abstract															
" "	3	To citizens, as per abstract...................															
" "	4	To sick in hospital, as per abstract..........															
" "	5	To extra issues, as per abstract															
" "	6	To sales to officers, as per abstract..........															
" 15	7	Capt. G T H, A. C. S. mil. service............															
" 13	8	H P C, Agent Subs. Dept.															
" 23	9	Capt W W, A. Qr. M. for transportation........															
" 31	10	Wastage, as per certific'e															
		Total issued.....................															
		Balance on hand.................															

Subsistence Department.——Forms.

FORM 1.

———————— during the month of ————————, by ————————,
United States Army.

TEA.		SUGAR.	VINEGAR.			CANDLES.			SOAP.		SALT.			POTATOES, DE-SICCATED.	MIXED VEGE-TABLES.	WHISKEY.		MOLASSES.		FORAGE.		NIOUTT.	PICKLES.	DRIED APPLES.					REMARKS.
Pounds.	Ounces.	Pounds.	Ounces.	Gallons.	Quarts.	Gills.	Sperm.	Adamantine.	Tallow.	Pounds.	Ounces.	Bushels.	Quarts.	Gills.	Pounds	Pounds.	Gallons.	Quarts.	Gallons.	Quarts.	Pounds hay.	Pounds corn.	Gallons.	Gallons.	Pounds.					

I certify that the above return is correct and just.

A. C. S.

Subsistence Department.——Forms.

FORM 3.

Abstract of Provisions issued during the month of ————, 186 , *to men*
U. S. Army, by

Number of return.	Number of men.	Number of days drawn for.	Commencing.	Ending.	Total number of rations due hospital.	RATIONS ACTUALLY REQUIRED FOR CONSUMPTION IN THE HOS-								
						Rations of pork.	Rations of fresh beef.	Rations of flour.	Rations of hard bread.	Rations of rice.	Rations of coffee.	Rations of sugar.	Rations of vinegar.	Rations of candles.
1	5	8	Oct. 18	Oct. 25	40	40	.....	30	10	40	40	40	40	40
2	.....	...	18	....	.....	.....	.....	.....	.....	.....	.....	.....	.....	.....
3	27	4	20	Oct. 23	108	108	.....	108	.....	108	108	108	108	108
4	78	6	20	25	468	100	168	468	.....	368	200	468	300	468
5	46	4	22	25	184	.....	84	130	.....	184	184	184	.....	184
6	122	6	26	. 31	732	130	300	697	.....	.....	402	732	.....	732
7	.....	...	....	....	......	.....	.....	.....	.....	.....	.....	.....	.....	.....
8	.....	...	....	....	......	.....	.....	.....	.....	.....	.....	84	.....	.....

Total rations due hospital 1532

Total quantity issued..............	378	552	1,433	10	700	934	1,616	448	1,532

	Barrels.	Pounds.	Ounces.	Pounds.	Barrels.	Pounds.	Ounces.	Pounds.	Pounds.	Pounds.	Pounds.	Ounces.	Gallons.	Quarts.	Gills.	Pounds.	Ounces.
Quantity in bulk..................	1	83	8	690	8	44	2	10	70	56	193	14	4	1	7	15	5

I certify that I have carefully compared the above "abstract" with the original returns now in my hundred and fifty-two rations of fresh beef, fourteen hundred and thirty-three rations of flour, ten sixteen hundred and sixteen rations of sugar, four hundred and forty-eight rations of vinegar, fifteen hundred and forty-eight rations of salt, and that the purchases, amounting to two dollars and seventy-actually required for consumption in the hospital.

Compared with returns of men in hospital and found correct.

———— ———— ——————, *Commanding.*

FORM 3.

in hospital at ——, under the charge of ——, Assistant Surgeon A. C. S., U. S. A.

PITAL.				
Rations of soap.		Rations of salt.		Gallons of molasses.
40		40		......
....		....		2
108		108		......
468		200		......
184		....		......
732		400		......
....		....		10
....		100		......
1,532		848		12
Pounds.	Ounces.	Quarts.	Gills.	Gallons.
61	4	16	7	12

REMARKS.

A MONTHLY STATEMENT OF THE HOSPITAL FUND.

Dr. To balance due hospital last month..........					$0	00
1,532 rations, being whole amount due this month, at 9½ cents per ration..........					145	54
ISSUED.						
Cr. By the following provisions at contract prices:—						
283½ pounds of pork, at 6 cents per pound..........			$17	01		
690 pounds of fresh beef, at 4 cents per pound........			27	60		
1,612 2-16 pounds of flour, at 2 cents per pound......			32	24¼		
10 pounds of hard bread, at 3½ cents per pound......				35		
70 pounds of rice, at 6 cents per pound..........			4	20		
56 pounds of coffee, at 9 cents per pound..........			5	04		
193 14-16 pounds of sugar, at 8 cents per pound......			15	51		
17⅛ quarts of vinegar, at 5 cents per quart..........				85⅝		
15 5-16 pounds of candles, at 12 cents per pound......			1	83¾		
61¼ pounds of soap, at 6 cents per pound..........			3	67½		
16⅞ quarts of salt, at 3 cents per quart..........				50⅝		
			108	82¾		
PURCHASED.						
2 pairs of chickens, at 87½ cents per pair	$1	75				
4 quarts of milk, at 7 cents per quart....		28				
3 dozen oranges, at 25 cents per dozen....		75				
			2	78		
Total expended..........	......	......	......	......	111	60¾
Balance due this month..........	......	......	......	......	33	93¼

possession, and find that they amount to three hundred and seventy-eight rations of pork, five rations of hard bread, seven hundred rations of rice, nine hundred and thirty-four rations of coffee, hundred and thirty-two rations of candles, fifteen hundred and thirty-two rations of soap, eight eight cents, were required by me for, and issued to, the sick, and that the rations drawn in kind were

(Duplicates.)

—— ——, *Asst. Surgeon, U. S. Army.*

Subsistence Department.——Forms.

FORM 2.

Abstract of Provisions issued from the ———, 18 , to the ———, 18 , to the troops of the United States stationed at the post of ———, by ———, Commissary of Subsistence.

Date.	No. of return.	No. of men.	No. of women.	Total.	No. of days drawn for.	Commencing.	Ending.	Rations of pork.		Rations of fresh beef.		Rations of bacon.		Rations of flour.		Rations of hard bread.		Rations of beans.		Rations of rice.		Rations of coffee.		Rations of sugar.		Rations of vinegar.		Rations of candles, (sperm or tallow.)		Rations of soap.		Rations of salt.		Remarks.
								bbls.	lbs.	lbs.	oz.	lbs.	oz.	bbls.	lbs.	lbs.	oz.	bush.	qts.	lbs.	oz.	lbs.	oz.	lbs.	oz.	gals.	qts.	lbs.	oz.	lbs.	oz.	bush.	qts.	
Total No. of rations........																																		
Quantity in bulk........																																		

I hereby certify that I have carefully compared the above abstract with the original returns now in my possession, and find that they amount to ——— rations of fresh beef, ——— rations of pork, ——— rations of bacon, ——— rations of flour, ——— rations of hard bread, ——— rations of beans, ——— rations of rice, ——— rations of coffee, ——— rations of sugar, ——— rations of vinegar, ——— rations of candles (sperm or tallow), ——— rations of soap, ——— rations of salt.

————————. *Commanding*

Subsistence Department.——Forms.

FORM 4.

Abstract of extra issues to the troops at ———, during the month of ———, by ———, A. C. S.

Date.	No. of return.	Number of rations.	Number of pounds of candles.		Remarks.
					Guard at ———.

I certify that I have carefully compared the above abstract with the original returns now in my possession, and find that they amount to ———, and that the issues were made by my order.

———, Commanding.

Subsistence Department.——Forms.

FORM 5.

Abstract of Provisions sold to officers at ——, *during the month of* ——, *by* ——*A. C. S.*

Articles and quantities sold.	Amount.	
	Dollars.	Cents.
—— pounds of pork............		
—— pounds of fresh beef......		
—— barrels of flour..........		
—— bushels of beans..........		
—— pounds of soap...........		
—— pounds of candles........		
—— bushels of salt..........		
—— gallons of vinegar.......		
—— pounds of sugar..........		
—— pounds of coffee.........		
Total........		

I certify that the above is a correct statement of all sales of subsistence stores made to officers at this post during the month of ——, 18 .

——————————, *A. C. S.*

I certify that I have compared the above abstract with the officers' certified list of purchases for their own use and the use of their families, and find the abstract correct.

Commanding.

FORM 6.

Monthly Summary Statement of Funds received and disbursed at ——, in ——, 18 .

DR.				CR.	
1861.	Dolls.	Cts.	1861.	Dolls.	Cts.
To amount disbursed this month..........			By balance as per last statement......		
			By cash received from the Treasury of the United States this month....		
			By cash from agents, sales, &c........		
To balance due the United States..........					
	$			$	

I certify that the above is a true statement of all moneys received and expended by me on account subsistence during the month, and the balance is in

Assistant Commissary of Subsistence.

Subsistence Department.——Forms.

FORM 7.

The United States, on account of Army Subsistence, in the quarter ending the ——— day of ———, 18 ——, in account
Dr. with Lieutenant ———, Regiment ———, Assistant Commissary of Subsistence, at Fort ———. Cr.

Date. 186 .	Dolls.	Cts.	Date. 186 .	Dolls.	Cts.
June 30th. To amount of Abstract No. 1.........			March 31st. By amount on hand, as per last return.........		
" " 2.........					
" " 3.........					
" " To balance on hand.........					
$			$		

I certify that the above account current exhibits an accurate and true statement of all money received and expended by me on account of the subsistence of the army, not heretofore accounted for; and that the balance of ——— dollars and ——— cents is due from ———, and is deposited in ——— in ———.

———, Assistant Commissary of Subsistence.

Subsistence Department.——Forms.

FORM 8.

Abstract of purchases made on account of Subsistence of the Army, by ———, at ———, in the quarter ending ———, 186 .

Date.	Number.	From whom purchased.	Fresh Beef. Pounds.	Pork. Barrels.	Flour. Barrels.	Beans. Bushels.	Rice. Pounds.	Coffee. Pounds.	Tea. Lbs.—oz.	Sugar. Pounds.	Vinegar. Gallons.	Candles. Pounds.	Soap. Pounds.	Salt. Bushels.	Hay. Pounds.	Corn. Bushels.	Chickens. Pairs of.	Amount. Dollars.	Cents.
		Total amount......																

I certify that the purchases were made agreeably to the above abstract, and that the sums were actually paid as charged; and, also, that I was wholly uninterested in the purchases, and that the articles were purchased at the lowest market price.

A. B., Lieut. Regt., and A. C. S.

Subsistence Department.——Forms.

FORM 9.

Abstract of Disbursements, on account of Contingencies, by Lieut. ————, Assistant Commissary of Subsistence, in the ———— quarter, ending the ———— day of ————, 18 .

Date.	Number of voucher.	To whom paid.	On what account.	Remarks.	Amount.
			Commutation of rations.		
			Weights and measures.		
			Clerk..............	By authority, October 16.	
			Stationery.		
			Per diem to extra-duty men.		

Acting Commissary of Subsistence.

FORM 10.

Consolidated Abstract of Provisions sold to officers at ——— , by ——— , in the quarter ending ——— , A. C. S.

Month.	Fresh beef, pounds of.	Bacon, pounds of.	Pork, pounds of.	Salt beef, pounds of.	Flour, pounds of.	Coffee, pounds of.	Sugar, pounds of.	Hard bread, pounds of.	Rice, pounds of.	Candles, pounds of.	Soap, pounds of.	Salt, quarts of.	Vinegar, gallons.	Total Amount. Dolls.	Cts.	Remarks.
1861.																Pounds of fresh beef, at ....
January														3	00	Pounds of bacon, at ....
February														5	20	Pounds of pork, at ....
March														4	10	Pounds of salt beef, at ....
Total																Pounds of flour, at ....
Price														$12	30	Pounds of coffee, at ....

Pounds of sugar, at ....
Pounds of hard bread, at ....
Pounds of rice, at ....
Pounds of candles, at ....
Pounds of soap, at ....

I certify that the above is correct.

Commissary.

FORM 11.

Estimate of Funds required for purchasing fresh beef, and for contingencies for the troops stationed at ——— for the quarter ending ———, 18 .

Troops.	Strength.	Number of weeks.	Number of rations per week.	Number of pounds per week.	Total number of pounds required.	Price per pound. Cts.	Total amount. Dolls.	Total amount. Cts.	Stationery. Dolls.	Hospital. Dolls.	Total amount required. Dolls.	Total amount required. Cts.	Remarks.
Company of ———													
Hospital contingencies......													
Amount.............													

Deduct the probable amount that will remain on hand, quarter ending ———

Total amount required to meet the expenditures in the quarter ending ———

———, *Commissary.*

Subsistence Department.——Forms.

FORM 12.

Return of Commissary Property received, issued, and remaining on hand at ——, during the quarter ending the —— day of ——, 186 , by ——, U. S. A.

From whom received.	Date.	No. of voucher.	Stationery.				Office Furniture.				Scales, Weights, etc.				Tools.			
On hand per last return......																		
Total to be accounted for...																		
Total issued and expended...																		
Remaining on hand......																		

I certify that the above return is correct, and that the articles specified were actually and necessarily expended in the public service.

—————————— A. C. S.

Subsistence Department.——Forms.

FORM 13.

Provision Return for Captain ——————, Company ——————, Regiment of —————— , for —————— days, commencing —————— day of —————— , 186 , and ending —————— day of —————— , 186 .

Post or Station.	Number of men.	Number of women.	Total.	Number of days.	Number of rations.	Pork.	Salt beef.	Fresh beef.	Bacon.	Hard bread.	Flour.	Beans.	Rice.	Coffee.	Tea.	Sugar.	Vinegar.	Sperm.	Adamantine.	Tallow.	Soap.	Salt.	Desic'd potatoes.	Mixed vegetables.	Remarks.

RATIONS OF— Candles.

Commanding Company.

Com-anding Post.

The A. C. S. will issue agreeably to the above return.

NOTE.—A similar return is made for detachments and hospital; and if rations are drawn for a commissioned officer, his name, rank, and regiment or corps must be mentioned under Remarks.

FORM 14.

Consolidated Provision Return for ——— *Regiment of* ———, *for* ——— *days, commencing* ——— *day of* ———, 186 , *and ending* ——— *day of* ———, 186 .

Post or Station.	Number of men.	Number of women.	Total.	Number of days.	Number of rations.	RATIONS OF—																					Remarks.
						Pork.	Salt beef.	Fresh beef.	Bacon.	Hard bread.	Flour.	Beans.	Rice.	Coffee.	Tea.	Sugar.	Vinegar.	Candles. Sperm.	Candles. Adamantine.	Candles. Tallow.	Soap.	Salt.	Desic'd potatoes.	Mixed vegetables.			
Total..............																											

The A. C. S. will issue on the above return.

Commanding Officer.

Commanding Regiment.

NOTE.—If rations are drawn for a commissioned officer on this return, his name, rank, and regiment or corps must be mentioned under Remarks.

FORM 15.

Form of Commissary's receipt to Contractors.

COUNTY OF ————,
    State of ————, }

Personally appeared before me, ————, inspector for said county, and made oath that, at the request of the parties concerned, he inspected the quantity of provisions below enumerated, delivered as supplies for the troops at Fort ————, on the contract of ————, for the year ————, and found them to be of the quantity and quality under-mentioned :

———— barrels of corn-fed pork, excluding the parts directed in the contract, and in quality as therein designated.
———— barrels of superfine flour.
———— bushels of good sound beans.
———— gallons of good cider or wine vinegar.
———— pounds of good hard soap.
———— pounds of tallow candles with cotton wicks.
———— bushels of clean dry salt.

S. T., *Inspector.*

Sworn and subscribed before me
    this ———— day of ————. }

A. B., *Justice of the Peace.*

Received, Fort ————, ————, 186 , the provisions above enumerated.

C. D., *Lieut., and A. C. S.*

FORM 18.

THE UNITED STATES,

To ——————, Special Contractor, DR.

186 .

For rations issued to recruits under the command of ———, at ———, from ——— to ———, as per accompanying abstract:

Complete rations, at ——— cents.........................

——— lbs. extra soap, at ——— cents.........................

——— lbs. extra candles, at ——— cents.........................

Due contractor...................... $

Received from the United States [or Lieut. B., recruiting officer], at ———, 186 . ——— dollars and ——— cents, in full of the above account.

——————, *Special Contractor.*

(Duplicate.)

FORM 17.

Abstract of rations issued to recruits stationed at ———, under command of ———, from ——— to ———, by ———, special contract.

Date.	No. of return.	No. of men.	Commencing.	Ending.	No. of days drawn for.	No. of complete rations.	Remarks.

Total number of complete rations..................................

I certify that I have carefully compared the above abstract with the original returns now in my possession, and they amount to ——— complete rations.

——————, Recruiting Officer.

FORM 18.

THE UNITED STATES

To Sergeant JAMES H. MCMULLEN,   DR.

Date.		
186 . June 30.	For commutation of rations while on detached service, returning to his branch rendezvous, en route from ——— to ———, from the 8th to the 12th June, 1860—five days, at 75 cents per day...........	3 75
	$	3 75

(Duplicates.)

I certify that the above account is correct; that the commutation was made by my order, and was necessary for the public service, it being impracticable to take rations in kind.

———————, *Recruiting Officer.*

Received at ———, 30th June, 186 , from ———, A. C. S., three dollars and ——— cents, in full of the above account.

JAMES H. MCMULLEN.

NOTE.—A similar form to the above will be used without a certificate for all purchases. For services rendered, a similar form will be used with a certificate, signed as A. C. S., stating that the services were rendered as charged for, and were necessary for the public service.

FORM 19.

ARTICLES OF AGREEMENT made and entered into this   day
of   , anno Domini one thousand eight hundred and sixty-
     , between   , an officer of the United States
army, of the one part, and   , of the county
of   , and State of   , of the other
part.

This agreement witnesseth, That the said   , for and on
behalf of the United States of America, and the said
heirs, executors, and administrators, have covenanted and agreed, and
by these presents do mutually covenant and agree, to and with each
other, as follows, viz. :

First. That the said   heirs, executors, and administrators, shall supply, or cause to be supplied and issued, at   ,
all the rations, to consist of the articles hereinafter specified, that shall
be required for the use of the United States recruits stationed at the
place aforesaid, commencing on the   day of   , one
thousand eight hundred and sixty-   , and ending on the
of   , eighteen hundred and   , or such earlier day
as the Commissary-General may direct, at the price of   cents
     mills for each complete ration.

Second. That the ration to be furnished by virtue of this contract
shall consist of the following articles, viz.: One and a quarter pound of
fresh beef, or three-quarters of a pound of salted pork, eighteen ounces
of bread or flour, and at the rate of eight quarts of beans or ten pounds
of rice, ten pounds of coffee, fifteen pounds of sugar, four quarts of
vinegar, and one and a half pounds of tallow, or one pound of sperm
candles, four pounds of soap, and two quarts of salt, to every hundred
rations, or the contractor shall furnish the men with good and wholesome
board and lodgings, at the option of the recruiting officer; and the recruiting party shall have the privilege of hanging out a flag from the place of
rendezvous.

Third. That fresh beef shall be issued at least thrice in each week, if required by the commanding officer.

Fourth. It is clearly understood that the provisions stipulated to be furnished and delivered under this contract shall be of the first quality.

Fifth. Should any difficulty arise respecting the quality of the provisions stipulated to be delivered under this contract, then the commanding officer is to appoint a disinterested person to meet one of the same description to be appointed by the contractor. These two thus appointed will have power to decide on the quality of the provisions; but should they disagree, then a third person is to be chosen by the two already appointed, the whole to act under oath, and the opinion of the majority to be final in the case.

Sixth. No member of Congress shall be admitted to any share herein, or any benefit to arise therefrom.

In witness whereof, the undersigned have hereunto placed their hands and seals the day and date above written.

WITNESS:

———— ————. [L. S.]

———————— ———— ————. [L. S.]

FORM 20.

ARTICLES OF AGREEMENT made this   day of   , eighteen hundred and sixty-   , between   , Assistant Commissary of Subsistence in the service of the United States of America, of the one part, and   , of   , in the State of   , of the other part.

This agreement witnesseth, That the said   , for and on behalf of the United States of America, and the said   , for himself, his heirs, executors, and administrators, have mutually agreed, and by these presents do mutually covenant and agree, to and with each other, in manner following, viz.:

First. That the said   shall deliver at   *fresh beef,* of a good and wholesome quality, in quarters, with an equal proportion of each (necks and shanks to be excluded), in such quantities as may be from time to time required for the troops, not exceeding five times in each week, on such days as shall be designated by the Assistant Commissary of Subsistence.

This contract to be in force for   months, or such less time as the Commissary-General may direct, commencing on the   day of   , eighteen hundred and sixty-

Second. The said   shall receive   cents and   mills per pound for every pound of *fresh beef* delivered and accepted under this contract.

Third. Payment shall be made monthly for the amount of *fresh beef* furnished under this contract, but in the event of the Assistant Commissary of Subsistence being without funds, then payment to be made as soon after as funds may be received for that purpose.

Fourth. That whenever and as often as the *beef* specified to be issued by this contract shall, in the opinion of the commanding officer, be unfit for issue, or of a quality inferior to that required by the contract, a survey shall be held thereon by two officers, to be designated by the commanding officer; and in case of disagreement, a third person shall be chosen by those two officers; the three thus appointed and chosen shall have power to reject such parts or the whole of the *fresh beef* as to them appear unfit for issue, or of a quality inferior to that contracted for.

Fifth. That in case of failure or deficiency in the quality or quantity of the *fresh beef* stipulated to be delivered, then the Assistant Commissary of Subsistence shall have power to supply the deficiency by purchase, and the said   will be charged with the difference of cost.

Sixth. No member of Congress shall be admitted to any share herein, or any benefit to arise therefrom.

In witness whereof, the undersigned have hereunto placed their hands and seals the day and date above written

WITNESS:

——— ———. [L.S.]

——— ———. [L.S.]

FORM 21.

KNOW ALL MEN BY THESE PRESENTS, That we,   and
are held and firmly bound to the United States of America in the sum
of   dollars, lawful money of the United States; for which
payment well and truly to be made, we bind ourselves, and each of us,
our and each of our heirs, executors, and administrators, for and in the
whole, jointly and severally, firmly by these presents.

Sealed with our seals—dated the   day of   , in the year
of our Lord eighteen hundred and sixty- .

The nature of this obligation is such, that if the above-bounden
heirs, executors, and administrators, or any of them, shall and do in all
things well and truly observe, perform, fulfil, accomplish, and keep, all
and singular the covenants, conditions, and agreements whatsoever which
on the part of the said   heirs, executors, or administrators, are or
ought to be observed, performed, fulfilled, accomplished, and kept, com-
prised or mentioned in certain articles of agreement or contract bearing
date   , one thousand eight hundred and sixty-   , between
     and the said   , concerning the supply and delivery
of *fresh beef* to the troops at   , or rations to recruits at   ,
according to the true intent and meaning of the said articles of agreement or contract, then the above obligations to be void; otherwise, to
remain in full force and virtue.

                                         —— ——. [L.S.]

WITNESSES :   —— ——. [L.S.]

                                         —— ——. [L.S.]

MISCELLANEOUS ITEMS.

A box, 24 by 16 inches square, and 22 inches deep, will contain one barrel, or 10,752 cubic inches.

A box, 16 by 16.8 inches square, and 8 inches deep, will contain one bushel, or 2,150.4 cubic inches.

A box, 8 by 8.4 inches square, and 8 inches deep, will contain one peck, or 537.6 cubic inches.

A box, 7 by 4 inches square, and 4.8 inches deep, will contain a half-gallon, or 131.4 cubic inches.

A box, 4 by 4 inches square, and 4.2 inches deep, will contain one quart, or 67.2 inches.

A convenient package for bacon is made 16 inches high, 16 inches wide, and 26 inches long (the three dimensions being inside measure). Make of 1¼-inch material, plain on the inside, tongue, groove, and strap with iron.

Paint vinegar-kegs to prevent evaporation and to fill worm-holes; cap the bungs with tin. Block-tin liquid measures and scoops are, in the end, the most economical.

One bushel of corn weighs			56	pounds.
"	"	wheat "	60	"
"	"	rye "	56	"
"	"	buckwheat weighs	52	"
"	"	barley "	48	"
"	"	oats "	24	"
"	"	beans "	60	"
"	"	potatoes "	60	"
"	"	onions "	57	"
"	"	dried peaches "	33	"
"	"	dried apples "	22	"
"	"	salt "	50	"

TABLE SHOWING THE WEIGHT AND BULK OF RATIONS

No. of rations.	Tare in pounds.	Net weight in pounds.	Gross weight in pounds.	Bulk in barrels.	Kind of ration.
1,000	655.9301	2391.25	3047.1801	11.8224	Pork, flour, beans, and small rations.
1	.6559	2.3912	3.0471	.01182	Do. do. do.
1,000	402.9968	2016.25	2419.2468	16.2656	Bread, (12 oz.,) bacon, and
1	.4029	2.0162	2.4192	.01626	Do. do. do.
1,000	460.2257	2266.25	2726.4757	19.2827	Bread, (16 oz.,)
1	.4602	2.2662	2.7264	.01928	Do. do. do.
Pork.........	468.75	750.	1218.75	3.75	
Bacon.........	153.1861	750.	903.1861	4.9019	
Flour.........	109.0561	1125.	1234.0561	5.7397	
Pilot bread...	171.6867	750.	921.6867	9.031	¾ lb. to one ration.
Do.........	228.9156	1000.	1228.9156	12.048	1 lb. to one ration.
Beans	22.3187	155.	177.3187	0.7142	
Rice	14.5	100.	114.5	0.4629	
Coffee	10.901	100.	70.901	0.3488	
Sugar	15.625	150.	135.625	0.5	
Vinegar.........	15.	92.5	107.5	0.333	
Candles.........	2.5	15.	17.5	0.0925	Tallow candles.
Soap.........	6.8965	40.	46.8965	0.1877	
Salt.........	4.8828	33.75	38.6328	0.1562	

One thousand rations of

By A B E.

Subsistence Department.

Table, showing the Quantity and Bulk of any

NUMBER OF RATIONS	PORK.			BEEF.		FLOUR.			BEANS.			RICE AND COFFEE.		TEA.	
	Barrels.	Pounds.	Ounces.	Pounds.	Ounces.	Barrels.	Pounds.	Ounces.	Bushels.	Quarts.	Gills.	Pounds.	Ounces.	Pounds.	Ounces.
1	......	......	12	1	4	......	1	2	......	......	0.64	....	1.6	....	0.24
2	......	1	8	2	8	......,	2	4	......	......	·1.28	....	3.2	....	0.48
3	......	2	4	3	12	......	3	6	......	......	1.92	....	4.8	....	0.72
4	......	3	......	5	......	......	4	8	......	......	2.56	....	6.4	....	0.96
5	......	3	12	6	4	..,..	5	10	......	......	3.20	....	8.0	....	1.20
6	......	4	8	7	8	..,...	6	12	......	......	3.84	....	9.6	....	1.44
7	......	5	4	8	12	......	7	14	......	......	4.48	....	11.2	....	1.68
8	......	6	......	10	......	......	9	......	......	......	5.12	....	12.8	....	1.92
9	......	6	12	11	4	......	10	2	......	......	5.76	....	14.4	....	2.16
10	......	7	8	12	8	......	11	4	......	......	6.40	1	....	....	2.4
20	......	15	......	25	......	......	22	8	......	1	4.80	2	....	....	4.8
30	......	22	8	37	8	......	33	12	......	2	3.20	3	....	....	7.2
40	......	30	......	50	......	......	45	......	......	3	1.60	4	....	....	9.6
50	......	37	8	62	8	......	56	4	......	4	....	5	........:	....	12.0
60	......	45	......	75	......	......	67	8	......	4	6.40	6	....	....	14.4
70	......	52	8	87	8	......	78	12	......	5	4.80	7	....	1	0.8
80	......	60	......	100	......	......	90	......	......	6	3.20	8	....	1	3.2
90	......	67	8	112	8	......	101	4	......	7	1.60	9	....	1	5.6
100	......	75	......	125	......	......	112	8	......	8	....	10	....	1	8.0
1,000	3	150	......	1,250	......	5	145	......	2	16	....	100	....	15	....
10,000	37	100	......	12,500	......	57	178	......	25	......	....	1,000	... .	150	....
100,000	375	......	......	125,000	......	573	192	......	250	......	....	10,000	....	1,500	....

Subsistence Department.

Number of Rations, from 1 *to* 100,000.

SUGAR		VINEGAR			SPERM CANDLES		SOAP		SALT			DESICCATED POTATOES		MIXED VEGETABLES	
Pounds	Ounces	Gallons	Quarts	Gills	Pounds	Ounces	Pounds	Ounces	Bushels	Quarts	Gills	Pounds	Ounces	Pounds	Ounces
....	2.4	....	...	0.32	....	0.16	....	0.64	...	...	0.16	....	1.5	....	1
....	4.8	....	..	0.64	....	0.32	....	1.28	...	...	0.32	....	3.0	....	2
....	7.2	....	...	0.96	....	0.48	....	1.92	...	...	0.48	....	4.5	....	3
....	9.6	....	...	1.28	....	0.64	....	2.56	...	...	0.64	....	6.0	....	4
....	12.0	....	..	1.60	....	0.80	....	3.20	...	...	0.80	....	7.5	....	5
....	14.4	....	..	1.92	....	0.96	....	3.84	...	...	0.96	....	9.0	....	6
1	0.8	....	...	2.24	....	1.12	....	4.48	...	...	1.12	....	10.5	....	7
1	3.2	....	...	2.56	....	1.28	....	5.12	...	...	1.28	....	12.0	....	8
1	5.6	....	...	2.88	....	1.44	....	5.76	...	...	1.44	....	13.5	....	9
1	8.0	....	...	3.20	....	1.6	....	6.40	...	...	1.60	....	15.0	....	10
3	......	....	...	6.40	....	3.2	....	12.80	...	...	3.20	1	14.0	1	4
4	8.0	....	1	1.60	....	4.8	1	3.20	...	...	4.80	2	13.0	1	1¼
6	......	....	1	4.80	....	6.4	1	9.60	...	...	6.40	3	12.0	2	8
7	8.0	....	2	....	....	8.0	2	....	...	1	....	4	11.0	3	2
9	......	....	2	3.20	....	9.6	2	6.40	...	1	1.60	5	10.0	3	12
10	8.0	....	2	6.40	....	11.2	2	12.80	...	1	3.20	6	9.0	4	6
12	......	....	3	1.60	....	12.8	3	3.20	...	1	4.80	7	8.0	5	....
13	8.0	....	3	4.80	....	14.4	3	9.60	...	1	6.40	8	7.0	5	10
15	......	1	...	....	1	....	4	....	...	2	....	9	6.0	6	4
150	......	10	...	....	10	....	40	....	...	20	....	93	12.0	62	8
1,500	......	100	...	....	100	....	400	....	6	8	....	937	8.0	625	....
15,000	......	1,000	...	....	1,000	....	4,000	....	62	16	....	9,375	....	6,250	....

ARTICLE XLIV.

MEDICAL DEPARTMENT.

1230. The medical supplies for the army are prescribed in the standard supply tables.

1231. The medical purveyors and the senior medical officer of each hospital, post, or command, will make the necessary requisitions for medical and hospital supplies, in duplicate (Form 1). If the supplies are to be obtained from the principal purveying depôts, the requisitions will be made upon the Surgeon-General on the 31st day of December annually; if from department or field depôts, they will be made upon the medical director at such times and for such periods as he may direct. Good vaccine matter will be kept on hand by timely requisition on the Surgeon-General.

1232. The medical purveyors at the principal depôts will issue medical and hospital supplies only on the order of the Surgeon-General; those at department or field depôts will issue on the order of a medical director. In particular and urgent cases, issues may be made on a special requisition (Form 2), approved by a commanding officer; a like authority will be required in transfers of medical supplies.

1233. When it is necessary to purchase medical supplies, and recourse cannot be had to a medical disbursing officer, they may be procured by the quartermaster on a special requisition (Form 2) and account (Form 3).

1234. When any requisition for medical supplies is not according to the supply table, the reason therefor must be set out.

1235. In every case of special requisition, a duplicate of the requisition shall, at the same time, be transmitted to the Surgeon-General, for his information, giving the name and station of the officer upon whom it is made.

1236. Medical purveyors will make to the Surgeon-General, at the end of each fiscal quarter, returns in duplicate (Form 4) of medical supplies received, issued, and remaining on hand, stating to whom, or from whom, and where and when issued or received; other medical officers in charge of medical supplies make similar returns of them annually, on the 31st December; and all officers, when relieved from the duty to which their returns relate. The returns will show the condition of the stores, and particularly of the instruments, bedding, and furniture. Medical purveyors will furnish abstracts of receipts and issues, with their returns (Form 5), giving the name of the person from whom received and to whom issued.

1237. An officer transferring medical supplies will furnish a certified invoice to the officer who is to receive them, and transmit a duplicate of it to the Surgeon-General. The receiving officer will furnish a receipt to the officer making the issue, with a report of the quality and condition of the articles, and transmit a duplicate of the receipt and report to the Surgeon-General. A medical officer who turns over medical supplies to a quartermaster for storage or transportation will forward to the Surgeon-General, with the invoice, the quartermaster's receipt for the packages.

1238. Medical officers will take up and account for all medical supplies of the army that come into their possession, and report, when they know it, to whose account they are to be credited.

1239. In all official lists of medical supplies the articles will be entered in the order of the supply table.

1240. Medical disbursing officers will, at the end of each fiscal quarter, render to the Surgeon-General, in duplicate, a quarterly account current of moneys received and expended, with the proper vouchers for the payments, and certificates that the services have been rendered, and the supplies purchased and received for the medical service, and transmit to him an estimate of the funds required for the next quarter.

1241. The senior medical officer of a hospital will distribute the patients, according to convenience and the nature of their complaints, into wards or divisions, under the particular charge of the several assistant surgeons, and will visit them himself each day, as frequently as the state of the sick may require, accompanied by the assistant, steward, and nurse.

1242. His prescriptions of medicine and diet are written down at once in the proper register, with the name of the patient and the number of his bed; the assistants fill up the diet table for the day, and direct the administration of the prescribed medicines. He will detail an assistant surgeon to remain at the hospital day and night, when the state of the sick requires it.

1243. In distributing the duties of his assistants, he will ordinarily require the aid of one in the care and preparation of the hospital reports, registers, and records, the rolls, and descriptive lists; and of another in the charge of the dispensary, instruments, medicines, hospital expenditures, and the preparation of the requisitions and annual returns.

1244. He will enforce the proper hospital regulations to promote health and prevent contagion, by ventilated and not crowded rooms, scrupulous cleanliness, frequent changes of bedding, linen, &c.

1245. He will require the steward to take due care of the hospital stores and supplies; to enter in a book, daily (Form 6), the issues to the ward-masters, cooks, and nurses; to prepare the provision returns, an receive and distribute the rations.

1246. He will require the ward-master to take charge of the effects of the patients; to register them in a book (Form 7); to have them numbered and labeled with the patient's name, rank, and company; to receive from the steward the furniture, bedding, cooking-utensils, &c., for use, and keep a record of them (Form 8), and how distributed to the wards and kitchens; and once a week to take an inventory of the articles in use, and report to him any loss or damage to them, and to return to the steward such as are not required for use.

1247. The cooks and nurses are under the orders of the steward; he is responsible for the cleanliness of the wards and kitchens, patients and attendants, and all articles in use. He will ascertain who are present at sunrise, and sunset, and tattoo, and report absentees.

1248. At surgeon's call the sick then in the companies will be conducted to the hospital by the first sergeants, who will each hand to the surgeon, in his company book, a list of all the sick of the company, on which the surgeon shall state who are to remain or go into hospital; who are to return to quarters as sick or convalescent; what duties the convalescents in quarters are capable of; what cases are feigned; and any other information in regard to the sick of the company he may have to communicate to the company commander.

1249. Soldiers in hospital, patients, or attendants, except stewards, shall be mustered on the rolls of their company, if it be present at the post.

1250. When a soldier in hospital is detached from his company so as not to be mustered with it for pay, his company commander shall certify and send to the hospital his descriptive list, and account of pay and clothing, containing all necessary information relating to his accounts with the United States, on which the surgeon shall enter all payments, stoppages, and issues of clothing to him in hospital. When he leaves the hospital, the medical officer shall certify and remit his descriptive list, showing the state of his accounts. If he is discharged from the service in hospital, the surgeon shall make out his final statements for pay and clothing. If he dies in hospital, the surgeon shall take charge of his effects, and make the reports required in the general regulations concerning soldiers who die absent from their companies.

1251. Patients in hospital are, if possible, to leave their arms and accoutrements with their companies, and in no case to take ammunition into the hospital.

1252. When a patient is transferred from one hospital to another, the medical officer shall send with him an account of his case, and the treatment.

1253. The regulations for the service of hospitals apply, as far as practicable, to the medical service in the field.

1254. The senior medical officer of each hospital, post, regiment, or detachment, will keep the following records, and deliver them to his successor: a register of patients (Form 9); a prescription book (Form 10); a diet book (Form 10); a case book; a meteorological register (Form 11); copies of his requisitions, annual returns, and quarterly reports of sick and wounded; and an order and letter book, in which will be transcribed all orders and letters relating to his duties.

1255. He will make up the muster and pay rolls of the medical cadets, hospital steward, female nurses, and matrons, and of all soldiers in hospital, sick or on duty, detached from their companies, on the forms furnished from the Adjutant-General's office, and according to the directions expressed on them.

1256. He will make the rolls of the cooks and nurses for extra-duty pay, which will be paid by the paymaster, in the absence of a medical disbursing officer, as in other cases of expenditures for the medical department (Form 12).

1257. The senior medical officer will select the cooks, nurses, and matrons (and, at posts where there is no hospital steward appointed by the Secretary of War, a soldier to act as steward), with the approval of the commanding officer. Cooks and nurses will be taken from the privates, and will be exempt from other duty, but shall attend the parades for muster and weekly inspections of their companies at the post, unless specially excused by the commanding officer.

1258. Ordinarily, hospital attendants are allowed as follows: to a general hospital, one steward, one nurse as ward-master, one nurse to ten patients, one matron to twenty, and one cook to thirty; to a hospital where the command exceeds five companies, one steward and ward-master, one cook, two matrons, and four nurses; to a post or garrison of one company, one steward and ward-master, one nurse, one cook, and one matron; and for every two companies more, one nurse; at arsenals where the number of enlisted men is not less than fourteen, one matron is allowed. The allowance of hospital attendants for troops in the field will be, for one company, one steward, one nurse, and one cook; for each additional company, one nurse; and for commands of over five companies, one additional cook.

1259. Medical officers, where on duty, will attend the officers and enlisted men, and the servants and laundresses authorized by law; and at stations where other medical attendance cannot be procured, and on marches, the hired men of the army, and the families of officers and soldiers. Medicines will be dispensed to the families of officers and soldiers, and to all persons entitled to medical attendance; hospital stores to enlisted men.

1260. Medical officers, in giving certificates of disability (Form 13), are to take particular care in all cases that have not been under their charge; and especially in epilepsy, convulsions, chronic rheumatism, derangement of the urinary organs, ophthalmia, ulcers, or any obscure disease liable to be feigned or purposely produced; and in no case shall such certificate be given until after sufficient time and examination to detect any attempt at deception.

1261. In passing a recruit the medical officer is to examine him stripped; to see that he has free use of all his limbs; that his chest is ample; that his hearing, vision, and speech are perfect; that he has no tumors, or ulcerated or extensively cicatrized legs; no rupture or chronic cutaneous affection; that he has not received any contusion, or wound of the head, that may impair his faculties; that he is not a drunkard; is not subject to convulsions; and has no infectious disorder, nor any other that may unfit him for military service.

1262. Medical officers attending recruiting rendezvous will keep a record (Form 14) of all the recruits examined by them. Books for this purpose will be procured by application to the Surgeon-General, to whom they will be returned when filled.

1263. As soon as a recruit joins any regiment or station, he shall be examined by the medical officer, and vaccinated when it is required.

1264. The senior medical officer of each hospital, post, regiment, or detachment, will make monthly to the medical director, and quarterly to the Surgeon-General, a report of sick and wounded, and of deaths, and of certificates for discharge for disability (Form 15), and transmit to him monthly a copy of the meteorological register (Form 11), and a copy of the "statement of the hospital fund" (Form 19).

1265. After surgeon's call, he will make a morning report of the sick to the commanding officer (Form 16).

1266. Every medical officer will report to the Surgeon-General and to the medical director the date when he arrives at a station, or when he leaves it, and his orders in the case, and at the end of each month whenever not at his station, whether on service or on leave of absence, and when on leave of absence his post-office address for the next month.

1267. The medical director will make to the Surgeon-General a monthly return of the medical officers of the command (Form 17), and a consolidated monthly report of the sick and wounded (Form 15) from the several reports made to him.

1268. When it is necessary to employ a private physician as medical officer, the commanding officer may do it by written contract, conditioned as in Form 18, at a stated compensation not to exceed $50 a month when the number of officers and men, with authorized servants and laundresses, is 100 or more; $40 when it is from 50 to 100, and $30 when it is under 50.

1269. But when he is required to abandon his own business, and give his whole time to the public service, the contract may be not to exceed $80 a month; and not to exceed $100, besides transportation in kind, to be furnished by the Quartermaster's Department, where he is required to accompany troops on marches or transports.　But a private physician will not be employed to accompany troops on marches or transports, except by orders from the War Department, or in particular and urgent cases by the order of the officer directing the movement, when a particular statement of the circumstances which make it necessary will be appended to the contract.

1270. And when a private physician is required to furnish medicines, he will be allowed, besides the stipulated pay, from 25 to 50 per cent. on it, to be determined by the Surgeon-General.

1271. In all cases, a duplicate of the contract will be transmitted forthwith by the commanding officer to the Surgeon-General, and the commanding officer for the time being will at once discontinue it, whenever the necessity for it ceases, or the Surgeon-General may so direct.

1272. The physician's account of pay due must be sent to the Surgeon-General for payment, vouched by the certificate of the commanding officer that it is correct and agreeable to contract, and that the services have been duly rendered.　But when it cannot conveniently be submitted to the Surgeon-General from the frontier or the field, it may be paid on the order of the commanding officer, not to exceed the regulated amount, by a medical disbursing officer, or a quartermaster.

1273. When medical attendance is required by officers or enlisted men on service, or for the authorized servants of such officers, and the attendance of a medical officer cannot be had, the officer, or, if there be no officer, then the enlisted man, may employ a private physician, and a just account therefor will be paid by the medical bureau.

1274. The account will set out the name of the patient, the date of and charge for each visit and for medicines.　The physician will make a certificate to the account in case of an officer, or affidavit in the case of an enlisted man, that the account is correct, and the charges are the customary charges of the place.

1275. The officer will make his certificate, or the enlisted man his affidavit, to the correctness of the account, that he was on service at the place, and stating the circumstances preventing him from receiving the services of a medical officer.

1276. When the charge is against an officer, he will pay the account if practicable, and transmit it to the medical bureau for reimbursement; in all other cases the account will be transmitted to the medical bureau for settlement.

Medical Department.

1277. If the charge is against a deceased officer or enlisted man, the physician will make the affidavit, before required, to the account, and that he has been paid no part of it.

1278. No charges for consultation fees will be paid by the medical bureau, nor will any account for medical attendance or medicines be paid, if the officer or enlisted man be not on service.

1279. A board of not less than three medical officers will be appointed from time to time by the Secretary of War, to examine applicants for appointment of assistant surgeons, and assistant surgeons for promotion. And no one shall be so appointed or promoted until so examined and found qualified.

1280. The board will scrutinize rigidly the moral habits, professional acquirements, and physical qualifications of the candidates, and report favorably, either for appointment or promotion, in no case admitting of a reasonable doubt.

1281. The Secretary of War will designate the applicants to be examined for appointment of assistant surgeon. They must be between 21 and 28 years of age. The board will report their respective merits in the several branches of the examination, and their relative merit from the whole; agreeably whereto, if vacancies happen within two years thereafter, they will receive appointments and take rank in the medical corps.

1282. When an assistant surgeon has served five years, he is subject to be examined for promotion. If he decline the examination, or be found not qualified by moral habits or professional acquirements, he ceases to be a medical officer of the army.

1283. An applicant for appointment failing at one examination, may be allowed a second, after two years; but never a third.

1284. Medical Cadets will be selected, from among the applicants who have been examined and approved by a Medical Board, by the Surgeon-General, who will assign them to duty at such places and in such numbers as the service may require. These candidates will be enlisted for the full term, by the Surgeon-General, or by a medical officer of the army authorized by him, who will at once cause to be administered to the Cadet the following oath:

I, —— ——, appointed a —— in the army of the United States, do solemnly swear, or affirm, that I will bear true allegiance to the United States of America, and that I will serve them honestly and faithfully against all their enemies or opposers whatsoever; and observe and obey the orders of the President of the United States, and the orders of the officers appointed over me, according to the rules and articles for the government of the armies of the United States.

Sworn to and subscribed before me, at ——, this —— day of ——, 186 .

—— ——, *Justice of the Peace.*

Medical Department.

1285. Medical Cadets will have the rank and pay of the Cadets at the Military Academy, and be under the direction and control of medical officers alone. They will be entitled each to one room as quarters, and fuel therefor, as allowed a Sergeant-Major, and will take choice next after Brevet Second Lieutenants in the selection of quarters. Transportation will be allowed them as in cases of paymaster's clerks.

1286. On the fifteenth day of the last month of his term of service, each Medical Cadet will report the fact to the medical officer in charge, whose duty it is to report the same to the Surgeon-General, together with a report of the general character and competency of the Cadet.

1287. The Secretary of War will appoint from the enlisted men of the army, or cause to be enlisted, as many competent hospital stewards as the service may require, not to exceed one for each post.

1288. The senior medical officer of a hospital requiring a steward may recommend a competent non-commissioned officer or soldier to be appointed, which recommendation the commanding officer shall forward to the Adjutant-General of the army, with his remarks thereon, and with the remarks of the company commander. And, as the object of these more permanent appointments is to procure the services of a more competent body of hospital stewards, no soldier, nor citizen, must henceforth be recommended for appointment who is not *known* to be temperate, honest, and in every way reliable, as well as sufficiently intelligent, and skilled in pharmacy, for the proper discharge of the responsible duties likely to be devolved upon him.

1289. When no competent enlisted man can be procured, the medical officer will report the fact to the Surgeon-General.* Applications and testimonials of competency, from persons seeking to be enlisted for hospital stewards, may be addressed to the Surgeon-General.

1290. The commanding officer may re-enlist a hospital steward at the expiration of his term of service, on the recommendation of the medical officer.

1291. Hospital stewards, whenever stationed in places whence no post return is made to the Adjutant-General's office, or when on furlough, will, at the end of every month, report themselves by letter to the Adjutant-General and Surgeon-General, as well as to the medical director of the military department in which they may be serving; to each of whom

---

* The current wants of the service may, however, be supplied by a detail from the command, on the recommendation of the medical officer, of a soldier to act as temporary steward, thus affording the means of a careful probation of all soldiers so detailed, who are ambitious of one day deserving a permanent appointment. Stewards thus detailed at posts, or with a body of troops of more than four companies, will receive the pay and allowances of a sergeant of ordnance; and at all other posts, or with smaller bodies of troops, the pay and allowances of a sergeant of infantry. (See Act July 5, 1838, sec. 12.)

they will also report each new assignment to duty, or change of station, ordered in their case, noting carefully the number, date, and source of the order directing the same. They will likewise report monthly, when on furlough, to the medical officer in charge of the hospital to which they are attached.

1293. The accounts of pay, clothing, &c., of hospital stewards must be kept by the medical officers under whose immediate direction they are serving, who are, also, responsible for certified statements of such accounts, and correct descriptive lists of such stewards, to accompany them in case of transfer—as, also, that their final statements and certificates of discharge are accurately made out, when they are, at length, discharged from service.

AMBULANCES.

1294. The following amount and kind of transportation for the sick and wounded may be provided for troops on marches and in campaigns against Indians:

1. For commands of less than five companies, to each company, one two-wheeled ambulance.
2. For a battalion, of five companies, one four-wheeled and five two-wheeled ambulances.
3. For a regiment, two four-wheeled and ten two-wheeled ambulances.

1295. The following schedule of transports for the sick and wounded and for hospital supplies will be adopted for a state of war with a civilized enemy:

1. For commands of less than three companies, one two-wheeled transport cart for hospital supplies, and to each company one two-wheeled ambulance.
2. For commands of more than three and less than five companies, two two-wheeled transport carts, and to each company one two-wheeled ambulance.
3. For a battalion of five companies, one four-wheeled ambulance, five two-wheeled ambulances, and two two-wheeled transport carts. For each additional company less than ten, one two-wheeled transport cart.
4. For a regiment of ten companies, two four-wheeled ambulances, ten two-wheeled ambulances, and four two-wheeled transport carts; and for greater commands in proportion.

1296. Ambulances will not be used for any other than the specific purpose for which they are designed, viz.: the transportation of the sick and wounded; and those hereafter provided for the army, will be made according to a pattern to be furnished the Quartermaster's Department by the Surgeon-General.

1297. The transport carts must be made after the models of the two-wheeled ambulances (their interior arrangement for the sick excepted), and to have solid board flooring to the body.

1298. Horse-litters may be prepared and furnished to posts whence they may be required for service on ground not admitting the employment of two-wheeled carriages; said litters to be composed of a canvas bed similar to the present stretcher, and of two poles each sixteen feet long, to be made in sections, with head and foot pieces constructed to act as stretchers to keep the poles apart.

1299. The allowance of hospital attendants in the field will be, for one company, one steward, one nurse, and one cook; for each additional company, one nurse; and for commands of over five companies, one additional cook.

HOSPITAL TENTS.

1300. Hospital tents must in future be made according to the pattern of the present tent and of the same material, but smaller, and having on one end a lapel so as to admit of two or more tents being joined and thrown into one with a continuous covering or roof. The dimensions to be these: In length, 14 feet; in width, 15 feet; in height (centre), 11 feet, with a wall 4½ feet, and a "fly" of appropriate size. The ridge-pole to be made in two sections after the present pattern; and to measure 14 feet when joined. Such a tent will accommodate from 8 to 10 patients comfortably.

1301. The following will be the allowance of tents for the sick, their attendants and hospital supplies:

Commands.	Hospital tents.	Sibley tents.	Common tents.
For one company.....	...	1	1
For three companies	1	1	1
For five companies.........................	2	1	1
For seven companies...................... .	2	1	1
For ten companies.....................,	3	1	1

1302. Upon the march or in battle, medical officers will habitually be attended by an orderly, carrying a hospital knapsack. This knapsack to be made of light wood and of the ordinary size; to be divided into four compartments or drawers, and to be covered with canvas or other suitable material: the object being to carry in an accessible shape such instruments, dressings, and medicines as may be needed in an emergency on the march or in the field.

STANDARD SUPPLY TABLE FOR GENERAL AND POST HOSPITALS.

Articles.	Quantities for one year for commands of—					Memoranda.
	From 100 to 200.	From 200 to 300.	From 300 to 400.	500 men.	1,000 men.	
MEDICINES.						
Acaciæ ....lb.	2	4	6	8	16	
Acidi acetici............lb.	1½	1	2	2½	5	
" arseniosi............oz.	½	1	2	2½	5	
" benzoici ....oz.	½	2	2	4	8	
' citrici ....lb.	1	2	3	4	8	
" muriatici............lb.	½	1	2	2½	5	
" nitrici............lb.	1	2	2	4	8	
" sulphurici ....lb.	1	2	3	4	8	
" " aromatici............lb.	1	2	3	4	8	
" tannici............oz.	2	4	6	8	16	
" tartarici............lb.	2	4	6	8	16	
Aetheris sulphurici loti............lb.	2	4	6	8	16	
Alcoholis ....bott.	24	48	72	96	192	
Aluminis ....lb.	1	2	3	4	8	
Ammoniaci ....lb.	½	1	2	2½	5	
Ammoniæ carbonatis............oz.	8	16	24	32	64	
" muriatis............lb.	½	1	2	2½	5	
Anthemidis............lb.	1	2	2	4	8	
Antimonii et potass: tartratis............oz.	3	6	9	12	24	
Argentii nitratis (crystals) ....oz.	1	2	3	4	8	
" " (fused) ....oz.	1	2	3	4	8	
Arnicæ ....lb.	1	2	3	4	8	

Medical Department.

						To be issued to posts where simple cerate cannot be sent without becoming rancid.
Assafœtidæ	oz.	32	16	12	8	4
Bismuthi subnitratis	oz.	32	16	12	8	4
Camphoræ	lb.	16	8	6	4	2
Cardamomi	oz.	64	32	24	16	8
Catechu	lb.	5	2¼	2	1	½
Ceræ albæ	lb.	16	8	6	4	2
Cerati resinæ	lb.	16	8	6	4	2
" simplicis	lb.	64	32	24	16	8
" zinci carbonatis	lb.	16	8	6	4	2
Chloroformi	lb.	8	4	3	2	1
Collodii	oz.	16	8	6	4	2
Copaibæ	lb.	40	20	15	10	5
Creasoti	oz.	16	8	6	4	2
Cretæ preparatæ	lb.	8	4	3	2	1
Cupri sulphatis	oz.	16	8	6	4	2
Emplastri adhæsivi	yds.	40	20	15	10	5
" cantharidis	lb.	24	12	9	6	3
" ferri	lb.	8	4	3	2	1
" hydrargyri	lb.	5	2½	2	1	½
" ichthyocollæ	yds.	24	12	9	6	3
Extracti belladonnæ	oz.	16	8	6	4	2
" buchu fluidi	lb.	8	4	3	2	1
" colchici acetici	oz.	8	4	3	2	1
" colocynthidis comp.	oz.	64	32	24	16	8
" colombæ fluidi	lb.	8	4	3	2	1
" conii	oz.	8	4	3	2	1
" cubebæ fluidi	lb.	8	4	3	2	1
" gentianæ fluidi	lb.	8	4	3	2	1
" glycyrrhizæ	lb.	48	24	18	12	6
" hyoscyami	oz.	16	8	6	4	2
" ipecacuanhæ fluidi	lb.	5	2½	2	1	½
" piperis fluidi	oz.	8	4	3	2	1
" pruni virg. fluidi	lb.	8	4	3	2	1
" rhei fluidi	lb.	8	4	3	2	1
" sarsaparillæ fluidi	lb.	16	8	6	4	2
" senegæ fluidi	lb.	5	2½	2	1	½

TABLE FOR GENERAL AND POST HOSPITALS.—CONTINUED.

ARTICLES.	From 100 to 200.	From 200 to 300.	From 300 to 400.	500 men.	1,000 men.	MEMORANDA.
Extracti sennæ fluidi..............lb.	1	2	3	4	8	
" taraxaci fluidi...............lb.	1	2	3	4	8	
" valerianæ fluidi............oz.	8	16	24	32	64	
" zingiberis fluidi............lb.	1½	1	2	2½	5	
Ferri iodidi........................oz.	2½	4	6	8	16	
" et quiniæ citratis...........oz.	4	8	12	16	32	
" sulphatis.....................oz.	2	4	6	8	16	
Gambogiæ..........................oz.	½	1	2	2½	5	
Guaiaci resinæ.....................lb.	¾	1	2	2½	5	
Hydrargyri chloridi corr:.........oz.	¾	1	2	2½	5	
" mitis.........lb.	1	2	3	4	8	
" cum cretâ.............lb.	¾	1	2	2½	5	
" iodidi.................oz.	1	2	3	4	8	
" oxidi rubri..........oz.	1	2	3	4	8	
Iodinii..............................oz.	2	4	6	8	16	
Lini................................lb.	4	8	12	16	32	
Liquoris ammoniæ.................lb.	4	8	12	16	32	
" ferri iodidi..............lb.	1	2	3	4	8	
" potass: arsenitis.......oz.	2	4	6	8	16	
" sodæ chlorinatæ.......bott.	3	6	9	12	24	
" zinci chloridi..........bott.	3	6	9	12	24	
Magnesiæ..........................lb.	½	1	2	2½	5	
" sulphatis...................lb.	25	50	75	100	200	

Medical Department.

Massæ pil: hydrargyri	oz.	8	16	24	32	64
Mellis despumati	lb.	2	4	6	8	16
Morphiæ sulphatis	dr.	2	4	6	8	16
Myrrhæ	lb.	½	1	2	2½	5
Olei anisi	oz.	1	2	3	4	8
" cajuputi	oz.	1	2	3	4	8
" caryophilli	oz.	1	2	3	4	8
" cinnamomi	oz.	2	2	3	8	8
" menthæ piperitæ	oz.	2	4	6	8	16
" morrhuæ	bott.	8	16	24	32	64
" olivæ	bott.	8	16	24	32	64
" origani	oz.	4	8	12	16	32
" ricini	qt. bott.	12	24	36	48	96
" terebinthinæ	qt. bott.	4	8	12	16	32
" tiglii	dr.	2	4	6	2½	16
Opii	lb.	½	1	2	2½	5
Picis abietis	lb.	1	2	3	4	8
Plumbi acetatis	lb.	1	2	3	4	8
Potassæ acetatis	lb.	1	2	3	4	8
" bicarbonatis	lb.	2	4	6	8	16
" bitartratis	lb.	1	2	3	4	8
" chloratis	lb.	1	2	3	4	8
" nitratis	lb.	½	1	2	2½	5
" sulphatis	lb.	1	2	3	4	8
Potassii cyanureti	dr.	8	16	24	32	64
" iodidi	oz.	1	1	2	2	5
Pruni virginianæ	lb.	2	4	6	8	16
Pulveris acaciæ	lb.	4	8	12	16	32
" aloës	oz.	2	4	6	8	16
" cantharidis	oz.	1	2	3	4	8
" capsici	lb.	1	2	3	4	8
" cinchonæ	lb.	2	2	6	8	16
" ferri	oz.	1	4	3	4	8
" " per sulphatis	oz.	2	2	6	16	32
" glycyrrhizæ	oz.	4	8	12	16	32
" ipecacuanhæ	lb.	½	1	2	2½	5

Medical Department.

TABLE FOR GENERAL AND POST HOSPITALS.—CONTINUED.

Articles.	Quantities for one year for commands of—					Memoranda.
	From 100 to 200.	From 200 to 300.	From 300 to 400.	500 men.	1,000 men.	
Pulveris ipecacuanhæ et opii ....lb.	½	1	2	2½	5	
" jalapæ ....oz.	4	8	12	16	32	
" lini.........lb.	8	16	24	32	64	
" opii.........lb.	½	1	2	2½	5	
" rhei.........oz.	4	8	12	16	32	
" sabinæ.........oz.	1	2	3	4	8	
" sinapis nigræ.........lb.	6	12	18	24	48	
" ulmi.........lb.	2	4	6	8	16	
Quassiæ.........oz.	½	1	2	2⅔	5	
Quiniæ sulphatis.........oz.	10–20	20–40	30–60	40–80	80–160	
Rhei.........lb.	4	8	12	16	32	
Sacchari.........lb.	20	40	60	80	160	
Saponis.........oz.	4	8	12	16	32	
Scillæ.........oz.	4	8	12	16	32	
Serpentariæ.........lb.	1½	1	2	2½	5	
Sodæ bicarbonatis.........lb.	2	4	6	8	16	
" boratis.........lb.	1⅓	1	2	2½	5	
" et potass: tartratis.........lb.	3	6	9	12	24	
Spigeliæ.........lb.	1½	1	2	2½	5	
Spiritus ammon: aromatici ....oz.	2½	4	6	8	16	
" ætheris compositi.........lb.	1½	1	2	2½	5	
" " nitrici.........lb.	2½	4	6	8	16	
" lavandulæ comp: ....lb.	½	1	2	2½	5	

Medical Department.

	Unit						Remarks
Spiritus vini gallici	bott.	12	24	36	48	96	
Strychniae	dr.	1	2	3	4	8	
Sulphuris loti	lb.	1	2	3	4	8	
Syrupi scillae	lb.	3	6	9	12	24	
Tincturae aconiti radicis	oz.	1	2	3	4	8	
" digitalis	oz.	4	8	12	16	32	
" ergotae (Dublin)	oz.	4	8	12	16	32	
" ferri chloridi	lb.	½	1	2	2½	5	
" veratri viridis	oz.	4	8	12	16	32	
Unguenti hydrargyri	lb.	1	2	3	4	8	
" " nitratis	lb.	½	1	2	2½	5	
Veratriae	dr.	1	2	3	4	8	
Vini colchici seminis	lb.	½	1	2	2½	5	
Zinci acetatis	oz.	1	2	3	4	8	
" sulphatis	oz.	1	2	3	4	8	
INSTRUMENTS.							
Buck's Spongeholder for the throat	no.	1	1	1	1	1	
Cupping glasses or tins	no.	12	12	18	18	24	
Dissecting	sets.	1	1	1	1	1	
Lancets, spring	no.	1	1	2	2	4	Four extra fleams to each lancet.
" thumb	no.	4	6	8	8	12	
Obstetrical	sets.	1	1	1	1	1	With cases.
Pocket	sets.	1	1	1	1	1	
Probangs	no.	6	6	6	6	6	
Pulleys	sets.	1	1	1	1	1	
Scarificators	no.	2	2	2	3	4	
Splints (assorted)	sets.	1	1	1	1	2	
Stethoscopes	no.	1	1	1	1	1	
Stomach-pump and case	no.	1	1	1	1	1	
Syringes, enema	no.	3	3	3	3	6	1 Davidson's; 1, 4-oz.; 1, 8-oz.
" penis, glass	no.	2	4	6	8	16	
" " metallic	no.	6	12	18	24	36	
" vagina	no.	3	3	3	3	6	Hard India-rubber, 1; glass, 2.
Teeth extracting	sets.	1	1	1	1	2	

Medical Department.

TABLE FOR GENERAL AND POST HOSPITALS.—Continued.

Articles.	Quantities for one year for commands of—					Memoranda.
	From 100 to 200.	From 200 to 300.	From 300 to 400.	500 men.	1,000 men.	
Tongue-depressor (hinge)..........no.	1	1	1	1	2	
Tourniquets, field ....no.	4	4	6	6	10	
" spiral..........no.	1	1	2	2	4	
Trusses, hernia...........no.	3	6	9	12	24	
Books.						
Anatomy...........cop.	1	1	1	1	1	
Chemistry ....cop.	1	1	1	1	1	
Dispensatory...........cop.	1	1	1	1	1	
Medical Dictionary ......cop.	1	1	1	1	1	
" Formulary ....cop.	1	1	1	1	1	
" Jurisprudence and Toxicology....cop.	1	1	1	1	1	
" Practice...........cop.	1	1	1	1	1	
Obstetricy ....cop.	1	1	1	1	1	
Regulations for Medical Department.......cop.	1	1	1	1	2	
Surgery ....cop.	2	2	2	2	2	
Blank...........no.	1	1	1	3	4	
Case...........no.	1	1	1	1	1	
Meteorological Register..........no.	1	1	1	1	1	
Order and Letter...........no.	1	1	1	1	1	
Prescription ....no.	1	1	1	1	1	
Register ....no.	1	1	1	1	1	

Medical Department.

		1	1	1	1	1	
Requisitions / Returns / Reports of sick	no.	1					
HOSPITAL STORES.							
Arrow-root	lb.	5	10	15	20	40	
Barley	lb.	20	40	60	80	160	
Cinnamon	lb.	¼	1	2	2½	5	
Cloves	oz.	4	8	12	16	32	
Cocoa	lb.	10	20	30	40	80	
Farina	lb.	5	10	15	20	40	
Ginger, ground (Jamaica)	lb.	¼	1	2	2½	5	
Nutmegs	oz.	4	8	12	16	32	
Tea	lb.	20	40	60	80	160	
Whisky, bottles of	doz.	2	4	6	8	16	
Wine, bottles of	doz.	2	4	6	8	16	
BEDDING.							
Bed-sacks	no.	10	20	30	40	80	
Bedsteads, iron	no.	6–10	12–20	18–30	24–40	48–80	
Blankets, woolen	no.	10–20	20–40	30–60	40–80	80–160	
Coverlets	no.	10	20	30	40	80	
Gutta-percha cloth	yds.	4	6	8	10	16	
Mattresses	no.	2	4	6	8	16	
Mosquito bars	no.	6–10	12–20	18–30	24–40	48–80	
Pillow-cases	no.	25	50	75	100	200	
" ticks	no.	10	20	30	40	80	
Sheets	no.	40	80	120	200	400	
FURNITURE, DRESSINGS, &C.							
Bandages, suspensory	no.	4	8	12	16	32	
Binder's boards	no.	4	6	8	12	16	18 inches by 4.
Corks, assorted	doz.	12	24	36	48	96	Assorted.
Corkscrews	no.	1	1	2	2	3	
Cotton batting	lb.	1	2	3	4	8	
" wadding	lb.	1	2	3	4	8	

Medical Department.

TABLE FOR GENERAL AND POST HOSPITALS.—CONTINUED.

ARTICLES.	Quantities for one year for commands of—					MEMORANDA.
	From 100 to 200.	From 200 to 300.	From 300 to 400.	500 men.	1,000 men.	
Flannel, red..........yds.	5	10	15	20	40	
Funnels, glass..........no.	1	1	2	2	4	
" tin..........no.	1	1	2	2	2	
Hatchets..........no.	1	1	2	2	2	
Hones (in wood)..........no.	1	2	1	1	1	4 inches by 1.
Ink-powder..........papers.	2	2	3	3	4	
Inkstands..........no.	1	1	2	2	2	
Linen..........yds.	5	10	15	20	40	
Lint..........lb.	4	6	8	10	20	
Measures, graduated..........no.	3	3	4	6	6	
" tin..........sets.	1	1	1	1	1	
Medicine cups and glasses..........no.	3	6	9	12	24	2 cups to 1 glass.
Mills, coffee..........no.	2	2	2	3	4	
Mortars and pestles, glass..........no.	1	1	2	2	2	
" " iron..........no.	1	1	1	1	1	
" " wedgewood..........no.	1	2	2	3	3	
Muslin..........yds.	25	50	75	100	200	
Needles, sewing..........no.	25	25	25	25	50	
Oiled silk, or gutta-percha tissue, or India-rubber tissue..........yds.	4	6	6	8	12	
Pans, bed..........no.	2	2	3	4	5	
Paper envelopes..........no.	100	125	150	200	250	Assorted, 3 sizes. "Official business" printed on each.

Medical Department.

Paper, filtering	quires.		3	2	2	1	½
" wrapping	quires.		20	15	15	12	10
" writing	quires.	[Foolscap, letter, and note—white; blue ruled.]	30	20	20	20	12
Pencils, hair	no.		50	30	24	18	12
" lead	no.		18	12	10	8	6
Pens, steel	doz.		6	4	3	3	2
Pill-boxes	papers.		24	12	9	6	3
" machine	no.		1	1	1	1	1
Pins, assorted	papers.		16	8	6	4	2
Quills	no.		50	50	50	25	25
Rain-gauges	no.		1	1	1	1	1
Razors	no.		2	1	1	1	1
Razor-strops	no.		2	1	1	1	1
Scales and weights, apothecary's	sets.		2	2	2	1	1
" " shop	sets.		1	1	1	1	1
Scissors	no.		4	3	2	2	2
Sheepskins, dressed	no.		12	10	8	6	4
Silk, surgeon's	oz.		1	½	½	¼	¼
" green	yds.		5	2½	2	1	⅜
Spatulas	lb.		12	6	4	3	3
Sponge	lb.		1	¾	¾	½	½
Tape	pieces.	{ ¼ woolen. { ¾ cotton.	32	16	12	8	4
Thermometers and hygrometers	no.		2	2	2	2	2
Thermometers	no.		1	1	1	1	1
Thread, linen	oz.		8	6	6	4	4
Tiles	no.		4	3	3	3	2
Tow	lb.		5	3	2	2	1
Towels	no.		150	75	50	30	20
Twine	lb.		3	1½	1½	1	1
Urinals	no.		10	6	5	3	2
Vials, assorted	doz.		48	24	18	12	6
Wafers (½ oz. boxes)	no.		3	2	2	1	1
Wax, sealing	sticks.		6	4	4	3	3

1303. Each medical officer will also be supplied with the following surgical instruments for his personal use, which he will retain in his immediate possession so long as he remains in the army, and for the complete and serviceable condition of which, at all times, he will be held responsible :

AMPUTATING.

1 Capital Saw.
1 Metacarpal Saw.
1 Capital Amputating Knife
1 Medium   "   "
1 Small   "   "
1 Large Catling.
1 Small   "
1 Scalpel.
1 Tenaculum.
1 Artery Needle.
1   "   Forceps.
1 Bone   "
1 Spiral Tourniquet.
12 Surgeon's Needles.
1 Mahogany Case, brass bound.
1 Gutta-Percha Pouch.

TREPHINING.

2 Trephines.
1 Scalpel, with Raspitor.
1 Heys' Saw.
1 Elevator.
1 Brush.
1 Mahogany Case, brass bound.

EXSECTING.

1 Bone Forceps, Liston's.
2 Bone Forceps, sharp, assorted.
1 Bone Forceps, for sequestra.
1 Chain Saw.
1 Chisel.
1 Gouge.
1 Lenticular Knife.
2 Spatulas, protecting.
1 Trephine, small crown.
1 Ecraseur.
1 Mahogany Case, brass bound.
1 Gutta-Percha Pouch.

GENERAL OPERATING

1 Metacarpal Saw.
1 Trocar.
1 Ball Forceps.
1 Gullet   "
1 Artery   "
1 Dressing "
2 Scissors, straight, and curved.
1 Artery Needle, with 4 points.
12 Surgeon's Needles.
1 Tourniquet.
1 Small Amputating Knife.
1   "   Catling.
3 Bistouries.
1 Hernia Knife.
3 Scalpels.
1 Cataract Knife.
1   "   Needle.
1 Tenaculum.
1 Double Hook.
6 Steel Bougies, silvered, double curve, Nos. 1 and 2, 3 and 4, 5 and 6, 7 and 8, 9 and 10, 11 and 12.
6 Wax Bougies, Nos. 2, 4, 6, 8, 10.
3 Silver Catheters, Nos. 3, 6, 9.
6 Gum-elastic Catheters, Nos. 1, 3, 5, 7, 9, 11.
2 Mahogany Cases, brass bound
1 Gutta-Percha Pouch.

POCKET.

1 Large Scalpel.
1 Small   "
1 Artery Forceps.
1 Bull-dog   "
1 Curved   "
1 Dressing   "
1 Needle.
1 Sharp-pointed Bistoury.

Medical Department.

1 Probe-pointed Bistoury.	1 Exploring Trocar.
1 Long Probe-pointed Bistoury.	1 Seton Needle.
1 Straight Scissors.	1 Spatula.
1 Knee "	2 Probes.
1 Flat-curved Scissors.	1 Director.
1 Gum Lancet.	1 Double Canula.
1 Tenaculum.	1 Comp'd Silver Catheter.
1 Tenotomy Knife.	6 Surgeon's Needles.
1 Abscess Lancet.	1 Artery Needle.
1 Exploring Needle.	1 Morocco Case.

1 Leather Trunk.

1304. The transfer of the surgical instruments issued to each medical officer for his personal use, is positively forbidden. These instruments will be accounted for to the Surgeon-General on the 31st day of December annually in a special return, in which the true condition of each must be stated; and if any be lost or damaged, a report of the facts and circumstances attending such loss or damage, must be given.

1305. To each General and Post Hospital, one ounce of *brominium*, with printed directions for preparing and administering Bibron's antidote to the poison of *serpents*. Also one bottle of *liquor ferri per sulphatis*, and one bottle of *liquor ammoniæ*, in equal proportions, with printed directions for preparing speedily and for administering the *hydrated sesqui-oxide of iron*, as an antidote to poisoning by *arsenic*.

1306. If the following articles of hospital furniture cannot be obtained with the hospital fund, they shall be procured from a quartermaster or medical disbursing officer, by special requisition :

ARTICLES.

Basins, wash.	Mugs.
Bowls.	Pans, frying.
Brushes.	—— sauce.
Buckets.	Pitchers.
Candlesticks.	Plates and Dishes.
Clothes-Lines.	Pots, chamber and chair.
Cups.	—— coffee and tea.
Dippers and Ladles.	Sadirons.
Graters.	Shovels, fire.
Gridirons.	Snuffers.
Kettles, tea.	Spoons.
Knives and Forks.	Tongs and Pokers.
Lamps and Lanterns.	Tumblers.
Locks and Keys.	Woodsaws.

Medical Department.

STANDARD SUPPLY TABLE FOR FIELD SERVICE.

Articles.	Reg't 3 mos.	Bat. 3 mos.	Comp. 3 mos.	Memoranda.
MEDICINES.				
Acidi acetici ....lb.	1	½	¼	
" sulph. aromatici ....lb.	1	½	¼	
" tannici ....oz.	2	1	1	
Alcoholis ....bott.	10	5	3	
Aluminis ....lb.	1	½	¼	
Ammoniæ carbonatis ....oz.	16	8	4	
Antimonii et potass. tartratis ....oz.	2	1	1	
Argenti nitratis (crystals) ....oz.	2	1	½	
" (fused) ....oz.	2	1	½	
Brominii ....oz.	1	1	1	
Camphoræ ....lb.	4	2	1	
Ceræ albæ ....oz.	2	2	1	
Cerati resinæ ....lb.	2	1	1	
" simplicis ....lb.	8	4	2	
Chloroformi ....lb.	2	1	1	
Copaibæ ....lb.	2	1	1	
Creasoti ....oz.	2	1	1	
Cupri sulphatis ....oz.	4	2	1	
Emplastri adhæsivi ....yds.	10	5	3	
" cantharidis ....lb.	4	2	1	
" ichthyocollæ ....yds.	10	5	3	
Extracti belladonnæ ....oz.	1	1	1	
" buchu fluidi ....lb.	1	½	¼	
" colchici acetici ....oz.	2	1	1	
" colocynthidis comp. ....oz.	16	8	4	
" glycyrrhizæ ....lb.	2	1	½	

" rhei fluidi.................lb.	4	1	2
" senegæ fluidi............oz.	4	4	8
" sennæ fluidi.............lb.	½	1	2
Hydrargyri chloridi corrosivi.....oz.	½	½	½
" mitis.................lb.	1	2	4
Iodinii.......................oz.	1	2	4
Liquoris ammoniæ..............lb.	1	2	—
" potass. arsenitis......oz.	5	10	20
Magnesiæ sulphatis............lb.	4	8	16
Massæ pil: hydrargyri.........oz.	1	1	4
Morphiæ sulphatis.............dr.	1	1	1
Olei caryophylli..............oz.	1	4	2
" menthæ piperitæ........oz.	2	6	8
" olivæ...............bott.	3	4	12
" ricini.............qt. bott.	2	1	8
" terebinthinæ........qt. bott.	1	4	2
" tiglii................dr.	2	4	8
Pilul: cathartic: comp: (U.S.)....doz.	2	4	8
" opii (U.S.)..........doz.	2	4	8
" quiniæ sulphatis (3 grs.)..doz.	½	1	2
Plumbi acetatis...............lb.	1	½	1
Potassæ bicarbonatis..........lb.	1	1	2
" chloratis...........lb.	½	½	1
" nitratis............lb.	1	1	1
Potassii cyanureti............dr.	2	4	8
" iodidi..............oz.	1	2	4
Pulveris acaciæ...............lb.	½	½	½
" capsici.............lb.	½	1	1
" ferri per sulphatis....oz.	½	4	8
" ipecacuanhæ.........lb.	4	8	16
" et opii.............oz.	4	1	2
" lini................lb.	½	½	½
" opii................lb.	3	6	12
" rhei................lb.	6	12	24
" sinapis nigræ.......lb.			
Quiniæ sulphatis..............oz.			

TABLE FOR FIELD SERVICE.—Continued.

Articles.	Reg't 3 mos.	Bat. 3 mos.	Comp. 3 mos.	Memoranda.
Sacchari ...lb.	10	5	2	
Saponis ...lb.	8	4	2	
Sodæ bicarbonatis ...lb.	1	½	¼	
Spiritus ammoniæ aromatici ...oz.	4	2	1	
" ætheris comp: ...lb.	1	½	¼	
" " nitrici ...lb.	2	1	½	
" vini gallici ...bott.	24	12	6	
Strychniæ ...dr.	1	1	1	
Tincturæ aconiti radicis ...lb.	1	½	¼	
" ferri chloridi ...lb.	1	½	¼	
" opii ...oz.	16	8	6	
" veratri viridis ...oz.	8	4	2	
Unguenti hydrargyri ...lb.	1	½	¼	
" nitratis ...lb.	½	¼	¼	
Zinci acetatis ...oz.	2	1	1	
" sulphatis ...oz.	2	1	1	
INSTRUMENTS.				
Buck's Spongeholder for the throat ...no.	1	1	1	
Cupping-glasses and tins ...no.	16	8	4	Half glass, half tin.
Lancets, spring ...no.	1	1	1	
" thumb (with cases) ...no.	6	4	2	
Pocket ...sets.	1	1	1	
Probangs (whalebone) ...no.	12	6	2	
Scarificators ...no.	4	2	1	
Splints (major) ...sets.	1	1	1	
Stomach-pump and case ...no.	1	1	1	
Syringes, enema ...no.	4	2	1	1 Davidson's; 1 hard rubber, 6 oz

Medical Department.

Item	Unit				Remarks
" penis, glass	no.	8	4	2	
" India-rubber	no.	8	4	2	
Teeth extracting	sets.	1	1	1	
Tongue-depressor (hinge)	no.	1	1	1	
Tourniquets, field	no.	8	4	2	
" spiral	no.	2	2	1	
Trusses, hernia	no.	6	3	2	
BOOKS.					
Anatomy (surgical)	cop.	1	1	1	
Medical Practice	cop.	1	1	1	
Regulations for Medical Department	cop.	1	1	1	
Surgery (operative)	cop.	1	1	1	
Thompson's Conspectus	cop.	1	1	1	
Blank	no.	4	4	4	
HOSPITAL STORES.					
Arrow-root	lb.	10	5	3	
Candles (sperm)	lb.	2	1	1	
Farina	lb.	10	5	3	
Ginger (fluid extract)	lb.	1	½	¼	
Nutmegs	oz.	8	4	1	
Tea	lb.	30	15	7	
Whisky, bottles of	doz.	2	1	½	
BEDDING.					
Blankets, woolen	no.	20–40	10–20	10	Brown.
Blanket-cases	no.	1 for 10 bla		nkets.	Of canvas, after pattern.
Gutta-percha cloth	yds.	8	4	2	{ So constructed as to form, when united, a continuous spread or covering.
" " bed-covers	no.	8	4	2	
Mosquito-bars	no.	12	6	4	
FURNITURE AND DRESSINGS.					
Bandages, roller, assorted	doz.	14	7	4	(See Mem. p. 308.)
" suspensory, assorted	no.	12	6	4	

Medical Department.

TABLE FOR FIELD SERVICE.—Continued.

Articles.	Reg't 3 mos.	Bat. 3 mos.	Comp. 3 mos.	Memoranda.
Binders' boards .... no.	18	9	5	18 inches by 4.
Buckets, leather .... no.	4	2	2	
Corks, assorted .... doz.	12	6	3	
Corkscrews .... no.	2	1	1	BANDAGES.
Cotton batting .... lb.	2	1	½	1 dozen, 1 inch wide, 1 yard long.
" wadding .... lb.	2	1	½	2 " 2 " "
Flannel (red) .... yds.	5	3	2	2 " 2½ " "
Hatchets .... no.	2	1	1	1 " 3 " "
Hones .... no.	1	1	1	½ " 3½ " "
Ink, 2-ounce bottles .... no.	12	6	3	½ " 4 " "
Knapsacks, hospital .... no.	...	...	...	4 " 6 " "
Lanterns .... no.	4	2	1	4 inches by 1, in wood.
Lint .... lb.	8	4	2	According to pattern.
Litters and stretchers, hand .... no.	...	...	...	
" horse .... no.	4	2	2	According to pattern.
Measures, graduated, assorted .... no.	...	...	...	6 oz., 2 oz., minim.
Medicine-chests .... no.	6	3	2	
" cups and glasses .... no.	...	...	...	2 cups to 1 glass.
" panniers .... no.	...	...	...	See note.
Mess-chests .... no.	...	...	...	
Mills, coffee .... no.	2	1	1	Small.
Mortars and pestles, wedgewood .... no.	2	1	1	
Muslin .... yds.	20	10	5	Assorted, in a case.
Needles, sewing .... no.	25	25	25	
Oiled silk or gutta-percha tissue, or India-rubber tissue .... yds.	8	4	2	Of hard India-rubber or other material. Shovel.
Pans, bed .... no.	2	1	1	
Paper envelopes, assorted .... no.	100	50	25	{ 50 letter, 25 note, 25 large. "Official Business" printed on each.

Medical Department.

Article					Remarks
Paper, wrapping......quires.	6			
" writing......quires.	12				{2 foolscap, 6 letter, 4 note, white; blue ruled.
Pencils, hair......no.	24	12	6		
" lead......no.	12	6	3		Of Faber's make, No. 2.
Pens, steel......doz.	2	2	3		
Pill-boxes (wood)......papers.	2	1	1		
" (tin)......no.	6	1	1		
Pins, assorted......papers.	4	6	6		
Razors......no.	1	2	2		
Razor-strops......no.	1	1	1		
Scales and weights, apothecary's......sets.	1	1	1		Large and medium.
Scissors......no.	4	2	2		
Sheep-skins, dressed......no.	4	2	1		
Silk, surgeons'......oz.	½	½	½		
Silk, green......yds.	1	3	2		
Spatulas......no.	6	½	½		
Sponge (washed)......lb.	1	½	¼		
Tape......pieces.	4	2	1		
Thread, linen......oz.	2	1	1		
Tiles......no.	2	1	1		
Towels......no.	40	20	10		
Twine......lb.	¼	½	¼		
Urinals......no.	4	2	1		
Vials, assorted......doz.	4	2	1		1 oz. and 2 oz.
Wafers (½-ounce boxes)......no.	1	1	1		
Wax, sealing......sticks.	2	1	1		

NOTE.—*Furniture of Mess Chest.*

8 Basins, tin.	2 Dippers and ladles.	6 Mugs (Britannia, ½-pint).	2 Pots, coffee and tea, tin.
2 Boxes, pepper and salt.	1 Grater.	1 Pan, frying.	12 Spoons, iron (table [6] and tea [6]).
6 Cups, tin.	1 Gridiron.	1 Pan, sauce.	1 Tray, tin.
4 Canisters (for tea, coffee, sugar, and butter).	1 Kettle, tea, Iron.	8 Plates (6) and dishes (2), tin	6 Tumblers, tin.
	12 Knives and forks.	1 Pot, iron.	

The Standard Supply Tables contain all the articles to be purchased by medical purveyors, except on the orders of the Surgeon-General; but any less quantity may be required or any article omitted at the discretion of the medical officer.

FORM 1.

Requisition for Medical and Hospital Supplies.

Station : ———, Period : ———.

From ——— to ———.

Command : Officers, ———; Enlisted Men, ———; All others entitled to Medicines, ———; Total, ———.

Articles, and characters or quantities.	On hand.	Wanted.	Articles, and characters or quantities.	On hand.	Wanted.
Acaciæ ....lb.					
Acidi acetici...................lb.					
" arseniosi................oz.					

Date : ———

———, Surgeon U. S. Army.

N.B.—Requisitions will exhibit the quantity of each and every article "on hand," whether more be wanted or not. They will be transmitted in duplicate, and by different mails.

FORM 2.

SPECIAL REQUISITION FOR SUPPLIES OF MEDICINES, ETC.

Requisition for Medicines (hospital stores, &c.) required at ———, *for* ———.

Acet. plumbi, lb. i.
Pulv. cinchonæ, lbs. x.
&c., &c.
&c., &c.

I certify that the medicines above required are necessary for the sick at ———, in consequence of [here state whether from loss, damage, &c., &c.], and that the requisition is agreeable to the supply table.

——————, *Surgeon.*

Approved:

——————, *Commanding Officer.*

Received, ———, 18—, of ———, the articles above enumerated.

——————, *Surgeon.*

FORM 3.

Account for Medicines, &c., purchased by a Surgeon or an Officer of the Quartermaster's Department.

The United States,

To A. B.,   Dr.

Acet. plumbi, lb. i, at 50 cts........ $0 50
Pulv. cinchonæ, lbs. x, at $2 ...... 20 00
&c., &c., &c.

I certify that the articles above charged, for the use of the sick at ——, are agreeable to the foregoing requisition, and that the charges are reasonable and just.

——————, *Surgeon.*

Received, ——, 18—, of ——————, —————— dollars and —————— cents, in full of the above account.

A. B.

NOTE.—The above certificate may be signed by the Surgeon making the requisition, or by any Surgeon or Assistant Surgeon belonging to the army.

Medical Department.——Forms.

FORM 4.

Return of Medical and Hospital Property.

Articles, and characters or quantities.	On hand at last return.	Received since last return.	Total.	Expended with the sick.	Issued.	Lost or destroyed by unavoidable accident.	Worn out, or unfit for use.	Total expended, &c.	On hand.	Remarks.

I certify that the above return is correct, to the best of my knowledge, and that the medicines and stores have been expended with the sick belonging to the army alone.

———— Surgeon.

N.B.—Returns will always be transmitted in duplicate, and by different mails.

FORM 5.

Abstract of Medical and Hospital Property received and issued at ——— in the quarter ending on the —— day of ———, 18—, by ———, Medical Purveyor, United States Army.

Articles, and characters or quantities.	RECEIVED.						ISSUED								
	Vou. No. 1. (Name.)	Vou. No. 2. (Name.)	Vou. No. 3. (Name.)	Vou. No. 4. (Name.)	Vou. No. 5. (Name.)	Total.	Vou. No. 1. (Name.)	Vou. No. 2. (Name.)	Vou. No. 3. (Name.)	Vou. No. 4. (Name.)	Vou. No. 5. (Name.)	Vou. No. 6. (Name.)	Vou. No. 7. (Name.)	Vou. No. 8. (Name.)	Total.
Acaciæ..........lb.															
Acidi acetici.....lb.															

I certify that the above abstract is correct.

N.B.—Invoices and receipts must accompany this abstract.

———, Medical Purveyor, U. S. A.

Medical Department.——Forms.

FORM 6.

Account of Hospital Stores, Furniture, &c., issued

Date.	Rice.	Sugar.	Tea.	Wine.	Brandy.	Coffee.	&c.	&c.	&c.			Remarks.
	Lbs.	Lbs.	Oz.	Qts.	Qts.	Lbs.	&c.	&c.	&c.			

FORM 7.

Account of Clothing, Arms, Equipments, &c., of Patients in Hospital.

Date.	Number.	Names.	Rank.	Regiment or corps.	Company.	Coats.	Jackets.	Overalls.	&c.	Muskets.	Knapsacks.	&c.	&c.	&c.	When delivered.	Remarks.
																The remarks will note to whom the articles were delivered; what money, &c., were left by those who die; and to whom they were given.

Medical Department.——Forms.

FORM 8.

Account of Furniture, Cooking Utensils, Bedding, &c., in Use.

No. of ward or kitchen.	Bunks.	Bed-sacks.	Sheets.	Blankets.	Kettles.	Spoons.	Knives.	Forks.	&c.	&c.									Lost.	Worn out.	Destroyed by order.	Returned to steward.	Remarks.
																							The remarks will state how articles have been lost, and by whom destroyed, or the persons suspected, &c.

Medical Department.——Forms.

FORM 9.
Register.

Names.	Rank.	Regiment or corps.	Company.	Complaint.	Admitted.	Returned to duty.	Deserted.	Discharged from service.	Sent to general hospital.	On furlough.	Died.	Remarks.

N.B.—Both Christian and sur-name will be registered.

FORM 10.

Prescription Book, Diet Book, and Diet Table.

Names.	Sunday.	Monday.	Tuesday.	Wednesday.	Thursday.	Friday.	Saturday.

The spaces in the Prescription Book are to be filled up with the prescriptions at length, the times of administering the medicines, and the quantities to be given at each time. The diet of the patients will be divided into full, half, and low, to be designated in the Diet Book by the letters F, H, and L.; and in order that the steward may have precise instructions for delivering the hospital stores, &c., the surgeon will, from time to time, insert in the Diet Book written directions of the quantity of each article in his store-room, which he may think necessary to each degree of diet. To each ten patients, for example, on low diet, a certain quantity of tea, sugar, &c. To each ten on half diet, a certain quantity of rice, milk, &c. These proportions will soon become familiar to the steward, who has only to refer to the letters in the Diet Book to ascertain the whole quantity of any article to be delivered for the day, as well as the quantity for each ward. When any liquor is directed, or any other article not contained in these general instructions of the surgeon, the precise quantity directed for each patient will be noted in the Diet Book. The Diet Tables are to be filled up daily from the Diet Book, and hung up in each ward of a general hospital

Medical Department.——Forms.

FORM 11.

METEOROLOGICAL

Station _____, *Lat.* _____, *Long.* _____,

186 .	Barometer.			Therm. attd.			Thermometer.				Hygrometer.			
Month.	7 A.M.	2 P.M.	9 P.M.	7 A.M.	2 P.M.	9 P.M.	7 A.M.	2 P.M.	9 P.M.	Daily mean.	7 A.M.	2 P.M.	9 P.M.	Daily mean.
1														
2														
3														
4														
5														
6														
7														
8														
9														
10														
11														
12														
13														
14														
15														
16														
17														
18														
19														
20														
21														
22														
23														
24														
25														
26														
27														
28														
29														
30														
31														
Monthly mean.														

FORM 11.

REGISTER

Alt. of Bar. above _____ *feet.*

Winds.						Weather.			Rain.			Remarks.
7 A.M.		2 P.M.		9 P.M.		7 A.M.	2 P.M.	9 P.M.	Began.	Ended.	Quantity.	
D.	F.	D.	F.	D.	F.							

FORM 11.—(Meteorological

SUMMARY OF WINDS AND WEATHER.

N.		N.E.		E.		S.E.		S.		S.W.		W.		N.W.	
Number.	Days.	Number.	Days.	Number.	Days.	Number.	Days.	Number.	Days.	Number.	Days.	Number.	Days.	Number.	Days.

No. of days FAIR.	No. of days CLOUDY.	No. of days of RAIN.	No. of days of SNOW.

REGISTER.)—Continued.

REMARKS.

This register is to be mailed to the Surgeon-General monthly without a letter of transmittal. All fractions are to be expressed in decimals carried out two points. The thermometer and hygrometer, if not connected, will be suspended side by side. One-third of the sum of the three daily observations will be registered as the daily mean. The direction (D.) and force (F.) of the winds will be expressed in accordance with existing regulations. The whole number of times any point of the compass is recorded during the month gives the "number of observations;" and that number divided by 3 gives the number of days from that point. The results thus obtained are to be recorded under "Summary of winds and weather." Observations on the weather will be recorded as FAIR or CLOUDY; and the number of fair and cloudy days during the month will be ascertained by dividing the sum total of each record by 3. The number of days on which it rains or snows will be noted separately.

SURGEON-GENERAL'S OFFICE, March, 1860.

Surgeon U. S. Army.

(ENDORSEMENT.)

Station :

METEOROLOGICAL REGISTER

FOR THE

Month of _____, 18—.

Transmitted by

Surgeon U. S. Army.

Rec'd S. G. Office, _____, 18—.

FORM 12.

Roll of Soldiers employed on extra duty as Cooks and Nurses in the Hospital at —— during the month of ——, 186 , by ——— ———, Surgeon.

No.	Names.	Rank or designation.	Company.	Regiment.	By whose order employed.	Nature of service.	Term of service.			Rate of pay or compensation.				How employed.
							From —	To —	No. of days.	Per diem. Cts.	Dolls.	Cts.		Remarks.

I certify that the above is a correct roll of the enlisted men employed on extra duty, under my direction, during the month of ——, 186 , and that the remarks opposite their names are accurate and just.

    Examined:

——————— ———, Surgeon.

——————— ———, Commanding.

FORM 13.
ARMY OF THE UNITED STATES.

Coat of Arms.

Certificate of Disability for Discharge.

(*To be used, in duplicate, in all cases of discharge on account of disability.*)

A. B., of Captain ———'s company (—), of the —— regiment of United States ———, was enlisted by —— ——, of the —— regiment of ——, at ——, on the —— day of ———, to serve —— years; he was born in ———, in the State of ———, is —— years of age, —— feet —— inches high, —— complexion, —— eyes, —— hair, and by occupation when enlisted ————. During the last two months said soldier has been unfit for duty —— days.

(The company commander will here add a statement of all the *facts* known to him concerning the disease or wound, or cause of disability of the soldier; the time, place, manner, and all the circumstances under which the injury occurred, or disease originated or appeared; the duty, or service, or situation of the soldier at the time the injury was received or disease contracted, or supposed to be contracted; and whatever facts may aid a judgment as to the cause, immediate or remote, of the disability, and the circumstances attending it.)

C. D., *Commanding Company.*

When the *facts* are not known to the company commander, the certificate of any officer, or affidavit of other person having such knowledge, will be appended.

I CERTIFY that I have carefully examined the said —— of Captain ———'s company, and find him incapable of performing the duties of a soldier, because of [here describe particularly the disability, wound, or disease; the extent to which it deprives him of the use of any limb or faculty, or affects his health, strength, activity, constitution, or capacity to labor or earn his subsistence. The surgeon will add, from his knowledge of the facts and circumstances, and from the evidence in the case, his professional opinion of the cause or origin of the disability.]

E. F., *Surgeon.*

(Duplicates.)

DISCHARGED this —— day of ———, 186 , at ————.

Commanding the Post.

NOTE 1.—When a *probable* case for *pension*, *special care* must be taken to state the *degree* of disability.

NOTE 2.—The *place* where the *soldier* desires to be *addressed* may be here added.

Town—   *County—*   *State—*

Medical Department.——Forms.

FORM 14.

Record of Recruits examined by ——, *at* ——

| Date. | Name. | WHERE BORN. | | Age. | Profession. | By whom enlisted. | Remarks. |
		Town or county.	State or kingdom.				
							The remarks will state the cause of rejecting any who are examined, &c., &c.

——, *Surgeon.*

FORM 15.

Report of the Sick and Wounded at ——, for the quarter ending ——, 186 .

Classes of Diseases.	Specific Diseases.	TAKEN SICK OR RECEIVED INTO HOSPITAL DURING THE QUARTER.										
		First.		Second.		Third.		Total by each disease.		Total by each class.	
	Month..........	Cases.	Deaths.	Cases.	Deaths.	Cases.	Deaths.	Cases.	Deaths.	Cases.	Deaths.
Fevers..........	Febris Congestiva............										
	Febris Continua Communis....										
	Febris Intermittens Quotidiana										
	Febris Intermittens Tertiana...										
	Febris Intermittens Quartana..										
	Febris Remittens.............										
	Febris Typhoides										
	Febris Typhus................										
	Febris Typhus Icterodes.......										
	All other diseases of this class.										
Eruptive Fevers	Erysipelas										
	Rubeola										
	Scarlatina...................										
	Variola......................										
	Varioloides..................										
	All other diseases of this class.										
	Carry forward.........										

FORM 15.—Continued.

TAKEN SICK OR RECEIVED INTO HOSPITAL DURING THE QUARTER.

Classes of Diseases.	Specific Diseases.	Month	First.		Second.		Third.		Total by each disease.		Total by each class.	
			Cases.	Deaths.	Cases.	Deaths.	Cases.	Deaths.	Cases.	Deaths.	Cases.	Deaths.
	Brought forward											
Diseases of the organs connected with the digestive system.	Cholera Asiatica											
	Cholera Morbus											
	Colica											
	Constipatio											
	Diarrhœa Acuta											
	Diarrhœa Chronica											
	Dysenteria Acuta											
	Dysenteria Chronica											
	Dyspepsia											
	Enteritis											
	Gastritis											
	Hæmatemesis											
	Hepatitis Acuta											
	Hepatitis Chronica											
	Icterus											
	Parotitis											
	Peritonitis											
	Splenitis											
	Tonsilitis											
	All other diseases of this class.											
	Asthma											
	Bronchitis Acuta											
	Bronchitis Chronica											

Medical Department.——Forms.

Diseases of the respiratory system..........	Catarrhus Epidemicus............
	Catarrhus.......................
	Hæmoptysis.....................
	Laryngitis......................
	Phthisis Pulmonalis.............
	Pleuritis.......................
	Pneumonia......................
	All other diseases of this class..
Diseases of the circulatory system..........	Anæmia.........................
	Aneurisma......................
	Angina Pectoris.................
	Carditis........................
	Endocarditis....................
	Pericarditis.....................
	Phlebitis.......................
	Varicocele......................
	Varix...........................
	All other diseases of this class..
Diseases of the brain and nervous system............	Apoplexia.......................
	Cephalalgia.....................
	Cerebritis......................
	Chorea.........................
	Delirium Tremens...............
	Epilepsia.......................
	Ictus Solis.....................
	Irritatio Spinalis...............
	Mania..........................
	Melancholia....................
	Meningitis......................
	Neuralgia......................
	Paralysis.......................
	Tetanus........................
	All other diseases of this class..

Carry forward..........

Medical Department.——Forms.

FORM 15.—Continued.

TAKEN SICK OR RECEIVED INTO HOSPITAL DURING THE QUARTER.

Classes of Diseases.	Specific Diseases. Month............	First.		Second.		Third.		Total by each disease.		Total by each class.	
		Cases.	Deaths.	Cases.	Deaths.	Cases.	Deaths.	Cases.	Deaths.	Cases.	Deaths.
Diseases of the urinary and genital organs, and venereal affections......	Brought forward...........										
	Bubo Syphiliticum.........										
	Calculus...................										
	Cystitis...................										
	Diabetes...................										
	Enuresis..........										
	Gonorrhœa................										
	Ischuria et Dysuria.......										
	Nephritis.................										
	Orchitis..................										
	Sarcocele.................										
	Strictura Urethræ........										
	Syphilis Primitiva........										
	Syphilis Consecutiva......										
	Ulcus Penis non Syphiliticum...										
	All other diseases of this class....										
Diseases of the serous exhalent vessels.....	Anasarca										
	Ascites...................										
	Hydrarthrus										
	Hydrocele.................										
	Hydrothorax..............										
	All other diseases of this class....										
Diseases of the fibrous and muscular structures...	Lumbago..................										
	Podagra..................										
	Rheumatismus Acutus.....										
	Rheumatismus Chronicus...										
	All other diseases of this class....										

Medical Department.——Forms.

Abscesses and ulcers.........
- Abscessus
- Anthrax
- Fistula
- Paronychia
- Phlegmon
- Ulcus
- All other diseases of this class

Wounds and injuries.........
- Ambustio
- Concussio Cerebri
- Compressio Cerebri
- Contusio
- Fractura
- Gelatio
- Hernia
- Luxatio
- Morsus Serpentis
- Punitio
- Sub-luxatio
- Vulnus Incisum
- Vulnus contusum vel Laceratum
- Vulnus Punctum
- Vulnus Sclopeticum
- All other diseases of this class

Diseases of the eye.........
- Amaurosis
- Cataracta
- Hemeralopia
- Iritis
- Nyctalopia
- Ophthalmia
- Retinitis
- All other diseases of this class

Diseases of the ear.........
- Otalgia
- Otitis
- Otorrhœa
- Surditas
- All other diseases of this class

Carry forward.........

FORM 15.—Continued.

TAKEN SICK OR RECEIVED INTO HOSPITAL DURING THE QUARTER.

Classes of Diseases.	Specific Diseases.	Month...........	First.		Second.		Third.		Total by each disease.		Total by each class.	
			Cases.	Deaths.	Cases.	Deaths.	Cases.	Deaths.	Cases.	Deaths.	Cases.	Deaths.
	Brought forward.........											
	Anchylosis.........											
	Atrophia.........											
	Bubo simplex.........											
	Cachexia.........											
	Debilitas.........											
	Ebrietas.........											
	Epistaxis.........											
	Exostosis.........											
	Hæmorrhois.........											
	Hematocele.........											
	Morbi Cutis.........											
All other diseases.........	Necrosis.........											
	Nostalgia.........											
	Odontalgia.........											
	Prolapsus ani.........											
	Scirrhus.........											
	Scorbutus.........											
	Scrofula.........											
	Suicidium.........											
	Toxicum.........											
	Tumores.........											
	Vermes.........											
	Morbi Varii.........											
	Total.........											

Medical Department.——Forms.

FORM 15.—Continued.
General Summary.

Remaining last report.			Taken sick during the quarter.	Aggregate.	Sent to general hospital.	Returned to duty.	On furlough.	Discharged.	Deserted.	Died.	Remaining.				Mean strength.				Number treated.		Ratio per 1000 of mean strength.	
Sick.	Convalescent.	Total.									Sick.	Convalescent.	Total.		Months.	Officers.	Enlisted men.	Total.		Deaths.	Cases.	Deaths.
														Total...								
														Ratio per qr.								

DIRECTIONS.—In regard to this Report, the utmost punctuality and exactness will be required, and its nomenclature will be strictly observed. It will be accompanied with a general Sanitary Report, to be written on alternate pages of foolscap paper, with a margin of one inch on the left side of each page, and to be folded in four equal folds; in which the medical officer will furnish information respecting all those agencies which may have influenced the sickness and mortality of the troops—such as the medical topography of the station; the climate; prevalent diseases in the vicinity; the duty and employment of the troops; the nature of their barrack and hospital accommodations; diet, water, clothing, and general habits of the men as to cleanliness, temperance, &c. Cases of unusual interest will be reported in detail. Diseases of women and children, if given, must be reported separately. No duplicate of this report is required. In consolidated and other monthly reports of sick and wounded, the general arrangement and the nomenclature of this form will be followed.

Medical Department.——Forms.

FORM 15.—Continued.

Discharges on Surgeon's Certificate and Deaths.

Name.		Rank.	Regiment.	Company.	Disease.	Date of discharge from service.	Date of death.
Surname.	Christian name.						

REMARKS.

NOTES.—Discharges on Surgeon's certificate, and deaths occurring among those of the command *not* on sick report, will also be reported, but separated from the others by a double line drawn across the page. The remarks will in each case specify the manner in which the disease originated, when it is known.

In every case of the death of an officer, whether on duty or not, a special report is to be made to the Surgeon-General.

FORM 15.—Continued.

(*Endorsement.*)

REPORT OF SICK AND WOUNDED

FOR THE

Quarter ending   , 186 .

Station:

SURGEON U. S. ARMY.

COMMAND.

REGIMENTS.	COMPANIES.

Medical Department.——Forms.

FORM 16.

Morning Report of the Surgeon of a Regiment, Post, or Garrison.

Date.	Company.	Remaining at last report.		Taken sick.	Total.		Returned to duty.	Discharged.	Sent to general hospital.	Died.	Remaining.		Remarks.
		In hospital.	In quarters.		In hospital.	In quarters.					In hospital.	In quarters.	

FORM 17

Return of the Medical Officers of the Regular Army, Volunteer Corps, and Militia, including Physicians employed under contract, serving in the Department of ——, for the month of ——, 186 .

Number.	Names.	Rank.	Post or station.	With what troops serving.	Remarks

———, Surgeon.

NOTE.—The names will be arranged in the following order: 1st. Medical Officers of the Regular Army; 2d. Those of Volunteer Corps and Militia; 3d. Private Physicians. In the column of "Remarks" will be noted all changes in the position of Medical Officers and Private Physicians, whether on duty or on leave of absence; giving the number, date, and source of the order directing or authorizing such change, the time of the departure of the officers from their posts, and the date of their return to duty. If to a new post, its position must be indicated by reference to some known point, as —— miles north from —— river, town, or post-office. The remarks opposite the names of Private Physicians will state, in addition to the above, the name and rank of the party making the contract, the date thereof, the monthly compensation, and the date of their discharge from service.

The Medical Directors will require from the Medical Officers and Private Physicians in their respective Departments, monthly reports to enable them to make out and transmit this Return to the Surgeon-General.

FORM 18.

Contract with a Private Physician.

This contract, entered into this —— day of ———, 18—, at ———, State of ———, between ——— ———, of the United States Army, and Dr. ——— ———, of ———, in the State of ———, witnesseth, that for the consideration hereafter mentioned, the said Dr. ——— promises and agrees to perform the duties of a medical officer, agreeably to the Army Regulations, at ——— (*and to furnish the necessary medicines*). And the said ——— promises and agrees, on behalf of the United States, to pay, or cause to be paid, to the said Dr. ——— the sum of —— dollars for each and every month he shall continue to perform the services above stated, which shall be his full compensation, and in lieu of all allowances and emoluments whatsoever (*except that for medicines furnished, which shall be at the rate of — per cent. on his monthly pay, to be determined by the Surgeon-General*). This contract to continue till determined by the said doctor, or the commanding officer for the time being, or the Surgeon-General.

[SEAL.]

Signed, sealed, and delivered }
   in presence of   }

[SEAL.]

——————

I certify that the number of persons entitled to medical attendance, agreeably to regulations, at ———, is ——, and that no competent physician can be obtained at a lower rate.

——— ———, *Commanding Officer.*

FORM 19.

A Monthly Statement of the Hospital Fund at ——, for the month of ——, 186 .

DR. To balance due hospital last month					$0	00
1532 rations, being whole amount due this month, at $9\frac{1}{2}$ cents per ration					145	54
ISSUED.						
CR. By the following provisions, at contract prices:						
$283\frac{1}{2}$ lbs. of pork, at 6 cents per pound			$17	01		
690 lbs. of fresh beef, at 4 cents per pound			27	60		
$1612\frac{2}{16}$ lbs. of flour, at 2 cents per pound			32	$24\frac{1}{4}$		
10 lbs. of hard bread, at $3\frac{1}{2}$ cents per pound				35		
70 lbs. of rice, at 6 cents per pound			4	20		
56 lbs. of coffee, at 9 cents per pound			5	04		
$193\frac{14}{16}$ lbs. of sugar, at 8 cents per pound			15	51		
$17\frac{1}{8}$ quarts of vinegar, at 5 cents per quart				$85\frac{5}{8}$		
$15\frac{5}{16}$ lbs. of candles, at 12 cents per pound			1	$83\frac{3}{4}$		
$61\frac{1}{4}$ lbs. of soap, at 6 cents per pound			3	$67\frac{1}{2}$		
$16\frac{7}{8}$ quarts of salt, at 3 cents per quart				$50\frac{5}{8}$		
12 gallons of molasses, at 28 cents per gallon			3	36		
			112	$18\frac{3}{4}$		
PURCHASED.						
2 pairs of chickens, at $87\frac{1}{2}$ cents per pair	$1	75				
4 quarts of milk, at 7 cents per quart	......	28				
3 dozen oranges, at 25 cents per dozen	......	75	2	78		
Total expended	......	.....	......	......	114	$96\frac{3}{4}$
Balance due this month					30	$57\frac{1}{4}$

—— ——, *Surgeon U. S. Army.*

[Date.]

(No letter of transmittal required.)

FORM 20.

Form of a Medical Certificate.

———— ————, of the —— regiment of ————, having applied for a certificate on which to ground an application for leave of absence, I do hereby certify that I have carefully examined this officer, and find that ————. [Here the nature of the disease, wound, or disability, is to be fully stated, and the period during which the officer has suffered under its effects.] And that, in consequence thereof, he is, in my opinion, unfit for duty. I further declare my belief that he will not be able to resume his duties in a less period than ————. [Here state candidly and explicitly the opinion as to the period which will probably elapse before the officer will be able to resume his duties. When there is no reason to expect a recovery, or when the prospect of recovery is distant and uncertain, it must be so stated.]

Dated at ————, this —— day of ————.

Signature of the }
Medical Officer. } ———— ————.

ARTICLE XLV.

PAY DEPARTMENT.

1307. The troops will be paid in such manner that the arrears shall at no time exceed two months, unless the circumstances of the case render it unavoidable, which the paymaster charged with the payment shall promptly report to the Paymaster-General.

1308. The Paymaster-General shall take care, by timely remittances, that the paymasters have the necessary funds to pay the troops, and shall notify the remittances to the paymasters and commanding officers of the respective pay districts.

1309. The payments, except to officers and discharged soldiers, shall be made on muster and pay rolls; those of companies and detachments, signed by the company or detachment commander; of the hospital, signed by the surgeon; and all muster and pay rolls, signed by the mustering and inspecting officer.

1310. When a company is paraded for payment, the officer in command of it shall attend at the pay-table.

1311. When a receipt on a pay-roll or account is not signed by the hand of the party, the payment must be witnessed. The witness to be a commissioned officer when practicable.

1312. Officers are paid on certified accounts, as in Form 3; discharged soldiers, on accounts according to Form 5, and certificates, Form 4. An officer retiring from service must make affidavit to his pay account, and to the certificate annexed to it, and state his place of residence, and the date when his resignation or removal takes effect. Pay accounts of post chaplains are to be certified by the commanding officer of the post.

1313. When an officer is dismissed from the service, he shall not be entitled to pay beyond the day on which the order announcing his dismissal is received at the post where he may be stationed, unless a particular day beyond the time is mentioned in the order.

1314. No officer shall receive pay for two staff appointments for the same time.

1315. Officers are entitled to pay from the date of the acceptance of their appointments, and from the date of promotion.

1316. No account of a restored officer for time he was out of service can be paid, without order of the War Department.

1317. As far as practicable, officers are to draw their pay from the paymaster of the district where they may be on duty.

1318. No officer shall pass away or transfer his pay account not actually due at the time; and when an officer transfers his pay account, he shall report the fact to the Paymaster-General, and to the paymaster expected to pay it.

1319. No person in the military service, while in arrears to the United States, shall draw pay. When the Secretary of War shall find by report of the Comptroller of the Treasury, or otherwise, that an officer of the army is in arrears to the United States, the Paymaster-General shall be directed to stop his pay to the amount of such arrears, by giving notice thereof to the paymasters of the army, and to the officer, who may pay over the amount to any paymaster. And no paymaster shall make to him any payment on account of *pay* until he exhibits evidence of having refunded the amount of the arrears, or that his pay accrued and stopped is equal to it, or until the stoppage is removed by the Paymaster-General.

1320. Officers having brevet commissions are entitled to their brevet pay and emoluments *when on duty and having a command according to their brevet rank, and at no other time.* (Act April 16, 1818.)

1321. Officers are *on duty and have a command according to their brevet* rank only when assigned to their brevet rank by the President with the appropriate actual command composed of different corps, or when serving on detachments composed of different corps, with such appropriate command. But in the regiment, troop, or company to which officers belong, they do duty and draw pay according to the commissions by which they are mustered in their own corps.

1322. The following are the appropriate commands to each grade:

1. For a captain, at least a company.
2. For a major, at least 2 companies.
3. For a lieutenant-colonel, at least 4 companies.
4. For a colonel, at least 1 regiment, or 10 companies.
5. For a brigadier-general, 2 regiments, or 20 companies.
6. For a major-general, 4 regiments, or 40 companies.
7. For a lieutenant-general, 8 regiments, or 80 companies.

1323. Officers charging brevet pay will state on their pay accounts the regiments and companies composing their commands.

1324. Double rations are allowed to the major-general commanding the army, and to every officer commanding in chief a separate army actually in the field; to the generals commanding the eastern and western geographical divisions; to the Quartermaster-General and the Adjutant-General; to the colonels or other officers commanding military geographical departments.

1325. Commanding officers of companies will not forfeit the allowances to which they are entitled by reason of such command when temporarily absent on duty, provided the absence is less than one month.

1326. No officer or soldier shall receive pay or allowances for any time during which he was absent without leave, unless a satisfactory excuse for such absence be rendered to his commanding officer, evidence of which, in case of an officer, shall be annexed to his pay account.

1327. Every deserter shall forfeit all pay and allowances due at the time of desertion. Stoppages and fines shall be paid from his future earnings, if he is apprehended and continued in service and if they are adjudged by a court-martial; otherwise, from his arrears of pay.

1328. No deserter shall receive pay before trial, or till restored to duty without trial by the authority competent to order the trial.

1329. In case of a soldier's death, desertion, or discharge without pay, or the forfeiture of his pay by sentence of court-martial, the amount due the laundress and sutler will be noted on the muster-roll.

1330. The extra pay allowed to soldiers acting as cooks and nurses in hospitals will be paid by the Pay Department. Such extra services will be noted on the hospital muster-rolls, and for the sums thus expended, the Pay Department will be reimbursed by the Medical Department.

1331. When an improper payment has been made to any enlisted soldier, and disallowed in the settlement of the paymaster's accounts, the paymaster n ay report the fact to the commander of the company in which the soldier is mustered, who will note on the muster-rolls the amount to be stopped from the pay of the soldier, that it may be re-funded to the paymaster in whose accounts the improper payment has been disallowed.

1332. Authorized stoppages to reimburse the United States, as for loss or damage to arms, equipments, or other public property; for extra issues of clothing; for the expense of apprehending deserters, or to reimburse individuals (as the paymaster, laundress, &c.); forfeitures for desertion, and fines by sentence of court-martial, will be entered on the roll and paid in the order stated.

1333. The paymaster will deduct from the pay of all enlisted men twelve and a half cents per month for the support of the "Soldiers' Home," and also the amount of the authorized stoppages entered on the muster-roll, descriptive list, or certificate of discharge.

1334. The additional pay of two dollars a month to a private soldier in virtue of a certificate of merit (Act March 3, 1847), commences at the date of the service for which the certificate is given, and continues while he remains a private soldier, if he has been continuously in service, or has a certificate of merit given for service in the war with Mexico. (Act August 4, 1854.)

1335. Non-commissioned officers who were recommended by the com-manding officer of their regiment f r promotion by brevet for distinguished service in the war with Mexico, and not promoted, receive two dollars a month additional pay, while in service as non-commissioned officers. (Act August 4, 1854.)

1336. The muster-rolls are to embrace all the data necessary to insure justice to the soldier, and to guide the paymaster in making his payments. Thus, when a man is entitled to the benefits of the 2d section of the Act of August 4, 1854, the following remark should be placed opposite his name: "$2 pr. mo. for 1st re-enlistment." If he be entitled to $1 additional for re-enlisting subsequent to its date, the remark will then be, "$3 pr. mo. for 2d re-enlistment;" for a third re-enlistment, "$4 pr. mo. for 3d re-enlistment," &c. For soldiers coming under the provisions of the 3d and 4th sections of the act, note as follows: "$2 pr. mo. for cert. merit;" "$2 pr. mo. for 1st re-enlistment, $2 for cert. merit," &c., according to the facts of the case.

1337. The retained pay is due to a discharged soldier unless forfeited by sentence of a court-martial, or as provided in paragraph 1340.

1338. The traveling pay is due to a discharged officer or soldier unless forfeited by sentence of a court-martial, or as provided in paragraph 1340, or the discharge is by way of punishment for an offense.

1339. In reckoning the traveling allowance to discharged officers or soldiers, the distance is to be estimated by the shortest mail route; if there is no mail route, by the shortest practicable route. Rations of soldiers, if not drawn in kind, are estimated at the contract price at the place of discharge. The price of the ration shall be stated on the certificate.

1340. Every enlisted man discharged as a minor, or for other cause involving fraud on his part in the enlistment, or discharged by the civil authority, shall forfeit all pay and allowances due at the time of the discharge, and shall not receive any final statements.

1341. Paymasters or other officers to whom a discharged soldier may apply, shall transmit to the Paymaster-General, with their remarks, any evidence the soldier may furnish relating to his not having received or having lost his certificates of pay due. The Paymaster-General will transmit the evidence to the Second Comptroller for the settlement of the account.

1342. No paymaster or other officer shall be interested in the purchase of any soldier's certificate of pay due, or other claim against the United States.

1343. The Paymaster-General will report to the Adjutant-General any case of neglect of company officers to furnish the proper certificates to soldiers entitled to discharge.

1344. Whenever the garrison is withdrawn from any post at which a chaplain is authorized to be employed, his pay and emoluments shall cease on the last day of the month next ensuing after the withdrawal of the troops. The Paymaster-General will be duly informed from the Adjutant-General's office whenever the appointment and pay of the post chaplain will cease under this regulation.

1345. Funds turned over to other paymasters, or refunded to the Treasury, are to be entered in accounts current, but not in the abstracts of payments.

1346. Whenever money is refunded to the Treasury, the name of the person refunding, and the purpose for which it is done, should be stated, in order that the officers of that Department may give the proper credits.

1347. When an officer of the army receives a temporary appointment from the proper authority to a grade in the militia then in actual service of the United States higher in rank than that held by him in the army, he shall be entitled to the pay and emoluments of the grade in which he serves. But in no case can an officer receive the compensation of two military commissions or appointments at the same time.

1348. Whenever the Paymaster-General shall discover that an officer has drawn pay twice for the same time, he shall report it to the Adjutant General.

1349. The Paymaster-General shall transmit to the Second Auditor, in the month of May, a statement exhibiting the total amount during the year up to the 31st December preceding, of stoppages against officers and soldiers on account of ordnance and ordnance stores, that the amount may be refunded to the proper appropriations. These stoppages will be regulated by the tables of cost published by the chief of the Ordnance Department, and shall have precedence of all other claims on the pay of officers or soldiers.

1350. The following returns are to be transmitted to the Paymaster General after each payment :

1st. Estimate for succeeding months (Form 1).

2d. Abstracts of payments (Form 6), accompanied by the vouchers

3d. General account current (Form 7).

4th. Monthly statement of funds, disbursements, &c. (Form 9).

1351. The accounts and vouchers for the expenditures to the regular army must be kept separate and distinct from those to volunteers and militia.

1352. Pay-roll of militia will be according to Form 8, the certificate at the foot to be signed by all the company officers present.

1353. No militia or volunteers shall be paid till regularly mustered into service, as provided in the General Regulations.*

---

* But see chap. 16, July 24, 1861, vol. xii. p. 274.

1354. In order to afford enlisted men of the army a secure deposit for the amounts from their pay, and to relieve the muster and pay rolls from accumulated credits of pay, the following provisions are made :

1. All enlisted men present with their companies or detachments at the time of payment shall hereafter sign the receipt for their monthly pay.

2. Soldiers may deposit with the paymaster any portion of their pay, not less than $5 at one time, provided that no amount so deposited shall be withdrawn until the expiration of the soldier's enlistment.

3. At the time of first deposit, a check-book will be given to the soldier, and a certificate of every deposit made, signed by the paymaster and company commander, shall be entered therein at the time of making the same.

4. The company commander shall keep an account of every deposit made by a soldier on the company book, and shall transmit to the Paymaster-General, after each payment, a list of the depositors and the amounts deposited by them respectively.

5. In case of the transfer of a soldier, his descriptive roll shall exhibit the several amounts deposited by him.

6. On the discharge of a soldier, the amount of his deposits shall be entered on his final statements, and paid on settlement of the same.

7. On the death of a soldier, his deposits shall be accounted for in the inventory of his effects and on the accompanying final statements.

8. The money deposited by any soldier shall not be liable to forfeiture by sentence of court-martial.

9. Paymasters will receive the deposits of the soldiers in their respective districts, credit the same in their accounts current, and furnish a list of the depositors, with the several sums deposited by each, to accompany their accounts and vouchers of disbursements. The sums thus received by the paymasters may be again used by them in the payment of troops.

10. The Paymaster-General shall keep in his office such record as may be necessary to show the deposits made by the enlisted men of each company.

1355. Paymasters will afford Sutlers every facility in the collection of the amounts due them in accordance with regulations 217 and 218.

1356. Officers absent from their appropriate duties, either with or without leave, for six months, will thereby forfeit all the emoluments and allowances to which they would otherwise be entitled.

Pay Department.

TABLE OF PAY, SUBSISTENCE, FORAGE, &c. OF THE U. S. ARMY.

GRADE.	Pay. Per month.	Subsistence. No. of rations per day.	Forage. No. of horses allowed in time of war.	Forage. No. of horses allowed in time of peace.	No. of servants allowed.
Lieutenant-General	$270 00	40	7		4
Major General	220 00	15	4	3	4
Senior Aide-de-Camp to General-in-Chief	80 00	4	2	1	2
Aide-de-Camp, in addition to pay, &c., of Lieutenant	24 00	....	3	3	..
Brigadier-General	124 00	12	5	1	3
Aide-de-Camp to Brigadier, in addition to pay, &c., of Lieutenant*	20 00	....	2	1	..
Adjutant-General	124 00	12	5	3	3
Assistant Adjutant-General, with the rank of Colonel	110 00	6	5	3	2
Assistant Adjutant-General, with the rank of Lieutenant-Colonel	95 00	5	4	3	2
Assistant Adjutant-General, with the rank of Major	80 00	4	4	3	2
Assistant Adjutant-General, with the rank of Captain	70 00	4	3	1	1
Judge Advocate	80 00	4	4	3	2
Inspector-General	110 00	6	5	3	2
Assistant Inspector-General, with the rank of Major	80 00	4	4	3	2
Signal Officer, with the rank of Major	80 00	4	5	3	2
Quartermaster-General	124 00	12	5	3	3
Assistant Quartermaster-General	110 00	6	4	3	2
Deputy Quartermaster-General	95 00	5	4	3	2
Quartermaster	80 00	4	4	3	2
Assistant Quartermaster	70 00	4	3	1	1
Paymaster-General, $2740 per annum					
Deputy Paymaster-General	95 00	5	4	3	2

$50 a mo. for forage.

Pay Department.

					Pay per month
Paymaster	2	3	4	4	80 00
Commissary-General of Subsistence	2	3	5	6	110 00
Assistant Commissary-General of Subsistence	2	3	4	5	95 00
Commissary of Subsistence, with the rank of Major	2	3	4	4	80 00
Commissary of Subsistence, with the rank of Captain	1	1	3	4	70 00
Assistant Commissary of Subsistence, in addition to pay, &c., of Lieutenant*					20 00
Surgeon-General, $2740 per annum.	2	3	4	8	
Surgeon of ten years' service in that grade	2	3	4	4	80 00
Surgeon, less than ten years' service	1	1	3	8	80 00
Assistant Surgeon of ten years' service	1	1	3	4	70 00
Assistant Surgeon of five years' service	1	1	2	4	70 00
Assistant Surgeon, less than five years' service					53 33⅓
MILITARY ACADEMY.					
Superintendent, not less than the Professor of Natural and Experimental Philosophy. The Commander of Corps of Cadets, not less than the Professor of Mathematics.					
Professor of Natural and Experimental Philosophy, $2240 per annum.	1	1	3	4	
Assistant Professor of Natural and Experimental Philosophy					70 00
Professor of Mathematics, $2240 per annum.	1	1	3	4	
Assistant Professor of Mathematics					70 00
Professor of Engineering, $2240 per annum.	1	1	3	4	
Assistant Professor of Engineering, and Instructor of Practical Engineering, each					70 00
Professor of Chemistry, Mineralogy, and Geology, $2240 per annum.	1	1	3	4	
Assistant Professor of Chemistry, Mineralogy, and Geology, and Assistant Professor of Ethics, each					70 00
Chaplain and Professor of Ethics, $2240 per annum.	1	1	3	4	
Professor of French, and Professor of Drawing, each $2240 per annum.	1	1	3	4	
Assistant Professor of French, and Assistant Professor of Drawing, each					70 00
Professor of Spanish, $2240 per annum.	1	2	2	4	
Instructor of Cavalry and Artillery Tactics					70 00
Adjutant of the Military Academy					63 33⅓
Master of the Sword, $1500 per annum.					60 00
Teacher of Music					30 00
Cadet					

TABLE OF PAY, SUBSISTENCE, FORAGE, &c.,—Continued.

Pay Department.

Grade.	Pay. Per month.	Subsistence. No. of rations per day.	Forage. No. of horses allowed in time of war.	Forage. No. of horses allowed in time of peace.	No. of servants allowed.
ENGINEERS AND TOPOGRAPHICAL ENGINEERS.					
Colonel	$110 00	6	5	3	2
Lieutenant-Colonel	95 00	5	4	3	2
Major	80 00	4	4	3	2
Captain	70 00	4	3	1	1
Lieutenants, 1st and 2d, and Brevet 2d	53 33	4	1	1	..
Enlisted men, same as Sappers and Miners.					
ORDNANCE.					
Chief of Ordnance	124 00	12	5	3	3
Colonel	110 00	6	5	3	2
Lieutenant-Colonel	95 00	5	4	3	2
Major	80 00	4	4	3	2
Captain	70 00	4	3	..	1
Lieutenants, 1st and 2d, and Brevet 2d	53 33⅓	4	2	..	1
Master Armorer, Master Carriage-Maker, or Master Blacksmith	34 00	..	..	..	..
Armorer, Carriage-Maker, or Blacksmith	20 00	..	..	..	..
Artificer	17 00	..	..	..	..
Laborer	18 00	..	..	..	..

Pay Department.

CAVALRY.

Rank					Pay
Colonel	2	3	5	6	$110 00
Lieutenant-Colonel	2	3	4	5	95 00
Major	2	3	4	4	80 00
Captain	1	2	3	4	70 00
Lieutenants, 1st and 2d, and Brevet 2d		2	1	4	53 33
Adjutant, in addition to pay, &c., of Lieutenant					10 00
Regimental Quartermaster, " " "					10 00
Sergeant-Major					21 00
Quartermaster-Sergeant					21 00
Chief Bugler					21 00
First Sergeant					20 00
Sergeant and Saddle Sergeant, Veterinary Sergeant, and Company Quartermaster-Sergeant					17 00
Corporal					14 00
Bugler					13 00
Farrier and Blacksmith					15 00
Private					13 00

ARTILLERY AND INFANTRY.

Rank					Pay
Colonel	2	3	4	6	95 00
Lieutenant-Colonel	2	3	3	5	80 00
Major	2	3	3	4	70 00
Adjutant, in addition to pay, &c., of Lieutenant		1	2		10 00
Regimental Quartermaster, in addition to pay, &c., of Lieutenant		2	2		10 00
Captain	1			4	60 00
First Lieutenant	1			4	50 00
Second Lieutenant	1			4	45 00
Sergeant-Major					21 00
Quartermaster-Sergeant					21 00
Principal Musician of Infantry					21 00
First Sergeant					20 00
Ordnance Sergeant, in addition to pay of Sergeant					5 00
Sergeant, and Company Quartermaster-Sergeant					17 00
Corporal					13 00

TABLE OF PAY, SUBSISTENCE, FORAGE, &c.,—Continued.

Pay Department.

Grade.	Pay. Per month.	Subsistence. No. of rations per day.	Forage. No. of horses allowed in time of war.	Forage. No. of horses allowed in time of peace.	No. of servants allowed.
Artificer of Artillery	$15 00				
Private	13 00				
Musician	12 00				
SAPPERS, MINERS, AND PONTONIERS.					
Sergeant	34 00				
Corporal	20 00				
Private of the 1st class	17 00				
Private of the 2d class	13 00				
Musician	12 00				
MILITARY STOREKEEPERS, &C.					
Military Store-keepers attached to the Quartermaster's Department; at armories, and at arsenals of construction; the store-keeper at Watertown arsenal, and store-keepers of ordnance serving in Oregon, California, and New Mexico, $1440 per annum.					
At all other arsenals, $1040 per annum.					
Post Chaplain, to be determined by the Council of Administration, not to exceed	60 00	4			
Medical Cadet	30 00				
Hospital Steward, appointed by the Secretary of War, and at posts of more than four companies, pay of Ordnance Sergeant	22 00				
Other Hospital Stewards	20 00				

Pay Department.

	Pay				
Matron	$6 00	...	...	...	...
Female Nurses, 40 cents per day and one ration.					
Master Wagoners (by Act 3d August, 1861)	17 00	...	...	...	...
Wagoners (by Act 3d August, 1861)	14 00	...	...	...	...
BANDS.					
Leader	45 00	4	...	...	1
One-fourth of the Musicians	34 00	...	...	...	...
One-fourth of " "	20 00	...	...	...	...
One-half of " "	17 00	...	...	...	...
Drum-Major	17 00	...	...	...	...

The commanding officer of a company is entitled to $10 per month for responsibility of arms and clothing.

Officers' subsistence is commuted at thirty cents per ration; forage, $8 per month for each horse actually owned and kept in service.

Officers are entitled to the pay of private soldier, $2 50 per month, clothing, and one ration per day for each private servant actually employed.

Every commissioned officer below the rank of Brigadier-General is entitled to one additional ration per day for every five years' service.

Two dollars per month is to be retained from the pay of each private soldier until the expiration of his term of enlistment, and 12½ cents per month from all enlisted men, for the support of the "Soldier's Home."

All enlisted men are entitled to $2 per month additional pay for re-enlisting, and $1 per month for each subsequent period of five years' service, provided they re-enlist within one month.

Paymaster's clerks, $700 per annum, and 75 cents per day when actually on duty.

The Adjutants, Quartermasters, and Commissaries of Battalions will receive the emoluments now provided by law for Regimental Adjutants.

* Entitled to only three rations per day as Lieutenant.

NOTE.—Chaplains, $40 per month and 4 rations. Upon the recommendation of the Council of Administration, the Secretary of War may allow Chaplains $20 per month in addition. Chaplains in volunteers, by Act of July, 1861, are paid as Captains of Cavalry.

For Army Pay List, see Appendix, pages 524–526.

Pay Department.

TABLES OF THE DAILY

Days.	$5 per month.	$6 per month.	$6⅔ per month.	$7 per month.	$7½ per month.	$8 per month.	$9 per month.	$10 per month.	$11 per month.	$12 per month.	$13 per month.
I.	16	20	22	23	24	26	30	33	36	40	43
II.	33	40	44	46	48	53	60	66	73	80	86
III.	50	60	66	70	73	80	90	1 00	1 10	1 20	1 30
IV.	66	80	88	93	97	1 06	1 20	1 33	1 46	1 60	1 73
V.	83	1 00	1 11	1 16	1 22	1 33	1 50	1 66	1 83	2 00	2 16
VI.	1 00	1 20	1 33	1 40	1 46	1 60	1 80	2 00	2 20	2 40	2 60
VII.	1 16	1 40	1 55	1 63	1 71	1 86	2 10	2 33	2 56	2 80	3 03
VIII.	1 33	1 60	1 77	1 86	1 95	2 13	2 40	2 66	2 93	3 20	3 46
IX.	1 50	1 80	1 99	2 10	2 19	2 40	2 70	3 00	3 30	3 60	3 90
X.	1 66	2 00	2 22	2 33	2 44	2 66	3 00	3 33	3 66	4 00	4 33
XI.	1 83	2 20	2 44	2 56	2 68	2 93	3 30	3 66	4 03	4 40	4 76
XII.	2 00	2 40	2 66	2 80	2 93	3 20	3 60	4 00	4 40	4 80	5 20
XIII.	2 16	2 60	2 88	3 03	3 17	3 46	3 90	4 33	4 76	5 20	5 63
XIV.	2 33	2 80	3 10	3 26	3 42	3 73	4 20	4 66	5 13	5 60	6 06
XV.	2 50	3 00	3 33	3 50	3 66	4 00	4 50	5 00	5 50	6 00	6 50
XVI.	2 66	3 20	3 55	3 73	3 90	4 26	4 80	5 33	5 86	6 40	6 93
XVII.	2 83	3 40	3 77	3 96	4 15	4 53	5 10	5 66	6 23	6 80	7 36
XVIII.	3 00	3 60	3 99	4 20	4 39	4 80	5 40	6 00	6 60	7 20	7 80
XIX.	3 16	3 80	4 21	4 43	4 64	5 06	5 70	6 33	6 96	7 60	8 23
XX.	3 33	4 00	4 44	4 66	4 88	5 33	6 00	6 66	7 33	8 00	8 66
XXI.	3 50	4 20	4 66	4 90	5 13	5 60	6 30	7 00	7 70	8 40	9 10
XXII.	3 66	4 40	4 88	5 13	5 37	5 86	6 60	7 33	8 06	8 80	9 53
XXIII.	3 83	4 60	5 10	5 36	5 61	6 13	6 90	7 66	8 43	9 20	9 96
XXIV.	4 00	4 80	5 22	5 60	5 86	6 40	7 20	8 00	8 80	9 60	10 40
XXV.	4 16	5 00	5 55	5 83	6 10	6 66	7 50	8 33	9 16	10 00	10 83
XXVI.	4 33	5 20	5 77	6 06	6 35	6 93	7 80	8 66	9 53	10 40	11 26
XXVII.	4 50	5 40	5 99	6 30	6 59	7 20	8 10	9 00	9 90	10 80	11 70
XXVIII.	4 66	5 60	6 21	6 53	6 84	7 46	8 40	9 33	10 26	11 20	12 13
XXIX.	4 83	5 80	6 43	6 76	7 08	7 73	8 70	9 66	10 63	11 60	12 56
XXX.	5 00	6 00	6 66	7 00	7 33	8 00	9 00	10 00	11 00	12 00	13 00

PAY OF THE ARMY.

$16 per month.	$20 per month.	$23 per month.	$25 per month.	$26⅔ per month.	$30 per month.	$33⅓ per month.	$40 per month.	$50 per month.	$60 per month.	$75 per month.
53	66	76	83	88	1 00	1 11	1 33	1 66	2 00	2 50
1 06	1 33	1 53	1 66	1 77	2 00	2 22	2 66	3 33	4 00	5 00
1 60	2 00	2 30	2 50	2 66	3 00	3 33	4 00	5 00	6 00	7 50
2 13	2 66	3 06	3 33	3 55	4 00	4 44	5 33	6 66	8 00	10 00
2 66	3 33	3 83	4 16	4 44	5 00	5 55	6 66	8 33	10 00	12 50
3 20	4 00	4 60	5 00	5 33	6 00	6 66	8 00	10 00	12 00	15 00
3 73	4 66	5 36	5 83	6 22	7 00	7 77	9 33	11 66	14 00	17 50
4 26	5 33	6 13	6 66	7 10	8 00	8 88	10 66	13 33	16 00	20 00
4 80	6 00	6 90	7 50	7 99	9 00	9 99	12 00	15 00	18 00	22 50
5 33	6 66	7 66	8 33	8 88	10 00	11 11	13 33	16 66	20 00	25 00
5 86	7 33	8 43	9 16	9 77	11 00	12 22	14 66	18 33	22 00	27 50
6 40	8 00	9 20	10 00	10 66	12 00	13 33	16 00	20 00	24 00	30 00
6 93	8 66	9 96	10 83	11 55	13 00	14 44	17 33	21 66	26 00	32 50
7 46	9 33	10 73	11 66	12 44	14 00	15 55	18 66	23 33	28 00	35 00
8 00	10 00	11 50	12 50	13 33	15 00	16 66	20 00	25 00	30 00	37 50
8 53	10 66	12 26	13 33	14 21	16 00	17 77	21 33	26 66	32 00	40 00
9 06	11 33	13 03	14 16	15 10	17 00	18 88	22 66	28 33	34 00	42 50
9 60	12 00	13 80	15 00	15 99	18 00	19 99	24 00	30 00	36 00	45 00
10 13	12 66	14 56	15 83	16 88	19 00	21 11	25 33	31 66	38 00	47 50
10 66	13 33	15 33	16 66	17 77	20 00	22 22	26 66	33 33	40 00	50 00
11 20	14 00	16 10	17 50	18 66	21 00	23 33	28 00	35 00	42 00	52 50
11 73	14 66	16 86	18 33	19 55	22 00	24 44	29 33	36 66	44 00	55 00
12 26	15 33	17 63	19 16	20 43	23 00	25 55	30 66	38 33	46 00	57 50
12 80	16 00	18 40	20 00	21 32	24 00	26 66	32 00	40 00	48 00	60 00
13 33	16 66	19 16	20 83	22 21	25 00	27 77	33 33	41 66	50 00	62 50
13 86	17 33	19 93	21 66	23 10	26 00	28 88	34 66	43 33	52 00	65 00
14 40	18 00	20 70	22 50	23 99	27 00	29 99	36 00	45 00	54 00	67 50
14 93	18 66	21 46	23 33	24 88	28 00	31 11	37 33	46 66	56 00	70 00
15 46	19 33	22 23	24 16	25 77	29 00	32 22	38 66	48 33	58 00	72 50
16 00	20 00	23 00	25 00	26 66	30 00	33 33	40 00	50 00	60 00	75 00

FORM 1.—(Estimate for Funds.)

Estimate of Funds required for the pay, subsistence, forage, and clothing of the troops of the United States, of which ———— is Paymaster, from the 1st of ————, 18—, to the 1st of ————, 18—, two months, founded on the actual number of said troops.

Description and enumeration of troops.	Commencement.	Expiration.	Pay.		Subsistence.		Forage.		Clothing for officers' servants, or money in lieu thereof.		Amount.	
			Dolls.	Cts.	Dolls.	Cts.	Dolls.	Cts.	Dolls.	Cts.	Dolls.	Cts.
Dead and discharged men....												
Casual payments............												
Arrears due prior to commencement of this estimate.......												
Aggregate amount..........												
Deduct balance on hand......												
Amount required..........												

I certify that the above estimate is founded on the best data, as to the actual number of troops, to be obtained.

————, *Paymaster U. S. A.*

FORM 2.

Receipts to be rendered by Paymasters for remittances.

Received of ——, this —— day of ——, 18—, at ——, in the State of ——, on ——, dated the —— day of ——, 18—, the sum of —— dollars and —— cents, on account of the pay, &c., of the Army of the United States, as follows:

Pay..................	$
Subsistence	
Forage..............	
Clothing.............	
Amount......	. $

For which amount I am accountable

(Signed triplicates.)

——————, *Paymaster.*

NOTE.—One receipt for the Paymaster-General, one for the Second Auditor, and one for the Treasurer.

Pay Department.——Forms.

FORM 3.—(Officers' Pay Account.)

The United States to ———— ,   Dr.

On what account.	Commencement and expiration.		Term of service charged.		Pay per month.		Amount.		Remarks.
	From —	To —	Months.	Days.	Dolls.	Cts.	Dolls.	Cts.	
Pay—									
For myself............									
For private servant, not soldier........									
Forage —									
For horse..........									
Clothing—									
For private servant, not soldier.........									
Subsistence—									
For myself for —— years' service									
For private servant, not soldier.............									

No. of days.	No. of rations per day.	Total number of rations.	Post or place where due.	Price of ration. Cts.

Pay Department.——Forms.

I hereby certify that the foregoing account is accurate and just; that I have not been absent without leave during any part of the time charged for; that I have not received pay, nor drawn rations, forage, or clothing in kind, or received money in lieu of any part thereof, for any part of the time therein charged; that I actually owned and kept in service, the horses, and employed the private servants for which I charge, for the whole of the time charged; and that I did not, during the term so charged, or any part thereof, keep or employ a soldier as a waiter or servant; that the annexed is an accurate description of my servant; that, for the whole period charged for my staff appointment, I actually and legally held the appointment and did duty in the department; that I was the actual and only commanding officer at the double-ration post charged for; and that no officer, within my knowledge, has a right to claim, or does claim, for said services, for any part of the period charged; that for the whole time brevet pay is claimed, I had the command stated; that I was actually in the command of a company for the whole time additional pay is charged; that I have not been in the performance of any staff duty for which I claim, or have received, extra compensation during the time an additional ration is charged for; that I have been in the United States Army as a commissioned officer for the number of years stated in the charge for extra rations; that I am not in arrears with the United States on any account whatsoever; and that the last payment I received was from Paymaster ———, and to the —— day of ———, 18—.

I at the same time acknowledge that I have received of ———, Paymaster, this —— day of ———, 18—, the sum of ——— $\frac{}{100}$ dollars, being the amount in full of said account.

(*Signed duplicates.*)

DESCRIPTION OF SERVANTS.

Name.	Complexion.	Height.		Eyes.	Hair.
		Feet.	Inches.		

Pay........................
Subsistence.............
Forage....................
Clothing.................

Amount..........$

Pay Department.——Forms.

FORM 4.

Certificate to be given a soldier at the time of his discharge.

I CERTIFY that the within named —— ——, a —— of Captain —— —— company (—) of the —— regiment of ——, born in ——, in the State of ——, aged —— years, —— feet —— inches high, —— complexion, —— eyes, —— hair, and by profession a ——, was enlisted by —— ——, at ——, on the —— day of ——, eighteen hundred and ——, to serve for —— years, and is now entitled to a discharge by reason of ——.

The said —— —— was last paid by Paymaster —— ——, to include the —— day of ——, eighteen hundred and ——, and has pay due from that time to the present date.

There is due to him —— dollars retained pay.

There is due to him —— dollars on account of clothing not drawn in kind.

He is indebted to the United States —— dollars on account of extra clothing, &c.

He is indebted to —— ——, laundress at ——, —— dollars.

The contract price of the ration at —— is —— cents.

Given in duplicate at ——, this —— day of ——, 18—.

—— ——,

Commanding Company.

NOTE.—When a soldier transfers his certificates, the transfer must be made on them, witnessed by a commissioned officer, when practicable, or by some other reputable person known to the Paymaster.

NOTE 1. The amount of additional pay per month, if any, *for former services* under the Act of *August* 4, 1854, must be carefully noted in the exact words used on the Muster-Roll.

2. Likewise, the amount due the soldier for a *certificate of merit* ; or in lieu of a *commission*, under sec. 4, *Act of August* 4, 1854.

3. So, also, of any other *extra* pay, for which he may be mustered ; *ex. gr.* as acting *Hospital Steward*, as *saddler, &c.*, and which may be *still due* him.

4. Stoppages for *loss* or *damage* done to *arms*, or other *public property*, must be noted, and the *articles*, and *particular damage* to each, specified.

5. Stoppages due, under the sentence of a court-martial, must be *carefully* stated, with No. and date of order.

6. In cases of *desertion*, the *date*, and that of *delivery*, or *apprehension*, must be given, together with a correct transcript of the order of *sentence or pardon*, whenever the final settlement of the man's accounts may be affected by either.

FORM 5.

The United States,

To —— ——, discharged from —— Company, —— Regiment of ——, DR.

	Dolls.	Cents.
For pay from —— of ——, 18—, to —— of ——, 18—, being —— months, —— days, at —— dollars per month..		
For retained pay due...		
For pay for traveling from ——, the place of my discharge, to ——, the place of my residence, —— miles, at twenty miles per day, equal to —— days, at —— dollars per month..		
For subsistence for traveling as above, —— days, at —— cents per ration or day..................................		
For clothing not drawn		
Amount..................................		
Deduct for Army Asylum...........................$ Deduct for clothing overdrawn....................		
Balance due		

Received of —— ——, Paymaster United States Army, this —— day of ——, 18—, —— dollars and - —— cents, in full of the above account.

Pay.......................
Subsistence.............
Clothing..................

Dollars. ....

(Signed in duplicate.)

FORM 6.

Abstract of Payments made by ——— ————,

No. of vouchers.	Date of payment.	To whom paid.	Rank or grade.	Corps.	Commencement and expiration.		Pay.		Subsistence.	
					From —	To —	Dolls.	Cts.	Dolls.	Cts.

I do hereby certify that he foregoing Abstract contains an accurate state-

Pay Department.——Forms.

FORM 6.

Paymaster, for the ——— months of ———.

Forage.		Clothing of servants.		Clothing of soldiers.						Amount.		Remarks.
Dolls.	Cts.	Dolls	Cts.	Dolls.	Cts.	Dolls.	Cts.	Dolls.	Cts.	Dolls.	Cts.	

ment of the payments made by me, as there:n expressed.

———,
Paymaster.

Pay Department.——Forms.

FORM 7.—(Account Current.)

——————, *Paymaster United States Army.*

The United States, *in account current with* ——————

DR.

Date.		Pay.		Subsistence.		Forage.		Clothing.		Amount.	
		Dolls.	Cts.	Dolls.	Cts.	Dolls.	Cts.	Dolls.	Cts.	Dolls.	Cts.
186	For amount expended, as per abstract and vouchers herewith, in paying the troops since the —— of ——, 186 , the date of the last account rendered										
	For amount turned over to ——										
	Due the U. States, to be accounted for in next account.......										

CR.

Date.		Pay.		Subsistence.		Forage.		Clothing.		Amount.	
		Dolls.	Cts.	Dolls.	Cts.	Dolls.	Cts.	Dolls.	Cts.	Dolls.	Cts.
	By balance to be accounted for, as stated in last account......										
186	By cash received of ——, as per my receipt dated the —— of ——, 186										
186	By amount received of —— for										

Pay Department.——Forms.

Amount.........$

By balance brought down.............

Amount.........$

I certify that the above is a true account of all public money received by me, not heretofore accounted for, and that the disbursements have been faithfully made.

Stated at ——, this —— of ——, 186 .

(Duplicate.)

————, *Paymaster.*

FORM 8.—

We, the subscribers, do hereby acknowledge to have received of ————
the full of our pay and allowances for the period

Number.	Names.	Rank.	Period of service.				Pay per month.	Amount of pay.	Clothing.	Subsistence.	Forage.	40 cents per day, use of horse, arms, &c.	25 cents per day for rations and forage, or 12½ cents for either.
			Commencement.	Expiration.	Months.	Days.							

We certify that we actually employed the servants, and owned and kept in charged, and did not, during any part of the time, employ a soldier as a servant. non-commissioned officers and privates of the company to which we belong, who them in service for the time paid for, although, in some cases, they may not have company.

Pay Department.——Forms.

(Pay Roll of Militia.)

-————, *Paymaster, the sums annexed to our names respectively, being herein expressed, having signed duplicates thereof.*

Traveling allowances.			Total amount.	Stoppages.	Balances paid.	Signature.	Witness.	Remarks.
Pay.	Subsistence.							

service the horses, for which we have received payment, for the whole of the time The names and description of our servants are below. We also certify that the are made up for pay, &c., as having horses and arms, actually owned and had been valued. We also certify that we witnessed the payment of the whole

———— ————, *Captain,* s·rvant named ———— ————.
———— ————, *1st Lieut.,* do. ———— ————.
———— ————, *2d Lieut.,* do. ———— ————.
———— ————, *Ensign,* do. — —— —————,

Pay Department.——Forms.

FORM 9.

Statement of moneys received and expended, and on hand, for the month ending ——.

Date.		Pay.	Subsistence.	Forage.	Servants' clothing.	Soldiers' clothing.	Effects of deceased soldiers.	Overdrawn clothing.	Ordnance.	Equipments.	Quartermaster's stores.	Militia.	Amount.	Remarks.
	Amount on hand from last month													
	Received from the Treasurer....													
	Received from Paymaster.........													
	Received from ——													
	Total received.............$													
	Expended in paying the troops													
	Turned over to Paymaster......													
	Total expended...........$													
	Balance to be accounted for....$													

Accountable for —— iron safe.

——————, *Paymaster.*

ARTICLE XLVI.

CORPS OF ENGINEERS AND TOPOGRAPHICAL ENGINEERS.

1357. The duties of these corps usually relate to the construction of permanent and field fortifications; works for the attack and defense of places; for the passage of rivers; for the movements and operations of armies in the field; and such reconnoissances and surveys as may be required for these objects, or for any other duty which may be assigned to them. By special direction of the President of the United States, officers of engineers may be employed on any other duty whatsoever. (See 63d Article of War.)

1358. All quarters for officers and soldiers at permanent fortifications will be estimated for and built by the Engineer Department, and then turned over to the Quartermaster's Department for preservation and assignment according to regulations; workshops and store-houses, which do not form part of the defenses, will be built and retained by the department for whose special use they are intended, but the location and character of the structure will be determined by the Engineer Bureau.

1359. No permanent fortification, or other important work assigned to either corps, shall be undertaken, until the plans have been submitted to a board composed of such officers of the corps as the Secretary of War may designate. The report of the board, with complete drawings and specifications of the work, and detailed estimates of the cost, shall be made to the bureau of the corps in the War Department, and be submitted to the Secretary of War, without whose sanction no plan shall be adopted. A dissenting member of the board may present his own project, memoir, plans, and estimates.

1360. The chief engineer, with the approbation of the Secretary of War, will regulate and determine the number, quality, form, and dimensions, &c., of the necessary vehicles, pontons, tools, implements, arms, and other supplies for the use and service of the engineer company of sappers, miners, and pontoniers, to be procured, as far as practicable, by fabrication in the government establishments of the Engineer and Ordnance Departments.

1361. In any work carried on under the direction of the chief of either corps, his authority must be obtained for the erection of any temporary buildings required in the progress of the work, or the purchase of any vessel or boat, or for furnishing medicines or medical attendance to hired men, and to determine the number and wages of clerks, foremen, and overseers.

1362. An engineer superintending a work or operation shall disburse the money for the same, and when informed of the funds applicable to the work, he will furnish to the bureau or office through which he receives his instructions, a detailed report of the manner in which he proposes to apply the funds.

1363. Public works in charge of either corps shall be inspected once a year, and when completed, by such officers of the corps as the Secretary of War shall designate. A report of each inspection shall be made to the Secretary of War through the bureau of the corps.

1364. On the completion of any fortification or other work, the officer in charge will transmit to the appropriate bureau all the books, papers, and drawings relating to it. Of fortifications, the following drawings are required: a plan of the finished work and the environs within the scope of investment, on a scale of 12 inches to a mile; a plan of the main work and outworks, on a scale of 1 inch to 50 feet, with sections, profiles, and elevations, on a scale of 1 inch to 25 feet; and a plan of the masonry, on a scale of 1 inch to 50 feet, with profiles and elevations, on a scale of 1 inch to 25 feet; and such other drawings as may be necessary to show important details of the work.

1365. An officer charged with a survey will procure the books and instruments for the execution of the duty by requisition on the appropriate bureau, and upon his return from field operations will report to it the condition of the instruments in his charge; on the completion of the survey, he will transmit to the bureau a full report thereof, with the field notes, and all necessary drawings.

1366. The following reports and returns for a work or operation under the direction of the chief of either corps are to be sent to the appropriate bureau of the corps by the officer in charge:

1367. Monthly returns, within five days after the month to which they relate, viz.: report of operations (Form 1); return of officers and hired men (Form 2); money statement (Form 3);

1368. An estimate of funds for one month, in time to receive the remittance for the service of the month;

1369. Quarterly returns, within twenty days after the quarter to which they relate, viz.: a money account current (Form 4); with abstract of disbursements (Form 5), and vouchers (Forms 6, 7, 8); and a return of property (Form 9), with abstracts of receipts and issues (Forms 10, 11, 12, 13, and 14);

1370. A quarterly return of instruments, books, &c. (Form 15) by every officer accountable for them;

1371. A report, in time to reach the bureau by the 20th of October, of the operations on the work or survey during the year ending 30th of June, with the necessary drawings, and showing the condition of the work, the extent and cost of the principal operations (as brick-work, stone-work, earth-work, surveys), accompanied by a summary statement of the expenditures during the year, with an estimate of the funds required for the next year, and an estimate of the amount required to complete the work.

1372. When disbursements are made by the same individual on account of different works, a separate set of accounts for each must be kept and rendered, as above required, as well as separate estimates, returns, and reports; the quarterly accounts being accompanied by a general statement (Form 3) of receipts and expenditures during the quarter on all the works.

1373. The following books and files for each work will be kept by the officer in charge: a letter-book, for copies of his official letters; file of letters received; file of orders received; a journal, containing a daily record of the occupations of the persons employed on the work; a book of materials, in which must be entered, under the appropriate head, every kind of material received, specifying date of delivery and payment, from whom received, the kind, quality, price, and cost—in this book the various articles will be entered under the same heads as in the quarterly return of property; a ledger, in which an account will be opened with every person of whom materials or supplies are purchased for the work, including every person not on the rolls; an account-book, containing entries, according to Form 5, of all expenditures and copies of the quarterly accounts current, and estimates of funds; a roll-book, showing the name, occupation, rate of pay, of each hired person, and time made by him daily in each month; a book of miscellanies, containing accounts of experiments and miscellaneous information relating to the work.

1374. Printed forms allowed will be furnished from the bureaus, unless otherwise directed, on requisition in May for a year's supply.

FORM 1.

Report of Operations at Fort Jay for the month of September, 1860.

MASONS have been employed in setting coping, N. and W. fronts; roofing case-mated traverse, S. W. exterior front; building breast-height and traverse walls, covert way, S. E. front; pointing interior counterscarps, S. E. and S. W. fronts.

LABORERS, embanking breakwater, S. W. front; embanking parapet of high covert way; excavating for and laying foundations of breast-height walls, covert way, S. E. front; sodding S. E. glacis coupé; quarrying stone for masons at S. E. quarry; aiding masons and carpenters; receiving materials.

TEAMSTERS, leveling S. E. glacis; transporting stone for and embanking break-water, S. W. front; aiding masons and carpenters; receiving materials

CARPENTERS, on quarters, E. front; making and repairing tools and machinery.

WHEELWRIGHTS and SMITHS, making and repairing tools and machinery.

PLUMBERS, covering arches, W. front; leading breast-height walls, covert way, S. E. front.

State any important result during the month, as the condition of a front, bastion, battery, &c.; progress of a survey.

Probable operations of the month of October.

MASONS, as in September: to commence laying the foundations of S. E. exterior front, and to lay the traverse circles in the exterior battery of N. front.

LABORERS, as in September: to finish breakwater, S. W. front, and commence the embankment of parapet of W. front.

TEAMSTERS, as in September.

CARPENTERS, making and repairing tools and machinery.

WHEELWRIGHTS and SMITHS,   do.   do.   do.

PLUMBERS, covering arches: to finish the W. front, and commence the S. W. front.

————— —————,

Maj. Engineers.

FORT JAY, NEW YORK,
        October 10, 1861.

Endorsement to be as follows:

FORT JAY.

Report of Operations for the month of September, 1860.

FORM 2.

Return of Officers and Hired Men at Fort Jay, for the Month of September, 1860.

OFFICERS.

Present.	Absent.
Major A. B. relieved Lieutenant E. F., in charge September 15, by special order No. 14, of August 2. Post-office address for October, Fort Jay.	Lieutenant E. F. at G. Island on service by order of Major A. B. Post-office address for October, Fort Jay. Lieutenant O. P. left September 10, on leave of absence by order——. Post-office address for October, Indianola, Texas.

HIRED MEN.

No.	Trade or occupation.	Time or piece work.	Wages.	Amount.
30	Masons	700 days	$2 25	$1575 00
10	Do.	200 days	1 75	350 00
20	Do. at piece work ..	700 sup. feet of granite..	at 15 c.	105 00
10	Carpenters	....	2 00	....
	Do.	....	1 50	....
	Laborers	....	1 00	....
	Do.	....	90	....
1	Clerk	1 month.....................	60 00	....
2	Foremen	1 do.	80 00	....
1	Overseer	1 do.	40 00	....
	Amount............	....	....	$...........

C. D., *Major Engineers.*

Endorsement:
Officers and Hired Men.
Fort Jay,
September, 1860.

FORM 3.

Statement of Money received and expended, under each appropriation, in the month of September, 1860.

	Fort Jay.	Fort B.	Contingencies of fortifications.	Total
Due U. S. from last month	$70 00	$80 00	....	$150 00
Received in the month......	450 00	8000 00	$300 00	8750 00
Total to be accounted for	520 00	8080 00	300 00	8900 00
Due from U. S. last month	....	....	400 00	400 00
Expended in the month.....	400 00	7000 00	....	7400 00
Total accounted for	400 00	7000 00	400 00	7800 00
Due 1st. Oct. to the U. S....	120 00	1080 00	....	1200 00
Do. from the U. S.	....	....	100 00	100 00
			Due U. S.	1100 00

C. D. *Major Engineers*

Engineers and Topographical Engineers.——Forms.

FORM 4.

The United States in account current with Major C. D., Corps of Engineers, at Fort Jay.

DR.					CR.
1860. Sept.	30	To amount paid for purchases and expenditures during the 3d quarter of 1860, as per accompanying vouchers and abstracts............ Balance........	1860. July	1	Due the United States, as per account current rendered for the 2d quarter of 1860:
			"	4	By the following Treasury drafts on War Warrant No. 5868,—viz.: No. 8169, on Collector of —— 8170, on Collector of —— 8171, on Treasurer of U. S.
			August	3	By the following articles sold from Fort Jay,—viz.: 4950 lbs. scrap iron, at 1½ cent per lb. 26 wheelbarrows, $5 each, sold A. B., as per accompanying certificate of sale
			Sept.	30	By this amount disallowed at the Treasury Department, being the item in Voucher No. 16 of the accounts for Fort Jay for the 2d quarter of 1860,—viz.:
			October	1	Due the United States............

I certify that the foregoing is a true account of all money received by me for Fort Jay not heretofore accounted for, and that the disbursements have been faithfully made.

E. E.

FORT JAY, NEW YORK,
October 4, 1860.
C. D., Major Engineers.

Endorsement to be as follows :
FORT JAY.
Account current of
Major C. D., U. S. Engineers, for the 3d quarter 1860.

FORM 5.

Abstract of Disbursements on account of Fort Jay during the quarter ending on the 30th of September, 1860.

No. of voucher.	Nature of purchase or expenditure.	To whom paid or of whom purchased.	AMOUNT.	
			Dolls.	Cts.
1	Lime...........................	Henry King....................	200	00
2	Stone..........................	Jones & King..............	500	00
8	Bricks.........................	Stephenson & Co.............	800	00
4	Sundries......................	Smith & Co..................	60	00
5	Cement........................	Samuel Jones................	100	00
6	Services......................	Hired men....................	826	52
7	Granite, lime, and bricks	Aaron Brown.................	3737	50
		Dollars......	5724	02

E. E.

C. D., *Major Engineers.*

FORT JAY, NEW YORK,
    October 4, 1860.

———

Endorsement to be as follows :

FORT JAY.
Abstract of Disbursements
by
Major C. D., U. S. Engineers, during the 3d quarter, 1860.

FORM 6.

The United States, for Fort Jay,

TO AARON BROWN,   DR.

Date.	Designation.	Application.	Cost. Dolls.	Cts.
1860. July 4.	For 600 cubic yards dressed Granite, at —— per yard.	Scarp wall	....	.....
	For 30 tons broken Granite, at —— per ton.	Backing of scarp	....	.....
	For cutting 700 feet of Granite, at —— per foot.	Scarp	....	.....
August 1.	For 20 M. hard Bricks, at —— per M.	Casemate arches	....	.....
	For 100 barrels Lime, 8 bushels each, at —— per barrel.	Foundation of scarp and piers		
		Dollars......	3737	50

I certify that the above account is correct and just; the articles to be (or have been) accounted for in my property return for —— quarter of ——.

(Signed)   C. D., *Major Engineers.*

Received at Fort Jay, this 24th day of September, 1860, from Major C. D., Corps of Engineers, the sum of three thousand seven hundred and thirty-seven dollars and fifty cents, in full payment of the above account.

(Signed in duplicate.)

$3737 50.   AARON BROWN.

Endorsement to be as follows:

Fort Jay.
Voucher No. 8.
Aaron Brown.
September 24th, 1860.
Granite, Lime, Bricks, $3737 50.

FORM 7.

We, the subscribers, hereby acknowledge to have received of ———————— the sums set opposite our names respectively, being in full for our services at Fort A————————, during the month of ————, 18—, having signed duplicate receipts.

No.	Name.	Occupation.	Time employed.	Rate of pay.	AMOUNT. Dolls.	AMOUNT. Cts.	Signatures.	Witness.
1	A. B.....	Clerk.............	1 month...	$80 00	80	00	A. B....	....
2	C. D.....	Overseer........	1 do.......	40 00	40	00	C. D. ...	....
3	E. F.....	Master Mason	24 days....	2 50	60	00	E. F. ...	....
4	G. H.....	Mason...........	20 do.....	1 75	35	00	G. H....	....
5	I. K......	Laborer.........	24 do.....	1 00	24	00	I. x K..	A. B....
					239	00		

I certify that the foregoing pay-roll is correct and just.

J. M., *Captain Engineers*

Endorsement :
Fort A——.
No. —.
Pay-roll for ————, 18—.
$239 00.

FORM 8.

We, the subscribers, acknowledge to have received of Captain ———————— the sums set opposite our names respectively, being in full for the services of our slaves at Fort A———— during the month of ————, 18—, having signed duplicate receipts.

From whom hired.	Name and occupation.	Time employed.	Rate of wages.	Amount for each slave.	AMOUNT RECEIVED. Dolls.	AMOUNT RECEIVED. Cts.	Signature.
A. B...	A., mason......	1 month....	$40 00	$40 00			
Do.....	C., blacksmith	25 days.....	2 00	50 00			
Do.....	D., laborer	1 month....	20 00	20 00			
					$110	00	A. B........
E. F...	G., laborer	12 days.....	$25 a mo..	12 00			
Do.....	H., do...........	1 month....	20 00	20 00			
					32	00	E. F........
					142	00	

I certify that the above pay-roll is correct and just.

J. M., *Captain Engineers*

Endorsement :
Fort A——.
No. —.
Slave-roll for ————, 18—.
$142 00.

Engineers and Topographical Engineers.——Forms.

FORM 9.

Return of Engineer Property at Fort Jay for the quarter ending 30th June, 18 .

Date.	Vouchers or Abstract.	Second Quarter, 18	BUILDING MATERIALS. Stone. Granite, cubic yards.	Marble, tons.	Bricks, M.	Lime, casks.	Cement, casks.	LUMBER. Scantling, M.	Boards, white pine, M.	Boats, No.	Horses, No.	Carts.	Harness, sets.	TOOLS.			FORAGE. Corn, lbs.	Hay, lbs.	PROVISIONS. Pork.	Flour.	Potatoes.	MISCEL-LAN.
1856.	Abstract A	On hand..........																				
	Abstract B	Purchases paid for...																				
		Purchases not paid for...																				
	Abstract C	Fabricated............																				
	Abstract D	Received from other posts																				
		Total to be accounted for..........																				
	Abstract E	Materials used........																				
	Abstract F	Forage issued.........																				
	Abstract G	Provisions issued																				
		Total issued and expended																				
		Remaining on hand 30th June.....																				

I certify that the foregoing return is a true statement of the public property in my charge at Fort A——, ending the —— quarter, 18—.

J. M., *Captain Engineers.*

FORM 10.

Abstract of Purchases received and paid for at Fort A——, in the —— quarter of 18 .

No of voucher.	To whom paid.	Granite, cubic yards.	Coping, superficial feet.	Bricks, M.	Hay, pounds.	Flour, barrels.	Screws, No.	Nails, pounds.	Hinges, No.	Locks, No.	Bar iron, pounds.	Steel, pounds.
		Stone.					Ironmongery.					
1	A. B.	800		10,000								
2	C. D.		700									
3	E. F.				4000							
4	M. N.					20						
5	O. P.						500	1000	50	20	2000	100
	Total	800	700	10,000	4000	20	500	1000	50	20	2000	100

I certify that the above abstract is correct.

J. M., *Major Engineers.*

FORM 11.

*Abstract of Purchases received, and not paid for, at Fort A ———, ———
quarter, 18—.*

Of whom purchased.	Bricks, M.	Bar iron, pounds.	Oats, bushels.	Hay, pounds.			
R....................	50,000	....	....	....			
S.....................	....	4000	....	....			
T.....................	....	....	100	2000			
X....................	....	....	....	....			
Y....................	....	....	....	....			
Amount............	50,000	4000	100	2000			

I certify that the above abstract is correct.

J. M., *Captain Engineers.*

FORM 12.

Abstract of Materials expended at Fort A———, ——— quarter, 18—.

For what purpose.	Stone, cubic yards.	Bricks, M.	Lime, barrels.	White pine boards, feet.	Yellow pine scantling, M.		
Scarp wall Bastion 1............	2000	....	....	....	....		
Casemates do.....................	....	50,000	50	....	....		
Stable	....	....	....	1500	800		
Amount............	2000	50,000	50	1500	800		

I certify that the above abstract is correct; that the issues and expenditures were made, and were necessary.

J. M., *Captain Engineers*

FORM 13.

Abstract of Forage issued at Fort Jay during the quarter ending on the 30th September, 1860.

Description of Forage.	Issued during the quarter.	Number of rations.	Distribution of the issues.							Remarks.
			Horses.	Days.	Mules.	Days.	Oxen.	Days.	Rations.	
Hay, lbs.	13,664	976	6	92	....	....	....	....	552	Half rations —horses at grass.
			2	65	....	....	....	....	130	
			4	40	....	....	....	....	80	
			....	....	3	10	....	....	30	
			....	....	....	....	2	92	184–976	
Oats, bu.	233¼	862	6	92	....	....	....	....	552	
			2	65	....	....	....	....	130	
			2	....	3	60	....	....	180–862	
Corn, bu.	210	440	4	40	....	....	....	....	160	
			....	....	3	32	....	....	96	
							2	92	184–440	

I certify that the above abstract is correct; that the issues were made, and were necessary.

C. D., *Major Engineers.*

FORT JAY, NEW YORK,
        October 1, 1860.

Endorsement to be as follows:
FORT JAY.
Forage Return for the 3d quarter of 1860.

FORM 14.

Abstract of Provisions issued at Fort Jay during the quarter ending on the 30th September, 1860.

Description of provisions.	Issued in the quarter.	Number of rations.	Number of men to whom issued	Remarks.
Pork.........pounds.	1500	2000		
Beef—fresh....do...	2500	2000		
Beef—salt......do...	....	....	40 men employed 92 days, 3680 rations, 40 " 40 " 320 " } 4000 rations. 40 " 8 "	
Flour ....do...	....	....		
Meal.......... ....do...	....	....		
Bread.............do...	4500	4000		
Beans.........quarts.	320	4000		
Vinegar ....do...	160	4000		
&c.........				

I certify that the above abstract is correct; that the issues were made, and were necessary.

C. D., *Major of Engineers.*

FORT JAY, NEW YORK,
 October 1, 1860.

Endorsement to be as follows:

FORT JAY.
Provision Return for the 3d quarter of 1860.

FORM

Return of Instruments, Books, Maps, Charts, and Plans, belonging to the Engineers, for the quarter ending

POST OR PLACE.		Sextants.	Box sextants.	Artificial horizons.	Theodolites.	Spirit levels.	Level staffs.	Surveyor's com-passes.	Pocket compasses.	Boat compasses.	Azimuth compasses.	Reconnoitring or spy-glass.	Boxes drawing in-struments.	Cases drawing in-struments.	Beam compasses.
Fort Jay, New York.															
On hand per last return...... Received during the quarter															
To be accounted for........... Disposed of since last return															
On hand the 30th September, 1860........															

BOOKS, MAPS, CHARTS,

		Vauban's Fortification.	Bousmard's Fortification.	Army Regulations.	Eng. Dep. Regulations.	Map of New York.	Map of New York Harbor.	General plan of Fort Jay.	Sheets of detailed draw-ings of Fort Jay.					
On hand per last return...... Received during the quarter														
To be accounted for........... Disposed of since last return														
On hand the 30th September, 1860........														

Endorsement to be as follows :

Return of Instruments, &c.,
in charge of
Major C. D., U. S. Engineers, in 3d quarter, 1860.

15.

United States, received and accounted for by Major C. D., of the Corps of on the 30th of September, 1860.

MENTS.																REMARKS.
Proportional compasses.	Triangular compasses.	Dividers.	Protractors.	Boxes of colors.	Brass scales.	Ivory scales.	Surveying chains.	Measuring tapes.	Barometers.	Thermometers.	Tin paper-cases.					Exhibiting the purchase, repair, disposition, &c., of the articles.
AND PLANS.																

I certify that the foregoing return is correct.

C. D , *Major Engineers.*

NEW YORK, *October* 1, 1860.

ARTICLE XLVII.

ORDNANCE DEPARTMENT.

1375. The Ordnance Department has charge of the arsenals and armories, and furnishes all ordnance and ordnance stores for the military service.

1376. The general denomination, "Ordnance and Ordnance Stores," comprehends all cannon and artillery carriages and equipments; all apparatus and machines for the service and manœuvres of artillery; all small arms and accoutrements and horse equipments; all ammunition; all tools and materials for the ordnance service; horse medicines, materials for shoeing, and all horse equipments whatever for the light artillery.

1377. Models or patterns proposed by the Ordnance Board and approved by the Secretary of War, of all ordnance and ordnance stores for the land service of the United States, with the standard gauges, weights, and measures, shall be deposited in the model office at the Washington arsenal; and no change or variation from them shall be allowed, except on the recommendation of the board, approved by the Secretary of War. The ordnance board is composed of such officers of that department as the Secretary of War may designate.

1378. Directions in detail for the inspection and proof of all ordnance and ordnance stores shall be issued by the chief of ordnance, with the approbation of the Secretary of War. Ordnance and ordnance stores procured by contract or open purchase are required to pass the same inspection and proof as if fabricated at the arsenals. (See Ordnance Manual.)

1379. The purchases and contracts for cannon, projectiles, powder, small arms, and accoutrements are made, or specially ordered by the chief of ordnance, under the direction of the Secretary of War.

1380. In each case the inspector shall give to the contractor triplicate inspection certificates (Forms 30, 34, 38), and transmit to the ordnance bureau an inspection report (Forms 31, 32, 39).

1381. The inspecting officers shall transmit to the ordnance bureau a consolidated report, in July (Form 33), of their inspections of ordnance and projectiles during the year ending 30th June, and quarterly and annual reports (Forms 35, 36, 37) of their inspections of small arms, barrels, &c. Inspectors shall retain copies of their inspection reports, to be turned over to their successors; at an armory, the quarterly and annual inspection reports (35, 36, 37) are signed by the superintendent and master armorer.

1382. Reports of defects in the quality or condition of ordnance supplies will, in all cases, besides naming the articles, describe the particular pattern or model, when and where made, and whence, when, and from whom received, with such other information as will aid the Ordnance Department in taking the proper measures for correcting the defect.

1383. The inspectors of small arms will procure necessary assistants from the national armories. No assistant shall inspect oftener than twice in succession the arms made at the same private establishment. The inspector will have the accepted arms boxed and sealed in his presence.

1384. In time of peace, ordnance and ordnance stores are to be issued from the arsenals and armories only by authority from the ordnance bureau of the War Department; in war, to supply troops in service, on the order of any general or field officer commanding an army, garrison, or detachment; provided, in issues to the militia, that they shall have been regularly mustered into the service, and the requisition (Form 23) be approved by the mustering and inspecting officer of the United States, or a general or field officer commanding in the regular service. In case of an issue not specially directed from the ordnance bureau, the order for the issue will be promptly transmitted to the bureau by the issuing officer.

1385. The arms, accoutrements, and horse equipments required by an officer for his own use in the public service may be issued to him on payment of the regulated price (Form 19), to be passed to the credit of the proper appropriation at the ordnance bureau.

1386. Requisitions (Form 22) for ordnance and ordnance stores for companies or posts may, in urgent cases, be sent direct to the Adjutant-General's office, a duplicate being forwarded at the same time to Department head-quarters. Requisitions for the military academy are to be transmitted to the chief engineer. Requisitions for supplies for arsenals and armories are sent direct to the ordnance bureau.

1387. Requisitions for horse equipments will be made according to the form prescribed for ordnance requisitions, the various articles being classified in the requisitions and returns under heads, as follows:

Under the head of SADDLE will be included every thing embraced thereunder in the published statement of equipments, until further orders, (see "*General Orders*," No. 23, of 1859,) excepting *stirrups, saddle-bags, girths*, and *surcingles*, which will be entered separately.

CURB BRIDLES.

The various kinds of curb bits, as—

    Bits No. 1.
    Bits No. 2.
    Bits No. 3. } Brass scutcheons and curb-chains included.
    Bits No. 4.

    Leather fittings complete.

WATERING BRIDLES.

Snaffle-bits, chains and toggles included.	*Picket-pins.*
Watering reins.	*Lariat-ropes.*
Halters.	*Cavalry blankets.*
Spurs, straps included.	*Artillery blankets.*
Curry-combs.	*Nose-bags.*
Horse-brushes.	*Hitching-snaps.*

The minor parts of any article may be called for separately when neces-sary, and in that case will be borne on the return until expended to per-fect articles that are deficient. The injury or destruction of the minor parts of any article, particularly of leather, will not be a sufficient reason for condemning it, but, on the contrary, the necessary repairs will be made in the company by means of extra-duty men, or artificers, or at the depôts. (See "*General Orders*," No. 22, of 1859, paragraph 7.)

1388. When arms, accoutrements, and equipments need repairs that cannot be made by the troops, the commanding officer may send them to be repaired to the most convenient arsenal.

1389. The commander of each company or detachment will be account-able for all ordnance and ordnance stores issued to his command. The commander of each post will be accountable for all ordnance and ordnance stores at the post, not issued to the company or detachment commanders, or not in charge of an officer of ordnance or a store-keeper. Ordnance sergeants will account for ordnance property only where there is no com-missioned officer of the army or store-keeper.

1390. Commanding officers of the militia in service of the United States shall return and account for ordnance and ordnance stores in the use of troops as required in the regular service. And all arms and equipments issued to such militia shall be charged against the person to whom the issue is made on the muster-roll or pay account, to be accounted for to the mustering and inspecting officer, before receiving pay during service and on his discharge.

1391. Enlisted men who lose, or dispose of, the Colt's revolver pistols intrusted to their care, will hereafter be charged forty dollars in each case; that being the amount of pecuniary damage sustained by the United States, as estimated by the Ordnance Department.

1392. When a mustering and inspecting officer relieves such person from charge for loss or damage to his arms or equipments, satisfactory evidence, by affidavit or otherwise, setting out the facts of the loss or damage, and showing that it was not by his fault, shall be annexed to the pay-roll or account.

1393. When charges on account of ordnance stores are made against a soldier, the property return shall give his name and the pay-roll or account in which the charge is made.

1394. Arm-chests are to be preserved and accounted for as other ordnance stores.

1395. Every officer commanding a regiment, corps, garrison, or detachment shall make, at the end of February, April, June, August, October, and December, a report to the chief of ordnance, stating all damages to arms, equipments, and implements belonging to his command, noting those occasioned by negligence or abuse, and naming the officer or soldier by whose negligence or abuse the said damages were occasioned (Act of February 8, 1815), from which reports the necessary instructions shall be issued to the armories and the ordnance inspectors to correct defects in the manufacture.

1396. Inspections shall be made of the armories and arsenals of construction annually, and of other arsenals every two years, by such officers of the department as the Secretary of War shall designate, and a report of each inspection made to the ordnance bureau.

1397. The charge of an armory in the absence of the superintendent devolves on the master armorer, unless the chief of ordnance shall otherwise direct; of an arsenal, on the military store-keeper in the absence of an officer of ordnance.

1398. The officer in charge of an arsenal or armory shall, under the direction of the chief of ordnance, make and publish the rules for its internal government; procure the necessary materials and tools; engage the workmen, assign their grade, and appoint the necessary foremen. The cause for discharging or displacing a foreman shall be reported to the ordnance bureau.

1399. The military store-keeper shall disburse the funds on the certificate of the officer in charge upon each pay-roll or other account, stating the sum total in words, and, under the direction of the officer in charge, have the care and custody and make the returns of the ordnance and ordnance stores, except those in the current service, for which, including draft animals, the officer in charge is accountable.

1400. Where there is no store-keeper, the commanding officer is accountable for all the ordnance property, unless authorized by the ordnance bureau to devolve the accountability on another officer.

1401. Orders for the issue of supplies from an arsenal or armory are directed to the officer in charge, who shall transmit them to the store-keeper, and see to their execution. For transportation, the stores will be turned over to the Quartermaster's Department, with duplicate invoices (Form 2); a third shall be transmitted to the officer who is to receive the stores.

1402. Materials to be consumed or expended are issued on the written orders of the officer in charge to the store-keeper, who shall make quarterly abstracts of such issues (Form 9) as his voucher, to be certified by the officer in charge.

1403. The officer in charge shall turn over to the store-keeper the invoices (Form 2) of stores received, to be receipted for by him (Form 7), and shall furnish to him invoices of articles fabricated, purchased, repaired, &c., from which the store-keeper shall make the quarterly abstracts to be certified by the officer in charge (Forms 3, 4, 5, 6). At an armory, all articles purchased, fabricated, or repaired are to be inspected by the master armorer before being paid for, or turned into store.

1404. The date when orders for supplies are received, or stores received at or issued from an arsenal or armory, shall be reported on the report of work done (Form 27).

1405. Hired men in the ordnance service (except slaves) shall be engaged on daily wages, except men on piece-work, and paid only for such days or parts of days as they actually work. Working time, by daylight only, shall average ten hours throughout the year. When men are paid for extra time or night-work, the necessity shall be explained on the pay-roll.

1406. Workmen in an armory shall be paid, as far as practicable, by piece-work. The price of piece-work shall be fixed, according to the skill and labor it requires, by the superintendent, under the direction of the chief of ordnance.

1407. Any increase of wages shall be promptly reported to the ordnance bureau, with the necessary explanations.

1408. The money value of any piece of work spoiled by the fault or incompetency of a workman shall be charged to him on the pay-roll.

1409. A fair rent shall be charged monthly on the pay-roll to the hired men who occupy public quarters, except the master armorer and clerks at an armory. The rent-roll (Form 12) shall be returned quarterly to the ordnance bureau.

1410. Armory officers and hired men in the ordnance service will receive ten cents mileage for travel on duty under orders.

1411. No buildings or other permanent works or improvements will be undertaken without the sanction of the Secretary of War. The plans and estimates for them are to be sent to the ordnance bureau by the month of August.

1412. No trees on the public grounds will be removed or destroyed without authority from the ordnance bureau.

1413. None but strong draft horses are to be purchased for the ordnance service, nor without authority from the chief of ordnance.

1414. The enlisted men of ordnance shall be enlisted in the grade of laborer. They may be mustered, at the discretion of the officer in command, in any grade for which they are competent, except the grade of master workman. Promotions to that grade require the sanction of the chief of ordnance. Enlistments (Form 24) are to be in duplicate; one filed at the post, the other forwarded to the ordnance bureau. The number of enlisted men at each arsenal will be directed by the chief of ordnance.

1415. Expenses of the issue and delivery of ordnance and ordnance stores to the States, at any point within the State designated by the governor, if on navigable water or otherwise easily accessible, are paid by the United States from the appropriation for arming and equipping the militia. The officers of the Ordnance Department provide for the transportation and the payment of the expenses.

1416. The accounts with the several States and Territories are kept in terms of muskets; but other small arms, accoutrements, field artillery, and equipments of equal value and of the patterns adopted for the troops of the United States, may be issued at the request of the State or Territory, if the government supplies will permit.

1417. Receipts (Form 8) will be prepared in triplicate by the issuing officer, and transmitted for the signature of the governor, or officer or agent appointed by him to receive the stores; one of which, when returned, shall be forwarded by the issuing officer to the ordnance bureau.

1418. The returns and reports prescribed in the following articles are required to be sent to the ordnance bureau.

1419. Monthly returns, within five days after the quarter to which they relate, viz.: by the officer in charge of an arsenal: 1st, of the officers and men of ordnance (Form 25); 2d, of hired men (Form 26); 3d, of work done (Form 27); and by the officer in charge of an armory, a return of armory officers and men, and small arms and appendages manufactured (Form 28); and by the officer in charge of an arsenal or armory, a summary statement by the disbursing officer of money received and expended (Form 20).

1420. An estimate by the officer in charge of an arsenal or armory, at the beginning of the quarter, of the funds required during the quarter (Form 21).

1421. Quarterly returns, within twenty days after the quarter, viz.: 1st, by every disbursing officer, a money account current (Form 18), with abstract of disbursements (Form 17), and vouchers (Forms 13, 14, 15, 16), and a duplicate of the abstract and of the account current, with endorsed statement (Form 20); 2d, a property return (Form 1), with vouchers (Forms 2, 3, 4, 5, 6, 7, 8, 9, 10, and 19), by every person accountable for ordnance and ordnance stores, except those in current service at arsenals and armories. The return for a post will be distinct from that for a company or detachment.

1422. An annual return, in July, by the officer in charge of an arsenal or armory, of all ordnance stores, tools, and draft animals in current service (Form 1).

1423. An annual inventory, in August, by the officer in charge of an arsenal or armory (Form 29), with a report, in a condensed form, of the principal operations of the post during the year ending 30th June, including an account of experiments, of the construction and repairs of buildings, machinery, &c.

1424. Letters of transmittal are to accompany reports and returns to the ordnance bureau.

1425. Every officer required to make a return of ordnance and ordnance stores shall take an inventory of them (Form 11) in the month of June, and certify on his return for the second quarter that the inventory has been taken and his return made in conformity with it. The same form of inventory is to be used at inspections.

1426. In all official lists, ordnance and ordnance stores are to be arranged according to the classification in Article 1432.

1427. The following records of their reports and returns are required to be kept by ordnance officers and turned over to their successors :

1. A company return book, consisting of the retained duplicates, bound together;
2. A monthly return book, containing the other monthly returns and statements;
3. An account book, containing copies of the quarterly accounts current and their endorsed statements, of abstracts of money disbursed, and of estimates for funds;
4. A letter book of copies of all letters sent;
5. Files of letters received;
6. Files of orders received;
7. An annual inventory book, by binding together the retained inventories;
8. At armories and arsenals of construction, such other books may be kept as may be necessary to show the details of the operations.

1428. All books and files are to be submitted to inspecting officers, when called for.

1429. Printed blanks allowed will be furnished from the ordnance office, unless otherwise directed, on requisitions in May for a year's supply.

Ordnance Department.——Prices of Small Arms.

1430.   PRICES OF SMALL ARMS.

PARTS.	PERCUSSION LOCK.						
	Musket.	Rifle.	Hall's carbine.	Artillery musketoon.	Cavalry musketoon.	Sappers' musketoon.	Pistol.
	D. C.	D. C.	D. C.	D. C.	D. C.	D. C.	D. C.
Barrel with sight, without breech screw	4 10	4 40	4 48	3 50	3 55	3 55	2 00
Breech screw	10	10	......	10	10	10	08
Bayonet or band stud	01	......	......	01	......	01	......
Tang screw	05	05	......	05	05	05	04
Breech sight	......	06	......	......	......	......	......
Cone	09	09	09	09	09	09	09
Lock plate	50	50	......	50	50	50	40
Tumbler	27	27	......	27	27	27	25
Tumbler screw	03	03	......	03	03	03	03
Bridle	16	16	......	16	16	16	14
Sear	20	20	13	20	20	20	17
Sear spring	10	10	13	10	10	10	08
Main spring	27	27	20	27	27	27	25
Lock screw, each	03	03	04	03	03	03	03
Hammer	60	60	60	60	60	60	45
Side plate (with band, for pistol)	07	10	......	07	12	07	40
Side screws, each	04	04	03	04	04	04	03
Upper band	38	45	23	38	38	58	......
Middle band	23	......	......	......	......	......	......
Lower band	15	18	11	21	28	21	......
Upper band spring	09	09	05	09	09	09	......
Middle band spring	08	......	......	......	......	......	......
Lower band spring	08	08	......	08	......	08	......
Guard plate	42	50	47	40	50	40	35
Guard plate screw, each	03	03	03	03	03	03	02
Guard bow without swivels	30	35	20	20	25	20	20
Guard bow nut, each	02	02	02	02	02	02	02
Swivels and rivets, each	10	10	......	10	......	10	......
Swivel plate	......	......	......	10	......	10	......
Swivel plate screw, each	......	......	......	03	......	03	......
Trigger	12	12	12	12	12	12	09
Trigger screw	02	02	......	02	02	02	02
Butt plate	30	53	29	30	50	30	28
Butt plate screw, each	03	03	05	03	03	03	02
Ramrod	50	50	50	40	50	40	25
Ramrod spring	12	12	12	12	......	12	......
Ramrod wires	01	01	......	01	......	01	......
Ramrod stop	01	01	......	01	......	01	......
Stock	1 45	1 85	2 25	1 36	1 36	1 36	90
Bayonet	1 45	......	......	......	......	......	......
Bayonet clasp	16	......	......	......	......	......	......
Bayonet clasp screw	02	......	......	......	......	......	......
Box plate	......	72	......	......	......	......	......
Box catch	......	05	......	......	......	......	......
Box spring	......	10	......	......	......	......	......
Box spring screw	......	02	......	......	......	......	......
Box screw, each	......	03	......	......	......	......	......
Ramrod swivel and rivet	......	......	......	......	25	......	25
Ramrod swivel and rivet screw	......	......	......	......	03	......	02
Swivel bar	......	......	24	......	24	......	......
Swivel nut	......	......	02	......	02	......	......
Swivel screw	......	......	03	......	03	......	......
Swivel ring	......	......	03	......	03	......	......

Ordnance Department.——Prices of Small Arms.

PRICES OF SMALL ARMS.—*Continued.*

PARTS.	Musket.	Rifle.	Hall's car-bine.	Artillery musketoon.	Cavalry musketoon.	Sappers' musketoon.	Pistol.
	D. C.	D. C.	D. C.	D. C.	D. C.	D. C.	D. C.
Sword bayonet blade	......	......	......	......	......	2 13	......
Sword bayonet hilt, without clasp ...	......	......	......	......	......	1 60	......
Sword bayonet clasp.....................	......	......	......	......	......	21	......
Sword bayonet clasp screw...........	......	......	......	......	......	02	......
Guide.....................................	......	......	06	......	......	......	......
Bridge....................................	......	......	65	......	......	......	......
Supporters, each.......................	......	......	43	......	......	......	......
Supporter screws, each................	......	......	02	......	......	......	......
Chocks, each	......	......	07	......	. .....	......	......
Chock screws, each....................	......	......	03	......	......	......	......
Receiver.................................	......	......	2 66	......	......	......	......
Butt piece...............................	......	......	08	......	......	......	......
Butt piece screw.......................	......	......	05	......	......	......	......
Strap.....................................	......	......	25	......	......	......	......
Strap screw.............................	......	......	05	......	......	......	......
Set screw................................	......	......	03	......	......	......	......
Link......................................	......	......	09	......	......	......	......
Link screw..............................	......	......	03	......	......	......	......
Stop......................................	......	......	14	......	......	......	......
Apron	......	......	13	......	......	......	......
Apron screw	......	......	03	......	......	......	......
Catch	......	......	19	......	......	......	......
Catch screw............................	......	......	03	......	......	......	......
Catch spring............................	......	......	12	......	......	......	......
Catch spring screw....................	......	......	04	......	......	......	......
Catch plate..............................	......	......	16	......	......	......	......
Catch plate screw	......	......	03	......	......	......	......
Lever.....................................	......	......	20	......	......	......	2 17
Barrel complete........	4 30	4 65	4 57	3 70	3 74	3 75	2 17
Lock complete..........................	2 25	2 25	1 46	2 25	2 25	2 25	1 89
Guard complete.........................	1 06	1 16	......	84	99	84	72
Bayonet complete	1 63	......	.....	......	......	......	......
Box plate complete.....................	......	98	......	......	......	......	......
Arm complete	13 00	13 25	17 00	10 37	11 00	10 62*	7 00

* Without sword bayonet.

Appendages. {
  Screw-driver and cone wrench................ .... 46 cents }
  Wiper... 20 " } For all arms.
  Ball screw .... 12 " }
  Spring vice .... 35 " }
  Bullet mould (rifle calibre).................. .... 50 " }

Ordnance Department.——Prices of Small Arms.

PRICES OF SMALL ARMS.—*Continued.*

COLT'S REVOLVER.

PARTS.	D. C.	PARTS.	D. C.
Barrel	7 00	Key screw	02
Sight	01	Lever	1 00
Cylinder	4 00	Rammer	30
Cone	06	Lever screw	02
Base pin	35	Catch spring	01
Lock frame	5 00	Catch on barrel	04
Lock screw	02	Catch on lever	06
Hammer and tumbler	88	Stock strap	50
Bolt	33	Stock strap screw	02
Bolt spring and sear	10	Guard plate	75
Bolt spring screw	02	Guard plate screw	02
Hand	31	Trigger	30
Hand spring	02	Stock	50
Main spring	50	Screw driver and cone wrench	42
Key	31	Ring or spring vice	01
Main spring screw	02	Bullet mould	1 00
Key spring and rivet	10	Pistol and appendages	24 00

SWORDS AND SABRES.

PARTS.		Cavalry sabre.	Horse artillery sabre.	Artillery sword.	Musketoon sword bayonet.	Non-commissioned officer's sword.	Musician's sword.
		D. C.	D. C.	D. C.	D. C.	D. C.	D. C.
Hilt	Gripe	20	17	......	......	24	20
	Head	70	44	87	1 60	50	44
	Guard	1 10	58	......	......	1 20	44
Blade		2 80	1 98	2 13	2 13	2 20	1 92
	Mouth piece	20	10	......	......	......	......
	Body	1 20	1 00	50	62	66	50
Scabbard	Bands and rings	60	60	......	......	......	......
	Ferrule and stud	15	13	25	40	35	25
	Tip	......	......	25	25	35	25
Arm complete		7 00	5 00	4 00	5 00	5 50	4 00

1431. PRICES OF ACCOUTREMENTS.

BLACK LEATHER BELTS.

PARTS.	Infantry.	Artillery.	Cavalry.	Rifle.
	D. C.	D. C.	D. C.	D. C.
Cartridge box	1 10	......	......	95
Cartridge box plate..	10	......	10	10
Cartridge box belt...	69	......	......	......
Cartridge box belt plate...	10	......	......	......
Bayonet scabbard and frog...	56	......	......	......
Waist belt, private's	25	......	......	37
Waist belt plate...	10	......	......	10
Cap pouch and pick..	40	......	40	40
Gun sling	16	......	......	16
Sabre belt	......	1 03	1 35	......
Sabre belt plate...	......	60	60	......
Sword belt...	......	1 00	......	......
Sword belt plate...	......	10	......	......
Sword belt, non-commissioned officer's and musician's.......	62	......	......	62
Sword belt plate do. do.	10	......	......	10
Waist belt do. do.	37	......	......	37
Waist belt plate do. do.	60	......	......	60
Carbine cartridge box	......	......	87	......
Pistol do	......	......	75	......
Holsters, with soft leather caps...	......	......	2 63	......
Carbine sling...	......	......	95	......
Carbine swivel..	......	......	88	......
Sabre knot..	......	......	30	......
Bullet pouch	......	......	......	53
Flask and pouch belt..	......	......	......	40
Powder flask	......	......	......	1 20
Waist belt, sapper's, with frog for sword bayonet, $1				

1432   CLASSIFICATION OF ORDNANCE AND ORDNANCE STORES.

PART FIRST.

ARTILLERY, SMALL ARMS, AMMUNITION, AND OTHER ORDNANCE STORES.

CLASS I.
Cannon.

18 pdr. brass cannon,	Mexican trophy,		weight.	lbs.
12 pdr.	do.	French,	do.	do.
9 pdr.	do.	Spanish,	do.	do.
8 pdr.	do.	French,	do.	do.
6 pdr.	do.	English trophy,	do.	do.
4 pdr.	do.	French,	do.	do.
3 pdr.	do.	English trophy,	do.	do.
12 pdr.	do.	field, U. S., pattern 1840,	do.	do.
6 pdr.	do.	do. do.	do.	do.
6 pdr.	do.	old pattern,	do.	do.
8 inch brass howitzers,	English trophy,		do.	do.
6 inch	do.	French,	do.	do.
24 pdr.	do.	field, U. S., pattern 1840,	do.	do.
12 pdr.	do.	do. do.	do.	do.
16 inch brass stone mortars,	French,		do.	do.
13 inch brass mortar,	do.		do.	do.
42 pdr. iron cannon,	U. S., pattern 1831,		do.	do.
42 pdr.	do.	do. 1819,	do.	do.
42 pdr.	do.	do. 1840,	do.	do.
32 pdr.	do.	do. 1840,	do.	do.
24 pdr.	do.	do. 1819,	do.	do.
24 pdr.	do.	do. 1839,	do.	do.
24 pdr.	do.	old pattern, round breech,	do.	do.
18 pdr.	do.	do. do.	do.	do.
18 pdr.	do.	model 1819,	do.	do.
18 pdr.	do.	do. 1839,	do.	do.
12 pdr.	do.	garrison, model 1819,	do.	do.
12 pdr.	do.	do. do. 1839,	do.	do
12 pdr.	do.	field, do. 1819,	do.	do
12 pdr.	do.	do. inspected 1834,	do.	do.
6 pdr.	do.	do. do. do	do.	do
100 pdr. columbiads,			do.	do.
50 pdr.	do.		do.	do

Ordnance Department.——Classification of Stores.

	weight.	lbs.
10 inch columbiads,	weight.	lbs.
8 inch do.	do.	do.
8 inch iron howitzers, sea-coast, model 1840,	do.	do
8 inch do. do. do. 1839,	do.	do
8 inch do. siege, do. 1839,	do.	do
24 pdr. do. field, inspected 1834,	do.	do.
24 pdr. do. for flank defense,	do.	do
24 pdr. do. field, old pattern, light,	do.	do.
12 pdr. do. do. inspected 1834,	do.	do.
10 inch iron mortars, sea-coast, model 1839,	do.	do.
10 inch do. do. do. 1819,	do.	do.
8 inch do. siege, do. 1840,	do.	do.

Unserviceable.

9 pdr. brass cannon, field,	do.	do.
6 pdr. do. do.	do.	do.
8 inch brass howitzers, American, old,	do.	do.
24 pdr. do. do. do.	do.	do.
10 inch brass mortars,	do.	do.
24 pdr. iron cannon, cascable broken,	do.	do.
6 pdr. do. old, various patterns,	do.	do.
6 pdr. do. wrought iron,	do.	do.

NOTE.—The mean weight of each kind of ordnance, as well as the number of pieces, should be entered on the inventories.

CLASS II.

Artillery Carriages.

12 pdr. field gun carriages, complete, stocktrail, pattern 1835.

12 pdr. do. do. do. do. 1840.					
6 pdr. do. do. do. do. do.					
24 pdr. howitzer field carriages, do. do. do. do.					
12 pdr. do. do. do. do. do. do.					
24 pdr. siege gun carriages, do. do. do. do.					
Mountain howitzer carriages, do. do. do. do.					
Caissons for 12 pdr. guns, do. do. do. do.					
Do. 6 pdr. do. do. do. do. do.					
Do. 24 pdr. howitzers, do. do. do. do.					
Do. 12 pdr. do. do. do. do. do. do.					
Do. without interior divisions, do. do. do.					

Traveling forges.

Battery wagons.

Portable forges for mountain service.

Chests with carriage-makers' tools, for mountain service.
Field battery wagons, with tools and stores, complete, C.
Field traveling forges, with   do.   do.   A
Mortar wagons, for siege service, complete.
 8 inch columbiad casemate gun carriages.
 8 inch   do.   do.   chassis.
32 pdr. casemate gun carriages.
32 pdr.   do.   chassis.
24 pdr. casemate gun carriages, wood.
24 pdr.   do.   do.   cast iron.
24 pdr.   do.   chassis.
24 pdr. howitzer casemate carriages, for flank defense, complete.
 8 inch sea-coast howitzer barbette carriages and chassis.
32 pdr. barbette gun carriages.
32 pdr.   do.   chassis.
24 pdr.   do.   gun carriages.
24 pdr.   do.   chassis.
10 inch sea-coast mortar beds, iron.
10 inch   do.   do.   wood.
10 inch siege   do.   iron.
 8 inch do.   do.   iron.

Unserviceable.

6 pdr. field carriages, Gribeauval pattern, require repairs.
6 pdr.   do.   stocktrail, ⎫
Caissons,   ⎬ Major ——'s battery.
Battery wagons,   ⎭
Traveling forges,

NOTE.—The "*field carriage, complete,*" includes the limber and ammunition chest, but no implements. The "*casemate or barbette carriage, complete,*" includes the upper or gun carriage, and the chassis, with all the wheels, but no implements. It is better, however, to enter the gun carriages and the chassis separately, as above.

CLASS III.

Artillery Implements and Equipments.

Axes, felling.
Bricoles.
Buckets, sponge, iron, for field guns.
   Do.   do.   wood, for garrison guns.
   Do.   tar,   iron, for field guns.
   Do.   water,   for field forge.
   Do.   watering, leather

Budge barrels.
Cannon locks, left side, for guns with lock pieces.
    Do.   do.   do.   without do.
Cannon spikes.
Chocks for casemate carriages.
Drag ropes.
Fuze augers.
 Do. extractors.
 Do. gimlets.
 Do. mallets.
 Do. plug reamers.
 Do. rasps.
 Do. saws.
 Do. setters, brass.
 Do.   do. wood.
Gunner's callipers.
    Do.   gimlets, for siege and garrison guns.
    Do.   do.   for field guns.
    Do.   haversacks.
    Do.   levels.
    Do.   pincers.
    Do.   quadrants.
Handspikes, trail, for field carriages.
    Do.   manœuvring, for garrison carriages.
    Do.   shod,   do.   do.
    Do.   truck, iron,   casemate do.
    Do.   roller, do.   do.   do.
Harness, viz.:
 Sets for two wheel horses, pattern 1840.
    Do.   leading do.   do.
    Do.   wheel do. with Grimsley's saddles, &c.
    Do.   leading do.   do.
Draft for mountain howitzer carriage.
Pack-saddles and bridles for   do.
Nose bags.
Whips.
Ladles and staves for 32 pdr. gun.
       Do.   24 pdr. gun.
       Do.   12 pdr. gun.
Lanterns, common.
    Do. dark.
Lanyards for friction primers.

Lead aprons and straps.
Linstocks.
Lock covers.
Men's harness.
Pass boxes.
Pendulum hausses for 12 pdr. field guns.
  Do.   6 pdr. do.
  Do.   32 pdr. field howitzers.
  Do.   24 pdr. do.
  Do.   12 pdr. do.
Pick axes.
Plummets.
Pointing wires.
Portfire cases.
Portfire shears.
Portfire stocks.
Powder funnels, copper.
Powder measures, do.
Priming horns.
Priming wires for siege and garrison guns.
  do. for field   do.
Prolonges.
Rammers and staves, viz. :
 For 32 pdr. garrison guns.
 For 24 pdr. do.
 For 12 pdr. do.
 For 10 inch columbiads.
 For 8 inch sea-coast howitzers.
Shell hooks.
Shell plug screws.
Splints.
Shovels.
Sponges, woolen, 8 inch.
 Do. do. 32 pdr.
 Do. do. 24 pdr.
 Do. do. 12 pdr.
 Do. do. 6 pdr.
Sponge covers, 32 pdr.
 Do. do. 24 pdr.
 Do. do. 6 pdr.
Sponges and rammers, viz. :
 For 8 inch siege howitzers.

For 24 pdr. field howitzers.
For 12 pdr. field guns.
For 6 pdr.   do.
Sponges and staves, viz. :
   For 42 pdr. gun.
   For 32 pdr. gun.
   For 12 pdr. gun, siege and garrison.
   For 10 inch columbiad, bore.
     Do.   do.   chamber.
   For 8 inch sea-coast howitzer.
Tangent scales for 12 pdr. field guns.
     Do.   6 pdr.   do.
     Do.   24 pdr. field howitzer.
     Do.   12 pdr.   do.
Tarpaulins, large.
     Do.   small.
Thumb stalls.
Tompions and collars for 12 pdr. field guns.
     Do.   do.   6 pdr.   do.
     Do.   for 8 inch mortars.
Tow hooks.
Tube pouches.
Vent covers.
Vent punches.
Worms and staves, viz.:
   For siege and garrison guns.
   For 12 pdr. field guns.
   For 6 pdr.   do.

NOTE.—A set of harness for two horses includes every thing required for them except *whips* and *nose bags*, which are reported separately.

CLASS IV.

Artillery Projectiles, and their Appendages, unprepared for Service.

42 pdr. cannon balls.	24 pdr. shells.
32 pdr. do.	12 pdr. do.
24 pdr. do.	32 pdr. spherical case shot.
12 pdr. do.	24 pdr. do. do.
6 pdr. do.	12 pdr. spherical case shot.
10 inch shells for columbiads.	6 pdr. do. do.
8 inch shells for mortars.	42 pdr. grape shot, loose, No.
32 pdr. shells.	24 pdr. do. do. do.

12 pdr. grape shot, loose, No.		For 12 pdr. do.	pounds.
Canister shot, loose, viz. :		For 6 pdr. do.	do.
For 32 pdr. gun,	pounds.	For 24 pdr. howitzer,	do.
For 24 pdr. do.	do.	For 12 pdr. do.	do.

CLASS V.

Artillery Projectiles, with their Appendages, prepared for Service.

12 pdr. shot for 12 pdr. gun,	fixed, rounds.
12 pdr. spherical case shot for 12 pdr. gun,	do. do.
12 pdr. canisters for 12 pdr. gun,	do. do.
6 pdr. shot,	do. do.
6 pdr. spherical case shot,	do. do.
6 pdr. canisters,	do. do.
12 pdr. howitzer shells,	do. do.
12 pdr. do. spherical case shot,	do. do.
12 pdr. do. canisters,	do. do.
32 pdr. do. spherical case shot, with metal fuzes,	do. do.
12 pdr. spherical case for 12 pdr. field gun,	do. do.
12 pdr. shells do. do.	do. do.

8 inch shells, strapped, for columbiad.
8 inch do.   do.   sea-coast howitzer.
12 pdr. howitzer shells, strapped.
12 pounder howitzer spherical case shot, strapped.
12 pdr. canisters for 12 pdr. field guns.
6 pdr. shot, strapped.
6 pdr. canisters.
12 pdr. grape shot, stands of.
42 pdr. cannon wads, junk.
32 pdr.   do.   hay.
24 pdr.   do.   grommet.

NOTE.—A *"round of fixed ammunition"* is here used to indicate the *projectile with its cartridge* prepared for use, although, in some cases, they are not actually connected together. A *"shot strapped"* or a *"canister," "stand of grape,"* &c., indicates the projectile prepared for making fixed ammunition, or for service.

CLASS VI.

Small Arms

Muskets, complete, VIZ. :
National armory, bright, percussion, new.
Do.   brown, flint, 4th class, short.
Do.   bright, altered to percussion
National armory, brown, altered to percussion.

Contract, brown, altered to percussion.
    Do.   bright,   do.
Musketoons, artillery, percussion.
    Do.   cavalry,   do.
    Do.   sappers,   do.
Rifles, viz.:
  Harper's Ferry, percussion, new.
    Do.   do.   repaired.
  Contract, full stocked, brown, flint.
  Hall's patent, new, without bayonets.
    Do.   do. with   do.
Pistols, viz.:
  Percussion, new model.
  Colt's patent.
Hall's carbines, new, percussion.
Wall pieces, rifle, 4 oz. calibre.
Cavalry sabres, pattern 1840.
Horse artillery sabres, privates', pattern 1840.
Non-commissioned officers' swords,   do.
Musicians' swords,   do.
Artillery swords, new pattern.
Cavalry sabres, English.
Regulation artillery swords, English.
Sergeants' swords, Prussian.
Foot officers' swords, new pattern, $30\frac{1}{2}$ inches.
    Do.   do.   32 do.
Field officers' swords.

Unserviceable.

Muskets, without bayonets.
Rifles, require repairs.
Carbines, Hall's patent, irreparable.

CLASS VII.

Accoutrements, Implements, and Equipments for Small Arms, and Horse Equipments for Cavalry.

Infantry cartridge-boxes.	Bayonet scabbards, 18 inches, black
Cartridge-box plates.	frogs.
Cartridge-box belts, black leather.	Gun slings.
Do. do. white do.	Waist belts, black leather.
Cartridge-box belt plates.	Do. belt plates, inf. privates'.
Bayonet scabbards, 16 inches.	Waist belt plates, inf. sergeants'.

Wipers for percussion muskets.
Ball screws,   do.
Screw drivers,   do.
Spring vices for muskets.
Cones for new muskets.
    Do.   altered do.
Cap pouches.
Cone picks.
Rifle cartridge boxes.
Rifle cartridge-box plates.
Rifle flasks.
Rifle ball pouches.
Rifle pouch and flask belts, white.
    Do.   do.   black.
Bayonet scabbards, Hall's rifles.
Bayonet scabbard belts, do.
Wipers for percussion rifles.
Screw drivers,   do.
Spare cones for rifles.
Ball screws,   do.
Bullet moulds, do.   round balls.
Bullet moulds, do.   con.   do.
Spring vices.
Cartridge boxes for pistols.

Cartridge-box plates for pistols.
Spring vices,   do.
Screw drivers,   do.
Bullet moulds,   do.
Ball screws,   do.
Spare cones,   do.
Screw drivers for Colt's pistols.
Spring vices,   do.
Powder flasks,   do.
Bullet moulds,   do.
Artillery sword belts.
Cavalry sabre belts, white, old pat.
Cavalry sabre belt plates,   do.
Non-com'd officers' sword belts
    double frogs, black leather.
Non-com'd officers' sword-belt plates
Horse artillery sabre belts, black.
Holsters.
Housings.
Musket flints.
Rifle flints.
Cavalry equipments, { saddles.
                      { bridles.

CLASS VIII.

Powder, Ammunition for Small Arms, &c., and Materials.

Cannon powder,   lbs.
Musket powder,   do.
Rifle powder,   do.
Mealed powder,   do.
Fulminate of mercury,   do.
Nitre, refined,   do.
Sulphur, crude,   do.
Sulphur, roll,   do.
Sulphur, flowers,   do.
Sulphur, pulverized,   do.
Pulverized charcoal,   do.
24 pdr. cartridges, 6 lbs.
12 pdr.   do.   2½ do.
 6 pdr.   do.   1¼ do.

42 pdr. cartridge bags, paper, with
    flannel bottoms.
32 pdr. cartridge bags, paper, with
    flannel bottoms.
24 pdr. cartridge bags, flannel.
12 pdr.   do.   field, do.
 6 pdr.   do.   do. do.
Musket buck and ball cartridges for
    percussion arms.
Musket buck and ball cartridges for
    flint lock arms.
Rifle ball cartridges for perc'n arms.
Pistol do.   do.   do.
Musketoon ball cartridges, perc'n.

Pistol ball cartridges, flint.

Musket blank cartridges.

Rifle   do.

Cartridges for Colt's pistols.

Musket balls, pressed (for proving muskets),   lbs.

Musket balls, pressed,   do.

Rifle   do.   do.

Buckshot,   do.

Laboratory paper, viz.:

  No. 1 (musket cartridge),   do.

  No. 2 (wrapping),   do.

  No. 3 (blank cartridge),   do.

Wrapping paper (No. 2) waxed, do.

Wrapping paper,   quires.

Priming tubes, filled.

Portfires.

Quick match,   lbs.

Slow match,   lbs.

Percussion caps for small arms.

Do. caps for Colt's pistols.

Do. primers for Maynard's lock.

Do. primers for cannon, Hidden's.

Friction tubes.

Rockets, war, Congreve.

Rockets, Hale's, 3¼ inch.

Rockets, do. 2¼ do.

Rockets, 1 inch, signal.

Fuzes, 10 inch, filled.

Fuzes, 8 inch, filled.

Fuzes, paper, for field ammunition

Fuzes, wooden,   do.

Blue lights.

Fire balls.

CLASS IX.

Parts, or Incomplete Sets of any of the Articles inserted in the Preceding Classes.

Parts of barbette carriages, viz.:

Bevil washers for 32 pdr.

  Do.   24 pdr.

Elevating screws.

Iron work for 24 pdr. carriages and chassis, complete, sets.

Lunettes.

Naves.

Pintles.

Pintle plates, 32 pdr.

Pipes,   32 pdr.

Rollers,   32 pdr.

  Do.   24 pdr.

Traverse wheels.

Parts of casemate carriages, viz.:

Bed plates for elevating screws.

Elevating screws.

Handles for elevating screws.

Iron work for 32 pdr. carriages, complete, sets.

Pintles, cast iron

Traverse wheels, large.

  Do.   do.   small.

Truck wheels.

Trunnion plates, 32 pdr., pairs.

Parts of field carriages, viz.:

Airbacks for forges.

Axletrees for 6 pdr. gun carriages

  Do. for 6 pdr. limbers.

Cap squares, 6 pdr.

Cap square chains.

Cold shut S links, No. 3.

  Do.   No. 5.

Elevating screws and nuts.

Fellies.

Iron work for 6 pdr. carriages, complete, sets.

Keys for ammunition chests.

Linch pins.

Lock chains.

Nails, Nos. 1 and 2, lbs.

Nave bands.

Nave boxes, cast iron.
Nuts, assorted.
Pintle hooks, keys, and chains
Poles, spare, ironed.
Pole props.
Pole yokes.
Rondelles, 6 pdr., large.
    Do.   do. small.
Splinter bars.
Spokes.
Stocks, 6 pdr. carriage,   ironed.
    Do.   caisson,   do.
    Do.   battery wagon, do.
Tire bolts, nuts, and washers.
Washers for axletrees, linch.
    Do.   do.   shoulder.
    Do. for bolts, assorted.
Wheels, spare.
Parts of artillery implements:
42 pdr. rammer heads.
24 pdr.   do.
12 pdr.   do.
 6 pdr.   do.
42 pdr. sponge heads.
24 pdr.   do.
12 pdr.   do.
 6 pdr.   do.
 8 inch columbiad sponge heads
    and staves, for bore.
 8 inch columbiad sponge heads
    and staves, for chamber.
24 pdr. sponge heads and staves.
 6 pdr. sponge and rammer staves.
 6 pdr. worm staves.
12 pdr. ladles.
Worms for siege and garrison guns.

Thimbles for prolonges.
    Parts of artillery harness, viz. :
Drivers' saddles, Grimsley's pat'n.
Valise   do.   do.
Bridles, Grimsley's pattern
Bits, brass plated.
Halters.
Halter chains.
Collars.
Girths.
Traces, leading, leather.
Traces, wheel,   do.
Leg guards.
Breast straps.
Breech straps.
Hames, pairs.
    Parts of small arms, viz. :
Stocks for percussion muskets.
Tumbler screws,   do.
Bridle screws,   do.
Sears, for percussion muskets.
Sear screws,   do.
Main-springs,   do.
Main-spring screws, do.
Sear-springs,   do.
Sear-spring screws, do.
Bayonets for Hall's rifles.
    Parts of prepared ammunition, viz.:
Sabots for 12 pdr. field gun.
Sabots for 12 pdr. howitzer.
Cylinders and caps for 6 pdr. field
    ammunition.
Plates for 12 pdr. canisters.
Plates for 24 pdr. grape.
Rocket cases, 2½ inch, Hale's.
Rocket cases, paper, 1 in., signal.

CLASS X.

Miscellaneous.

Garrison gins, old pattern.
    Do. with ratchet windlass.
Casemate gins,   do.

Field and siege gins, with ratchet
    windlass.
Sling carts, large.

Ordnance Department.——Classification of Stores.

Sling carts, hand.
Casemate trucks.
Hand carts.
Store trucks.
Lifting jacks.
Falls for casemate gins.
Falls for garrison gins
Falls for field and siege gins.
Treble blocks, iron.
Double   do.
Single   do.
Gin handspikes.
Handspikes for mechan'l. man'rs.
Long rollers,   do.
Short rollers,   do.
Half rollers,   do.
Blocks,   do.
Half blocks,   do.
Quarter blocks,   do.
Gun chocks,   do.
Wheel chocks for mechan'l man'rs.
Roller   do.   do
Skids,   do.   do

Shifting planks for mechanical man-
    œuvres.
Trunnion chains.
Mortar eprouvettes.
Beds for   do.
Balls for   do.
Rocket conductors, Hale's.
Star gauges, with rings, for inspect-
    ing cannon.
42 pdr. ring gauges for shot, large.
    Do.   small, old.
    Do.   do. new.
13 in. ring gauges for shells, large.
    Do.   small, old.
    Do.   do. new.
42 pdr. grape shot gauges, large.
42 pdr.   do.   small.
Can'r. shot gauges for 12 pdr. gun.
    Do.   do.   how'r.
Shell callip'rs for thickness of sides.
    Do.   do.   bottom.
42 pdr. cylinder gauges for shot.
32 pdr.   do.   do.

PART SECOND.

TOOLS AND MATERIALS.

Cloths, Ropes, Thread, &c.

Canvas,   yards.
Cotton cloth,   do.
Duck, cotton,   do.
Linen, brown,   do.
Marline,   pounds.
Rope, hemp,   do.
Rope, Manilla,   do.
Sash cord,   do.

Thread, shoe,   pounds.
Thread, patent,   do.
Tow,   do.
Twine, bundling,   do.
Worsted stuff,   yards.
Yarn, cotton,   pounds.
Yarn, packing,   do.
Yarn, woolen,   do.

Forage.

Bran,   bush.
Hay,   lbs.

Oats,   bush.
Straw,   lbs.

Ironmongery.

Bolts, door,	No.	Mica, sheet,	pounds.
Brass, sheet,	pounds.	Nails, iron, cut,	do.
Buckles, iron,	No.	Do. wrought,	do.
Do. brass,	do.	Do. finishing,	do.
Chains, iron,	pounds.	Do. horseshoe,	do.
Chalk,	do.	Do. bellows,	do.
Copper, sheet,	do.	Do. copper,	do.
Do. bar,	do.	Pulleys, brass,	No.
Do. cake,	do.	Rasps,	do.
Do. scrap,	do.	Rivets and burrs, iron,	pounds.
Emery,	do.	Do. copper,	do.
Files, assorted,	No.	Sand paper,	quires.
Glue,	pounds.	Screws, wood, assorted,	No.
Hinges, iron, butt,	pairs.	Spelter solder,	pounds.
Do. brass, do.	do.	Steel, cast,	do.
Horseshoes,	pounds.	Do. blister,	do.
Iron, bar,	do.	Do. shear,	do.
Do. sheet,	do.	Do. scrap,	do.
Do. plate,	do.	Tacks, iron,	papers.
Do. scrap,	do.	Do. copper,	pounds
Do. castings,	do.	Tin, block,	do.
Lead, pig,	do.	Do. sheets,	do.
Do. sheet,	do.	Tubing, wrought iron,	feet.
Do. scrap,	do.	Wire, iron,	pounds.
Locks, assorted,	No.	Do. brass,	do.
Do. magazine,	do.	Do. steel,	do.

Laboratory Stores.

Acid, nitric,	pounds.	Gum shellac,	pounds.
Do. muriatic,	do.	Nitrate baryta,	do.
Alcohol,	do.	Nitrate strontia,	do.
Antimony, sulphuret,	do.	Quicksilver,	do.
Borax,	do.	Rosin,	do.
Beeswax,	do.	Sal ammoniac,	do.
Camphor,	do.	Soap,	do.
Chlorate potash,	do.	Sponge,	do.
Chloride lime,	do.	Tallow,	do.
Flour,	do.	Whisky,	gallons.
Gum arabic,	do.		

Lumber.—Gun Carriage Timber, and Building Materials.

For 12 pdr. stocktrail carriage.
Gun carriage stocks.
Axle bodies.

For six pdr. stocktrail carriage:
Gun carriage stocks.
Axle bodies.
Cheeks.

Axle bodies for limbers.
Poles,   do.
Hounds,   do.
Forks,   do.
Splinter bars,   do.
Front footboards,   do.

Axle bodies for caissons
Stocks,   do.
Middle rails,   do.
Side rails,   do.
Cross bars,   do.
Front footboards,   do.
Hind footboards,   do.

Stocks   for forges.
Axle bodies,   do.
Side rails,   do.
Middle rails,   do.
Cross bars,   do.
Studs, plates, and guides, do.

Ends for coal boxes.
Sides,   do.
Bottoms,   do.
Lids,   do

Axle bodies for battery wagons.
Stocks,   do.
Lower side rails,   do.
Upper do.   do.
Ridge poles,   do.

Ends   for ammunition chests.
Sides,   do.
Frames for covers,   do.
Panels,   do.
Bottoms,   do.
Cover linings,   do.

Principal partitions for ammunition
    chests.
Naves   for field carriages.
Spokes,   do.
Fellies,   do.
Trail handspikes,   do.

Legs for siege and garrison gins.
Pry poles,   do.
Windlasses,   do.
Upper braces,   do.
Middle do.   do.
Lower do.   do.
Handspikes for gins.

For 32 pdr. casemate gun carriage:
Cheeks.
Front transoms.
Rear   do.
Slides.
Axletrees.

For 32 pdr. casemate chassis·
Tongues.
Hurters and guides.
Rails.
Front transoms.
Rear   do.

For 32 pdr. barbette top car-
    riage:
Uprights.
Braces.
Front transoms.
Middle   do.

For 32 pdr. barbette chassis:
Tongues.
Rails.
Hurters.
Front transoms.
Middle   do.
Rear   do.
Props.
Spokes for barbette carriages.
Handspikes for   do.

Ordnance Department.——Classification of Stores.

Plank, poplar, for interior of ammunition chests,	feet.	Scantling, poplar, for sponge heads,	feet
Plank, ash, for implements,	do.	Scantling, ash,	do.
Do. walnut,	do.	Building materials:	
Do. cherry,	do.	Brick, red,	No.
Do. beech,	do.	Do. fire,	do.
Do. white pine,	do.	Fire clay,	barrels.
Do. yellow pine,	do.	Lime,	do.
Scantling, maple, for rammer heads,	feet.	Sand,	loads.
		Slates,	No.

NOTE.—The number of pieces of timber for each part of a gun carriage, &c., should be reported separately, as above. Miscellaneous plank, scantling, &c., should be stated in board measure.

Leather and Materials for Harness Work.

Leather, buff,	sides.	Leather, sole,	pounds.
Do. bridle,	do.	Sheep skins, with wool,	No.
Do. kip,	do.	Do. tanned,	do.
Do. thong,	do.	Black wax,	pounds.
Do. collar,	do.	Bristles,	do.
Do. harness,	pounds.	Hair,	do.
Do. band,	do.	Raw hides,	No.
Do. skirting,	do.	Whip stocks,	do.

Paints, Oils, Glass, &c.

Chrome green,	pounds.	Pumice stone,	pounds.
Coal tar,	gallons.	Prussian blue,	do.
Copperas,	pounds.	Paint, mixed, olive,	do.
Glass, window,	feet.	do. black,	do.
Lacker for cannon,	gallons.	Spirits of turpentine,	gallons.
Lampblack,	pounds.	Tar,	do.
Lead, white,	do.	Umber,	pounds.
Litharge,	do.	Varnish, copal,	gallons.
Oil, linseed,	gallons.	do. Japan,	do.
Oil, neatsfoot,	do.	Vermilion,	pounds.
Oil, sperm,	do.	Whiting,	do.
Ochre, yellow,	pounds.	Zinc paint, white,	do.
Putty,	pounds.		

Stationery.

Books, office, blank.		India-rubber,	pieces.
Ink, black,	gallons.	Paper, letter,	quires.
Ink, red,	pints.	Do. cap,	do.

Paper, envelope,	quires.	Quills,	No.
Do. blotting,	do.	Sealing-wax,	pounds.
Do. drawing,	sheets.	Tape,	pieces.
Pencils, lead,	No.	Wafers,	pounds.
Pens, steel,	do.	Ordnance Manual.	
Pasteboard,	pounds.	Ordnance Regulations.	

Tools.

Adzes, carpenters'.	Drawing knives.
Do. coopers'.	Dredging boxes.
Alphabets, sets.	Drifts, assorted.
Andirons, pairs.	Drills, do.
Anvils.	Drill bows.
Augers, assorted.	Figure stamps, sets.
Awls, saddlers'.	Fire buckets.
Axes, broad.	Fire engines.
Do. felling.	Flasks, moulders', wood.
Do. hand.	Do. do. iron.
Bellows, hand.	Flatteners.
Benches, laboratory.	Forks, hay.
Bevels, assorted.	Do. straining.
Bick irons.	Formers, cast iron, assorted.
Bits, auger.	Do. laboratory, do.
Blocks for tackle.	Do. for musket cartridges.
Braces.	Do. for rifle cartridges.
Brace bits.	Fullers, assorted.
Brushes, dusting.	Funnels, copper.
Do. paint.	Do. glass.
Do. whitewash.	Furnaces, tinners'.
Chasing tools.	Gauges, assorted.
Cherries.	Do. wire.
Chisels, cold.	Do. cutting.
Do. firmer.	Do. for rockets.
Do. framing.	Do. for portfires.
Do. splitting.	Gimlets, assorted.
Do. for turning wood.	Glue pots.
Clamps, wood.	Gouges, carpenters'.
Do. iron.	Do. turners'.
Claw tools.	Do. stockers'.
Compasses.	Grindstones.
Countersinks.	Hacksaw frames.
Diamonds, glaziers'.	Hammers, bench.

Hammers, copper.
  Do.   creasing.
  Do.   hand.
  Do.   planishing.
  Do.   trimming.
Hand barrows.
Hardies.
Hatchets, assorted.
Heading tools.
Hoes.
Holdfasts, bench.
Horses, draft.
  Do.   saddlers', wood.
Instruments, drawing, cases of.
Jugs.
Kettles, lead.
  Do.   copper.
  Do.   varnish.
Knives, pallet.
  Do.   putty.
  Do.   round, saddlers'
  Do.   shoe.
Ladders.
  Do.   step.
Ladles, large.
  Do.   lead.
Lanterns.
Lathes, hand.
  Do.   engine.
Level and plumb.
Mallets.
Mandrills, assorted.
Marlinespikes.
Measuring lines.
Milling tools.
Mortars and pestles, brass
Nippers, cutting
Oil stones.
Paint mills.
Pans, copper.
  Do.   paste.
  Do.   stone.

Pick axes.
Pincers, saddlers'.
Pliers.
Punches, saddlers'.
  Do.   for cutting rifle patches.
  Do.   for stencils.
Rakes.
Reamers, assorted.
Rules, carpenters'.
Saws, compass.
  Do.   cross-cut.
  Do.   circular.
  Do.   hand.
  Do.   tenon.
  Do.   web.
  Do.   whip.
Saw sets.
Scales and beams, large.
  Do.   do.   small
Scales, counter.
  Do.   graduated.
Scissors.
Scoops, copper.
Screw plates and taps.
Screw drivers.
Scythes.
Scythe snaths.
Sets, nail.
Shears, tinners .
  Do.   small.
Shovels.
Shoeing tools, sets of.
Sickles.
Sieves, composition.
  Do.   parchment.
  Do.   assorted.
Sledges.
Soldering irons.
Spades.
Spatulas.
Spirit levels.
Spoke shaves.

Ordnance Department.——Classification of Stores.

Spy glasses.
Squares, trying.
Stakes, bench.
Straight edges.
Swedges.
Sand screens.
Taps, screw.
Ticklers.
Tongs, tinners', grooving.
  Do.   smiths'.
Tools for cutting wood screws.
  Do. for turning iron.
  Do. for making paper fuzes.
  Do. for bending sheet iron.
  Do. for making metal fuzes.
Trammels.

Trestles.
Tube moulds.
Tube wires.
Vices, bevel.
  Do.   bench.
  Do.   breeching.
  Do.   hand.
Water buckets.
Watering pots.
Wheels, buffing.
Wheelbarrows.
Wheel cutters.
Wrenches, screw.
  Do.   tap.
  Do.   assorted.

Miscellaneous Articles.

Arm chests.
Barrels.
Baskets.
Boxes, packing
Brooms.
Canisters, tin.
Carboys.
Corks.
Coal, bituminous, bushels or tons.
Coal, anthracite, pounds.

Coal, charred, bushels.
Demijohns.
Lightning-rod points.
Oil cans, large.
Pumps.
Plows.
Safes, iron.
Salt, bushels.
Wood, oak, cords.
  Do. pine, do.

FORM 1.

RETURN

OF

ORDNANCE AND ORDNANCE STORES RECEIVED, ISSUED, AND REMAIN-
ING ON HAND, AT ——— ARSENAL, COMMANDED BY
MAJOR A. B., DURING THE QUARTER
ENDING ———, 18—.

PART FIRST.

ARTILLERY, SMALL ARMS, AMMUNITION, AND OTHER ORDNANCE STORES.

Ordnance Department.——Forms.

FORM 1.—

DATE. 18—.		No. of voucher.	SECOND QUARTER, 18—.	BRASS GUNS.					
				English trophies.		Mexican.	U. S.		
				6 pdr., weight 674 lbs.	3 pdr., weight 215 lbs.	18 pdr., trophies, weight 4384 lbs.	6 pdr., old pattern, 800 lbs.	12 pdr., pattern 1840, 1770 lbs.	6 pdr., pattern 1840, 885 lbs.
April	1		On hand from last quarter.......................						
"	15	1	Received from C. D., Military Storekeeper..						
May........	10	2	Do. do. E. F., contractor at ———						
"	22	3	Do. do. Capt. G. H., ——— regiment of artillery....................						
June.......	30	4	Fabricated at the post during the quarter, per abstract........................						
"	"	5	Purchased during the quarter, per abstract................						
"	"	6	Repaired during the quarter....................						
			Total to be accounted for...........						
May........	15	7	Condemned and dropped from the return by order of the President of the United States....................						
June........	30	8	Issued to sundry persons, per abstract......						
"	"	9	Expended at the post, per abstract............						
"	"	10	Issued for current service, per abstract.....						
"	"	6	Repaired during the quarter						
			Total issued and expended..........						
			Remaining on hand to be accounted for next quarter......................						

Ordnance Department.——Forms.

(PROPERTY RETURN.)

NANCE.																	CLASS II.——ARTILLERY					
BRASS HOWITZERS.		BRASS MORTARS.		IRON GUNS.							IRON HOW'RS.	UNSERVICEABLE.							FIELD ARTILLERY.				BAR-BETTE.
U. States.		French.										Brass guns.		Iron guns.									
24 pdr., 1312 lbs.	12 pdr., 783 lbs.	16 inch, stone, 1050 lbs.	10 inch, 785 lbs.	42 pdr., model of 1831.	42 pdr., model of 1840.	32 pdr., model of 1840.	24 pdr., model of 1819.	12 pdr., garrison, model of 1839.	10 inch, sea-coast, model of 1840.	8 inch, sea-coast, model of 1840.	24 pdr.	6 pdr., old pattern, weight 660 lbs.	3 pdr., old pattern, 318 lbs.	24 pdr., old pattern, 5376 lbs.	18 pdr., old pattern, 4238 lbs.	6 pdr., old pattern, 844 lbs.	12-pdr. stocktrail gun carriages, pattern 1840.	6-pdr. caissons, pattern 1840.	Traveling forges, pattern 1840.	Battery wagons, pattern 1840.	24-pdr. gun carriages.	24-pdr. chassis.

Ordnance Department.——Forms.

FORM 1.—

CARRIAGES.					CLASS III.—ARTILLERY EQUIPMENTS AND IMPLEMENTS.																
	CASEMATE.				CANNON LOCKS.		HANDSPIKES.						SPONGES.							WORMS AND STAVES.	
8-inch columbiad gun carriages.	8-inch columbiad chassis.	32-pdr. gun carriages.	32-pdr. chassis.	24-pdr. howitzer for flank defense, complete.	Percussion, left side, for guns, with lock pieces.	Percussion, left side, for guns, without lock pieces.	Trail, for field carriages.	Manoeuvring.	Shod.	Linstocks.	Port-fire cases.	Shell hooks.	32 pdr.	24 pdr.	10-inch columbiad, bore.	Tarpaulins, large.	Tarpaulins, small.	Tube pouches.	For siege and garrison guns.	For 12-pdr. field guns.	For 6-pdr. field guns.

Ordnance Department.——Forms.

(PROPERTY RETURN.)—Continued.

CLASS IV.——CANNON BALLS.								CL. V.——FIXED AMMUNITION, &C.									CLASS VI.——SMALL		
SHOT.			SHELLS.		SPHERICAL CASE.			SHOT, FIXED.	SPHERICAL CASE, FIXED.		STRAPPED SHOT.							MUSKETS.	RIFLES.	PISTOLS.
42 pdr.	32 pdr.	24 pdr.	10 inch.	8 inch.	24 pdr.	12 pdr.	6 pdr.	12-pdr. shot for 12-pdr. gun, rounds.	12-pdr. canister do.	For 12-pdr. gun do.	For 12-pdr. howitzer do.	For 6-pdr. gun do.	12-pdr. shot for 12-pdr. field gun.	6-pdr. shot.	12-pdr. canisters for 12-pdr. howitzer.	12-pdr. grape.		National Armory, percussion, bright.	National Armory, altered to percussion, brown.	Hall's patent, flint.	Percussion, new.	Percussion, new model.	Colt's.

Ordnance Department.—·Forms.

FORM 1.—

ARMS.			CLASS VII.—ACCOUTREMENTS.								CLASS VIII.—POWDER, &C.							
SWORDS AND SABRES.			FOR MUSKETS.			FOR RIFLES.			CAVALRY.		POWDER, LBS.			CARTRIDGES.			LEAD BALLS, LBS.	
Cavalry sabres, pattern 1840.	Horse artillery sabres, pattern 1840.	Non-commissioned officers' swords.	Infantry cartridge boxes.	Infantry cartridge box plates.	Cartridge box belts.	Wipers.	Ball screws.	Bullet moulds.	Holsters.	Cavalry cartridge boxes.	Cannon.	Rifle.	Fulminate of mercury.	Musket buck and ball.	Pistol ball.	Rifle blank.	Musket, pressed.	Buckshot.

Ordnance Department.——Forms.

(PROPERTY RETURN.)—Continued.

CLASS IX.—PARTS OF ARTILLERY CARRIAGES.									CLASS X.—MISCELLANEOUS.					
					SPARE PARTS FOR FIELD CARRIAGES.									
Elevating screws for barbette carriages.	Flange rollers for do.	Pintles for casemate chassis.	Sets of iron-work for 24-pdr. barbette carriages, complete.	Traverse wheels for barbette chassis.	Fellies.	Nave bands.	Pole yokes.	Spokes.	Sling carts, large.	Garrison gins.	Hand carts.	Casemate trucks.	Falls for garrison gins.	Double blocks, iron.

PART SECOND.

TOOLS AND MATERIALS.

Ordnance Department.——Forms.

FORM 1.—

CLOTH, ROPE, THREAD, &C.									FORAGE.		IRONMONGERY, &C.						
													IRON.		NAILS.		
yards.	pounds.	do.	do.	do.	yards.	pounds.					No.		pounds.	do.	do.	do.	
Cotton cloth,	Marline,	Rope, hemp,	Thread, patent,	Twine, bundling,	Worsted stuff,	Yarn, cotton,			Hay.	Oats.	Buckles,	Horse-shoes.	Bar,	Sheet,	Copper,	Iron, cut,	

Ordnance Department.——Forms.

(PROPERTY RETURN.)—Continued.

LABORATORY STORES.						GUN CARRIAGE TIMBER.											
						FOR FIELD CAR-RIAGES.				FOR 24-PDR. BARBETTE CARRIAGES.							
						12-pdr. gun carriages.		Caissons.		Gun carriages.			Chassis.				
Alcohol, pounds.	Beeswax, do.	Gum arabic, do.	Quicksilver, do.	Rosin, do.		Stocks.	Axle bodies.	Stocks.	Middle rails.	Uprights.	Braces.	Axle bodies.	Rails.	Tongues.	Front transoms.	Middle transoms.	

Ordnance Department.——Forms.

FORM 1.—(PROPERTY RETURN.)—Continued.

PAINTS AND OILS.					STATIONERY.				TOOLS.				MISCELLANEOUS.			
pounds.	do.	gallons.	do.	pounds.	quires.	sheets.	quarts.							tons.	barrels.	loads.
Lead, white,	Ochre, yellow,	Oil, linseed,	Oil, sperm,	Paint, olive,	Paper, letter,	Paper, drawing,	Ink, black,	Ordnance Regulations.	Axes, hand.	Hammers, saddlers'.	Planes, bench.	Rules, carpenters'.	Carboys.	Coal, bituminous,	Lime,	Sand,

I certify that the foregoing Return exhibits a correct statement of the public property in my charge during the —— quarter, 18—.

A. B., *Captain Commanding.*

U. S. ARSENAL (ARMORY OR POST),
——, 18—.

NOTE.—For the quarter ending 30th June add a certificate that an accurate inventory of property has been made, and the return corrected accordingly. Abstracts of the receipts and issues will be made when their number makes it more convenient.

FORM 2.

Invoice of Ordnance and Ordnance Stores turned over by A. B., Captain or Military Storekeeper, to Lieutenant C. D., —— Arsenal, in obedience to order for Supplies, No. ——.
Assistant Quartermaster, for transportation to ——

NO. OF BOXES OR PACKAGES.	MARKS.	TOTAL CONTENTS.	WEIGHT OR MEASUREMENT.
From 1 to 7................	Captain A. B., commanding —— arsenal, near P., Pennsylvania. ——	140 muskets, complete, N. A., new, brown..	2100 lbs.
From 8 to 10................	Lieutenant A. B., commanding —— arsenal, near R., Virginia.	300 cartridge boxes, infantry; 300 cart. box belts; 300 gun slings.	1000 "

I certify that the above is a correct invoice of ordnance and ordnance stores turned over by me, this —— day of ——, 18—, to Lieutenant C. D., Assistant Quartermaster, for transportation to —— Arsenal.

A. B.,
Captain Commanding, or Military Storekeeper.

(Signed duplicates.)

Endorsement to be as follows :

No. ——.

Invoice of stores turned over to Quartermaster for transportation,
—— quarter, ——, 18—.

Ordnance Department.——Forms.

FORM 3.

Abstract of Articles fabricated at ——— Arsenal during the ——— quarter of 18 .

Appropriation.	6-pounder field carriages.	32-pounder case-mate carriages.	24-pounder case-mate carriages.	10-inch sea-coast mortar-beds.	6-pounder strapped shot.	Rifle flasks.	Cavalry sabre-belts.	Holsters, pairs.	Musket-ball cartridges.	Port-fires.	Quick match, pounds.
Ordnance service	8					210	100	60			35
Arming the militia											
Armament of fortifications	2	2	1	4							
Ordnance and ordnance stores					200				10,000	250	
Total	10	2	1	4	200	210	100	60	10,000	250	35

I certify that the above is correct.

A. B., *Captain Commanding.*

NOTE.—This abstract is designed to include such articles only as are completed, and are in a suitable condition to be issued for service. (To be made in triplicate. Two to be forwarded with the return.)

Endorsement to be as follows :

No. ———.

Articles fabricated at ——— Arsenal,
——— quarter. 18—.

Ordnance Department.——Forms.

FORM 4.

Abstract of Articles purchased at ——— Arsenal during the ——— quarter of 18

Appropriation.	Hemp rope, lbs.	Hay, do.	Bar iron, do.	Screws (ass'd), No.	Gum arabic, lbs.	White pine boards, ft.	Harness leather, lbs.	White lead, do.	Linseed oil, galls.	Letter-paper, quires.	Axes, No.	Anthracite coal, lbs.
Ordnance service		1570			5				20	20		4480
Arsenals	300							150				
Armament of fortifications	250		1000	720		720		500	80			
Ordnance and ordnance stores			750	144		800	100	500	40		10	
Arming the militia												
Total	550	1570	1750	864	5	1520	100	1150	140	20	10	4480

I certify that the above abstract is correct. (See vouchers Nos. 2, 5, 7, 8, 12, of the cash accounts for this quarter.)

A. B., *Captain Commanding.*

(To be made in triplicate. Two to be forwarded with the return.)

Endorsement to be as follows:

No. ———.

Abstract of articles purchased

at ——— Arsenal,

——— quarter, 18——.

FORM 5,

Statement of Articles repaired at ——— during the ——— quarter of 18—.

ARTICLES.	Number transferred from unserviceable to serviceable, or made up from unserviceable articles into serviceable articles.	
	FROM	TO
6-pounder field carriages........	2 unserviceable	2 serviceable.
24 " barbette chassis........	5 "	5 "
12 " sponges and rammers........	7 "	6 "
Muskets........	170 }	170 muskets complete.
Bayonets........	170 }	

(Signed)   A. B., *Captain Commanding.*

I certify that the above statement is correct.

(Triplicate.   Two to be forwarded with the return.)

Endorsement to be as follows:

No. ———.

Articles repaired at ———
Arsenal,
——— quarter, ———, 18—.

FORM 6.

Statement of serviceable materials obtained from the breaking up of condemned Ordnance or Ordnance Stores, by order of the Secretary of War, of ——, 18—.

(See Form 10.)

400	lbs. wrought iron.
200	" cast iron.
50	" brass.
30	" copper.
50	" old rope for junk.
20	" leather.

(Signed) 　　A. B., *Captain Commanding.*

(In duplicate.)

Endorsement to be as follows:

No. —.
Materials obtained from
condemned stores,
—— quarter, ——, 18—.

FORM 7.

Received ——, this —— day of ——, 18—, of Captain —— ——, commanding —— ——, the following Ordnance and Ordnance Stores, &c.

4	32-pounder iron cannon.
3	24 " casemate carriages, complete.
3	24 " barbette carriages, complete.
500	muskets, new, brown.

C. D., *Major Commanding.*

(In duplicate.)

Endorsement to be as follows:

No. —.
Receipts for issues to the Army,
—— quarter, ——, 18—.

NOTE.—When the receipt of the officer to whom the stores are issued is not received by the issuing officer in time to accompany his property return, his certified invoice and the receipt of the quartermaster for the packages will be substituted for this voucher.

FORM 8.

I hereby acknowledge to have received of the United States, by the hands of
———— ————, of the United States Army, the following arms and accoutrements,
viz.:

100	common rifles, equal in value to.....................	123	1-13 muskets.
100	sets accoutrements (black leather) for rifles, equal in value to.....................................	21 11-13	do.
350	pistols......................equal in value to.........	215 5-13	do.
50	artillery swords..................do....................	16 4-13	do.
175	cavalry sabres......................do....................	80 10-13	do.
175	do. belts............do....................	15 4-13	do.
1000	muskets..........................do....................	1000	do.
500	sets accoutrements for muskets (black leather), equal in value to....................................	115 10-13	do.
4	6-pdr. iron cannon,		
4	6-pdr. field carriages, with } equal in value to	110 8-13	do.
	equipments complete,		
	Total......	1698 9-13	do.

The whole being equivalent to sixteen hundred and ninety-eight and nine-thir-
teenth muskets, which are received on account of the quota of arms due to the
———— of ————, under the Act of April, 1808, for arming the whole body of the
militia, and for which I have signed triplicate receipts.

Given at ————, this ———— day of ————, 18—.

(Signed) A. B., *Governor or Agent of the State of* ————.

(To be given in triplicate.)

Endorsement to be as follows:

No. ——.

Receipts for issues to the Militia.

Ordnance Department.——Forms.

FORM 9.

Abstract of Materials, &c., expended or consumed at ——— Arsenal during the ——— quarter of 18———

Expended or Consumed.	Powder, cannon, pounds.	Powder, rifle, pounds.	Musket-balls, pressed, pounds.	Bundling twine, pounds.	Hay, pounds.	Bar iron, pounds.	Cast steel, pounds.	Gum arabic, do.	Uprights for 32-pdr. barbette carriages.	White pine boards, feet.	Pressed bricks, No.	Calfskins, No.	White lead, pounds.	Letter-paper, quires.
In experimental firing.............ordnance.	39	50						4						
In making musket and rifle cartridges......do....		100	500	2										
In repair and preservation of the post.......do....										100				
In preservation of stores.....do....										260				
In repair of tools and machinery.....do....							38					2		
In office duties.....do....														20
On account of public horses.....do....					3500									
In repair and preservation of buildings...arsenals.											100		50	
In making sea-coast carriages.......fortifications.						270			20				230	
In making field and siege gins.....ordnance stores.						350							20	
In fixing ammunition.....do....			1000											
Total expended..............	39	150	1500	2	3500	620	38	4	20	360	100	2	300	20

I certify that the above abstract is correct, and that the stores were issued for the purposes stated.

(Two with the return.)

Endorsement to be as follows :
No. ———.
Abstract of articles expended or consumed at ———,
——— quarter, ———, 18———.

(To be signed in triplicate by the commanding officer of the Arsenal or Post.)

Ordnance Department.——Forms.

FORM 10.

List of Ordnance and Ordnance Stores condemned at ———, by ———, Inspector ———, at an inspection made on the ——— of ———, 18 .

Articles condemned.	In what manner disposed of.				Remarks.
	Broken up.	Sold.	Dropped.	Total.	
12-pounder brass guns, French........				2	Recast.
6-pounder field carriages............	2	1		3	
Sets of harness for two wheel horses....				2	
Muskets............................		170	2	170	
Infantry cartridge-boxes.............	54	26	5	85	

I certify that the above-enumerated articles have been inspected by me, in conformity to the regulations, and are hereby recommended to be disposed of as above.

(Duplicates.)

R. L. B., *Inspector.*

Approved: M. F., *President United States.*

NOTE.—The stores embraced in the above are to be retained on the property return until the purposes of the condemnation, as approved by the President, shall have been finally executed.

Endorsement to be as follows :

No. ——

Condemned Stores,

—— Arsenal,

—— quarter ——, 18

Ordnance Department.——Forms.

FORM 11.

Inventory of Ordnance and Ordnance Stores on hand at ———, *commanded by* ———, *inspected* ———, *18 .*

Number or quantity.	Articles.	Location.	Commanding Officer's Remarks.	Inspector's Recommendations.
6	12-pounder brass cannon...1770 pounds.	Arsenal yard......	Serviceable, model of 1840.........	
2	4-pounder.....do.......350....do....	......do............	...do......French.........	To be sold.
1	3-pounder.....do......216....do....	......do............	...do......English, trophy, captured at Yorktown.	
8	18-pounder iron cannon...3800....do....	......do............	Heavy, old pattern.........	
6	18-pounder.....do........3200....do....	......do............	Light....do.........	To be exchanged for new guns.
2	12-pounder brass cannon 1800....do....	......do............	Unserviceable, French, worn out.........	
1	6-pounder......do.......670....do....	......do............	...do......English, trophy, captured at Saratoga.	
8	6-pounder field carriages, stocktrail..	Gun-house.........	New, serviceable.........	To be broken up.
2	6-pounder.....do.........	......do............	Unserviceable, irreparable.........	
15 galls.	Linseed-oil.........	Store-house cellar.		
			(To be signed by the commanding officer.)	*(To be signed by the Inspector-General or other authorized inspector.)*

NOTE.—The stores will be entered on the inventory in the order of the classification, which order should be observed as nearly as practicable in the arrangement of the articles in store.

The commanding officer will describe, in the column of remarks, the kind, quality, and condition of the several articles, more in detail than it is practicable to do in the quarterly returns. He will also express his opinion, in the column of remarks, as to the manner in which the unserviceable stores should be disposed of.

Endorsement to be as follows :

No. ———.

Inventory for inspection, or for the correction of second quarter's return of property.

FORM 12.

RENT-ROLL.

Statement of Dwelling-Houses belonging to the United States at ————— Armory (or Arsenal), and of the rents due thereon, on ——— ———, 186 .

HOUSES.		BY WHOM OCCUPIED.	TIME OC-CUPIED.	RENT PER QUARTER.	AMOUNT.
No.	Of what kind.		Months.		
				D. C.	D. C.
1	Brick, two story ...	A. B., Com'ding officer's clerk			
2	Wood......do.........	C. D., Master Armorer.			
3	Do.........do.........	E. F., Store-keeper.			
4	Do..... one story ...	G. H.	3	3 25	3 25
5	Brick......do.........	J. K.	2	4 00	2 67
6	Do.........do.........	L. M.	3	3 50	3 50
7	Do..... two story ...	N. O.	1½	3 00	1 50
		P. Q.	3	3 00	3 00
		R. S.	1½	3 00	1 50
8	Do..... one story ...	T. U., Paymaster's clerk.....			
9	Stone......do.........	V. W.	3	2 75	2 75
	Do.........do.........	X. Z.	2	2 75	1 83
10	Do.........do.........	Unoccupied.			

I certify that the foregoing roll exhibits a correct account of the dwelling-houses at this armory, and of their occupation, and of the amount of rent now due for each.

A. B., Commanding Officer.

——— Armory,
——, 186 . }

Endorsement to be as follows :

No. ———.
Rent ·roll.
——— Armory, ——— quarter

Ordnance Department.——Forms.

FORM 13.—(To be printed.)

The United States,

To ————————,

						REMARKS.
186 .		**NATIONAL ARMORIES.**				
September...	10th.	For 100 bushels charcoal, at 5 cents per bushel......	$5 00	......		Smith's shop.
November...	8th.	" 75 cords oak wood, at $3 50 per cord......	262 50	......		Fuel for workshops.
Do........	15th.	" 5560 feet of pine boards, at $10 50 per thousand......	58 38	88	$325 88	For arm-chests.
			$325 88			
		ARMING THE MILITIA.				
Date		For 2000 feet oak timber, at $40 per thousand......	80 00	00	80 00	Gun-carriages.
			80 00	$405 88		

(Dr. column)

ARSENAL OR ARMORY, }
———————, 186 . }

Received from ———————, Paymaster, ——— dollars ——— cents, in full of the above account.

(Signed in duplicates.)

I certify that the above account is correct and just, amounting to four hundred and five dollars and eighty-eight cents.

A. M., *Commanding Officer.*

Endorsement to be as follows:

No. ——, A. B.

November ——, 186 .

National Armories....... $325 88

Arming the militia........ 80 00

——————

$405 88

Ordnance Department.——Forms.

FORM 14.—(To be printed.)

We, the subscribers, hereby acknowledge to have received of ———— the sums set opposite our names, respectively, being in full for our services at ———— Arsenal during the month of ————, 18—, having signed duplicate receipts.

No.	Names.	Occupation.	No. of days employed.	PAY PER DAY.		AMOUNT.		Signatures.	Witnesses.
				Dollars.	Cents.	Dollars.	Cents.		
1	A. B.	Master armorer....	26	2	50	65	00		
2	C. D.	Blacksmith........	24	1	50	36	00		
3	E. F.	Carpenter........ &c.	20	1	20	24	00		
						325	00		

I certify that the foregoing pay-roll is correct and just, amounting to three hundred and twenty-five dollars — cents, to be charged as follows:

[Date.]

Ordnance.................... $105 00
Arming militia............... 64 10
Arsenals.................... 39 90
Armament of fortifications.... 116 00
                            $325 00

(Signed by commanding officer.)

Endorsement to be as follows:

No. ——, hired men for October ——, 18—.
Ordnance.................... $105 00
Arming militia............... 64 10
Arsenals.................... 39 90
Armament of fortifications.... 116 00
                            $325 00

Ordnance Department.——Forms.

FORM 15.—(To be printed.)

Pay-Roll of Clerks, Armorers, and others employed at the U. S. Armory, ————, during the month of ————, 18—.

We, the subscribers, acknowledge to have received from ————, Paymaster, the sums set opposite our respective names in the last column of figures, in full for our services during the month of ————, 18—.

Number.	Names.	Occupation or employment.	Time or number.	Wages or prices.	Amount.	NATIONAL ARMORIES.				SIGNED IN DUPLICATE.	
						Arms and appendages.		Special work.	Amount.	Signatures.	Witnesses.
						Musket.	Rifle.				
1	A. B......	Clerk, Com'g Officer's office.	1 month..	$55 00	$55 00	....	....	$55 00	$55 00	A. B.......	
2	C. D......	Foreman, Armorer..........	25 days.	2 00	50 00	$50 00	....	....	50 00	C. D.......	
3	E. F......	Machinist........	20 do...	1 50	30 00	....	....	....	30 00	E. F.......	
4	G. H...{	Forging barrels..........	248......	20	49 60	....	....	....			
		Dr. for bursted barrels......	16.......	30	4 80	$44 80	....	....	44 80	G. H.......	
									$179 80		

I certify that the foregoing pay-roll is correct and just, amounting to ———— dollars and ———— cents, to be charged as follows:

National armories.............. $00 00
Arming militia................ 00 00
Repairs and improvements...... 00 00
⠀⠀⠀⠀⠀⠀⠀⠀⠀⠀⠀⠀⠀⠀⠀⠀⠀⠀⠀⠀$00 00

A. B., *Superintendent.*

Endorsement to be as follows:
⠀⠀⠀⠀No. ————.
⠀⠀⠀⠀⠀⠀Hired men for ————, 18—.
Armories.............. $00 00
Arming militia.......... 00 00
Repairs and improvements....... 00 00
⠀⠀⠀⠀⠀⠀⠀⠀⠀⠀⠀⠀⠀⠀$00 00

NOTE.—The printed forms will contain the requisite heads for disbursements under various appropriations. The amount on each page of the roll will be footed up separately, and these several amounts will be recapitulated on the last page.

Ordnance Department.——Forms.

FORM 16.—(To be printed.)

We, the subscribers, hereby acknowledge to have received of ——— the sums set opposite our names, respectively, being in full for the services of our slaves at ——— Arsenal during the month of ———, 18—, having signed duplicate receipts.

From whom hired.	Name and occupation.	Time employed.	Wages per month.	Amount for each slave.	Amount received.		Signatures.
A. B.	A. Laborer	1 month.....	$12 00	$12 00			
	C. do.	22–26 do.	15 00	12 69			
	D. Blacksmith......	20–26 do.	18 50	14 23			
	E. Laborer	19–26 do.	14 00	10 23	$49	15	A. B.
C. D.	F. Laborer	25–26 do. ...	16 00	16 00			
	G. do.	1 do. ...	14 50	13 94			
	H. do.	1 do. ...	14 50	14 50	43	44	C. D.
					$92	59	

NOTE.—In cases where it may be difficult to obtain the proper signatures on the roll, because of the distant residence of the owners of the slaves, separate receipts may be taken and appended to the roll.

I certify that the above pay-roll is correct and just, amounting to ——— dollars ——— cents, to be charged as follows:

Arsenals $71 40
Armament of fortifications.............. 21 19
                       92 59

(Signed duplicates.)

A. B., *Commanding Officer.*

Endorsement to be as follows:

No. ———.

Slave-roll for ———, 18—.

Arsenals..................... $71 40
Armament of fortifications... 21 19
                 92 59

[Date.]

FORM 17.—(To be printed.)

Abstract of Disbursements at ——— Arsenal, by ———, in the quarter ending ———, 186 .

Date of payment.	Number of voucher.	To whom paid.	NATURE OF THE DISBURSEMENT. If the voucher is for *Services*, add from —— to ——, 18—, or for the month of ——, 18—. If for *Articles*, and there is sufficient room on the one line, state the quantity of each; or if not room for this, then say, "iron, nails, and paint-brushes," or whatever the voucher may be for.	Ordnance service.		Arsenals.		Armament of fortifications.		Ordnance, ordnance stores and supplies.		Total.	
				Dolls.	Cts.	Dolls.	Cts.	Dolls.	Cts.	Dolls.	Cts.	Dolls.	Cts.
18—. May 5 ...	1	A. B.	500 lbs. bar iron; 20 lbs. cast steel	10	00			15	00			25	00
" 10 ...	2	C. D.	100 lbs. harness leather; 4 calfskins							26	00	26	00
June 30 ...	3	E. F.	50 bushels oats; 1000 lbs. hay	35	00							35	00
" ...	4	Hired men......	Services for the month of June	300	00	50	00	250	00	400	00	1000	00
				345	00	50	00	265	00	426	00	1086	00

(To be signed in duplicate by the disbursing officer.)

Endorsement to be as follows:

Abstract of Disbursements.
—— quarter, 18—.

Ordnance service..........	$345 00
Arsenals	50 00
Armament of fortifications	265 00
Ordnance and ordnance stores......	426 00
	$1086 00

Ordnance Department.——Forms.

FORM 18.—(To be printed.)

The United States in account current with Captain A. B.,

Dr.				Cr.	
Dates.	To Expenditures.	Amount.	Dates.	By Cash received.	Amount.
186 . December 31....	For ordnance service, per abstract	$	186 . October 1...	Balance due from last account, per official statement...........	$
	Arming the militia...do..........		" 20...	Amount of Treasury Warrant, No. ——, issued on requisition No. ——	
	Arsenals............do..........		November 15...	Amount received of Major —— for a sword...........	
	Armament of fortifications..do..		December 31...	Amount of rent-roll for 4th quarter	
	Ordnance and ordnance stores.....			Dollars............	
	Balance to new account.........		December 31...	Balance due the United States carried to new account........	
	Dollars............				

I certify that the above is a true account of all money of the Ordnance Department received by me and not heretofore accounted for, and that the disbursements have been faithfully made.

—— Arsenal, }
——, 186 . }

(To be signed and furnished in duplicate by the disbursing officer.)

Endorsement to be as follows:

ACCOUNT CURRENT.

Captain A. B., ——— Arsenal,
——— quarter, 186 .

FORM 19.

Received, ——— Arsenal, ———, 186 , of Major ——— ———,
One field officer's sword,
One pair percussion pistols,
for which I have paid the said Major ——— ——— the cost price, ———
dollars.

W. A. N.,

(To be made in duplicate.)   *Major* ——— *Artillery*

———

Endorsement to be as follows

No. ———.

Receipt for stores
issued to Major W. A. N.
for his own use.

Ordnance Department.——Forms.

FORM 20.

Statement of Receipts and Expenditures, under each appropriation, for the month of ——— (or for the ——— quarter), 18—.

	Ordnance service.	Arming militia.	Arsenals.	Armament of fortifications.	Amount.
Due to the United States from last account, or last month.....	69 62	.....	87 21	.....	157 83
Received in —— quarter, or month.....	450 00	800 00	1000 00	300 00	2550 00
Total to be accounted for.....	519 62	800 00	1087 21	300 00	2706 83
Due from the United States from last account, or last month.....	.....	45 50	.....	.....	45 50
Expended in —— quarter, or month.....	519 62	716 20	1104 80	231 50	2572 12
Total accounted for.....	519 62	761 70	1104 80	231 50	2617 62
Balance due ——, 18—. { To the United States.....	.....	38 30	.....	68 50	106 80
{ From the United States.....	.....	.....	17 59	.....	17 59
Due United States.....					89 21

(To be signed by the disbursing officer.)

Endorsement on monthly statement to be.

Money received and expended,

—— Arsenal, Nov. —, 18—.

NOTE.—Quarterly statement to be endorsed on the quarterly account current intended for the Ordnance Office.

FORM 21.

Estimate of Funds required at ——— Arsenal during the fourth quarter of 18—.

ORDNANCE SERVICE.		
Police and preservation of Post...............................	$430 00	
Placing arms in racks..	500 00	
Tools and machinery...	300 00	
Fuel for steam-engine..	350 00	
Public horses..	150 00	
Office duties..	200 00	
	1930 68	
Due U. S. from last quarter..........	130 68	
Amount required.......................	....	$1800 00
ORDNANCE, ORDNANCE STORES, AND SUPPLIES.		
Making sling carts...............................	1027 48	
Making lifting jacks.............................	300 00	
Purchase of lumber for packing boxes, &c..............	150 00	
Due from U. S. last quarter..........	222 52	
Amount required.......................	....	1700 00
Total amount required.................	....	$3500 00

REQUIRED IN SUMS AS FOLLOWS:

Month.	Ordnance service.	Ordnance, ordnance stores, and supplies.	Amount.
October...............................	$500 00	$700 00	$1200 00
November.............................	500 00	500 00	1000 00
December	800 00	500 00	1300 00
Total.....................	$1800 00	$1700 00	$3500 00

(To be signed by the commanding officer.)

FORM 22.

Requisition for Ordnance and Ordnance Stores for —— Arsenal or Post, —— date.

Post or Place.	6-pdr. gun carriages.	Infantry cartridge boxes.	Cannon powder, pounds.	Slow match, pounds.	Shot gauges, sets.	&c. &c.	Remarks.
Required ——, 18—.........	3	106	1000	50	1	....	
On hand (date).........	2	100	200	5	....	....	
To be supplied.........	1	6	800	45	1	....	

[Here follow the explanations demanding the issue.]

(Signed) ——————

A. B., Commanding.

Endorsement to be as follows :

Requisition for Ordnance Stores for [post or place].

[Date].

Ordnance Department.——Forms.

FORM 23.

Requisition for Ordnance and Ordnance Stores for the use of —— of militia in the service of the United States.

6-pdr. brass cannon.	6-pdr. carriages.	Muskets, complete	Non-com'd officers' swords.	Cartridge boxes.	Cartridge box belts.	Bayonet scabbards.	Waist belt plates.	Gun slings.	6-pdr. shot, fixed.	Musket-ball cartridges.	Remarks.
2	2	....	....	....	....	....	....	....	120	....	Company of infantry of 58 non-commissioned officers and privates. Same form for Artillery, Riflemen, and Cavalry.
....	....	49	9	49	49	49	51	49	....	2500	
Total... 2	2	49	9	49	49	49	51	49	120	2500	

I certify that there are —— non-commissioned officers, musicians, and privates under my command, called into the service of the United States, and that the above requisition is made in conformity thereto.

(Signed)   A. B., *Captain of 5th Regiment of Militia of the State of Tennessee.*

NASHVILLE, *June 1, 18—.*

The above requisition has been examined in conformity to the Ordnance Regulations, and is approved.

(Signed)   C. D., *Major United States Army.*

NASHVILLE, *June 5, 18—.*

Endorsement to be as follows:

Requisition for Ordnance and Ordnance Stores, ——, 18—.

FORM 24.

STATE OF ——:

I —— ——, born in ——, aged —— years, and by occupation a ——,
do hereby acknowledge to have voluntarily enlisted this —— day of ——, 18 ,
as a —— of ordnance, in the army of the United States of America, for the
period of five years, unless sooner discharged by proper authority; do also agree
to accept such bounty, pay, rations, and clothing, as is or may be established by
law. And I, —— ——, do solemnly swear that I will bear true faith and
allegiance to the United States of America, and that I will serve them honestly
and faithfully against all their enemies and opposers whomsoever; and that I
will observe and obey the orders of the President of the United States, and the
orders of the officers appointed over me, according to the Rules and Articles of
War, and the regulations which govern enlisted men of the Ordnance Department.

J. G., *Recruit.*

Sworn and subscribed to, at ——,
this —— day of ——, 18 .

S. M., *Magistrate.*

I certify that I have carefully examined the above-named recruit, and that,
in my opinion, he is free from all *bodily defects* and mental infirmity which
would in *any way* disqualify him from performing the duties of a —— of ordnance.

A. B., *Examining Surgeon.*

I certify that I have minutely inspected the recruit, —— ——, *previously
to his enlistment,* who was *entirely sober* when enlisted; and that, to the best of my
judgment and belief, he is of lawful age, and a competent mechanic (carriage-
maker, or otherwise, as the case may be). This recruit has —— eyes, —— hair,
—— complexion; is —— feet —— inches high.

(Duplicates.)

C. D., *Recruiting (or Enlisting) Officer.*

————

Endorsement to be as follows:

Jonas Gould, —— Arsenal,
February ——, 18 .

NOTE.—In making up and endorsing enlistments, see General Regulations for
the Army.

FORM 25.—(To be printed.)

Return of a Company of Ordnance at the ——— *Arsenal, for the month of* ———, 18

Present.																								Absent.		Present and absent.			Total number of men authorized at the post.	Alterations since last return.							
For duty.														Sick.			In arrest or confinement.																				
Lieutenant-Colonels.	Majors.	Captains.	First Lieutenants.	Second Lieutenants.	Assistant Surgeon.	Store-keeper.	Master carriage-maker.	Master blacksmith.	Carriage-makers.	Blacksmiths.	Armorers.	Artificers.	Laborers.	Blacksmiths.	Artificer.	Laborer.	Blacksmiths.	Artificers.	Laborers.			Total enlisted men.	Aggregate.			Total enlisted men.	Aggregate.	Aggregate last month.		Joined.	Discharged.	Dropped.					

Officers present and absent, and absentees accounted for.		Remarks in explanation of alterations on the face of the return.					Orders and instructions received during the month.		
Names, rank, or grades.	Remarks.	No.	Rank.	Names.	Date.	Remarks.	No.	Date.	Description.

(To be signed by the commanding officer.)

Endorsement to be as follows:

Company,

——— Arsenal, December ——, 18 .

FORM 26.—(To be printed.)

Return of hired men employed at —— Arsenal for the month of ——, 18—.

No.	Names.	Trade and Employment.	Days employed.	WAGES.		AMOUNT.	
				Dolls.	Cts.	Dolls.	Cts.
1	A	Blacksmith, mounting cannon	25	1	50	37	50
2	B	Do......repairing and making tools	19	1	40	26	60
3	C	Wheelwright, making gun-carriages	26	1	70	44	20
4	D	Do......repairing....do	16	1	60	25	60
5	E	Armorer, repairing arms	18½	1	50	22	75
6	F	Do....cleaning arms	23	1	40	32	20
7	G	Carpenter, making packing-boxes	25	1	25	31	25
8	H	Painter, painting gun-carriages	17	1	25	21	25
9	I	Laborer, removing earth	13		70	9	10
10	K	Do...digging gravel	7		75	5	25
		Amount				255	70

(To be signed by the commanding officer.)

Endorsement to be as follows:

Hired men,

—— Arsenal. December, 18——

Ordnance Department.——Forms.

FORM 27.

Summary statement of work done at ——— *Arsenal in the month of* ———, 18—

Articles fabricated.	Other work done.
4 6-pounder field carriages.	500 pounds of powder proved.
200 12-pounder sponges.	50 24-pounder cannon lackered.
100 port-fires.	Inclosures repaired.
10,000 musket ball cartridges.	Barracks painted and cleaned, &c., &c.

Tools.

2 hand hammers.
20 powder measures.

Supplies forwarded to ——— , *in pursuance of Order No.* ——— , *received* ———.

Unfinished.

2 6-pounder field carriages.
1 6-pounder caisson.
10 sets iron work for barbette carriages, &c., &c.

Received from ———

Stairs finished in new store-house. This building is now completed, except plastering and painting.

50 24-pounder cannon.
500 pounds cannon powder.
1000 sets of infantry accoutrements.

Hired men.	Enlisted men.
8 master workmen.	1 master workman.
30 mechanics.	10 mechanics.
5 laborers.	6 laborers.

(To be signed by the commanding officer.)

NOTE.—This statement should exhibit such particulars as are necessary to give a correct view of what has been done at the post during the month, without descending into very minute details. Work may, when necessary, be reported in parts; but the articles reported as fabricated should accord with the quarterly abstract. In cases where new buildings or other extensive works are in progress, after stating the particulars of the work done, the extent to which the work has advanced, and its condition at the end of the month, should be stated.

Endorsement to be as follows:

Work done,
——— Arsenal,
December -——, 18—.

Ordnance Department.——Forms.

Return of the Officers, Armorers, and others employed at the ———
the month

	Commandant.	Master armorer.	Military store-keeper.	Clerks.	Foremen.	Machinists.	Barrel forgers.	Lock forgers.	Bayonet forgers.	Ramrod forgers.	Mounting forgers.	Trip-hammer men.
Musket work { On salaries or wages...												
At piece-work..........												
Rifle work.... { On salaries or wages...												
At piece-work..........												
Total........................												

ARMS AND APPENDAGES.

	Muskets.	Rifles.	Screw-drivers.	Wipers.	Ball-screws.	Spring-vices.	Cones.	Bullet-moulds.	Ammunition-flasks.	Musket-boxes.	Rifle-boxes.
Manufactured											
Delivered to store-keeper											
Manufactured at rifle factory.............											
Delivered to store-keeper											

Ordnance Department.——Forms.

(To be printed.)

Armory ; and also the arms and appendages manufactured during of ———, 186 .

Assistant forgers.	Annealers.	Borers.	Turners and drillers.	Grinders.	Barrel straighteners.	Lock filers.	Mounting filers.	Polishers.	Stockers.	Barrel finishers.	Lock finishers.	Arm finishers.	JOBBERS.				Total.
													Smiths.	Filers.	Carpenters.	Laborers.	

——— ARMORY,
  Office of Superintendent, ———, 186 .

                              A. B., *Superintendent.*

NOTE.—This return will be limited to such operations as are carried on under the appropriation for armories. Persons employed, or work done, at armories, under other appropriations, will be separately reported.

———

Endorsement to be as follows :
        MONTHLY RETURN.
——— Armory, October ———, 186 .

Ordnance Department.——Forms.

FORM 29.—

Inventory of Stores at – ——— Arsenal, 30th June, 186   , and report
inventory was

Articles.	Description, condition, and explanations.	Number or quantity on hand per last inventory.	Received since from other posts.	Saved from articles broken up.	Changed from unserviceable to serviceable.	Fabricated.	Purchased.	Taken up not before accounted for.	Total to be accounted for.
Class No.									

Prices which are not established by the regulations, or by instructions from the Ordnance Office, or the Inspector of Arsenals and Armories, will be determined by reference to the first cost of the property, when it can be ascertained, allowing for such alterations as may have affected the original value.

In estimating the cost of the labor of enlisted men, their time will be charged at the following rates:

Master workmen.................\$1 50 per day ⎫
Mechanics.........   90   "   ⎬ For the whole year, Sundays
Artificers.........   70   "   ⎪   included.
Laborers..........   60   "   ⎭

Ordnance Department.——Forms.

(To be printed.)

of operations causing an increase or decrease at any time since the last rendered.

Consumed and used in fabrication and for repairs.	Issued to other posts.	Sold.	Broken up and dropped.	Lost by unavoidable accident.	Number or quantity remaining on hand this 30th June.	Value per piece, per lb., &c.		Valuation of stores remaining.			
								Total value of each description.		Total value of each class.	
						Dollars.	Cts.	Dollars.	Cts.	Dollars.	Cts.
Amount carried forward.....											

NOTE.—In printing the inventories for the national armories, the necessary alterations are made in the headings of the several columns to adapt them to the circumstances of the case.

(Signed by the commanding officer.)

FORM 30.

I hereby certify that I have, this —— day of ———, 18—, inspected and proved twenty twenty-four pounder iron cannon (or other ordnance, or shot, or shells, as the case may be) manufactured by J. M., of C. D. C., under his contract (agreement, or open purchase, as the case may be) with the United States, dated ——.

And I do further certify that the said cannon (or other ordnance, or shot, or shells, as the case may be) have been inspected and proved by me in exact accordance with the regulations established in the Ordnance Department for the proof and inspection of ordnance before its reception for the service of the United States; that the said cannon have been numbered and weighed, and that their numbers and corresponding weights are as follows, viz.:

$$\begin{aligned}
\text{No. 20} &\ldots\ldots\ldots\ldots\ldots\ldots\ldots\ldots\ldots\ldots\ldots\ldots\ldots \quad \text{5660 lbs.}\\
21 &\ldots\ldots\ldots\ldots\ldots\ldots\ldots\ldots\ldots\ldots\ldots\ldots\ldots \quad \text{5652 "}\\
22 &\ldots\ldots\ldots\ldots\ldots\ldots\ldots\ldots\ldots\ldots\ldots\ldots\ldots \quad \text{5640 "}
\end{aligned}$$

&c., &c., &c.

Total weight.................   **lbs.**

The total weight of the cannon being equivalent to —— pounds.

I further certify that the total weight of the shot (or shells, as the case may be) used in the proof of said guns amounts to —— pounds.

Given under my hand, at the —— ——, this —— day of ——, 18—.

(Signed)   W. J. W., *Major of Ordnance,*
Inspector of Ordnance at the foundries.

RECAPITULATION.

20 24-pounder cannon (or other ordnance, or shot, or shells, as the case may be).

———

                               C. F., ———, 18—.

The United States,

            To J. M.,   **DR.**

For 20 24-pounder cannon, weight —— lbs., at $—— per 100 lbs...... $000 00
For 24-pounder shot used in proving the same, weighing —— lbs., at
—— per —— lb... 000 00

FORM 30.—Continued.

Received, ——, 18—, on the ground of the C. F., the above 20 24-pounder cannon.

(Signed)   A. M., Captain of Ordnance,
or Military Store-keeper.

(To be given in triplicate.)

NOTE.—Two of the triplicates are to be forwarded by the contractor to the Ordnance Office—one being intended for the Treasury, and one for the Ordnance Office; the third is retained by the contractor.

———

Endorsement to be as follows:
Certificate of Inspection
of —— pdr. cannon (or shot, or shells),
at —— Foundry, ——, 18—.

FORM 31.—

Inspection and Proof of ————

NUMBERS.		DIAMETERS—OF									
		Cascable.				First re-enforce.		Second re-enforce front.	Chase.		Muzzle.	
Foundry.	Register.	Knob.	Neck.	Fillet.	Base ring.	Rear.	Front.		Rear.	Front.	Neck.	Face.
Prescribed dimensions.												

Preponderance taken at the plane of the muzzle   **lbs.**

Order of firing.	PROOF CHARGES OF							
	Powder.		Balls.		Shells.		Number of	
	Lbs.	Proof range.	No.	Lbs.	No.	Lbs.	Wads.	Sabots.
First								
Second...................								
Third.....................								

Preponderance taken at the plane of the muzzle   **lbs.**

Ordnance Department.——Forms.

(To be printed.)

at the ——— Foundry, 18—.

Register number.	Trunnions.		Rimbases.		Cylinder of Bore.		Chamber.		Vent.	Distance between rimbases.	WIDTHS—OF	
	Right.	Left	Right.	Left.	Least.	Greatest.	Least.	Greatest.			Base ring.	Chase ring.

Ordnance Department.——Forms.

FORM 31.—(INSPECTION, &c.)—Continued.

LENGTH FROM REAR OF BASE RING—TO												LENGTH OF TRUNNIONS			AXIS OF TRUNNIONS			LENGTH OF BORE FROM FACE OF MUZZLE—TO					GREATEST ENLARGEMENT AFTER PROOF		
Register number.	Rear of breech.	End of cascable.	REAR OF TRUNNIONS: Right.	REAR OF TRUNNIONS: Left.	Centre of vent.	FIRST RE-ENFORCE: Rear.	FIRST RE-ENFORCE: Front.	2d re-enforce front.	CHASE: Rear.	CHASE: Front.	MUZZLE: Face.	Right.	Left.	Register number.	Below axis of bore.	Alignment.	Vent, interior, from bottom.	End of cylinder.	Mouth of chamber.	End of chamber cylinder.	Bottom of the bore.	Position of greatest enlargement.	Cylinder.	Chamber.	Weight, pounds.

I certify that the inspection and proof, as herein recorded, have been made in accordance with the regulations, and that this report is in all respects correct. —— Foundry, ——, 18—.

(*Signed by the inspecting officer.*)

Endorsement to be as follows:

Inspection report of —— pounder cannon, at —— Foundry, ——, 18—.

FORM 32.

—— FOUNDRY, ——, 18—.

Proof and Inspection of - —— *inch shells,* —— *pounder shot, &c.*

Number of — inch shells rejected in inspection.	Number of — inch shells rejected in the water and air proof.	Total number of —inch shells rejected.	Total number of —inch shells received.	Total weight of — inch shells received.	Weight of one of the heaviest — inch shells received.	Weight of one of the lightest — inch shells received.	Remarks.
				Pounds.	Pounds.	Pounds.	
10	15	25	200	15,000	77	72	

Total number of shells rejected, —— ⎫ as per certificate of inspection of this
Total number of shells received —— ⎰ date.

I certify that the proof and inspection above referred to have been carefully made, and that this report is in all respects correct.

(Signed)   W. J. W., *Major of Ordnance,*
Inspector of Cannon and Foundries.

———

Endorsement to be as follows :

Inspection Report of —— inch shells
at —— Foundry, ——, 18—.

FORM 33.

Annual Consolidated Report of the Inspection of Ordnance and Projectiles at the Foundries for the year ended June 30, 18—.

Names of Foundries.	POUNDER GUNS (OR OTHER ORDNANCE).					POUNDER ROUND SHOT.					INCH SHELLS.				
	Number examined.	Number rejected in the inspection.	Number burst.	Number received.	Ratio or number approved for each hundred examined.	Number examined.	Number rejected in the inspection.	Number broken in proof.	Number received.	Ratio or number approved for each hundred examined.	Number examined.	Number rejected in the inspection.	Number rejected in the water and air proof.	Number received.	Ratio or number approved for each hundred examined.
C. F.	150	5	2	143	90.53	2000	300	12	1688	84.04	200	10	15	175	87.05
W. P. F.	180	2	3	174	96.11	1500	150	10	1340	89.33	180	8	12	160	88.88

I certify that the above has been carefully made up from my several inspection reports of the year ended June 30, 18—.

(Signed)   W. J. W., *Major of Ordnance,*

Inspector of Ordnance at the Foundries.

Endorsement to be as follows:

Annual Consolidated Inspection Report of Ordnance and Projectiles at the foundries for the year ended June 30, 18—.

FORM 34.

I hereby certify that I have, this —— day of ———, 18—, inspected and approved three hundred and twenty muskets, three hundred and twenty screwdrivers, three hundred and twenty wipers, thirty-two ball-screws, thirty-two spring vices, and three hundred and twenty spare flint caps, and sixteen packing-boxes (or rifles, pistols, carbines, Hall's rifles, and their appendages, cavalry sabres or swords, accoutrements, &c., as the case may be), manufactured by A. W., of Millbury, Massachusetts, under his contract (agreement, or open purchase, as the case may be) with the United States, dated —— January, 18—.

And I further certify that the said arms and appendages have been inspected according to the regulations established in the Ordnance Department, and that they conform to the standard models and the established gauges; that they are of good quality and workmanship; that they are securely packed in good strong boxes; and that they are, in all respects, conformable to the contract.

I also certify that, according to my best judgment, the true value of each packing-box is —— dollars and —— cents.

Given under my hand at Millbury, ———, this —— day of ———, 18—.

(Signed)   J. M., *Ass't. to Inspector of Arms.*

Approved:

(Signed)   H. K. C., *Major of Ordnance,*
         Inspector of the contract service.

RECAPITULATION.

320 muskets and appendages (or other small arms, as the case may be), viz.:

320 muskets.	320 ramrods.
320 bayonets.	320 screw-drivers, &c.

———

MILLBURY, MASS., November, 18—.

The United States,

     To A. W.,   DR.

For 320 muskets, with bayonets and ramrods, at $12 each................... $000 00

320 screw-drivers, ⎫
320 wipers,   ⎬ Appendages, at —— cents for each musket...... 000 00
32 ball-screws, ⎪
32 spring vices, ⎭

16 packing-boxes, at $2 50 each.

Transportation of 16 boxes from Millbury, Massachusetts, to the Watertown Arsenal, at $1 20 per box.......... .... 000 00

Received, Watertown Arsenal, —— November, 18—, sixteen boxes, containing three hundred and twenty muskets and appendages above mentioned.

The transportation of arms from Millbury to Watertown Arsenal is estimated at one dollar and twenty cents per box.

(Signed)   H. K. C., Major of Ord. Com'g.

(To be given in triplicate.)

NOTES.—This form of certificate will be used for every species of small arms and accoutrements manufactured for the military service of the United States.

Two of the triplicates are forwarded by the contractor to the Ordnance Office, one being intended for the Treasury, and one for the Ordnance Office; the third is retained by the contractor.

Endorsement to be as follows:

Certificate of inspection of —— -
muskets (rifles, pistols, &c.),
—— quarter, ——, 18—.

Ordnance Department.——Forms.

FORM 35.—(To be printed.)

Quarterly Inspection Report of musket barrels (or carbine, rifle, or pistol barrels, as the case may be), manufactured for the United States by ———, of ———, proved and inspected by J. M., 18—.

Number examined.	REJECTED FOR DEFECTS.								POWDER.		Total number rejected.	BURST.		Total number burst.	Total number burst and rejected.	Total number received.	Ratio per 100 received.
	Below prescribed weight.	Below prescribed length.	Calibre too large.	Exterior dimensions too small.	Interior cinder-holes.	Deep ring-bores.	Exterior cinder-holes.	Cross cracks and flaws.	Proof-range eprouvette, No. —.	Date of proof.		1st charge.	2d charge.				
457							5	58	200	Jan. 20, 18—.........	63	11		11	74	383	83.8

I certify that the proof and inspection above referred to have been carefully made, and that this report is in all respects correct.

(Signed)   J. M., *Ass't to Inspector of Arms.*

Approved:

(Signed)   H. K. C., *Major of Ordnance, Inspector of the Contract Service.*

NOTE.—This form will be also used at the U. S. Armories. Its heading, when there used, will be so altered as to suit it to the National Armory service, in which it will be signed by the Master Armorer and the Superintendent.

Endorsement to be as follows:

Inspection Report of Musket (Rifle or Pistol) barrels, ——— quarter, ———, 18—.

FORM 36.—(To be printed.)

Quarterly Inspection Report of Muskets (Carbines, Rifles, Pistols, Swords, Sabres, &c., as the case may be), manufactured for the United States by ——, of ——, inspected ——, 18—.

TIME EMPLOYED IN THE INSPECTION. DAYS.	Number examined	REJECTED FOR DEFECTS IN			Total number rejected	Total number received	Ratio per 100 received.	Remarks.
		Workmanship.	Materials.	Dimensions.				
Stocks.........	325	......	5	......	5	320	98.4	
Barrels.........	343	2	21	......	23	320	93	
Breech-screws	320	......	......	......	......	320	......	
[Names of parts to be inserted according to the kind of arms inspected.]								

I certify that the proof and inspection above referred to have been carefully made, and that the 320 muskets, and their appendages, have been accepted.

(Signed)   H. K. C., *Major of Ordnance, Inspector of the Contract Service.*

Approved: (Signed)   J. M., *Assistant to Inspector of Arms.*

NOTE.—This form will be also used at the U. S. Armories. Its heading, when there used, will be so altered as to suit it to the National Armory service, in which it will be signed by the Master Armorer and the Superintendent.

Endorsement to be as follows:
Inspection Report of —— Muskets (Carbines, common Rifles, or Pistols), —— quarter, 18—.

FORM 37

Annual Consolidated Inspection Report of Muskets (or Carbines, Rifles, Pistols, Swords, Sabres, &c., as the case may be) manufactured on contract for the United States for the year ended the 30th June, 18——.

| | RATIO OR NUMBER APPROVED FOR EACH HUNDRED EXAMINED. | | | | | | | |
| | NAMES OF CONTRACTORS. | | | | | | | |
	A. B.	C. D.	E. F.	G. H.	J. K.	L. M.	N. O.	Mean.
Barrels from first inspection.........	100	100	100	100	100	100	100	100
Barrels from powder proof.........	96.75	97.88	99.54	99.41	99.48	83.90	94.32	95.88
Barrels from final inspection.........	75.19	85.95	90.08	91.23	87.60	83.14	89.12	86.04
[Names of parts to be inserted according to the kind of arms inspected.]								

I certify that the above report has been carefully made up from my several quarterly inspection reports.

(Signed)   H. K. C., *Major of Ordnance,*
and Inspector of the Contract Service.

NOTE.—This form will be also used at the National Armories. Its heading, when there used, will be so altered as to suit it to the National Armory service, in which it will be signed by the Master Armorer and the Superintendent.

This form for the Contract Service is represented with six or eight columns, but for the National Armory Service it will have but one; for the words "Names of Contractors" will be substituted "National Armory, Springfield," "National Armory, Harper's Ferry," &c.

Endorsement to be as follows :

Annual Consolidated Report of Muskets, &c.

for ——, 18——.

FORM 38.

I hereby certify that I have, this —— day of ———, 18—, inspected and proved ten barrels of cannon powder (or musket or rifle powder, as the case may be), numbered 1, 2, 3, 5, 7, 8, 9, 11, 13, and 15, manufactured by A. B., of ———, under his contract (agreement, or open purchase, as the case may be) with the United States, dated ———, 18—.

And I further certify that the said cannon (or musket or rifle powder, as the case may be) has been inspected and proved by me in exact accordance with the regulations established in the Ordnance Department for the proof and inspection of gunpowder before its reception for the service of the United States, and that the weight of the powder in each of the above-mentioned barrels, saving only so much as was used by me in the proof and inspection, is one hundred pounds.

Given under my hand, at the Powder Works of A. B., this —— day of ———, 18—.

(To be signed by the proving officer.)

RECAPITULATION.

10 barrels cannon (or musket or rifle powder, as the case may be).

A. B. POWDER WORKS.

The United States,

To A. B.,   DR.

For 10 barrels of cannon powder, weighing 1000 lbs., at 15 cents per lb.. $150 00
For 10 barrels, $1 00 each.. 10 00

                                                    $160 00

Received at the —— Arsenal, ———, 18—, of A. B., the above ten barrels of cannon powder.

            (Signed)   C. D., *Captain of Ordnance,*
                                          or Military Store-keeper.

(To be signed in triplicate.)

NOTE.—Two of the triplicates are forwarded by the contractor to the Ordnance Office—one being intended for the Treasury and one for the Ordnance Office; the third is retained by the contractor.

Endorsement to be as follows:
Certificate of Inspection
of —— barrels of cannon (or musket) powder,
at the Powder Works of A. B., ———, 18—.

Ordnance Department.——Forms.

FORM 39.

Report of the Proof and Inspection of Cannon (Musket or Rifle) Powder, manufactured by —— —— for the Ordnance Department at the Powder Works of —— —— (or at the —— Arsenal, as the case may be), this —— day of ——, 18—.

Number of barrels inspected. Eprouvette, No. —.	PROOF-RANGES.			BARRELS REJECTED.		BARRELS RECEIVED.
	First range.	Second range.	Medium range.	Giving ranges less than 225 yards.	Their ranges not entering into those forming the general mean range in next column.	Giving the general mean range of 262 yards.
1	318	306	312	....	....	Received...........
2	293	187	290	....	....	do. ....
3	200	210	205	Rejected.		
4	178	182	175	Rejected.		
5	268	268	268	....	....	do. ....
6	192	190	191	Rejected.		
7	261	265	263	....	....	do. ....
8	260	250	255	....	....	do. ....
9	243	241	242	....	....	do. ....
10	200	202	201	Rejected.		
11	235	235	235	....	....	do. ....
12	203	203	203	Rejected.		
13	212	208	210	Rejected.		
14	201	199	200	Rejected.		
15	232	228	230	....	....	do. ... .

Total number of barrels rejected, 7 ⎫ as per certificate of inspection of this date.
Total number of barrels received, 8 ⎭

I certify that the proof and inspection above referred to have been carefully made, and that this report is in all respects correct.

(*To be signed, in duplicate, by the proving officer.*)

NOTES.—1st. Quick match will be used in priming the eprouvette.

2d. When government powder is inspected at the arsenals, the first four columns only are used.

Endorsement to be as follows:

Inspection Report of —— barrels of Cannon
(or Musket) Powder, &c.,
at the Powder Works of A. B.,
(or at the —— Arsenal),
——, 18—.

ARTICLE XLVIII.
PROCEEDINGS IN CIVIL COURTS.

1433. When an officer is made a party to any action or proceeding in a civil court which may involve the interest of the United States; or when, by the performance of his public duty, he is involved in any action or proceeding in which he claims protection or indemnity from the United States, he shall promptly report the case to the Adjutant-General, to be laid before the Secretary of War.

1434. In ordinary cases, when an officer is called upon to show by what authority he holds a soldier in service, he can himself set forth the facts, and need not employ counsel. In important cases, if counsel be necessary, and there is not time to obtain the previous authority of the War Department, he will forthwith report the facts to the Adjutant-General.

ARTICLE XLIX.
ARMS OF THE UNITED STATES.

1435. *Arms*—Paleways of thirteen pieces, argent and gules; a chief, azure; the escutcheon on the breast of the American eagle displayed, proper, holding in his dexter talon an olive-branch, and in his sinister a bundle of thirteen arrows, all proper; and in his beak a scroll, inscribed with this motto: " E PLURIBUS UNUM."

For the *crest:* over the head of the eagle, which appears above the escutcheon, a glory breaking through a cloud, proper, and surrounding thirteen stars, forming a constellation, argent, and on an azure field

ARTICLE L.

FLAGS, COLORS, STANDARDS, GUIDONS.

GARRISON FLAG.

1436. The garrison flag is the national flag. It is made of bunting, thirty-six feet fly, and twenty feet hoist, in thirteen horizontal stripes of equal breadth, alternately red and white, beginning with the red. In the upper quarter, next the staff, is the Union, composed of a number of white stars, equal to the number of States, on a blue field, one-third the length of the flag, extending to the lower edge of the fourth red stripe from the top. The storm flag is twenty feet by ten feet; the recruiting flag, nine feet nine inches by four feet four inches.

COLORS OF ARTILLERY REGIMENTS.

1437. Each regiment of Artillery shall have two silken colors. The first, or the national color, of stars and stripes, as described for the garrison flag. The number and name of the regiment to be embroidered with gold on the centre stripe. The second, or regimental color, to be yellow, of the same dimensions as the first, bearing in the centre two cannon crossing, with the letters U. S. above, and the number of the regiment below; fringe, yellow. Each color to be six feet six inches fly, and six feet deep on the pike. The pike, including the spear and ferrule, to be nine feet ten inches in length. Cords and tassels, red and yellow silk intermixed

COLORS OF INFANTRY REGIMENTS.

1438. Each regiment of Infantry shall have two silken colors. The first, or the national color, of stars and stripes, as described for the garrison flag; the number and name of the regiment to be embroidered with silver on the centre stripe. The second, or regimental color, to be blue, with the arms of the United States embroidered in silk on the centre. The name of the regiment in a scroll, underneath the eagle. The size of each color to be six feet six inches fly, and six feet deep on the pike. The length of the pike, including the spear and ferrule, to be nine feet ten inches. The fringe yellow; cords and tassels, blue and white silk intermixed.

CAMP COLORS.

1439. The camp colors are of bunting, eighteen inches square; white for infantry, and red for artillery, with the number of the regiment on them. The pole eight feet long.

STANDARDS AND GUIDONS OF MOUNTED REGIMENTS.

1440. Each regiment will have a silken standard, and each company a silken guidon. The standard to bear the arms of the United States, embroidered in silk, on a blue ground, with the number and name of the regiment, in a scroll underneath the eagle. The flag of the standard to be two feet five inches wide, and two feet three inches on the lance, and to be edged with yellow silk fringe.

1441. The flag of the guidon is swallow-tailed, three feet five inches from the lance to the end of the swallow-tail; fifteen inches to the fork of the swallow-tail, and two feet three inches on the lance. To be half red and half white, dividing at the fork, the red above. On the red, the letters U. S. in white; and on the white, the letter of the company in red. The lance of the standards and guidons to be nine feet long, including spear and ferrule.

ARTICLE LI.

UNIFORM, DRESS, AND HORSE EQUIPMENTS.

COAT.

For Commissioned Officers.

1442. All officers shall wear a frock-coat of dark blue cloth, the skirt to extend from two-thirds to three-fourths of the distance from the top of the hip to the bend of the knee; single-breasted for Captains and Lieutenants; double-breasted for all other grades.

1443. For a Major-General—two rows of buttons on the breast, nine in each row, placed by threes; the distance between each row, five and one-half inches at top, and three and one-half inches at bottom; stand-up collar, to rise no higher than to permit the chin to turn freely over it, to hook in front at the bottom, and slope thence up and backward at an angle of thirty degrees on each side; cuffs two and one-half inches deep to go around the sleeves parallel with the lower edge, and to button with three small buttons at the under seam; pockets in the folds of the skirts, with one button at the hip, and one at the end of each pocket, making four buttons on the back and skirt of the coat, the hip button to range with the lowest buttons on the breast; collar and cuffs to be of dark blue velvet; lining of the coat black.

1444. For a Brigadier-General—the same as for a Major-General, except that there will be only eight buttons in each row on the breast, placed in pairs.

1445. For a Colonel—the same as for a Major-General, except that there will be only seven buttons in each row on the breast, placed at equal distances; collar and cuffs of the same color and material as the coat.

1446. *For a Lieutenant-Colonel*—the same as for a Colonel.

1447. *For a Major*—the same as for a Colonel.

1448. *For a Captain*—the same as for a Colonel, except that there will be only one row of nine buttons on the breast, placed at equal distances.

1449. *For a First Lieutenant*—the same as for a Captain.

1450. *For a Second Lieutenant*—the same as for a Captain.

1451. *For a Brevet Second Lieutenant*—the same as for a Captain.

1452. *For a Medical Cadet*—the same as for a Brevet Second Lieutenant.

1453. A round jacket, according to pattern, of dark blue cloth, trimmed with scarlet, with the Russian shoulder-knot, the prescribed insignia of rank to be worked in silver in the centre of the knot, may be worn on undress duty by officers of Light Artillery.

For Enlisted Men.

1454. The uniform coat for all enlisted *foot* men, shall be a single-breasted frock of dark blue cloth, made without plaits, with a skirt extending one-half the distance from the top of the hip to the bend of the knee; one row of nine buttons on the breast, placed at equal distances; stand-up collar to rise no higher than to permit the chin to turn freely over it, to hook in front at the bottom and then to slope up and backward at an angle of thirty degrees on each side; cuffs pointed according to pattern, and to button with two small buttons at the under seam; collar and cuffs edged with a cord or welt of cloth as follows, to wit: Scarlet *for Artillery;* sky-blue *for Infantry;* yellow *for Engineers;* crimson *for Ordnance* and *Hospital stewards.* On each shoulder a metallic scale according to pattern; narrow lining for skirt of the coat of the same color and material as the coat; pockets in the folds of the skirts with one button at each hip to range with the lowest buttons on the breast; no buttons at the ends of the pockets.

1455. *All Enlisted Men of the Cavalry and Light Artillery* shall wear a uniform jacket of dark blue cloth, with one row of twelve small buttons on the breast placed at equal distances; stand-up collar to rise no higher than to permit the chin to turn freely over it, to hook in front at the bottom, and to slope the same as the coat-collar; on the collar, on each side, two blind button-holes of lace, three-eighths of an inch wide, one small button on the button-hole, lower button-hole extending back four inches, upper button-hole three and a half inches; top button and front ends of collar bound with lace three-eighths of an inch wide, and a strip of the same extending down the front and around the whole lower edge of the jacket; the back seam laced with the same, and on the cuff a point of the same shape as that on the coat, but formed of the lace; jacket to extend to the waist, and to be lined with white flannel; two small buttons at the under seam of the cuff, as on the coat cuff; one hook and eye at the bottom of the collar; color of lace (worsted), yellow for *Cavalry*, and scarlet for *Light Artillery*.

1456. *For all Musicians*—the same as for other enlisted men of their respective corps, with the addition of a facing of lace three-eighths of an inch wide on the front of the *coat or jacket*, made in the following manner: bars of three-eighths of an inch worsted lace placed on a line with each button six and one-half inches wide at the bottom, and *thence* gradually expanding upward to the last button, counting from the waist up, and contracting from thence to the bottom of the collar, where it will be six and one-half inches wide, with a strip of the same lace following the bars at their outer extremity—the whole presenting something of what is called the herring-bone form; the color of the lace facing to correspond with the color of the trimming of the corps.

1457. *For Fatigue Purposes*—a sack coat of dark blue flannel extending half-way down the thigh, and made loose, without sleeve or body lining, falling collar, inside pocket on the left side, four coat buttons down the front.

1458. *For Recruits*—the sack coat will be made with sleeve and body lining, the latter of flannel.

1459. On all occasions of duty, except fatigue, and when out of quarters, the coat or jacket shall be buttoned and hooked at the collar.

BUTTONS.

1460. *For General Officers and Officers of the General Staff*—gilt, convex, with spread eagle and stars, and plain border; large size, seven-eighths of an inch in exterior diameter; small size, one-half inch.

1461. *For Officers of the Corps of Engineers*—gilt, nine-tenths of an inch in exterior diameter, slightly convex; a raised bright rim, one-thirtieth of an inch wide; device, an eagle holding in his beak a scroll, with the word "*Essayons,*" a bastion with embrasures in the distance surrounded by water, with a rising sun—the figures to be of dead gold upon a bright field. Small buttons of the same form and device, and fifty-five hundredths of an inch in exterior diameter.

1462. *For Officers of the Corps of Topographical Engineers*—gilt, seven-eighths of an inch exterior diameter, convex and solid; device, the shield of the United States, occupying one-half the diameter, and the letters 𝕿. 𝕰. in old English characters the other half; small buttons, one-half inch diameter, device and form the same.

1463. *For Officers of the Ordnance Department*—gilt, convex, plain border, cross cannon and bombshell, with a circular scroll over and across the cannon, containing the words "Ordnance Corps;" large size, seven-eighths of an inch in exterior diameter; small size, one-half inch.

1464. *For Officers of Artillery, Infantry, and Cavalry*—gilt, convex; device, a spread eagle with the letter A, for Artillery—I, for Infantry—C, for Cavalry, on the shield; large size, seven-eighths of an inch in exterior diameter; small size, one-half inch.

1465. *Aides-de-camp* may wear the button of the General Staff, or of their regiment or corps, at their option.

1466. *For Medical Cadets*—same as for Officers of the General Staff.

1467. *For all Enlisted Men*—yellow, the same as is used by the Artillery, &c., omitting the letter in the shield.

TROWSERS.

1468. *For General Officers and Officers of the Ordnance Department*—of dark blue cloth, plain, without stripe, welt, or cord down the outer seam.

1469. *For Officers of the General Staff and Staff Corps*, except the Ordnance—dark blue cloth, with a gold cord, one-eighth of an inch in diameter, along the outer seam.

1470. *For all Regimental Officers*—dark blue cloth, with a welt let into the outer seam, one-eighth of an inch in diameter, of colors corresponding to the facings of the respective regiments, viz.: *Cavalry*, yellow; *Artillery*, scarlet; *Infantry*, sky-blue.

1471. *For Medical Cadets*—same as for Officers of the General Staff, except a welt of buff cloth, instead of a gold cord.

1472. *For Enlisted Men*, except companies of Light Artillery—dark blue cloth; *sergeants* with a stripe one and one-half inch wide; *corporals* with a stripe one-half inch wide, of worsted lace, down and over the outer seam, of the color of the facings of the respective corps.

1473. *Ordnance Sergeants and Hospital Stewards*—stripe of crimson lace one and one-half inch wide.

1474. *Privates*—plain, without stripe or welt.

1475. *For Companies of Artillery equipped as Light Artillery*—sky-blue cloth.

All trowsers to be made loose, without plaits, and to spread well over the boot; to be re-enforced for all enlisted mounted men.

HAT.

1476. *For Officers*—of best black felt. The dimensions of medium size to be as follows:

Width of brim, 3¼ inches.

Height of crown, 6¼ inches.

Oval of tip, ½ inch.

Taper of crown, ¾ inch.

Curve of head, ⅜ inch.

The binding to be ½ inch deep, of best black ribbed silk.

1477. *For Enlisted Men*—of black felt, same shape and size as for officers, with double row of stitching, instead of binding, around the edge. To agree in quality with the pattern deposited in the clothing arsenal.

1478. *Medical Cadets* will wear a forage cap according to pattern.

Trimmings.

1479. *For General Officers*—gold cord, with acorn-shaped ends. The brim of the hat looped up on the right side, and fastened with an eagle attached to the side of the hat; three black ostrich-feathers on the left side; a gold-embroidered wreath in front, on black velvet ground, encircling the letters **U. S.** in silver, old English characters.

1480. *For Officers of the Adjutant-General's, Inspector-General's, Quartermaster's, Subsistence, Medical and Pay Departments, and the Judge Advocate, above the rank of Captain*—the same as for General Officers, except the cord, which will be of black silk and gold.

1481. *For the same Departments, below the rank of Field Officers* —the same as for Field Officers, except that there will be but two feathers.

1482. *For Officers of the Corps of Engineers*—the same as for the General Staff, except the ornament in front, which will be a gold-embroidered wreath of laurel and palm, encircling a silver turreted castle on black velvet ground.

1483. *For Officers of the Topographical Engineers*—the same as for the General Staff, except the ornament in front, which will be a gold-embroidered wreath of oak leaves, encircling a gold-embroidered shield, on black velvet ground.

1484. *For Officers of the Ordnance Department*—the same as for the General Staff, except the ornament in front, which will be a gold-embroidered shell and flame, on black velvet ground.

1485. *For Officers of Cavalry*—the same as for the General Staff, except the ornament in front, which will be two gold-embroidered sabres crossed, edges upward, on black velvet ground, with the number of the regiment in silver in the upper angle.

1486. *For Officers of Artillery*—the same as for the General Staff, except the ornament in front, which will be gold-embroidered cross-cannon, on black velvet ground, with the number of the regiment in silver at the intersection of the cross-cannon.

1487. *For Officers of Infantry*—the same as for Artillery, except the ornament in front, which will be a gold-embroidered bugle, on black velvet ground, with the number of the regiment in silver within the bend.

1488. *For Enlisted Men*, except companies of Light Artillery—the same as for officers of the respective corps, except that there will be but one feather, the cord will be of worsted, of the same color as that of the facing of the corps, three-sixteenths of an inch in diameter, running three times through a slide of the same material, and terminating with two tassels, not less than two inches long, on the side of the hat opposite the feather. The insignia of corps, in brass, in front of the hat, corresponding with those prescribed for officers, with the number of regiment, five-eighths of an inch long, in brass, and letter of company, one inch, in brass, arranged over insignia.

1489. *For Hospital Stewards* the cord will be of buff and green mixed. The wreath in front of brass, with the letters U. S. in Roman, of white metal. Brim to be looped up to side of hat with a brass eagle, having a hook attached to the bottom to secure the brim—on the right side for mounted men and left side for foot men. The feather to be worn on the side opposite the loop.

1490. All the trimmings of the hat are to be made so that they can be detached; but the eagle, badge of corps, and letter of company, are to be always worn.

1491. For companies of Artillery equipped as Light Artillery, the old pattern uniform cap, with red horsehair plume, cord and tassel.

1492. Officers of the General Staff, and Staff Corps, may wear, at their option, a light French chapeau, either stiff crown or flat, according to the pattern deposited in the Adjutant-General's office. Officers below the rank of field officers to wear but two feathers.

FORAGE CAPS.

1493. For fatigue purposes, forage caps, of pattern in the Quartermaster-General's office: dark blue cloth, with a welt of the same around the crown, and yellow metal letters in front to designate companies.

1494. Commissioned officers may wear forage caps of the same pattern, with the distinctive ornament of the corps and regiment in front.

CRAVAT OR STOCK.

1495. *For all Officers*—black; when a cravat is worn, the tie not to be visible at the opening of the collar.

1496. *For all Enlisted Men*—black leather, according to pattern.

BOOTS.

1497. *For all Officers*—ankle or Jefferson.

1498. *For Enlisted Men of Cavalry and Light Artillery*—ankle and Jefferson, rights and lefts, according to pattern.

1499. *For Enlisted Men of Artillery, Infantry, Engineers, and Ordnance*—Jefferson, rights and lefts, according to pattern.

SPURS.

1500. *For all Mounted Officers*—yellow metal, or gilt.

1501. *For all Enlisted Mounted Men*—yellow metal, according to pattern. (See par. 1620.)

GLOVES.

1502. *For General Officers and Officers of the General Staff and Staff Corps*—buff or white.

1503. *For Officers of Artillery, Infantry, Cavalry, Dragoons, and Riflemen*—white.

SASH.

1504. *For General Officers*—buff, silk net, with silk bullion fringe ends; sash to go twice around the waist, and to tie behind the left hip, pendent part not to extend more than eighteen inches below the tie.

1505. *For Officers of the Adjutant-General's, Inspector-General's, Quartermaster's, and Subsistence Departments, Corps of Engineers, Topographical Engineers, Ordnance, Artillery, Infantry, Cavalry, and the Judge Advocate of the Army*—crimson silk net; *for Officers of the Medical Department*—medium or emerald green silk net, with silk bullion fringe ends; to go around the waist and tie as for General Officers.

1506. *For all Sergeant Majors, Quartermaster Sergeants, Ordnance Sergeants, Hospital Stewards, First Sergeants, Principal or Chief Musicians and Chief Buglers*—red worsted sash, with worsted bullion fringe ends; to go twice around the waist, and to tie behind the left hip, pendent part not to extend more than eighteen inches below the tie.

1507. The sash will be worn (over the coat) on all occasions of duty of every description, except stable and fatigue.

1508. The sash will be worn by " *Officers of the Day*" across the body, scarf fashion, from the right shoulder to the left side, instead of around the waist, tying behind the left hip as prescribed.

SWORD-BELT.

1509. *For all Officers*—a waist-belt not less than one and one-half inch nor more than two inches wide to be worn over the sash; the sword to be suspended from it by slings of the same material as the belt, with a hook attached to the belt upon which the sword may be hung.

1510. *For General Officers* — Russia leather, with three stripes of gold embroidery; the slings embroidered on both sides.

1511. *For all other Officers*—black leather, plain.

1512. *For all Non-commissioned Officers*—black leather, plain.

SWORD-BELT PLATE.

1513. *For all Officers and Enlisted Men*—gilt, rectangular, two inches wide, with a raised bright rim; a silver wreath of laurel encircling the "Arms of the United States;" eagle, shield, scroll, edge of cloud and rays bright. The motto, "E PLURIBUS UNUM," in silver letters, upon the scroll; stars also of silver; according to pattern.

SWORD AND SCABBARD.

1514. *For General Officers*—straight sword, gilt hilt, silver grip, brass or steel scabbard.

1515. *For Officers of the Adjutant-General's, Inspector-General's, Quartermaster's, and Subsistence Departments, Corps of Engineers, Topographical Engineers, Ordnance, the Judge Advocate of the Army, Aides-de-Camp, Field Officers of Artillery, Infantry, and Foot Riflemen, and for the Light Artillery*—the sword of the pattern adopted by the War Department, April 9, 1850; or the one described in General Orders No. 21, of August 28, 1860, for officers therein designated.

1516. *For the Medical and Pay Departments*—small sword and scabbard, according to pattern in the Surgeon-General's office.

1517. *For Medical Cadets*, the sword and belt and plate will be the same as for non-commissioned officers.

1518. *For Officers of Cavalry*—sabre and scabbard now in use, according to pattern in the Ordnance Department.

1519. *For the Artillery, Infantry, and Foot Riflemen,* except the field officers—the sword of the pattern adopted by the War Department, April 9, 1850.

1520. The sword and sword-belt will be worn upon all occasions of duty, without exception.

1521. When on foot, the sabre will be suspended from the hook attached to the belt.

1522. When not on military duty, officers may wear swords of honor, or the prescribed sword, with a scabbard, gilt, or of leather with gilt mountings.

SWORD-KNOT.

1523. *For General Officers*—gold cord with acorn end.

1524. *For all other officers*—gold lace strap with gold bullion tassel.

BADGES TO DISTINGUISH RANK.

Epaulettes.

1525. *For the Major-General Commanding the Army*—gold, with solid crescent; device, three silver-embroidered stars, one, one and a half inches in diameter, one, one and one-fourth inches in diameter, and one, one and one-eighth inches in diameter, placed on the strap in a row, longitudinally, and equidistant, the largest star in the centre of the crescent, the smallest at the top; dead and bright gold bullion, one-half inch in diameter and three and one-half inches long.

1526. *For all other Major-Generals*—the same as for the Major-General Commanding the Army, except that there will be two stars on the strap instead of three, omitting the smallest.

1527. *For a Brigadier-General*—the same as for a Major-General, except that, instead of two, there shall be one star (omitting the smallest) placed upon the strap, and not within the crescent.

1528. *For a Colonel*—the same as for a Brigadier-General, substituting a silver-embroidered spread eagle for the star upon the strap ; and within the crescent for the *Medical Department*—a laurel wreath embroidered in gold, and the letters 𝕸. 𝕾., in old English characters, in silver, within the wreath; *Pay Department*—same as the Medical Department, with the letters 𝕻. 𝕯., in old English characters ; *Corps of Engineers*—a turreted castle of silver; *Corps of Topographical Engineers*—a shield embroidered in gold, and below it the letters 𝕿. 𝕰., in old English characters, in silver; *Ordnance Department*—shell and flame in silver embroidery ; *Regimental Officers*—the number of the regiment embroidered in gold, within a circlet of embroidered silver, one and three-fourths inches in diameter, upon cloth of the following colors: *for Artillery*—scarlet; *Infantry*—light or sky blue; *Cavalry*—yellow.

1529. *For a Lieutenant-Colonel*—the same as for a Colonel, according to corps, but substituting for the eagle a silver-embroidered leaf.

1530. *For a Major*—the same as for a Colonel, according to corps, omitting the eagle.

1531 *For a Captain*—the same as for a Colonel, according to corps, except that the bullion will be only one-fourth of an inch in diameter, and two and one-half inches long, and substituting for the eagle two silver-embroidered bars.

1532. *For a First Lieutenant*—the same as for a Colonel, according to corps, except that the bullion will be only one-eighth of an inch in diameter, and two and one-half inches long, and substituting for the eagle one silver-embroidered bar.

1533. *For a Second Lieutenant*—the same as for a First Lieutenant, omitting the bar.

1534. *For a Brevet Second Lieutenant*—the same as for a Second Lieutenant.

1535. All officers having military rank will wear an epaulette on each shoulder.

1536. The epaulette may be dispensed with when not on duty, and on certain duties off parade, to wit: at drills, at inspections of barracks and hospitals, on Courts of Inquiry and Boards, at inspections of articles and necessaries, on working parties and fatigue duties, and upon the march, except when, in war, there is immediate expectation of meeting the enemy, and also when the overcoat is worn.

Shoulder-Straps:

1537. *For the Major-General Commanding the Army*—dark blue cloth, one and three-eighths inches wide by four inches long; bordered with an embroidery of gold one-fourth of an inch wide; three silver-embroidered stars of five rays, one star on the centre of the strap, and one on each side equidistant between the centre and the outer edge of the strap; the centre star to be the largest.

1538. *For all other Major-Generals*—the same as for the Major-General Commanding the Army, except that there will be two stars instead of three; the centre of each star to be one inch from the outer edge of the gold embroidery on the ends of the strap; both stars of the same size.

1539. *For a Brigadier-General*—the same as for a Major-General, except that there will be one star instead of two; the centre of the star to be equidistant from the outer edge of the embroidery on the ends of the strap.

1540. *For a Colonel*—the same size as for a Major-General, and bordered in like manner with an embroidery of gold; a silver-embroidered spread eagle on the centre of the strap, two inches between the tips of the wings, having in the right talon an olive-branch, and in the left a bundle of arrows; an escutcheon on the breast, as represented in the arms of the United States; cloth of the strap as follows: for the *General Staff and Staff Corps*—dark blue; *Artillery*—scarlet; *Infantry*—light or sky blue; *Cavalry*—yellow.

1541. *For a Lieutenant-Colonel*—the same as for a Colonel, according to corps, omitting the eagle, and introducing a silver-embroidered leaf at each end, each leaf extending seven-eighths of an inch from the end border of the strap.

1542. *For a Major*—the same as for a Colonel, according to corps, omitting the eagle, and introducing a gold-embroidered leaf at each end, each leaf extending seven-eighths of an inch from the end border of the strap.

1543. *For a Captain*—the same as for a Colonel, according to corps, omitting the eagle, and introducing at each end two gold-embroidered bars of the same width as the border, placed parallel to the ends of the strap; the distance between them and from the border equal to the width of the border.

1544. *For a First Lieutenant*—the same as for a Colonel, according to corps, omitting the eagle, and introducing at each end one gold-embroidered bar of the same width as the border, placed parallel to the ends of the strap, at a distance from the border equal to its width.

1545. *For a Second Lieutenant*—the same as for a Colonel, according to corps, omitting the eagle.

1546. *For a Brevet Second Lieutenant*—the same as for a Second Lieutenant.

1547. *For a Medical Cadet*—a strip of gold lace three inches long, half an inch wide, placed in the middle of a strap of green cloth three and three-quarter inches long by one and one-quarter inches wide.

1548. The shoulder-strap will be worn whenever the epaulette is not.

Chevrons.

1549. The rank of non-commissioned officers will be marked by chevrons upon both sleeves of the uniform coat and overcoat, above the elbow, of silk or worsted binding one-half an inch wide, same color as the edging on the coat, points down, as follows:

1550. *For a Sergeant Major*—three bars and an arc, in silk.

1551. *For a Quartermaster Sergeant*—three bars and a tie, in silk.

1552. *For an Ordnance Sergeant*—three bars and a star, in silk.

1553. *For a Hospital Steward*—a half chevron of the following description,—viz.: of emerald green cloth, one and three-fourths inches wide, running obliquely downward from the outer to the inner seam of the sleeve, and at an angle of about thirty degrees with a horizontal, parallel to, and one-eighth of an inch distant from, both the upper and lower edge, an embroidery of yellow silk one-eighth of an inch wide, and in the centre a "caduceus" two inches long, embroidered also with yellow silk, the head toward the outer seam of the sleeve.

1554. *For a First Sergeant*—three bars and a lozenge, in worsted.

1555. *For a Sergeant*—three bars, in worsted.

1556. *For a Corporal*—two bars, in worsted.

1557. *For a Pioneer*—two crossed hatchets of cloth, same color and material as the edging of the collar, to be sewed on each arm above the elbow in the place indicated for a chevron (those of a corporal to be just above and resting on the chevron), the head of the hatchet upward, its edge outward, of the following dimensions, viz.: *Handle*—four and one-half inches long, one-fourth to one-third of an inch wide. *Hatchet*—two inches long, one inch wide at the edge.

1558. *To indicate service*—all non-commissioned officers, musicians, and privates, who have served faithfully for the term of five years, will wear, as a mark of distinction, upon both sleeves of the uniform coat, below the elbow, a diagonal half chevron, one-half an inch wide, extending from seam to seam, the front end nearest the cuff, and one-half an inch above the point of the cuff, to be of the same color as the edging on the coat. In like manner, an additional half chevron, above and parallel to the first, for every subsequent five years of faithful service; distance between each chevron one-fourth of an inch. Service in war will be indicated by a light or sky blue stripe on each side of the chevron for Artillery, and a red stripe for all other corps the stripe to be one-eighth of an inch wide.

OVERCOAT.

For Commissioned Officers.

1559. A "*cloak coat*" of dark blue cloth, closing by means of four frog buttons of black silk and loops of black silk cord down the breast, and at the throat by a long loop *à échelle*, without tassel or plate, on the left side, and a black silk frog button on the right; cord for the loops fifteen-hundredths of an inch in diameter; back, a single piece, slit up from the bottom, from fifteen to seventeen inches, according to the height of the wearer, and closing at will, by buttons, and button-holes cut in a concealed flap; collar of the same color and material as the coat, rounded at the edges, and to stand or fall; when standing, to be about five inches high; sleeves loose, of a single piece, and round at the bottom, without cuff or slit; lining, woolen; around the front and lower border, the edges of the pockets, the edges of the sleeves, collar, and slit in the back, a flat braid of black silk one-half an inch wide; and around each frog button on the breast, a knot two and one-quarter inches in diameter of black silk cord, seven-hundredths of an inch in diameter, arranged according to drawing; cape of the same color and material as the coat, removable at the pleasure of the wearer, and reaching to the cuff of the coat-sleeve when the arm is extended; coat to extend down the leg from six to eight inches below the knee, according to height. *To indicate rank*, there will be on both sleeves, near the lower edge, a knot of flat black silk braid not exceeding one-eighth of an inch in width, arranged according to drawing, and composed as follows:

1560. *For a General*—of five braids, double knot.

1561. *For a Colonel*—of five braids, single knot.

1562. *For a Lieutenant-Colonel*—of four braids, single knot.

1563. *For a Major*—of three braids, single knot.

1564. *For a Captain*—of two braids, single knot.

1565. *For a First Lieutenant*—of one braid, single knot.

1566. *For a Second Lieutenant and Brevet Second Lieutenant*—a plain sleeve, without knot or ornament.

For Enlisted Men.

1567. *Of all Mounted Corps*—of sky-blue cloth; stand-and-fall collar; double-breasted; cape to reach down to the cuff of the coat when the arm is extended, and to button all the way up; buttons (1467).

1568. *All other Enlisted Men*—of sky-blue cloth; stand-up collar; single-breasted; cape to reach down to the elbows when the arm is extended, and to button all the way up; buttons (1467).

1569. *For Cavalry*—a gutta-percha talma, or cloak extending to the knee, with long sleeves.

OTHER ARTICLES OF CLOTHING AND EQUIPMENT.

1570. *Flannel shirt, drawers, stockings, and stable-frock*—the same as now furnished.

1571. *Blanket*—woolen, gray, with letters U. S. in black, four inches long, in the centre; to be seven feet long, and five and a half feet wide, and to weigh five pounds.

1572. *Canvas overalls for Engineer soldiers*—of white cotton; one garment to cover the whole of the body below the waist, the breast, the shoulders, and the arms; sleeves loose, to allow a free play of the arms, with narrow wristband buttoning with one button; overalls to fasten at the neck behind with two buttons, and at the waist behind with buckle and tongue.

1573. *Belts of all Enlisted Men*—black leather.

1574. *Cartridge-box*—according to pattern in the Ordnance Department.

1575. *Drum-sling*—white webbing; to be provided with a brass drumstick carriage, according to pattern.

1576. *Knapsack*—of painted canvas, according to pattern now issued by the Quartermaster's Department; the great-coat, when carried, to be neatly folded, not rolled, and covered by the outer flap of the knapsack.

1577. *Haversack*—of painted canvas, with an inside sack unpainted, according to the pattern now issued by the Quartermaster's Department.

1578. *Canteen*—of tin, covered with woolen cloth, of the pattern now issued by the Quartermaster's Department.

TENTS.

1579. *For all Commissioned Officers*—wall tent, with a fly, pattern now issued by the Quartermaster's Department.

1580. *For Hospital purposes*—pattern described in " General Orders" No. 1, of January 19, 1860.

1581. *For all Enlisted Men*—Sibley's patent, according to the pattern now issued by the Quartermaster's Department, at the rate of one tent to 17 mounted or 20 foot men. Sheet-iron stoves will be issued with the tents in cold climates, or when specially ordered.

1582. *For Officers' Servants and Laundresses*—small common tent, old pattern.

HORSE FURNITURE.

For General Officers and the General Staff.

1583. *Housing for General Officers*—to be worn over the saddle; of dark blue cloth, trimmed with two rows of gold lace, the outer row one inch and five-eighths wide, the inner row two inches and one-fourth; to be made full, so as to cover the horse's haunches and forehands, and to bear on each flank corner the following ornaments, distinctive of rank, to wit: for the *Major-General Commanding the Army*—a gold-embroidered spread eagle and three stars; for other *Major-Generals*—a gold-embroidered spread eagle and two stars; for a *Brigadier-General*—a gold-embroidered spread eagle and one star.

1584. *Saddle-cloth for General Staff Officers*—dark blue cloth, of sufficient length to cover the saddle and holsters, and one foot ten inches in depth, with an edging of gold lace one inch wide.

1585. *Surcingle*—blue web.

1586. *Bridle*—black leather; bent branch bit, with gilt bosses; the front and roses yellow.

1587. *Collar*—yellow.

1588. *Holsters*—black leather, with gilt mountings.

1589. *Stirrups*—gilt or yellow metal.

For Officers of the Corps of Engineers and Topographical Engineers.

1590. The same as for General Staff Officers.

1591. In time of actual field service, General Officers and Officers of the General Staff and Staff Corps are permitted to use the horse equipments described for mounted service.

HORSE EQUIPMENTS FOR THE MOUNTED SERVICE.

1592. A complete set of horse equipments for mounted troops consists of 1 *bridle*, 1 *watering bridle*, 1 *halter*, 1 *saddle*, 1 *pair saddle bags*, 1 *saddle blanket*, 1 *surcingle*, 1 *pair spurs*, 1 *currycomb*, 1 *horse brush*, 1 *picket pin, and* 1 *lariat;* 1 link and 1 nose bag when specially required.

HEAD GEAR.

1593. All the *leather* is black bridle leather, and the buckles are malleable iron, flat, bar buckles, blued.

1594. BRIDLE—It is composed of 1 *headstall*, 1 *bit*, 1 *pair of reins*.

1595. HEADSTALL—1 *crown piece,* the ends split, forming 1 *cheek strap* and 1 *throat lash billet* on one side, and on the other, 1 *cheek strap* and 1 *throat lash*, with 1 *buckle*, .625 inch, 2 *chapes* and 2 *buckles*, .75 inch, sewed to the ends of cheek piece to attach the bit; 1 *brow band*, the ends doubled and sewed form 2 loops on each end through which the cheek straps and throat lash and throat lash billet pass.

1596. BIT (shear steel, blued)—2 *branches*, S shaped, pierced at top with an *eye* for the cheek strap billet, and with a small hole near the eye for the curb chain, terminated at the bottom by 2 *buttons*, into which are welded 2 *rings*, 1 inch, for the reins; 1 *mouth piece*, curved in the middle, its ends pass through the branches and are riveted to them; 1 *cross bar*, riveted to the branches near the lower ends; 2 *bosses* (cast brass), bearing the number and letter of the regiment and the letter of the company, riveted to the branches with 4 *rivets;* 1 *curb-chain hook*, steel wire, No. 10, fastened to the *near* branch; 1 *curb chain*, steel wire, No. 11, curb-chain links 0.7 inch wide, with 1 loose ring in the middle, fastened to the *off* branch by a S hook, coldshut; 1 *curb strap* (leather), fastened to the curb chain by 2 *standing loops*.

1597. 1 *curb ring* for bit No. 1 replaces the curb chain and curb strap. They are of two sizes: No. 1 has an interior diameter of 4 inches; No. 2, of 3.75 inches. The number is marked on the outside of the swell. No. 1 is the larger size.

1598. There are four bits, differing from each other in the arch of the mouth piece, and in the distance from the mouth piece to the eye for the cheek strap. The branches are alike below the mouth piece. No. 1 is a Spanish bit, No. 2 is the next severest, and No. 4 is the mildest. Height of arch is $2\frac{1}{4}$ inches in No. 1, 2 inches in No. 2, $1\frac{1}{2}$ inch in No. 3, and $\frac{1}{2}$ inch in No. 4. The distance between the branches is 4.5 inches in all the bits.

1599. REINS—2 *reins* sewed together at one end, the other ends sewed to the rings of the bit.

WATERING BRIDLE.

1600. The watering bridle is composed of 1 *bit* and 1 *pair of reins.*

1601. BIT (wrought iron, blued)—2 *mouth-piece sides* united in the middle by a loop hinge; their ends are pierced with 2 holes to receive 2 *rings* 1.7 inches diameter for the reins. 2 *chains and toggles*, 3 links, each 1 inch × 0.55 inch, welded into the rein rings.

1602. REINS—2 *reins* sewed together at one end, the other end sewed to rings of the bit.

HALTER.

1603. 2 *cheek pieces*, sewed at one end to 2 *square loops* 1.6 inches diameter, and the other to 2 *cheek rings* 1.6 inches diameter; 2 *standing loops* for the toggles of the watering bridle sewed to the cheek piece near to the square loops; 1 *crown piece* sewed to the *off* cheek ring, 1 buckle 1.12 inches, and *chape* sewed to the near cheek ring; 1 *nose band*, the ends sewed to the square loops; 1 *chin strap*, the ends sewed to the square loops and passing loose through the hitching-strap ring; 1 *throat strap*, folded on itself making two thicknesses, and forming at top a loop for the throat band to pass through, and embracing in the fold at the other end 1 *bolt* which holds 1 *hitching-strap ring ;* 1 *throat band* passes loose through the loop in the throat strap, and is sewed to the cheek rings; 1 *hitching strap* 6½ feet long, 1 *buckle* 1.25 inches, and 1 *standing loop*, 1 *billet* sewed to the buckle end by the same seam which holds the buckle.

SADDLE.

1604. All the *leather* is black bridle or harness leather, and the buckles are blued malleable iron.

1605. The *saddle* is composed of 1 *tree*, 2 *saddle skirts*, 2 *stirrups*, 1 *girth* and *girth strap*, 1 *surcingle*, 1 *crupper.*

SADDLE TREE.

1606. WOOD (beech)—1 *pommel* made of 2 pieces framed together at top and glued; 1 *cantle* formed of 2 pieces like the pommel; 2 *side bars* (poplar), each made of 3 pieces glued together; they are glued to the pommel and cantle, and fastened by 2 *rivets*, 2 *burrs*, and 4 *nails*, the burrs let in on the under side; 1 *strap mortise* in the pommel, 3 *strap mortises* in the cantle.

1607. There are three sizes of trees, varying in the length of the seat The number is marked on the pommel ornament.

Horse Equipments.

No. 1.   11 inches length of seat.   15 per cent.
No. 2.   11½   "   "   50   "
No. 3.   12   "   "   35   "

1608. IRON.—1 *pommel arc* 0.1 inch thick, with three small holes on top, fastened to the side bars by 4 *rivets*; 1 *pommel plate* 0.1 inch thick, semi-circular, fastened to the front of the pommel by 4 *rivets*; 1 *cantle arc* 0.1 inch thick, with three small holes on top, fastened to the side bars by 4 rivets; 1 *cantle plate* 0.1 inch thick, fastened to the rear of the cantle by 4 *rivets*; 2 *stirrup loops* hinged in 2 *holdfasts* which are fastened to the side bars by 6 *rivets*.

1609. The tree is painted with one coat of white lead. It is covered with the best quality kip skin raw hide, put on wet, sewed with thongs of the same and held in place by stitches through the wood along the junction of the pommel and cantle with the side bars. The seams are made on the edges of the side bars, where they will not chafe the horse or rider.

1610. 2 *crupper rings*, held by staples driven into the front ends of side bars; 2 *foot staples* for coat straps, fastened to the front of the pommel by 4 *brass screws*, ¾ inch; 2 *crupper rings* (japanned black), fastened by staples driven into the rear ends of side bars; 2 *foot staples*, fastened to the rear of cantle by 4 brass screws, ¾ inch; 1 *guard plate*, 1 *pommel ornament*, shield-shaped (sheet brass), fastened to the pommel, each, by 3 brass screw pins; 6 *guard plates*, fastened to the cantle by 12 *screw pins*; 2 *foot staples*, fastened on the back strap by 4 *brass screws*, ¾ inch; 1 *saddle-bag stud*, fastened on the back strap to the cantle arc by 2 copper rivets.

1611. Two SADDLE SKIRTS (thick harness leather), fastened to the side bars by 38 brass screws, ¾ inch; 2 *stay loops* for the saddle-bag straps, sewed to the rear edge of the skirts.

1612. Two STIRRUPS (hickory or oak), made of one piece bent, the ends separated by 1 *transom* and fastened by 2 *iron rivets*, each, 4 *burrs*; 2 *leather hoods*, fastened to the stirrups by 12 *copper rivets and burrs*— distance of hood from rear of stirrup, 6 inches; 2 *stirrup straps*, 2 *brass buckles*, 1.375 inches, 2 *sliding loops*, pass through the stirrup loops and through a hole cut in the skirts; 2 *sweat leathers*, each has 2 *standing loops*.

1613. GIRTH—2 *girth straps* pass over the pommel and cantle arcs, to which they are fastened by 4 *copper rivets* and 4 *burrs*; they are fastened to the side bars by 4 *brass screws*, ¾ inch; the ends are sewed into 2 D rings, 1.85 inches; 2 *girth billets*, sewed to the straight side of the D rings; 1 *girth*, 4.5 inches, blue woolen webbing; 1 *chape*, 1 *buckle*, 2 inches, 1 *standing loop*, and 1 *safe* on the off end; and 1 *chape*, 1 *buckle*, 1.5

inches, 1 D *ring*, 1.85 inches, 1 *standing loop*, 1 *safe* on the near side; 1 *standing loop* on the middle.

1614. SIX COAT STRAPS, 6 *buckles*, 0.625 inch, and stops. They pass through the mortises in the pommel and cantle and the foot staples.

1615. ONE CARBINE SOCKET, 1 *strap*, 1 *buckle*, 0.75 inch, sewed to the socket. The socket is buckled to the D ring on the off side of the saddle.

1616. ONE SURCINGLE, 3.25 inches, blue woolen webbing; 1 *chape*, 1 *buckle*, 1.5 inches, 1 *standing loop* on one end, and 1 *billet* on the other; 1 *billet* lining sewed over the end of webbing to the billet; 2 *standing loops* near the buckle end.

1617. CRUPPER—1 *dock*, made of a single piece and stuffed with hair, the ends sewed to the body of the crupper; 1 *body*, split at one end, has sewed to it 1 *chape*, 1 *ring*, 1.25 inches, 2 *back straps*—each has one buckle, 0.75 inch, and 2 *sliding loops*—they pass through the rings of the side bars and the ring on the body of the crupper.

1618. SADDLE BAGS (bag leather).—They are composed of 2 *pouches* and 1 *seat;* the ends of the seat are sewed to the pouches. Each pouch has 1 *back*, sewed to the gusset and upper part of inner front with a *welt;* 1 *gusset*, sewed to the back and to 1 *outer* and 1 *inner front* with a *welt;* 1 *flap*, sewed to the top of the back and to the seat by 2 seams; 1 *flap billet*, sewed to the point of the flap; 1 *chape and* 1 *buckle*, 0.625 inch, sewed to the outer front; 1 *billet*, 1 *buckle*, 0.625 inch, sewed to the chape. The seat is sewed to the pouch by the same seams which join the flap to the back of the pouch. It has 2 *holes* for the foot staples and 1 *hole* for the saddle-bag stud; 2 *key straps*, sewed to the seat near its ends; 4 *lacing thongs* for the pouches.

1619. SADDLE BLANKET.—To be of pure wool, close woven, of stout yarns of an indigo-blue color, with an orange border 3 inches wide, 3 inches from the edge. The letters U. S., 6 inches high, of orange color, in the centre of the blanket. Dimensions: 75 inches long, 67 inches wide; weight, 3.1875 pounds; variation allowed in weight, 0.1875 pounds.

1620. SPURS (brass).—2 *spurs*, 2 *rowels*, 2 *rivets*, 2 *spur straps*, 19 inches long, 2 *roller buckles*, 0.625 inch, 2 *standing loops*.
Length of heel for No. 1, 3¼ inches; for No. 2, 3¼ inches—inside meas.
Width of heel   "   3¼   "   "   3   "   "
Length of shank to centre of rowel, 1 inch.
Diameter of rowel, 0.85 inch.

1621. ONE HORSE BRUSH—1 *body* (maple), Russia bristles; 1 *cover*, glued and fastened to the body by 8 brass screws; 1 *hand strap*, fair leather, fastened to the sides of the body by 6 screws; 2 *leather washers* under the heads of screws. *Dimensions:* Body, 9.25 inches long, 4 inches wide, 0.5 inch thick; cover, 0.1 inch thick; bristles project 0.9 inch; hand strap, 2 inches wide.

1622. ONE CURRY COMB—iron, japanned black. The pattern of "Carpenter's, No. 333." 1 *body* (sheet iron, 0.4), the top and bottom edges turned at right angles, forming two rows of teeth; 3 *double rows* of teeth, riveted to the body by *six rivets;* 1 *cross bar*, riveted across the top by 2 rivets; 1 *handle shank*, riveted to the body by 3 rivets; 1 *handle* (wood), turned and painted, passes over the shank and is held by the riveted end of the shank; 1 *ferrule*, sheet iron. *Dimensions:* Length, 4 inches; width, 4.75 inches; thickness, 0.75 inch; length of handle, 4 inches; weight, 0.84 pound.

1623. ONE PICKET PIN (iron, painted black).—The parts are: *the body, the neck, the head, the swell, the point;* 1 *lariat ring* around the neck, 8-shaped, the larger opening for the lariat. *Dimensions:* Length, 14 inches; diameter at swell, 4 inches from point, 0.75 inch; at neck, 0.5 inch; at head, 1 inch; lariat ring, 0.2 inch wire, welded, interior diameter, 1 inch; weight of pin, 1.29 pounds.

1624. ONE LARIAT.—Best hemp 1¼-inch rope, 30 feet long, of 4 strands; an eye spliced in one end, the other end whipped with small twine; weight, 2.38 pounds.

1625. ONE LINK—1 *strap*, embracing in the fold at one end 1 *spring hook*, and at the other 1 *buckle*, 0.75 inch, and 1 *billet*.

1626. ONE NOSE BAG—same as for Light Artillery.

MILITARY STORE-KEEPERS.

1627. A citizen's frock-coat of blue cloth, with buttons of the department to which they are attached; round black hat; pantaloons and vest, plain, white or dark blue; cravat or stock, black.

MISCELLANEOUS.

1628. General Officers, and Colonels having the brevet rank of General Officers, may, on occasions of ceremony, and when not serving with troops, wear the "dress" and "undress" prescribed by existing regulations.

1629. Officers below the grade of Colonel having brevet rank, will wear the epaulettes and shoulder-straps distinctive of their army rank. In all other respects, their uniform and dress will be that of their respective regiments, corps, or departments, and according to their commissions in the same. Officers above the grade of Lieutenant-Colonel by ordinary commission, having brevet rank, may wear the uniform of their respective regiments or corps, or that of General Officers, according to their brevet rank.

1630. The uniform and dress of the Signal Officer will be that of a Major of the General Staff.

1631. Officers are permitted to wear a plain dark blue body-coat, with the button designating their respective corps, regiments, or departments, without any other mark or ornament upon it. Such a coat, however, is not to be considered as a dress for any military purpose.

1632. In like manner, officers are permitted to wear a buff, white, or blue vest, with the small button of their corps, regiment, or department.

1633. Officers serving with mounted troops are allowed to wear, for stable duty, a plain dark blue cloth jacket, with one or two rows of buttons down the front, according to rank; stand-up collar, sloped in front as that of the uniform coat; shoulder-straps according to rank, but no other ornament.

1634. The hair to be short; the beard to be worn at the pleasure of the individual; but, when worn, to be kept short and neatly trimmed.

1635. *A Band* will wear the uniform of the regiment or corps to which it belongs. The commanding officer may, at the expense of the corps, sanctioned by the Council of Administration, make such *additions* in ornaments as he may judge proper.

ARTICLE LII.

VOLUNTEERS AND MILITIA IN THE SERVICE OF THE UNITED STATES.

1636. Whenever volunteer or drafted militia are called into the service of the United States, by any officer authorized to make such call, the requisition must be made on the Governor of the State or Territory in which the militia are to be raised, and the number of officers, non-commissioned officers, and privates will be stated in the requisition, according to the organization prescribed by the law of the United States.

1637. Before militia are received in the service of the United States, they shall be mustered by an Inspector-General, or some other officer of the regular army, specially designated to muster them.

1638. When volunteers are to be mustered into the service of the United States, they will, at the same time, be minutely examined by the surgeon and assistant surgeon of the regiment, to ascertain whether they have the physical qualifications necessary for the military service. And in case any individual shall be discharged within three months after entering the service, for a disability which existed at that time, he shall receive neither pay nor allowances except subsistence and transportation to his home. The certificate given by the surgeon will, in all cases, state whether the disability existed prior to the date of muster, or was contracted after it.

1639. It shall be the duty of the officer designated to muster and inspect militia, to forward muster-rolls of each company, and of the field and staff of each regiment, *direct* to the Adjutant-General of the Army, Washington; and he will also immediately forward a consolidated return, by regiments and corps, of the force received into service, for the in formation of the War Department.

1640. *Mustering in.*—Reference will be made to the particular act or acts of Congress under which the militia are called into service. If there be no such act, then to the act May 8, 1792, amended by the acts April 18, 1814, and April 20, 1816. Mustering officers will not muster into service a greater number of officers, or of higher rank, than the law prescribes. No officers of the general staff will be mustered or received into service, except such general officers, with their aides-de-camp, as may be required to complete the organization of brigades or divisions.

1641. *Mustering out.*—The rolls for this purpose will be compared with those of the first muster. All persons on the first rolls, and absent at the final muster, must be accounted for—whether dead, captured, discharged, or otherwise absent; and if the mustering officer, in any particular case, shall have cause to doubt the report made to be entered on the rolls, he shall demand the oath of one or more persons to prove the fact to his satisfaction; further, he shall take care that not more persons of the several ranks be mustered out of service than were mustered in, if there be an excess over the requisition or beyond the law, nor recognize additions or substitutes, without full satisfaction that the additions or substitutions were regularly made, and at the time reported on the rolls.

1642. Officers mustering in troops will be careful that men from one company or detachment are not borrowed for the occasion, to swell the ranks of others about to be mustered. No volunteer will be mustered into the service who is unable to speak the English language.

1643. Officers charged with the duty of mustering militia will take care that the muster-rolls contain all the information that may in any way affect their pay; the distance from the places of residence to the place of rendezvous or organization, and the date of arrival, must be stated in each case; the date and place of discharge, and the distance thence to the place of residence; all stoppages for articles furnished by the Government must be noted on the rolls; and in cases of absence at the time of discharge of the company, the cause of absence must be stated. When the necessary information cannot be obtained, the mustering officer will state the reason.

1644. If, as has sometimes happened, militia, at the end of a term of service, shall, from the want of a mustering officer, disperse or return home without being regularly mustered out; and if, with a view to a payment, a muster shall afterward be ordered by competent authority, the officer sent for the purpose shall carefully verify all the facts affecting pay, by the oath of one or more of the officers belonging to such militia, in order that full justice may be done.

1645. In all cases of *muster* for *payment*, whether final or otherwise, the mustering officer will give his particular attention to the state and condition of the public property: such as quarters, camp-equipage, means of transportation, arms, accoutrements, ammunition, &c., which have been in the use or possession of the militia to be paid; and if any such public property shall appear to be damaged, or lost, beyond ordinary wear or unavoidable accident, such loss or damage shall be noted on the muster-rolls, in order that the injury or loss sustained by the United States may be stopped from the pay that would otherwise be due to the individual or detachment mustered for payment. *See regulations of the Ordnance Department.* This provision shall be read to all detachments of militia on being mustered into service, and as much oftener as may be deemed necessary.

1646. Payments will, in all cases, be made by the paymasters of the regular army.

1647. Officers of the volunteer service tendering their resignations, will forward them through the intermediate commanders to the officer commanding the department or *corps d'armée* in which they may be serving, who is authorized to grant them honorable discharges. This commander will immediately report his action to the Adjutant-General of the Army, who will communicate the same to the Governor of the State to which the officer belongs. A clear statement of the cause will accompany every resignation.

1648. Vacancies occurring among the commissioned officers in volunteer regiments will be filled by the Governors of the respective States by which the regiments were furnished. Information of such appointments will, in all cases, be furnished to the Adjutant-General of the Army.

APPENDIX.

ARTICLES OF WAR.

AN ACT FOR ESTABLISHING RULES AND ARTICLES FOR THE GOVERNMENT OF THE ARMIES OF THE UNITED STATES.*

SECTION 1. *Be it enacted, by the Senate and House of Representatives of the United States of America, in Congress assembled,* That, from and after the passing of this act, the following shall be the rules and articles by which the armies of the United States shall be governed:

ARTICLE 1. Every officer now in the army of the United States shall, in six months from the passing of this act, and every officer who shall hereafter be appointed shall, before he enters on the duties of his office, subscribe these rules and regulations.

ART. 2. It is earnestly recommended to all officers and soldiers diligently to attend divine service; and all officers who shall behave indecently or irreverently at any place of divine worship shall, if commissioned officers, be brought before a general court-martial, there to be publicly and severely reprimanded by the president; if non-commissioned officers or soldiers, every person so offending shall, for his first offense, forfeit one-sixth of a dollar, to be deducted out of his next pay; for the second offense, he shall not only forfeit a like sum, but be confined twenty-four hours; and for every like offense, shall suffer and pay in like manner; which money, so forfeited, shall be applied, by the captain or senior officer of the troop or company, to the use of the sick soldiers of the company or troop to which the offender belongs.

ART. 3. Any non-commissioned officer or soldier who shall use any profane oath or execration, shall incur the penalties expressed in the foregoing article; and a commissioned officer shall forfeit and pay, for each and every such offense, one dollar, to be applied as in the preceding article.

ART. 4. Every chaplain commissioned in the army or armies of the United States, who shall absent himself from the duties assigned him (excepting in cases of sickness or leave of absence), shall, on conviction thereof before a court-martial, be fined not exceeding one month's pay,

---

* These rules and articles, with the exceptions indicated by the notes annexed to articles 10, 20, 65, and 87, remain unaltered and in force at present.

besides the loss of his pay during his absence; or be discharged, as the said court-martial shall judge proper.

ART. 5. Any officer or soldier who shall use contemptuous or disrespectful words against the President of the United States, against the Vice-President thereof, against the Congress of the United States, or against the Chief Magistrate or Legislature of any of the United States, in which he may be quartered, if a commissioned officer, shall be cashiered, or otherwise punished, as a court-martial shall direct; if a non-commissioned officer or soldier, he shall suffer such punishment as shall be inflicted on him by the sentence of a court-martial.

ART. 6. Any officer or soldier who shall behave himself with contempt or disrespect toward his commanding officer, shall be punished, according to the nature of his offense, by the judgment of a court-martial.

ART. 7. Any officer or soldier who shall begin, excite, cause, or join in, any mutiny or sedition, in any troop or company in the service of the United States, or in any party, post, detachment, or guard, shall suffer death, or such other punishment as by a court-martial shall be inflicted.

ART. 8. Any officer, non-commissioned officer, or soldier, who, being present at any mutiny or sedition, does not use his utmost endeavor to suppress the same, or, coming to the knowledge of any intended mutiny, does not, without delay, give information thereof to his commanding officer, shall be punished by the sentence of a court-martial with death, or otherwise, according to the nature of his offense.

ART. 9. Any officer or soldier who shall strike his superior officer, or draw or lift up any weapon, or offer any violence against him, being in the execution of his office, on any pretense whatsoever, or shall disobey any lawful command of his superior officer, shall suffer death, or such other punishment as shall, according to the nature of his offense, be inflicted upon him by the sentence of a court-martial.

ART. 10. Every non-commissioned officer or soldier, who shall enlist himself in the service of the United States, shall, at the time of his so enlisting, or within six days afterward, have the Articles for the government of the armies of the United States read to him, and shall, by the officer who enlisted him, or by the commanding officer of the troop or company into which he was enlisted, be taken before the next justice of the peace, or chief magistrate of any city or town corporate, not being an officer of the army,* or where recourse cannot be had to the civil magistrate, before the judge advocate, and in his presence shall take the following oath or affirmation: "I, A. B., do solemnly swear, or affirm (as

---

* By Sect. 11 of Chap. 42 August 3, 1861, the oath of enlistment and re-enlistment may be administered by any commissioned officer of the army.

the case may be), that I will bear true allegiance to the United States of America, and that I will serve them honestly and faithfully against all their enemies or opposers whatsoever; and observe and obey the orders of the President of the United States, and the orders of the officers appointed over me, according to the Rules and Articles for the government of the armies of the United States." Which justice, magistrate, or judge advocate is to give to the officer a certificate, signifying that the man enlisted did take the said oath or affirmation.

ART. 11. After a non-commissioned officer or soldier shall have been duly enlisted and sworn, he shall not be dismissed the service without a discharge in writing; and no discharge granted to him shall be sufficient which is not signed by a field officer of the regiment to which he belongs, or commanding officer, where no field officer of the regiment is present; and no discharge shall be given to a non-commissioned officer or soldier before his term of service has expired, but by order of the President, the Secretary of War, the commanding officer of a department, or the sentence of a general court-martial; nor shall a commissioned officer be discharged the service but by order of the President of the United States, or by sentence of a general court-martial

ART. 12. Every colonel, or other officer commanding a regiment, troop, or company, and actually quartered with it, may give furloughs to non-commissioned officers or soldiers, in such numbers, and for so long a time, as he shall judge to be most consistent with the good of the service; and a captain, or other inferior officer, commanding a troop or company, or in any garrison, fort, or barrack of the United States (his field officer being absent), may give furloughs to non-commissioned officers or soldiers, for a time not exceeding twenty days in six months, but not to more than two persons to be absent at the same time, excepting some extraordinary occasion should require it.

ART. 13. At every muster, the commanding officer of each regiment, troop, or company, there present, shall give to the commissary of musters, or other officer who musters the said regiment, troop, or company, certificates signed by himself, signifying how long such officers, as shall not appear at the said muster, have been absent, and the reason of their absence. In like manner, the commanding officer of every troop or company shall give certificates, signifying the reasons of the absence of the non-commissioned officers and private soldiers; which reasons and time of absence shall be inserted in the muster-rolls, opposite the names of the respective absent officers and soldiers. The certificates shall, together with the muster-rolls, be remitted by the commissary of musters, or other officer mustering, to the Department of War, as speedily as the distance of the place will admit.

ART. 14. Every officer who shall be convicted before a general court-martial of having signed a false certificate relating to the absence of either officer or private soldier, or relative to his or their pay, shall be cashiered.

ART. 15. Every officer who shall knowingly make a false muster of man or horse, and every officer or commissary of musters who shall willingly sign, direct, or allow the signing of muster-rolls wherein such false muster is contained, shall, upon proof made thereof, by two witnesses, before a general court-martial, be cashiered, and shall be thereby utterly disabled to have or hold any office or employment in the service of the United States.

ART. 16. Any commissary of musters, or other officer, who shall be convicted of having taken money, or other thing, by way of gratification, on mustering any regiment, troop, or company, or on signing muster-rolls, shall be displaced from his office, and shall be thereby utterly disabled to have or hold any office or employment in the service of the United States.

ART. 17. Any officer who shall presume to muster a person as a soldier who is not a soldier, shall be deemed guilty of having made a false muster, and shall suffer accordingly.

ART. 18. Every officer who shall knowingly make a false return to the Department of War, or to any of his superior officers, authorized to call for such returns, of the state of the regiment, troop, or company, or garrison, under his command; or of the arms, ammunition, clothing, or other stores thereunto belonging, shall, on conviction thereof before a court-martial, be cashiered.

ART. 19. The commanding officer of every regiment, troop, or independent company, or garrison, of the United States, shall, in the begin ning of every month, remit, through the proper channels, to the Department of War, an exact return of the regiment, troop, independent company, or garrison, under his command, specifying the names of the officers then absent from their posts, with the reasons for and the time of their absence. And any officer who shall be convicted of having, through neglect or design, omitted sending such returns, shall be punished, according to the nature of his crime, by the judgment of a general court-martial.

ART. 20. All officers and soldiers who have received pay, or have been duly enlisted in the service of the United States, and shall be convicted of having deserted the same, shall suffer death, or such other punishment as, by sentence of a court-martial, shall be inflicted.*

---

* No officer or soldier in the army of the United States shall be subject to the punishment of death, for desertion in time of peace.—*Act 29th May*, 1830.

ART. 21. Any non-commissioned officer or soldier who shall, without leave from his commanding officer, absent himself from his troop, company, or detachment, shall, upon being convicted thereof, be punished according to the nature of his offense, at the discretion of a court-martial.

ART. 22. No non-commissioned officer or soldier shall enlist himself in any other regiment, troop, or company, without a regular discharge from the regiment, troop, or company in which he last served, on the penalty of being reputed a deserter, and suffering accordingly. And in case any officer shall knowingly receive and entertain such non-commissioned officer or soldier, or shall not, after his being discovered to be a deserter, immediately confine him, and give notice thereof to the corps in which he last served, the said officer shall, by a court-martial, be cashiered.

ART. 23. Any officer or soldier who shall be convicted of having advised or persuaded any other officer or soldier to desert the service of the United States, shall suffer death, or such other punishment as shall be inflicted upon him by the sentence of a court-martial.*

ART. 24. No officer or soldier shall use any reproachful or provoking speeches or gestures to another, upon pain, if an officer, of being put in arrest; if a soldier, confined, and of asking pardon of the party offended, in the presence of his commanding officer.

ART. 25. No officer or soldier shall send a challenge to another officer or soldier, to fight a duel, or accept a challenge if sent, upon pain, if a commissioned officer, of being cashiered; if a non-commissioned officer or soldier, of suffering corporeal punishment, at the discretion of a court-martial.

ART. 26. If any commissioned or non-commissioned officer commanding a guard shall knowingly or willingly suffer any person whatsoever to go forth to fight a duel, he shall be punished as a challenger; and all seconds, promoters, and carriers of challenges, in order to duels, shall be deemed principals, and be punished accordingly. And it shall be the duty of every officer commanding an army, regiment, company, post, or detachment, who is knowing to a challenge being given or accepted by any officer, non-commissioned officer, or soldier, under his command, or has reason to believe the same to be the case, immediately to arrest and bring to trial such offenders.

ART. 27. All officers, of what condition soever, have power to part and quell all quarrels, frays, and disorders, though the persons concerned should belong to another regiment, troop, or company; and either to order officers into arrest, or non-commissioned officers or soldiers into confinement, until their proper superior officers shall be acquainted there-

* See note on page 502.

with; and whosoever shall refuse to obey such officer (though of an inferior rank), or shall draw his sword upon him, shall be punished at the discretion of a general court-martial.

ART. 28. Any officer or soldier who shall upbraid another for refusing a challenge, shall himself be punished as a challenger; and all officers and soldiers are hereby discharged from any disgrace or opinion of disadvantage which might arise from their having refused to accept of challenges, as they will only have acted in obedience to the laws, and done their duty as good soldiers who subject themselves to discipline.

ART. 29. No sutler shall be permitted to sell any kind of liquors or victuals, or to keep their houses or shops open for the entertainment of soldiers, after nine at night, or before the beating of the reveille, or upon Sundays, during divine service or sermon, on the penalty of being dismissed from all future sutling.

ART. 30. All officers commanding in the field, forts, barracks, or garrisons of the United States, are hereby required to see that the persons permitted to suttle shall supply the soldiers with good and wholesome provisions, or other articles, at a reasonable price, as they shall be answerable for their neglect.

ART. 31. No officer commanding in any of the garrisons, forts, or barracks of the United States, shall exact exorbitant prices for houses or stalls, let out to sutlers, or connive at the like exactions in others; nor by his own authority, and for his private advantage, lay any duty or imposition upon, or be interested in, the sale of any victuals, liquors, or other necessaries of life brought into the garrison, fort, or barracks, for the use of the soldiers, on the penalty of being discharged from the service.

ART. 32. Every officer commanding in quarters, garrisons, or on the march, shall keep good order, and, to the utmost of his power, redress all abuses or disorders which may be committed by any officer or soldier under his command; if, upon complaint made to him of officers or soldiers beating or otherwise ill-treating any person, or disturbing fairs or markets, or of committing any kind of riots, to the disquieting of the citizens of the United States, he, the said commander, who shall refuse or omit to see justice done to the offender or offenders, and reparation made to the party or parties injured, as far as part of the offender's pay shall enable him or them, shall, upon proof thereof, be cashiered, or otherwise punished, as a general court-martial shall direct.

ART. 33. When any commissioned officer or soldier shall be accused of a capital crime, or of having used violence, or committed any offense against the person or property of any citizen of any of the United States, such as is punishable by the known laws of the land, the commanding officer and officers of every regiment, troop, or company, to which the person or persons so accused shall belong, are hereby required, upon application duly made by, or in behalf of, the party or parties injured, to use their utmost endeavors to deliver over such accused person or persons to the civil magistrate, and likewise to be aiding and assisting to the officers of justice in apprehending and securing the person or persons so accused, in order to bring him or them to trial. If any commanding officer or officers shall wilfully neglect, or shall refuse, upon the application aforesaid, to deliver over such accused person or persons to the civil magistrates, or to be aiding and assisting to the officers of justice in apprehending such person or persons, the officer or officers so offending shall be cashiered.

ART. 34. If any officer shall think himself wronged by his Colonel, or the commanding officer of the regiment, and shall, upon due application being made to him, be refused redress, he may complain to the General commanding in the State or Territory where such regiment shall be stationed, in order to obtain justice; who is hereby required to examine into said complaint, and take proper measures for redressing the wrong complained of, and transmit, as soon as possible, to the Department of War, a true state of such complaint, with the proceedings had thereon.

ART. 35. If any inferior officer or soldier shall think himself wronged by his Captain or other officer, he is to complain thereof to the commanding officer of the regiment, who is hereby required to summon a regimental court-martial, for the doing justice to the complainant; from which regimental court-martial either party may, if he thinks himself still aggrieved, appeal to a general court-martial. But if, upon a second hearing, the appeal shall appear vexatious and groundless, the person so appealing shall be punished at the discretion of the said court-martial.

ART. 36. Any commissioned officer, store-keeper, or commissary, who shall be convicted at a general court-martial of having sold, without a proper order for that purpose, embezzled, misapplied, or wilfully, or through neglect, suffered any of the provisions, forage, arms, clothing, ammunition, or other military stores belonging to the United States to be spoiled or damaged, shall, at his own expense, make good the loss or damage, and shall, moreover, forfeit all his pay, and be dismissed from the service.

ART. 37. Any non-commissioned officer or soldier who shall be convicted at a regimental court-martial of having sold, or designedly, or through neglect, wasted the ammunition delivered out to him, to be employed in the service of the United States, shall be punished at the discretion of such court.

ART. 38. Every non-commissioned officer or soldier who shall be convicted before a court-martial of having sold, lost, or spoiled, through neglect, his horse, arms, clothes, or accoutrements, shall undergo such weekly stoppages (not exceeding the half of his pay) as such court-martial shall judge sufficient, for repairing the loss or damage; and shall suffer confinement, or such other corporeal punishment as his crime shall deserve.

ART. 39. Every officer who shall be convicted before a court-martial of having embezzled or misapplied any money with which he may have been intrusted, for the payment of the men under his command, or for enlisting men into the service, or for other purposes, if a commissioned officer, shall be cashiered, and compelled to refund the money; if a non-commissioned officer, shall be reduced to the ranks, be put under stoppages until the money be made good, and suffer such corporeal punishment as such court-martial shall direct.

ART. 40. Every captain of a troop or company is charged with the arms, accoutrements, ammunition, clothing, or other warlike stores belonging to the troop or company under his command, which he is to be accountable for to his Colonel in case of their being lost, spoiled, or damaged, not by unavoidable accidents, or on actual service.

ART. 41. All non-commissioned officers and soldiers who shall be found one mile from the camp without leave, in writing, from their commanding officer, shall suffer such punishment as shall be inflicted upon them by the sentence of a court-martial.

ART. 42. No officer or soldier shall lie out of his quarters, garrison, or camp without leave from his superior officer, upon penalty of being punished according to the nature of his offense, by the sentence of a court-martial.

ART. 43. Every non-commissioned officer and soldier shall retire to his quarters or tent at the beating of the retreat; in default of which he shall be punished according to the nature of his offense.

ART. 44. No officer, non-commissioned officer, or soldier shall fail in repairing, at the time fixed, to the place of parade, of exercise, or other rendezvous appointed by his commanding officer, if not prevented by sickness or some other evident necessity, or shall go from the said place of rendezvous without leave from his commanding officer, before he shall be regularly dismissed or relieved, on the penalty of being punished, according to the nature of his offense, by the sentence of a court-martial.

ART. 45. Any commissioned officer who shall be found drunk on his guard, party, or other duty, shall be cashiered. Any non-commissioned officer or soldier so offending shall suffer such corporeal punishment as shall be inflicted by the sentence of a court-martial.

ART. 46. Any sentinel who shall be found sleeping upon his post, or shall leave it before he shall be regularly relieved, shall suffer death, or such other punishment as shall be inflicted by the sentence of a court-martial.

ART. 47. No soldier belonging to any regiment, troop, or company shall hire another to do his duty for him, or be excused from duty but in cases of sickness, disability, or leave of absence; and every such soldier found guilty of hiring his duty, as also the party so hired to do another's duty, shall be punished at the discretion of a regimental court-martial.

ART. 48. And every non-commissioned officer conniving at such hiring of duty aforesaid, shall be reduced; and every commissioned officer knowing and allowing such ill practices in the service, shall be punished by the judgment of a general court-martial.

ART. 49. Any officer belonging to the service of the United States, who, by discharging of firearms, drawing of swords, beating of drums, or by any other means whatsoever, shall occasion false alarms in camp, garrison, or quarters, shall suffer death, or such other punishment as shall be ordered by the sentence of a general court-martial.

ART. 50. Any officer or soldier who shall, without urgent necessity, or without the leave of his superior officer, quit his guard, platoon, or division, shall be punished, according to the nature of his offense, by the sentence of a court-martial.

ART. 51. No officer or soldier shall do violence to any person who brings provisions or other necessaries to the camp, garrison, or quarters of the forces of the United States, employed in any parts out of the said States, upon pain of death, or such other punishment as a court-martial shall direct.

ART. 52. Any officer or soldier who shall misbehave himself before the enemy, run away, or shamefully abandon any fort, post, or guard which he or they may be commanded to defend, or speak words inducing others to do the like, or shall cast away his arms and ammunition, or who shall quit his post or colors to plunder and pillage, every such offender, being duly convicted thereof, shall suffer death, or such other punishment as shall be ordered by the sentence of a general court-martial.

ART. 53. Any person belonging to the armies of the United States who shall make known the watchword to any person who is not entitled to receive it according to the rules and discipline of war, or shall presume to give a parole or watchword different from what he received, shall suffer death, or such other punishment as shall be ordered by the sentence of a general court-martial.

ART. 54. All officers and soldiers are to behave themselves orderly in quarters and on their march; and whoever shall commit any waste or spoil, either in walks of trees, parks, warrens, fish-ponds, houses, or gardens, corn-fields, inclosures of meadows, or shall maliciously destroy any property whatsoever belonging to the inhabitants of the United States, unless by order of the then commander-in-chief of the armies of the said States, shall (besides such penalties as they are liable to by law) be punished according to the nature and degree of the offense, by the judgment of a regimental or general court-martial.

ART. 55. Whosoever, belonging to the armies of the United States in foreign parts, shall force a safeguard, shall suffer death.

ART. 56. Whosoever shall relieve the enemy with money, victuals, or ammunition, or shall knowingly harbor or protect an enemy, shall suffer death, or such other punishment as shall be ordered by the sentence of a court-martial.

ART. 57. Whosoever shall be convicted of holding correspondence with, or giving intelligence to, the enemy, either directly or indirectly, shall suffer death, or such other punishment as shall be ordered by the sentence of a court-martial.

ART. 58. All public stores taken in the enemy's camp, towns, forts, or magazines, whether of artillery, ammunition, clothing, forage or provisions, shall be secured for the service of the United States; for the neglect of which the commanding officer is to be answerable.

ART. 59. If any commander of any garrison, fortress, or post shall be compelled, by the officers and soldiers under his command, to give up to the enemy, or to abandon it, the commissioned officers, non-commissioned officers, or soldiers who shall be convicted of having so offended, shall suffer death, or such other punishment as shall be inflicted upon them by the sentence of a court-martial.

ART. 60. All sutlers and retainers to the camp, and all persons whatsoever, serving with the armies of the United States in the field, though not enlisted soldiers, are to be subject to orders, according to the rules and discipline of war.

ART. 61. Officers having brevets or commissions of a prior date to those of the regiment in which they serve, may take place in courts-martial and on detachments, when composed of different corps, according to the ranks given them in their brevets or dates of their former commissions; but in the regiment, troop, or company to which such officers belong, they shall do duty and take rank both in courts-martial and on detachments which shall be composed of their own corps, according to the commissions by which they are mustered in the said corps.

ART. 62. If, upon marches, guards, or in quarters, different corps of the army shall happen to join, or do duty together, the officer highest in rank of the line of the army, marine corps, or militia, by commission, there on duty or in quarters, shall command the whole, and give orders for what is needful to the service, unless otherwise specially directed by the President of the United States, according to the nature of the case.

ART. 63. The functions of the engineers being generally confined to the most elevated branch of military science, they are not to assume, nor are they subject to be ordered on any duty beyond the line of their immediate profession, except by the special order of the President of the United States; but they are to receive every mark of respect to which their rank in the army may entitle them respectively, and are liable to be transferred, at the discretion of the President, from one corps to another, regard being paid to rank.

ART. 64. General courts-martial may consist of any number of commissioned officers, from five to thirteen, inclusively; but they shall not consist of less than thirteen where that number can be convened without manifest injury to the service.

ART. 65.* Any general officer commanding an army, or Colonel commanding a separate department, may appoint general courts-martial whenever necessary. But no sentence of a court-martial shall be carried into execution until after the whole proceedings shall have been laid before the officer ordering the same, or the officer commanding the troops for the time being; neither shall any sentence of a general court-martial, in the time of peace, extending to the loss of life, or the dismission of a commissioned officer, or which shall, either in time of peace or war, respect a general officer, be carried into execution, until after the whole proceedings shall have been transmitted to the Secretary of War, to be laid before the President of the United States for his confirmation or disapproval, and orders in the case. All other sentences may be confirmed and executed by the officer ordering the court to assemble, or the commanding officer for the time being, as the case may be.

ART. 66. Every officer commanding a regiment or corps may appoint, for his own regiment or corps, courts-martial, to consist of three commissioned officers, for the trial and punishment of offenses not capital, and

---

* Whenever a general officer commanding an army, or a colonel commanding a separate department, shall be the accuser or prosecutor of any officer in the army of the United States, under his command, the general court-martial for the trial of such officer shall be appointed by the President of the United States.

The proceedings and sentence of the said court shall be sent directly to the Secretary of War, to be by him laid before the President, for his confirmation or approval, or orders in the case.

So much of the sixty-fifth article of the first section of "An act for establishing rules and articles for the government of the armies of the United States," passed on the tenth of April, eighteen hundred and six, as is repugnant hereto, shall be, and the same is hereby, repealed.—*Act 29th May*, 1830, *Sects.* 1, 2, 3.

decide upon their sentences. For the same purpose, all officers commanding any of the garrisons, forts, barracks, or other places where the troops consist of different corps, may assemble courts-martial, to consist of three commissioned officers, and decide upon their sentences.

ART. 67. No garrison or regimental court-martial shall have the power to try capital cases or commissioned officers; neither shall they inflict a fine exceeding one month's pay, nor imprison, nor put to hard labor, any non-commissioned officer or soldier for a longer time than one month.

ART. 68. Whenever it may be found convenient and necessary to the public service, the officers of the marines shall be associated with the officers of the land forces, for the purpose of holding courts-martial, and trying offenders belonging to either; and, in such cases, the orders of the senior officer of either corps who may be present and duly authorized, shall be received and obeyed.

ART 69. The judge advocate, or some person deputed by him, or by the general, or officer commanding the army, detachment, or garrison, shall prosecute in the name of the United States, but shall so far consider himself as counsel for the prisoner, after the said prisoner shall have made his plea, as to object to any leading question to any of the witnesses, or any question to the prisoner, the answer to which might tend to criminate himself; and administer to each member of the court, before they proceed upon any trial, the following oath, which shall also be taken by all members of the regimental and garrison courts-martial:

"You, A. B., do swear that you will well and truly try and determine, according to evidence, the matter now before you, between the United States of America and the prisoner to be tried, and that you will duly administer justice, according to the provisions of 'An act establishing Rules and Articles for the government of the armies of the United States,' without partiality, favor, or affection; and if any doubt should arise, not explained by said Articles, according to your conscience, the best of your understanding, and the custom of war in like cases; and you do further swear that you will not divulge the sentence of the court until it shall be published by the proper authority; neither will you disclose or discover the vote or opinion of any particular member of the court-martial, unless required to give evidence thereof, as a witness, by a court of justice, in a due course of law. So help you God."

And as soon as the said oath shall have been administered to the respective members, the president of the court shall administer to the judge advocate, or person officiating as such, an oath in the following words:

"You, A. B., do swear, that you will not disclose or discover the vote or opinion of any particular member of the court-martial, unless required to give evidence thereof, as a witness, by a court of justice, in due course of law; nor divulge the sentence of the court to any but the proper authority, until it shall be duly disclosed by the same. So help you God."

ART. 70. When a prisoner, arraigned before a general court-martial shall, from obstinacy and deliberate design, stand mute, or answer foreign to the purpose, the court may proceed to trial and judgment as if the prisoner had regularly pleaded not guilty.

ART. 71. When a member shall be challenged by a prisoner, he must state his cause of challenge, of which the court shall, after due deliberation, determine the relevancy or validity, and decide accordingly; and no challenge to more than one member at a time shall be received by the court

ART. 72. All the members of a court-martial are to behave with decency and calmness; and in giving their votes are to begin with the youngest in commission.

ART. 73. All persons who give evidence before a court-martial are to be examined on oath or affirmation, in the following form:

"You swear, or affirm (as the case may be), the evidence you shall give in the cause now in hearing shall be the truth, the whole truth, and nothing but the truth. So help you God."

ART. 74. On the trials of cases not capital, before courts-martial, the deposition of witnesses, not in the line or staff of the army, may be taken before some justice of the peace, and read in evidence; provided the prosecutor and person accused are present at the taking the same, or are duly notified thereof.

ART. 75. No officer shall be tried but by a general court-martial, nor by officers of an inferior rank, if it can be avoided. Nor shall any pro ceedings of trials be carried on, excepting between the hours of eight in the morning and three in the afternoon, excepting in cases which, in the opinion of the officer appointing the court-martial, require immediate example.

ART. 76. No person whatsoever shall use any menacing words, signs, or gestures, in presence of a court-martial, or shall cause any disorder or riot, or disturb their proceedings, on the penalty of being punished at the discretion of the said court-martial.

ART. 77. Whenever any officer shall be charged with a crime, he shall be arrested and confined in his barracks, quarters, or tent, and deprived of his sword by the commanding officer. And any officer who shall leave his confinement before he shall be set at liberty by his commanding officer, or by a superior officer, shall be cashiered.

ART. 78. Non-commissioned officers and soldiers, charged with crimes, shall be confined until tried by a court-martial, or released by proper authority.

ART. 79. No officer or soldier who shall be put in arrest shall continue in confinement more than eight days, or until such time as a court-martial can be assembled.

ART. 80. No officer commanding a guard, or provost marshal, shall refuse to receive or keep any prisoner committed to his charge by an officer belonging to the forces of the United States; provided the officer committing shall, at the same time, deliver an account in writing, signed by himself, of the crime with which the said prisoner is charged.

ART. 81. No officer commanding a guard, or provost marshal, shall presume to release any person committed to his charge without proper authority for so doing, nor shall he suffer any person to escape, on the penalty of being punished for it by the sentence of a court-martial.

ART. 82. Every officer or provost marshal, to whose charge prisoners shall be committed, shall, within twenty-four hours after such commitment, or as soon as he shall be relieved from his guard, make report in writing, to the commanding officer, of their names, their crimes, and the names of the officers who committed them, on the penalty of being punished for disobedience or neglect, at the discretion of a court-martial.

ART. 83. Any commissioned officer convicted before a general court-martial of conduct unbecoming an officer and a gentleman, shall be dismissed the service.

ART. 84. In cases where a court-martial may think it proper to sentence a commissioned officer to be suspended from command, they shall have power also to suspend his pay and emoluments for the same time, according to the nature and heinousness of the offense.

ART. 85. In all cases where a commissioned officer is cashiered for cowardice or fraud, it shall be added in the sentence, that the crime, name, and place of abode, and punishment of the delinquent, be published in the newspapers in and about the camp, and of the particular State from which the offender came, or where he usually resides; after which it shall be deemed scandalous for an officer to associate with him.

ART. 86. The commanding officer of any post or detachment, in which there shall not be a number of officers adequate to form a general court-martial, shall, in cases which require the cognizance of such a court, report to the commanding officer of the department, who shall order a court to be assembled at the nearest post or department, and the party accused, with necessary witnesses, to be transported to the place where the said court shall be assembled.

ART. 87.* No person shall be sentenced to suffer death but by the

---

* So much of these rules and articles as authorizes the infliction of corporeal punishment by stripes or lashes, was specially repealed by Act of 16th May, 1812. By Act of 2d

concurrence of two-thirds of the members of a general court-martial, nor except in the cases herein expressly mentioned; *nor shall more than fifty lashes be inflicted on any offender, at the discretion of a court-martial;* and no officer, non-commissioned officer, soldier, or follower of the army, shall be tried a second time for the same offense.

ART. 88. No person shall be liable to be tried and punished by a general court-martial for any offense which shall appear to have been committed more than two years before the issuing of the order for such trial, unless the person, by reason of having absented himself, or some other manifest impediment, shall not have been amenable to justice within that period.

ART. 89. Every officer authorized to order a general court-martial shall have power to pardon or mitigate any punishment ordered by such court, except the sentence of death, or of cashiering an officer; which, in the cases where he has authority (by Article 65) to carry them into execution, he may suspend, until the pleasure of the President of the United States can be known; which suspension, together with copies of the proceedings of the court-martial, the said officer shall immediately transmit to the President for his determination. And the colonel or commanding officer of the regiment or garrison where any regimental or garrison court-martial shall be held, may pardon or mitigate any punishment ordered by such court to be inflicted.

ART. 90. Every judge advocate, or person officiating as such, at any general court-martial, shall transmit, with as much expedition as the opportunity of time and distance of place can admit, the original proceedings and sentence of such court-martial to the Secretary of War; which said original proceedings and sentence shall be carefully kept and preserved in the office of said Secretary, to the end that the persons entitled thereto may be enabled, upon application to the said office, to obtain copies thereof.

The party tried by any general court-martial shall, upon demand thereof, made by himself, or by any person or persons in his behalf, be entitled to a copy of the sentence and proceedings of such court-martial.

ART. 91. In cases where the general, or commanding officer may order a court of inquiry to examine into the nature of any transaction, accusation, or imputation against any officer or soldier, the said court shall consist of one or more officers, not exceeding three, and a judge advocate, or other suitable person, as a recorder, to reduce the proceedings and

March, 1853, the repealing act was repealed, so far as it applied to the crime of desertion, which, of course, revived the punishment by lashes for that offense. Flogging was totally abolished by Sec. 3 of Chap. 54, 5 August, 1861.

evidence to writing; all of whom shall be sworn to the faithful performance of their duty. This court shall have the same power to summon witnesses as a court-martial, and to examine them on oath. But they shall not give their opinion on the merits of the case, excepting they shall be thereto specially required. The parties accused shall also be permitted to cross-examine and interrogate the witnesses, so as to investigate fully the circumstances in the question.

ART. 92. The proceedings of a court of inquiry must be authenticated by the signature of the recorder and the president, and delivered to the commanding officer, and the said proceedings may be admitted as evidence by a court-martial, in cases not capital, or extending to the dismission of an officer, provided that the circumstances are such that oral testimony cannot be obtained. But as courts of inquiry may be perverted to dishonorable purposes, and may be considered as engines of destruction to military merit, in the hands of weak and envious commandants, they are hereby prohibited, unless directed by the President of the United States, or demanded by the accused.

ART. 93. The judge advocate or recorder shall administer to the members the following oath:

" You shall well and truly examine and inquire, according to your evidence, into the matter now before you, without partiality, favor, affection, prejudice, or hope of reward. So help you God."

After which the president shall administer to the judge advocate or recorder the following oath:

" You, A. B., do swear that you will, according to your best abilities, accurately and impartially record the proceedings of the court, and the evidence to be given in the case in hearing. So help you God."

The witnesses shall take the same oath as witnesses sworn before a court-martial.

ART. 94. When any commissioned officer shall die or be killed in the service of the United States, the major of the regiment, or the officer doing the major's duty in his absence, or in any post or garrison, the second officer in command, or the assistant military agent, shall immediately secure all his effects or equipage, then in camp or quarters, and shall make an inventory thereof, and forthwith transmit the same to the office of the Department of War, to the end that his executors or administrators may receive the same.

ART. 95. When any non-commissioned officer or soldier shall die, or be killed in the service of the United States, the then commanding officer of the troop or company shall, in the presence of two other commissioned officers, take an account of what effects he died possessed of, above his arms and accoutrements, and transmit the same to the office of the Department of War, which said effects are to be accounted for, and paid to the representatives of such deceased non-commissioned officer or soldier. And in case any of the officers, so authorized to take care of the effects of deceased officers and soldiers, should, before they have accounted to their representatives for the same, have occasion to leave the regiment or post, by preferment or otherwise, they shall, before they be permitted to quit the same, deposit in the hands of the commanding officer, or of the assistant military agent, all the effects of such deceased non-commissioned officers and soldiers, in order that the same may be secured for, and paid to, their respective representatives.

Art. 96. All officers, conductors, gunners, matrosses, drivers, or other persons whatsoever, receiving pay or hire in the service of the artillery, or corps of engineers of the United States, shall be governed by the aforesaid Rules and Articles, and shall be subject to be tried by courts-martial, in like manner with the officers and soldiers of the other troops in the service of the United States.

Art. 97. The officers and soldiers of any troops, whether militia or others, being mustered and in pay of the United States, shall, at all times and in all places, when joined, or acting in conjunction with the regular forces of the United States, be governed by these rules and articles of war, and shall be subject to be tried by courts-martial, in like manner with the officers and soldiers in the regular forces; save only that such courts-martial shall be composed entirely of militia officers.

Art. 98. All officers serving by commission from the authority of any particular State, shall, on all detachments, courts-martial, or other duty, wherein they may be employed in conjunction with the regular forces of the United States, take rank next after all officers of the like grade in said regular forces, notwithstanding the commissions of such militia or State officers may be elder than the commissions of the officers of the regular forces of the United States.

Art. 99. All crimes not capital, and all disorders and neglects which officers and soldiers may be guilty of, to the prejudice of good order and military discipline, though not mentioned in the foregoing articles of war, are to be taken cognizance of by a general or regimental court-martial, according to the nature and degree of the offense, and be punished at their discretion.

Art. 100. The President of the United States shall have power to prescribe the uniform of the army.

Art. 101. The foregoing articles are to be read and published, once in every six months, to every garrison, regiment, troop, or company, mustered, or to be mustered, in the service of the United States, and are to be duly observed and obeyed by all officers and soldiers who are, or shall be, in said service.

SEC. 2. *And be it further enacted,* That in time of war, all persons not citizens of, or owing allegiance to, the United States of America, who shall be found lurking as spies in or about the fortifications or encampments of the armies of the United States, or any of them, shall suffer death, according to the law and usage of nations, by sentence of a general court-martial.

SEC. 3. *And be it further enacted,* That the rules and regulations by which the armies of the United States have heretofore been governed, and the resolves of Congress thereunto annexed, and respecting the same, shall henceforth be void and of no effect, except so far as may relate to any transactions under them prior to the promulgation of this act, at the several posts and garrisons respective'y, occupied by any part of the army of the United States.   [APPROVED, April 10, 1806.]

EXTRACTS FROM ACTS OF CONGRESS.

1. IF any non-commissioned officer, musician, or private shall desert the service of the United States, he shall, in addition to the penalties mentioned in the Rules and Articles of War, be liable to serve for and during such a period as shall, with the time he may have served previous to his desertion, amount to the full term of his enlistment; and such soldier shall and may be tried by a court-martial, and punished, although the term of his enlistment may have elapsed previous to his being apprehended or tried.—*Act 16th March*, 1802, *Sec.* 18.

2. "That if any person shall sell, exchange, or give, barter or dispose of, any spirituous liquor or wine to an Indian (in the Indian country), such person shall forfeit and pay the sum of five hundred dollars; and if any person shall introduce, or attempt to introduce, any spirituous liquor or wine into the Indian country, except such supplies as shall be necessary for the officers of the United States and troops of the service, under the direction of the War Department, such person shall forfeit and pay a sum not exceeding three hundred dollars; and if any superintendent of Indian affairs, Indian agent, or sub-agent, or commanding officer of a military post, has reason to suspect, or is informed, that any white person or Indian is about to introduce, or has introduced, any spirituous liquor or wine into the Indian country, in violation of the provisions of this section, it shall be lawful for such superintendent, Indian agent, or sub-agent, or military officer, agreeably to such regulations as may be established by the President of the United States, to cause the boats, stores, packages, and places of deposit of such person to be searched, and if any such spirituous liquor or wine is found, the goods, boats, packages, and peltries of such persons shall be seized and delivered to the proper officer, and shall be proceeded against by libel, in the proper court, and forfeited, one half to the use of the informer, and the other half to the use of the United States; and if such person is a trader, his license shall be revoked and his bond put in suit. And it shall moreover be lawful for any person in the service of the United States, or for any Indian, to take and destroy any ardent spirits or wine found in the Indian country, excepting military supplies as mentioned in this section." —*Act 30th June*, 1834, *Sec.* 20.

3. "That if any person whatever shall, within the limits of the Indian country, set up or continue any distillery for manufacturing ardent spirits, he shall forfeit and pay a penalty of one thousand dollars, and it shall be the duty of the superintendent of Indian affairs, Indian agent, or sub-agent, within the limits of whose agency the same shall be set up or continued, forthwith to destroy and break up the same; and it shall be lawful to employ the military force of the United States in executing that duty."—*Act* 30*th June,* 1834, *Sec.* 21.

4. "That the twentieth section of the 'Act to regulate trade and intercourse with the Indian tribes, and to preserve peace on the frontiers,' approved June thirtieth, eighteen hundred and thirty-four, be and the same is hereby so amended, that, in addition to the fines thereby imposed, any person who shall sell, exchange, or barter, give, or dispose of, any spirituous liquor or wine to an Indian, in the Indian country, or who shall introduce, or attempt to introduce, any spirituous liquor or wine into the Indian country, except such supplies as may be necessary for the officers of the United States and the troops of the service, under the direction of the War Department, such person, on conviction thereof, before the proper district court of the United States, shall in the former case be subject to imprisonment for a period not exceeding two years, and in the latter case not exceeding one year, as shall be prescribed by the court, according to the extent and criminality of the offense. And in all prosecutions arising under this section, and under the twentieth section of the act to regulate trade and intercourse with the Indian tribes, and preserve peace on the frontiers, approved June thirtieth, eighteen hundred and thirty-four, to which this is an amendment, Indians shall be competent witnesses."—*Act* 3*d March,* 1847, *Sec.* 2.

5. "That no annuities, or moneys, or goods shall be paid or distributed to the Indians while they are under the influence of any description of intoxicating liquor; nor while there are good and sufficient reasons for the officers or agents, whose duty it may be to make such payments or distributions, for believing that there is any species of intoxicating liquor within convenient reach of the Indians; nor until the chiefs and head men of the tribe shall have pledged themselves to use all their influence, and to make all proper exertions to prevent the introduction and sale of such liquor in their country."—*Act* 3*d March,* 1847, *Sec.* 3.

AN ACT to authorize the employment of volunteers to aid in enforcing the laws and protecting public property.

WHEREAS, certain of the forts, arsenals, custom-houses, navy yards, and other property of the United States have been seized, and other viola tions of law have been committed and are threatened by organized bodies of men in several of the States, and a conspiracy has been entered into to overthrow the government of the United States: Therefore,

Be it enacted by the Senate and House of Representatives of the United States of America in Congress assembled, That the President be and he is hereby authorized to accept the services of volunteers, either as cavalry, infantry, or artillery, in such numbers,* not exceeding five hundred thousand, as he may deem necessary, for the purpose of repelling invasion, suppressing insurrection, enforcing the laws, and preserving and protecting the public property : *Provided,* That the services of the volunteers shall be for such time as the President may direct, not exceeding three years nor less than six months, and they shall be disbanded at the end of the war. And all provisions of law applicable to three years' volunteers shall apply to two years' volunteers, and to all volunteers who have been, or may be, accepted into the service of the United States for a period not less than six months, in the same manner as if such volunteers were specially named. Before receiving into service any number of volunteers exceeding those now called for and accepted, the President shall, from time to time, issue his proclamation, stating the number desired, either as cavalry, infantry, or artillery, and the States from which they are to be furnished, having reference, in any such requisition, to the number then in service from the several States, and to the exigencies of the service at the time, and equalizing, as far as practicable, the number furnished by the several States, according to Federal population.

Sec. 2. *And be it further enacted,* That the said volunteers shall be subject to the rules and regulations governing the army of the United States, and that they shall be formed, by the President, into regiments of infantry, with the exception of such numbers for cavalry and artillery, as he may direct, not to exceed the proportion of one company of each of those arms to every regiment of infantry, and to be organized as in the regular service. Each regiment of infantry shall have one colonel, one lieutenant-colonel, one major, one adjutant (a lieutenant), one quartermaster (a lieutenant), one surgeon and one assistant surgeon, one sergeant major, one regimental quartermaster sergeant, one regimental commissary sergeant, one hospital steward, two principal musicians, and twenty four musicians for a band ; and shall be composed of ten companies, each company to consist of one captain, one first lieutenant, one second lieutenant, one first sergeant, four sergeants, eight corporals, two musicians, one wagoner, and from sixty-four to eighty-two privates.

---

* As the exigencies of the service may, in his opinion, demand, not exceeding 500,000, by Sec. 1 of Chap. 17, July 25, 1861.

SEC. 3. *And be it further enacted,* That these forces, when accepted as herein authorized, shall be organized into divisions of three or more brigades each; and each division shall have a major-general, three aides-de-camp, and one assistant adjutant-general with the rank of major. Each brigade shall be composed of four or more regiments, and shall have one brigadier-general, two aides-de-camp, one assistant adjutant-general with the rank of captain, one surgeon, one assistant quartermaster, and one commissary of subsistence.

SEC. 4. *And be it further enacted,* That the President shall be authorized to appoint, by and with the advice and consent of the Senate, for the command of the forces provided for in this act, *a number of major-generals, not exceeding six, and a number of brigadier-generals, not exceeding eighteen,** and the other division and brigade officers required for the organization of these forces, except the aides-de-camp, who shall be selected by their respective generals from the officers of the army or volunteer corps: *Provided,* That the President may select the major generals and brigadier-generals provided for in this act from the line or staff of the regular army, and the officers so selected shall be permitted to retain their rank therein. The Governors of the States furnishing volunteers under this act, shall commission the field, staff, and company officers requisite for the said volunteers; but in cases where the State authorities refuse or omit to furnish volunteers at the call or on the proclamation of the President, and volunteers from such States offer their services under such call or proclamation, the President shall have power to accept such services, and to commission the proper field, staff, and company officers.

SEC. 5. *And be it further enacted,* That the officers, non-commissioned officers, and privates, organized as above set forth, shall, in all respects, be placed on the footing, as to pay and allowances, of similar corps of the regular army: *Provided,* That the allowances of non-commissioned officers and privates for clothing, when not furnished in kind, shall be three dollars and fifty cents per month, and that each company officer, non-commissioned officer, private, musician, and artificer of cavalry shall furnish his own horse and horse equipments, and shall receive forty cents per day for their use and risk, except that in case the horse shall become disabled, or shall die, the allowance shall cease until the disability be removed or another horse be supplied. Every volunteer non-commissioned officer, private, musician, and artificer, who enters the service of the United States under this act, shall be paid at the rate of fifty cents in lieu of subsistence, and if a cavalry volunteer, twenty-five cents additional, in

---

* "Such number of major-generals and of brigadier-generals as may, in his judgment, be required for their organization."—*Act July* 25, 1861.

lieu of forage, for every twenty miles of travel from his place of enrolment to the place of muster—the distance to be measured by the shortest usually traveled route; and when honorably discharged, an allowance at the same rate, from the place of his discharge to his place of enrolment, and, in addition thereto, if he shall have served for a period of two years, or during the war, if sooner ended, the sum of one hundred dollars: *Provided*, That such of the companies of cavalry herein provided for, as may require it, may be furnished with horses and horse equipments in the same manner as in the United States Army.

Sec. 6. *And be it further enacted*, That any volunteer who may be received into the service of the United States under this act, and who may be wounded or otherwise disabled in the service, shall be entitled to the benefits which have been or may be conferred on persons disabled in the regular service; and the widow, if there be one, and if not, the legal heirs of such as die, or may be killed in service, in addition to all arrears of pay and allowances, shall receive the sum of one hundred dollars.

Sec. 7. *And be it further enacted*, That the bands of the regiments of infantry and of the regiments of cavalry shall be paid as follows: one-fourth of each shall receive the pay and allowances of sergeants of engineer soldiers; one-fourth, those of corporals of engineer soldiers; and the remaining half, those of privates of engineer soldiers of the first class; and the leaders of the band shall receive the same pay and emoluments as second lieutenants of infantry.

Sec. 8. *And be it further enacted*, That the wagoners and saddlers shall receive the pay and allowances of corporals of cavalry. The regimental commissary sergeant shall receive the pay and allowances of regimental sergeant major, and the regimental* quartermaster sergeant shall receive the pay and allowances of a sergeant of cavalry.

Sec. 9. *And be it further enacted*, That there shall be allowed to each regiment one chaplain, who shall be appointed by the regimental commander on the vote of the field officers and company commanders on duty with the regiment at the time the appointment shall be made. The chaplain so appointed must be a regular ordained minister of a Christian denomination, and shall receive the pay and allowances of a captain of cavalry, and shall be required to report to the colonel commanding the regiment to which he is attached, at the end of each quarter, the moral and religious condition of the regiment, and such suggestions as may conduce to the social happiness and moral improvement of the troops.

Sec. 10. *And be it further enacted*, That the general commanding a separate department or a detached army is hereby authorized to appoint a military board or commission of not less than three nor more than five officers, whose duty it shall be to examine the capacity, qualifications,

---

* The word "regimental" is erroneously in erted.

propriety of conduct, and efficiency of any commissioned officer of volunteers within his department or army, who may be reported to the board or commission, and upon such report, if adverse to such officer, and if approved by the President of the United States, the commission of such officer shall be vacated: *Provided always,* That no officer shall be eligible to sit on such board or commission whose rank or promotion would in any way be affected by its proceedings, and two members at least, if practicable, shall be of equal rank of the officer being examined. *And when vacancies occur in any of the companies of volunteers, an election shall be called by the colonel of the regiment to fill such vacancies, and the men of each company shall vote in their respective companies for all officers as high as captain, and vacancies above captain shall be filled by the votes of the commissioned officers of the regiment, and all officers so elected shall be commissioned by the respective Governors of the States, or by the President of the United States.**

SEC. 11. *And be it further enacted,* That all letters written by soldiers in the service of the United States may be transmitted through the mails without pre-payment of postage, under such regulations as the Post-Office Department may prescribe, the postage thereon to be paid by the recipients.

SEC. 12. *And be it further enacted,* That the Secretary of War be, and he is hereby, authorized and directed to introduce among the volunteer forces in the service of the United States, the system of allotment tickets now used in the navy, or some equivalent system, by which the family of the volunteer may draw such portions of his pay as he may request.

[APPROVED July 22, 1861.]

AN ACT in addition to the "Act to authorize the employment of volunteers to aid in enforcing the laws and protecting public property," approved July twenty-second, eighteen hundred and sixty-one.

Be it enacted by the Senate and House of Representatives of the United States of America in Congress assembled, That the President of the United States be, and he is hereby, authorized to accept the services of volunteers, either as cavalry, infantry, or artillery, in such numbers as the exigencies of the public service may, in his opinion, demand, to be organized as authorized by the act of the twenty-second of July, eighteen hundred and sixty-one: *Provided,* That the number of troops hereby authorized shall not exceed five hundred thousand.

---

* All in italics repealed by Sect. 3 of Chapter 52, August 6, 1861.

SEC. 2. *And be it further enacted*, That the volunteers authorized by this act shall be armed as the President may direct; they shall be subject to the rules and articles of war, and shall be upon the footing, in all respects, with similar corps of the United States Army, and shall be mustered into the service for " during the war."

SEC. 3. *And be it further enacted*, That the President shall be authorized to appoint, by and with the advice and consent of the Senate, for the command of the volunteer forces, such number of major-generals and of brigadier-generals as may, in his judgment, be required for their organization.

[APPROVED July 25, 1861.]

TABLE OF PAY, SUBSISTENCE, FORAGE, ETC., ALLOWED BY LAW TO THE OFFICERS OF THE ARMY.

RANK AND CLASSIFICATION OF OFFICERS.	PAY. Per month.	SUBSISTENCE. 30 cents for each ration. Act Feb. 21, 1857, sec. 1.		FORAGE. $8 per mo. for each horse. Act Apr. 24, 1816, sec. 12.		SERVANTS. Pay, subsistence, and clothing of a private soldier, Act April 24, 1816, sec. 12.		Total monthly pay.
		Number of rations per day.	Monthly commutation value.	Number of horses allowed.	Monthly commutation value.	Number of servants allowed.	Monthly commutation value.	
	$ c.		$ c.		$ c.		$ c.	$ c.
General Officers.								
Lieutenant-General...........................	270 00	40	360 00	....	50 00	4	98 00	778 00
Aides-de-camp and Military Secretary to Lieutenant-General, *each*...................	80 00	5	45 00	3	24 00	2	49 00	198 00
Major-General...........................	220 00	15	135 00	3	24 00	4	98 00	477 00
Senior Aide-de-camp to General-in-Chief....	80 00	4	36 00	3	24 00	2	49 00	180 00
Aide-de-camp, in addition to pay, &c. of Lt..	24 00	....	....	1	8 00	....	....	32 00
Brigadier-General..........................	124 00	12	108 00	3	24 00	3	73 50	329 50
Aide-de-camp, in addition to pay, &c. of Lt.*	20 00	3	....	1	8 00	....	....	19 00
Adjutant-General's Department.								
Adjutant-General—Colonel..................	110 00	6	54 00	3	24 00	2	49 00	237 00
Assistant Adjutant-General—Lieut. Col.....	95 00	5	45 00	3	24 00	2	49 00	213 00
Assistant Adjutant-General—Major...........	80 00	4	36 00	3	24 00	2	49 00	189 00
Assistant Adjutant-General—Captain........	70 00	4	36 00	1	8 00	1	24 50	138 50
Judge-Advocate—Major..........................	80 00	4	36 00	3	24 00	2	49 00	189 00
Inspector-General's Department.								
Inspector-General—Colonel..................	110 00	6	54 00	3	24 00	2	49 00	237 00
Signal Department.								
Signal Officer—Major..........................	80 00	4	36 00	3	24 00	2	49 00	189 00
Quartermaster's Department.								
Quartermaster-General—Brig. General......	124 00	12	108 00	3	24 00	3	73 50	329 50
Assistant Quartermaster-General—Col.....	110 00	6	54 00	3	24 00	2	49 00	237 00
Deputy Quartermaster-General—Lt. Col.....	95 00	5	45 00	3	24 00	2	49 00	213 00
Quartermaster—Major..........................	80 00	4	36 00	3	24 00	2	49 00	189 00
Assistant Quartermaster—Captain...........	7)00	4	36 00	1	8 00	1	24 50	138 50
Subsistence Department.								
Commissary-General of Subsistence—Col...	110 00	6	54 00	3	24 00	2	49 00	237 00
Assistant Commissary-General of Subsistence—Lieut. Colonel..........................	95 00	5	45 00	3	24 00	2	49 00	213 00
Commissary of Subsistence—Major...........	80 00	4	36 00	3	24 00	2	49 00	189 00
Commissary of Subsistence—Captain........	70 00	4	36 00	1	8 00	1	24 50	138 50
Assistant Commissary of Subsistence, in addition to pay, &c. of Lieut.*............	20 00	3	....	....	....	....	....	11 00
Medical Department.								
Surgeon-General, $2740 per annum...........	....	....	....	....	....	....	....	228 33
Surgeons of ten years' service	80 00	8	72 00	3	24 00	2	49 00	225 00
Surgeons of less than ten years' service....	80 00	4	36 00	3	24 00	2	49 00	189 00
Assistant Surgeons of ten years' service....	70 00	8	72 00	1	8 00	1	24 50	174 50
Assistant Surgeons of five years' service....	70 00	4	36 00	1	8 00	1	24 50	138 50
Asst. Surg. of less than five years' service..	53 33	4	36 00	1	8 00	1	24 50	121 83

* Entitled to only 3 rations per day as Lieutenants.

Table of Pay, Forage, &c.

TABLE OF PAY, SUBSISTENCE, FORAGE, &c.—Continued.

Rank and Classification of Officers.	Pay. Per month	Subsistence. 30 cents for each ration. Act Feb. 21, 1857, sec. 1. Number of rations per day.	Monthly commutation value.	Forage. $8 per mo. for each horse. Act Apr. 24, 1816, sec. 12. Number of horses allowed.	Monthly commutation value.	Servants. Pay, subsistence, and clothing of a private soldier. Act April 24, 1816, sec. 12. Number of servants allowed.	Monthly commutation value.	Total monthly pay.
Pay Department.	$ c.		$ c.		$ c.		$ c.	$ c.
Paymaster-General, $2740 per annum........	....	....	....	....	....	....	....	228 83
Deputy Paymaster-General	95 00	5	45 00	3	24 00	2	49 00	213 00
Paymaster..	80 00	4	36 00	3	24 00	2	49 00	189 00
Officers of the Corps of Engineers, Corps of Topographical Engineers, and Ordnance Department.								
Colonel...	110 00	6	54 00	3	24 00	2	49 00	237 00
Lieutenant-Colonel...............................	95 00	5	45 00	3	24 00	2	49 00	213 00
Major..	80 00	4	36 00	3	24 00	2	49 00	189 00
Captain	70 00	4	36 00	1	8 00	1	24 50	138 50
First Lieutenant	53 33	4	36 00	1	8 00	1	24 50	121 83
Second Lieutenant................................	53 33	4	36 00	1	8 00	1	24 50	121 83
Brevet Second Lieutenant.......................	53 33	4	36 00	1	8 00	1	24 50	121 83
Officers of Mounted Dragoons, Cavalry, Riflemen, and Light Artillery.								
Colonel...	110 00	6	54 00	3	24 00	2	49 00	237 00
Lieutenant-Colonel	95 00	5	45 00	3	24 00	2	49 00	213 00
Major..	80 00	4	36 00	3	24 00	2	49 00	189 00
Captain..	70 00	4	36 00	2	16 00	1	24 50	146 50
First Lieutenant..................................	53 33	4	36 00	2	16 00	1	24 50	129 83
Second Lieutenant................................	53 33	4	36 00	2	16 00	1	24 50	129 83
Brevet Second Lieutenant.......................	53 33	4	36 00	2	16 00	1	24 50	129 83
Adjutant { in addition to pay of } Reg'l Qr. Master { Lieutenant............ }	10 00	....	....	....	....	....	....	10 00
Officers of Artillery and Infantry.								
Colonel...	95 00	6	54 00	3	24 00	2	49 00	222 00
Lieutenant-Colonel	80 00	5	45 00	3	24 00	2	49 00	198 00
Major..	70 00	4	36 00	3	24 00	2	49 00	179 00
Captain	60 00	4	36 00	....	....	1	24 50	120 50
First Lieutenant	50 00	4	36 00	....	....	1	24 50	110 50
Second Lieutenant................................	45 00	4	36 00	....	....	1	24 50	105 50
Brevet Second Lieutenant.......................	45 00	4	36 00	....	....	1	24 50	105 50
Adjutant, in addition to pay, &c. of Lieut...	10 00	....	....	1	8 00	....	....	18 00
Reg'l Quartermaster, in addition to pay, } &c. of Lieutenant........................ }	10 00	....	....	2	16 00	....	....	26 00

1. The officer in command of a company is allowed $10 per month for the responsibility of clothing, arms, and accoutrements.—Act March 2, 1827, Sec. 2.

2. Every commissioned officer below the rank of Brigadier-General is entitled to one additional ration per day for every five years' service.

3. Paymaster's clerks, $700 per annum, and 75 cents per day when actually on duty.

4. Chaplains in army, $10 to $60 per month and four rations a day.

5. Chaplains in volunteers, same as captain of cavalry.

MONTHLY PAY OF NON-COMMISSIONED OFFICERS, PRIVATES, &c.

CAVALRY.

Sergeant-Major	$21 00	Corporal	$14 00
Quartermaster-Sergeant	21 00	Bugler	13 00
Chief Bugler	21 00	Farrier and Blacksmith	15 00
First Sergeant	20 00	Private	13 00
Sergeant	17 00		

ORDNANCE.

Master Armorer, Master Carriage-Maker, or Master Blacksmith	$34 00	Artificer	$17 00
		Laborer	13 00
Armorer, Carriage-Maker, or Blacksmith	20 00		

ARTILLERY AND INFANTRY.

Sergeant-Major	$21 00	Artificer, artillery	$15 00
Quartermaster-Sergeant	17 00	Private	13 00
First Sergeant	20 00	Principal Musician	21 00
Sergeant	17 00	Musician	12 00
Corporal	13 00		

SAPPERS, MINERS, AND PONTONIERS.

Sergeant	$34 00	Private, second class	$13 00
Corporal	20 00	Musician	12 00
Private, first class	17 00		

Medical Cadets	$30 00	Matron	$6 00
Hospital Steward, first class	22 00	Female Nurses, 40 cents per day and one ration.
" " second class	20 00	

Two dollars per month is to be retained from the pay of each private soldier until the expiration of his term of enlistment, and 12½ cents per month from all enlisted men, for the support of the "Soldier's Home."

All enlisted men are entitled to $2 per month additional pay for re-enlisting, and $1 per month for each subsequent period of five years' service, provided they re-enlist within one month after the expiration of their term.

Volunteers and militia, when called into service of the United States, are entitled to the same pay, allowances, &c., as regulars.

INDEX.

Officer of the day visits guards, when, 62.
  prevented from joining post by sickness, 33.
  recruiting, form of receipt of, 145.
  regimental recruiting, duties of, 141.
  registered as a deserter, when, 12.
  removal of, from station assigned to him, 67.
  restored, account of, 341.
  senior medical, duties of, 282–285.
    records kept by, 284.
  who succeeds to command, duties of, 11.
Officers, account of stoppages against, 345.
  and men in ordnance service, mileage for, 391.
  appointment of, 11.
  bear cost of their own transportation, when, 165.
  caution to, 19.
  cavalry, duties of, during march, 97.
  commanding, powers of, to arrest, 38.
    to examine stores, 35.
  command not assumed by what, 10.
  commissioned, appointment and promotion of, 11.
  commissioned by a State, 10.
    by the United States, 10.
    forage caps for, 481.
    one, always in a company, 31.
    two, in a garrisoned post, 31.
    uniform coat for, 476.
  company, in arrest on a march, 39.
  deceased, 28.
  disbursing, duties of, 147.
  disposition of, in camp of infantry, 66.
  dress allowed to, 494.
  duties of, during battle, 106.
  duties of mustering, 496.
    recruiting, 130.
  entitled to brevet pay, when, 342.
  entitled to pay, when, 341.
  epaulettes for, 484.
  exchange or transfer of, 12.
  field and company, present at dress parade, 53.
  field, of the trenches, duties of, 114.
    under arrest on a march, 39.
  form of report of, whose quarters, &c., are commuted, Quartermaster's Department, 180.
  general, trimmings for uniform of, 480.
  having brevets, duties of, 10.
  in camp, when permitted to occupy a vacant house, 76.

Officers, inexperienced, on guard as what, 62.
  in the field not entitled to commutation, 162.
  inventories of effects of deceased, 28.
  leave of absence, granted, when, 12.
  leaves of absence to, 31.
  light offenses of, how treated, 38.
  medical, duties of, 284, 286.
  military, forbidden to make contracts for the service, 149.
  named on rosters, how, 83.
  non-commissioned, 18.
    and privates, Quartermaster's Department, form of roll of, 176.
    board for examination of, 18.
    certificates of, 19.
    disabled, 30.
    furnished with certificate of rank, 19.
    in arrest on a march, 39.
    in command of squads, 21.
    inventories of effects of deceased, 28.
    not employed in menial service, 24.
    not sent to guard-house, 19.
    privates, &c., pay of, 526.
    promotion of, 12, 18.
    rank of, 9.
    receive additional pay, when, 343.
    reduced, how, 19.
    responsibilities of, 21.
    staff, funeral escort of, 44.
    treatment of, 19.
  not to leave the United States, 32.
  of artillery assigned to head-quarters, 73.
    tents of, 80.
  of corps of engineers, books kept by, 371.
    buttons for, 478.
    charged with a survey, duties of, 370.
    may assume command, when, 10.
  of corps of topographical engineers, books kept by, 371.
  of engineers assigned to head-quarters, 73.
  of engineers, duties of, 10.
    reports of, 370.
  of foreign service, honors paid to, 41.
  of general staff and staff corps, trowsers for, 479.
  of general staff, buttons for, 478.
  of Inspector-General's Department, duties of, 10.
  of light artillery, jacket worn on undress duty, 477.

Service, regimental recruiting, 140.
Shambles, designated by staff officer, 76.
Shell, time of flight and range, how noted, 16.
Shells, time of bursting of charged, 17.
Shot-furnaces, masonry, when heated, 15.
Shots and shells, number allowed for annual practice, 17.
Shoulder-straps, uniform, 485.
Sick and wounded, reports of, made by senior medical officer, 285.
   diet of, in hospitals, 244.
   march, how, 98.
Sickness, leave of absence on account of, 32.
   of officers, 33.
Siege, general commanding, duties of, 118.
   general plan of, drawn, by whom, 114.
   journal of, 118.
   materials for, how furnished, 115.
   service, 115.
Sieges, 113.
Signal officer, 157.
   uniform and dress of, 495.
Signals, 39.
   telegraphic, by whom worked, 90.
Single company, review of, 57.
Skirmishers, grand guard act as, when, 92.
Small arms, prices of, 394–396.
   and other ordnance stores, classification of, 398.
Soldier, discharge of, absent from his company, 31.
   effects of one who dies in hospital, 283.
   furniture for, in the field, 23.
   name and number of each, how placed, 21.
Soldier's account rendered immediately, when, 38.
   Home, fund paid over to, 244.
Soldiers, deceased, 28.
   disabled, 30.
   effects of deceased, 28.
   furloughs not granted to, when, 34.
   in hospital, muster and pay rolls of, how made, 284.
   insane, 31.
   inventories of effects of deceased, 28.
   mustered as artificers, 19.
   mustered in hospital, how, 283.
   on furlough, prohibitions of, 34.
   re-enlistment of, 137.
   return of deceased, 70.
   to pay compliments to officers, 41.
   transfer of, 27.
   uniform of, 23.

Soldiers without arms, salutation of, 42.
Soldiers' children at post school, 35.
   debts, payment of, 38.
   mess, 23.
Southern posts, pork for, 248.
Speaker of House of Representatives of United States, honors paid to, 41.
Special contractor, form of bill of, 142.
   form of bill of, Subsistence Department, 272.
   duty, officer detached for, 31.
   orders, 66.
   reconnoissances, 94.
Spies, treatment, 96.
Spring wagons or carriages used, only when, 164.
Spurs, uniform, 482.
Squads, how quartered, 21.
   non-commissioned officers in command of, 21.
Stable guard, duties of, 85.
   guards in cavalry, 83.
Staff, appointments on, 13.
Staff officers, reports of, 73.
   reports of appointments, &c., of, 70.
Standard, place of, in camp, 75.
Standard supply table for general and post hospitals, 292–301.
Standards and guidons of mounted regiments, 476.
Statement, form of, of articles repaired, &c., Ordnance Department, 434.
   form of, of moneys received, expended, &c., Pay Department, 368.
   form of, of receipts and expenditures, Ordnance Department, 448.
   form of, of serviceable materials, &c., Ordnance Department, 435.
   of work done, &c., form of, Ordnance Department, 455.
Stationery, 167.
   and furniture, 134.
Steward, hospital, temporary, appointment of, 288.
   of hospital at posts, sometimes appointed by senior medical officer, 284.
   of hospital, duties of, 282.
Stewards, hospital, pay of, 288.
Stoppages against officers, account of, 345.
   entered on pay-roll, 343.
Storage of packages, 242.
Store-keeper, duties of military, 390.
   Ordnance Department, duties of, 391.